Tony Horwitz

Tony Horwitz, who won a Pulitzer Prize for his reporting for the *Wall Street Journal*, is the author of *Confederates in the Attic*, *Baghdad without a Map*, *One for the Road* and *Into the Blue*, a *New York Times* bestseller. He lives in Martha's Vineyard with his wife, Geraldine Brooks, and their sons, Nathaniel and Bizu.

Praise for *A Voyage Long and Strange*

'Enlightening and entertaining . . . perhaps the most enjoyable aspect of this exemplary popular history is the way it shows that wisdom is all ᴜnd us, if only we'd take the trouble to learn' *Guardian*

ihralling' *Scotland on Sunday*

'*A Voyage Long and Strange* is a history-fuelled, self-imposed mission rediscovery, a travelogue that sets out to explore the surprisingly long list of explorers who discovered America, and what discovered means anyway . . . surprisingly fun and funny' *Publishers Weekly*

ɪɪreverent, effervescent re-examination of early exploration in the Americas by peripatetic, Pulitzer Prize-winning journalist Horwitz . . . Accessible to all ages, hands-on and immensely readable, this book invites readers to search out America's story for themselves' *Kirkus*

'This has been one of my best non-fiction reads for a while: really ᴜ ᴏught provoking' *Historical Novels Review*

'Well researched, perceptive . . . and sprinkled with acerbic humour' *Traveller*

'Horwi   sy to read'
*The Aɴ

A VOYAGE LONG AND STRANGE

REDISCOVERING THE NEW WORLD

TONY HORWITZ

JOHN MURRAY

First pub

© Tony Horwitz 2008

Sections of chapters 8 and 9 were originally published in different form in *Men's Journal*

Designed by Meryl Sussman Levavi

A CIP catalogue record for this title is available from the British Library

ISBN 978-0-7195-6636-3

Printed and bound by Clays Ltd, St Ives plc

John Murray policy is to use papers that are natural, renewable and recyclable products and made from wood grown in sustainable forests. The logging and manufacturing processes are expected to conform to the environmental regulations of the country of origin.

John Murray (Publishers)
338 Euston Road
London NW1 3BH

www.voyagelongandstrange.com
www.johnmurray.co.uk

To Erica and Josh, bread in the backseat
sandwich of our childhood travels.

Mistakes ... are the portals of discovery.

James Joyce, *Ulysses*

"Pray look better, sir," quoth Sancho; "those
things yonder are no giants, but windmills."

Miguel de Cervantes, *Don Quixote*

CONTENTS

PART I
DISCOVERY

PART II
CONQUEST

PART III
SETTLEMENT

MAPS

A VOYAGE
LONG AND
STRANGE

THE LOST CENTURY

T HE PILGRIMS DIDN'T think much of Cape Cod. "A hideous
and desolate wilderness," William Bradford called it. "Full of
wild beasts and wild men." Rather than stay, a small party
from the *Mayflower* sailed ahead, searching for a winter haven. In December 1620, they reached Plymouth, a place "fit for situation," Bradford wrote. "At least it was the best they could find."

On a New England road trip a few summers ago, I washed up in
Plymouth, too. It could have been Dedham or Braintree or some other
pit stop on the highway near Boston. But a Red Sox game pulsed on
the radio, so I drove until it ended at the Plymouth exit. Stopping for
beer at Myles Standish Liquor, I was directed to the William Bradford
Motor Inn, the best I could find in peak tourist season.

Early the next morning I went for a walk along the waterfront, past
a chowder house, a saltwater taffy shop, a wax museum, and a replica
Mayflower moored in the bay. Near the water stood a gray historic
marker that was terse even by New England standards.

Plymouth Rock. Landing Place of the Pilgrims. 1620.

I looked around and couldn't see anything except asphalt and a few stones small enough for skipping. Then I spotted a lone speed-walker racing down the sidewalk. "Excuse me," I said, chasing after him, "but where's Plymouth Rock?"

Without breaking stride, he thrust a thumb over his shoulder. "You just passed it."

Twenty yards back was a columned enclosure, between the side-walk and shoreline. Stepping inside, I came to a rail overlooking a shallow pit. At the bottom sat a lump of granite, the wet sand around it strewn with cigarette butts and ticket stubs from the wax museum. The boulder, about five feet square, had a badly mended cleft in the middle. It looked like a fossilized potato.

A few minutes later a family arrived. As they entered the portico, the father intoned to his children, "This is where it all began." Then they peered over the rail.

"*That's* it?"

"Guess so."

"It's, like, nothing."

"We've got rocks bigger than that in our yard."

Before long, the portico was packed: tour bus groups, foreign sightseers, summer campers. Their response followed the same arc, from solemnity to shock to hilarity. But Plymouth Rock was an icon of American history. So visitors dutifully snapped pictures or pointed video cameras down at the static granite.

"That's going to be one heckuva home movie."

"Yeah. *My Visit to Plymouth Pebble.*"

"The Pilgrims must have had small feet."

I went over to chat with a woman in green shorts and tan shirt standing outside the enclosure, counting visitors with a hand clicker. Claire Olsen was a veteran park ranger at Plymouth, accustomed to hearing tourists abuse the sacred stone. "A lot of people come here ex-pecting the Rock of Gibraltar," she said. "Maybe that's where they went on their last vacation."

She was also accustomed to fielding odd questions. Was it true that the *Mayflower* crashed into Plymouth Rock? Did the Pilgrims serve Thanksgiving on top of it? The bronze, ten-foot-tall Indian on a hill overlooking the rock—was he life-sized?

The most common question, though, concerned the date etched into the rock's surface. Why did it say 1620, visitors wondered, rather than 1492? Wasn't that when Columbus arrived?

"Or they ask, 'Is this where the three ships landed?' " Claire said. "They mean the *Niña,* the *Pinta,* and the *Santa María.* People think Columbus dropped off the Pilgrims and sailed home."

Claire had to patiently explain that Columbus's landing and the Pilgrims' arrival occurred a thousand miles and 128 years apart. "Americans learn about 1492 and 1620 as kids and that's all they remember as adults," she said. "The rest of the story is blank."

As she returned to counting tourists, I returned to the Governor Bradford, chuckling over visitors' questions. America, great land of idiocy! But Claire's parting comment gave me pause. Back on the road, winding past cranberry bogs, I scanned the data stored in my own brain about America's founding by Europeans. *In fourteen hundred and ninety-two, Columbus sailed the ocean blue . . .* John Smith and Jamestown . . . the Mayflower Compact . . . Pilgrims in funny hats . . . Of the Indians who met the English, I of course knew Pocahontas, Squanto, and . . . Hiawatha?

That was the sum of what I dredged up. Scraps from elementary school and the Thanksgiving table. Plus some fuzzy, picture-book images of black-robed friars and armored conquistadors I couldn't identify. As for dates, I'd mislaid an entire century, the one separating Columbus's sail in 1492 from Jamestown's founding in 16-0-something. Maybe nothing happened in the period between. Still, it was distressing not to know. Expensively educated at a private school and university—a history major, no less!—I'd matriculated to middle age with a third grader's grasp of early America.

Returning home to Virginia, I resolved to undertake some remedial study. At first, this proved deceptively easy: most of what I wanted to know was hiding in plain sight, at my local library. After skimming a few histories, I dug deeper, reading the letters and journals of early explorers. A cinch, really—except, an awful lot happened between

Columbus and the Pilgrims. Incredible stories I'd known nothing about. This wasn't a gap in my education; it was a chasm.

By the time the first English settled, other Europeans had already reached *half* of the forty-eight states that today make up the continental United States. One of the earliest arrivals was Giovanni da Verrazzano, who toured the Eastern Seaboard in 1524, almost a full century before the Pilgrims arrived. Verrazzano, an Italian in command of a French ship, smelled America before he saw it: "A sweet fragrance," he wrote, wafted out to sea from the dense cedar forests of the Carolinas.

Reaching the coast, Verrazzano dispatched one of his men to swim ashore and greet some people gathered on the dunes. The natives promptly carried the Frenchman to a fire on the beach and stripped off his clothes—not to "roast him for food," as his shipmates feared, but to warm the sailor while "looking at the whiteness of his flesh and examining him from head to toe."

Coasting north, Verrazzano was favorably impressed by a wide bay he called Santa Margarita, better known today as New York harbor. "A very agreeable place," he wrote, presciently observing that its well-populated shore "was not without some properties of value." Only at the end of his east coast cruise was Verrazzano disappointed. Natives bared their buttocks at sailors and lowered trade goods onto "rocks where the breakers were most violent." Verrazzano called this "Land of Bad People," a name since changed to Maine.

In 1528, on a return voyage to America, Verrazzano went ashore on a Caribbean island that appeared deserted. He was quickly seized by natives, then "cut into pieces and eaten down to the smallest bone." Or so claims the only surviving account of his landing, which concludes: "Such a sad death had the seeker of new lands."

History has been cruel to Verrazzano, too. In his own time, the navigator was so renowned that his name appeared on an early globe, spanning the east coast of North America. Today, he is forgotten, except as the namesake of a New York bridge that arcs over the narrows he sailed through in 1524.

Even less remembered are the Portuguese pilots who steered Spanish ships along *both* coasts of the continent in the sixteenth century, probing upriver to Bangor, Maine, and all the way to Oregon. En route, in 1542, one diarist wrote of California, "The country appears to be very fine," but its inhabitants "live very swinishly." That same year, Spanish conquistadors completed a reconnaissance of the continent's interior: scaling the Appalachians, rafting the Mississippi, peering down the Grand Canyon, and galloping as far inland as central Kansas (much to the surprise of the Plains Indians, who had never seen horses).

The Spanish didn't just explore: they settled, from the Rio Grande to the Atlantic. Upon founding St. Augustine, the first permanent European city on U.S. soil, the Spanish gave thanks and dined with Indians—fifty-six years before the Pilgrim Thanksgiving at Plymouth. The Spanish also established a Jesuit mission in Virginia, a few miles from the future Jamestown. Nor were Spaniards the only Europeans on the premises. French Protestants, fleeing persecution at home, founded a Florida colony in 1564, before all but two of the Pilgrims were born.

The more I read about pre-*Mayflower* America, the more I wondered why I'd learned so little of it before. This wasn't a clot of esoteric names and dates I'd dozed through in high school history, like the Habsburg Succession or the War of Jenkins's Ear. This was the forgotten first chapter of my own country's founding by Europeans, a chapter mysteriously redacted from the textbooks of my youth—and, as far as I knew, from national memory.

Anglo bias seemed the obvious culprit, but it didn't altogether explain Americans' amnesia. Jamestown preceded Plymouth by thirteen years as the first permanent English colony on the continent. Yet, like most Americans, I was ignorant of the Jamestown story, even though I'd spent much of my life in Virginia. Almost everyone knows the *Mayflower,* even new immigrants; the Pilgrim ship features prominently in citizenship tests. How many Americans can name the three ships that brought the first English to Jamestown? Or recall anything about the colony, except perhaps Pocahontas and John Smith?

Plymouth, it turned out, wasn't even the first English colony in New England. That distinction belonged to Fort St. George, in Popham, Maine—a place I'd never heard of. Nor were Pilgrims the first to settle Massachusetts. In 1602, a band of English built a fort on the island of Cuttyhunk. They came, not for religious freedom, but to get rich from digging sassafras, a commodity prized in Europe as a cure for the clap.

History isn't sport, where coming first means everything. The outposts at Popham and Cuttyhunk were quickly abandoned, as were most of the early French and Spanish settlements. Plymouth endured, the English prevailed in the contest for the continent, and Anglo-American Protestants—New Englanders, in particular—molded the new nation's memory. And so a creation myth arose, of Pilgrim Fathers seeding a new land with their piety and work ethic. The winners wrote the history.

But losers matter, especially in the history of early America. It was Spanish, French, and Portuguese voyages that spurred the English across the Atlantic in the first place, and that determined where they settled. Early Europeans also introduced horses, pigs, weeds, swords, guns—and, most lethally, diseases to which Indians had no resistance.

Plymouth was "fit for situation," as William Bradford put it, because an "extraordinary plague" had recently wiped out coastal natives. This left the shoreline undefended and fields conveniently cleared for corn. In the South and the Mississippi Valley, the devastation was even greater. Sixteenth-century conquistadors cut a swath through ancient civilizations that had once rivaled those of the Aztec and Inca. The Pilgrims, and later, the Americans who pushed west from the Atlantic, didn't pioneer a virgin wilderness. They occupied a land long since transformed by European contact.

There was another side to the story, just as dramatic and not so depressing. To early Europeans, America seemed a world truly new, and their words give voice to the strangeness and wonder of discovery. What to make of luminous insects that seemed at night a "flame of fire"? Or of "hump-backed cows" with goatlike beards that pounded across the Plains? Even the endless prairie, derided today as "flyover country," astonished those who first rode across it. "If a man lay down on his back he lost sight of the ground," one Spanish horseman marveled of the flatness.

Most exotic of all were America's people, whom Columbus named *los Indios,* Verrazzano called *la genta de la terra,* and the early English referred to as the Naturals. To the filthy, malnourished, and over-dressed Europeans, natives seemed shockingly large, clean, and bare. Indians were likewise astounded by Europeans. Natives fingered the strangers' beards, patted flat the wrinkles on their garments (perhaps thinking the cloth was skin), and wondered at their trade goods. When given hand mirrors, Verrazzano wrote, "They would look at them quickly, and then refuse them, laughing." Exchanges of food were also bewildering. "They misliked nothing but our mustard," an Englishman wrote of Cuttyhunk islanders in 1602, "whereat they made many a sowre face."

The Pilgrims who arrived in Massachusetts eighteen years later had a very different experience. Samoset, the first Indian they met at Plymouth, greeted the settlers in English. The first thing he asked for was beer.

If the drama of first contact was denied the late-arriving Pilgrims, it is even less available to travelers today. Encounters between alien cultures don't occur anymore, outside of science fiction. All that's needed to explore other hemispheres is a search engine.

But roaming the annals of early America, I'd discovered a world that was new and strange to me. What would it be like to explore this New World, not only in books but on the ground? To take a pre-Pilgrimage through early America that ended at Plymouth Rock instead of beginning there? To make landfall where the first Europeans had, meet the Naturals, mine the past, and map its memory in the present? To rediscover my native land, the U.S. continent?

I had no idea where this would lead, or what I'd find. But I'd read enough to know there'd be detours outside modern boundaries and textbook timelines. Columbus, for starters, was yet another latecomer. To begin at the beginning, I had to go back, way back, to the first Europeans who crossed the ocean blue, long before fourteen hundred and ninety-two.

PART I
DISCOVERY

A woodcut published in 1493 to illustrate Columbus's account of his landing the year before. It is believed to be the oldest European artwork imagining "the Indies" and its people.

CHAPTER I

VINLAND

FIRST CONTACT

> There was now much talk of looking for new
> lands.
> —*The Saga of the Greenlanders*

THE STORY OF America's discovery by Europeans begins with a fugitive. Eirik the Red fled his native Norway, the sagas say, "because of some killings." Settling in Iceland, Eirik took up farming and feuded with a neighbor, Filth-Eyjolf. Then he slew Filth, as well as Hrafn the Dueller. Banished for the murders, Eirik moved to islands off Iceland's coast and lent bedsteads to a man named Thorgest. When the loan went bad, Eirik killed Thorgest's sons, "along with several other men."

Exiled again—this time by the *Thing,* or regional assembly—Eirik headed west, like so many outlaws a millennium later. He sailed from Iceland to pioneer a glacial frontier he called Greenland, "as he said people would be attracted to go there if it had a favorable name."

Greenland today has no arable soil; three-quarters of its surface is sheet ice. Eirik, however, arrived during a long warming trend in the North Atlantic. Greenland in A.D. 985 wasn't a garden spot, but nor was volcanic Iceland or the treeless Faeroe Islands, another extremity the Vikings had settled. Eirik and his followers raised stock along

Greenland's coastal fringe, founding a colony that would grow to several thousand Norse and carry on a lively trade with Europe in luxury goods, such as polar bears and walrus tusks.

Eirik seems to have mellowed in Greenland, or at least stopped killing. The only strife following his arrival was domestic; Eirik's wife converted to Christianity and refused to sleep with her pagan husband, "much to his displeasure." By then, the couple had several grown sons, including Leif, who was large, strong, "and wise, as well as being a man of moderation in all things." Eirik the Red also had an illegitimate daughter, Freydis, who took after her hotheaded and homicidal father. Her moment comes later in this saga.

There are two versions of what happened next. Both tell of mariners who became lost while sailing the North Atlantic (the Norse word *hafvalla,* meaning "disoriented at sea," appears often in the sagas). In *Eirik the Red's Saga,* known in abridged form to many Americans, Leif Eiriksson left Norway for Greenland and "chanced upon land where he had not expected any to be found." He gathered wondrous plants and on his way home rescued shipwrecked sailors. "Afterwards he became known as Leif the Lucky."

But *The Saga of the Greenlanders* tells a fuller and less gallant story. In this version, it was a storm-tossed mariner named Bjarni Herjólfsson, who, while sailing for Greenland, first stumbled on a shore unknown to the Norse. For five days, Bjarni sailed along the coast, resisting the entreaties of his men, who wanted to go ashore. "No," Bjarni replied. "For this country seems to me to be worthless."

Even without a thousand years' hindsight, Bjarni's instincts seemed suspect. "Many people thought him short on curiosity," the saga says of Bjarni's cool reception upon reaching Greenland, "since he had nothing to tell of these lands." Leif, a more intrepid soul, bought Bjarni's ship and sailed with thirty-five men to explore the mysterious territory. He arrived at a mountainous shore where a "single flat slab of rock" ran from glaciers to the water. Leif hadn't yet developed his father's flair for salesmanship. He named his find Stone Slab Land.

After a second stop, at a wooded shore Leif called Forest Land, the Norse reached an island where "they found dew on the grass, which they collected in their hands and drank of, and thought they had never tasted anything as sweet." Nearby lay a headland and a river full of salmon. The Norse built "large houses" and settled in. "It seemed to them the land was so good, that livestock would need no fodder during winter. The temperature never dropped below freezing and the grass only withered slightly." To Nordic eyes, a terrestrial Valhalla.

Forays inland revealed another marvel. A man called Tyrkir, who hailed "from a more southerly country" than the Norse, wandered off and returned "pleased about something." At first he babbled in German and made strange faces. Then Tyrkir reported in Norse that he'd found grapes. From the description of his mood and manner, it seems he'd somehow become drunk on them.

"Are you really sure of this?" Leif asked about the fruit. Norsemen loved wine but lived too far north to recognize the plant it came from. "I'm absolutely sure," Tyrkir replied, "because where I was born there was no lack of grapevines and grapes."

Leif put his men to work collecting the fruit, cutting vines, and felling trees to load his ship. Then he sailed for Greenland. "It is said that the boat which was drawn behind the ship was filled with grapes." Leif also carried home an appealing name for his discovery: Vinland, or Land of Wine.

WHEN THE FOG lifted, fifteen minutes' drive from the airport, I caught my first glimpse of the newfound land. A sign appeared by the Trans-Canada Highway, bearing a pictograph of a huge antlered beast looming over a crushed sedan. "Caution: Moose May Wander onto Highway." The road dipped into a swale between two lakes, and fog enveloped me again. It was 4:30 A.M., dawn in midsummer Newfoundland, and rush hour for moose. For the next fifty miles, the only vehicle on the road apart from my rental car was an ambulance streaking the other way, its siren screaming. Sleep-deprived after my flight through the night, I imagined a moose-crushed motorist inside.

The next sign I saw was for the "Dildo B & B," and then a road marker, reporting the distance to the nearest town: 170 kilometers. Strange that the first territory in America discovered by Europeans should become, a millennium later, among its least inhabited. To keep myself awake, I turned on the Canadian Broadcasting Service, which filled the early-morning hours with English-language broadcasts from around the world. I tuned in just in time for Radio Sweden and a program on Nordic cuisine.

The show opened with a woman yoiking, then segued to an interview with a Swedish Jew. "Do you eat moose?" the host asked.

"I am not certain it is kosher," his guest replied. "But most Jews will eat moose if they feel like it."

A Saami followed, talking about reindeer tongue. Then Swedish radio gave way to Czech radio and then the BBC, carrying me through to the breakfast hour. Finally reaching a sliver of civilization, I slowed beside a small restaurant and store. The sign in front of it read:

Live Worms

Soft-serve

Cod Tongues

Like moose being kosher, cods having tongues wasn't something I'd ever considered. Opting for coffee, I drove on, past another warning sign, recording the alarming toll of "Moose/Vehicle Accidents" over the past year. Snowcapped mountains rose in the distance. Then I saw what I'd come for: a sign decorated with a logo of a longship and the words "Viking Trail." Steering onto the trail, I headed toward the most northeasterly point on the continent reachable by car: L'Anse aux Meadows, site of the first European settlement in America.

"SAGA" STEMS FROM a Norse word for "say." It refers to spoken accounts of the Viking Age (roughly, A.D. 800 to 1050) that were later written down by medieval clerics. Sagas tell of real people, real places, and real events, typically feuds. The prose is matter-of-fact. But sagas also inhabit a twilight zone where the normal and the paranormal intersect.

In *Eirik the Red's Saga,* a woman heads for the outhouse, only to find her way blocked by ghosts. In Vinland, a Viking is slain by a one-legged man-beast wielding a bow and arrow. "There was a man named Ulf," one saga begins, "son of Bjalfi and of Hallbera, the daughter of Ulf the Fearless. She was the sister of Hallbjorn Half-troll from Hrafnista."

Needless to say, such passages have cast doubt on the sagas' reliability as historical sources. Adding to the doubt is the way sagas were transmitted. The Christian scribes who first recorded them, several centuries after the events they describe, thought little of massaging tales about their pagan forebears. Later editors and translators added their own spin, differing on the sequence of scenes and the meaning of Norse phrases. In short, the sagas we read today are many generations removed from the stories first told around hearths in the far North Atlantic a thousand years ago.

The sagas also have a history of inspiring romantic fictions. When English translations of the Vinland sagas reached a wide American audience in the 1830s, evidence of Vikings suddenly began surfacing across New England. Antiquarians declared that a mysterious stone tower in Newport, Rhode Island, was actually Norse-built, and that a nearby grave containing both bones and metal belonged to an ancient warrior. "I was a Viking old!" Henry Wadsworth Longfellow wrote of the grave in his popular poem "The Skeleton in Armor."

Later in the nineteenth century, the locus of Viking finds moved to the upper Midwest, home to Scandinavian émigrés who were eager to elevate one of their own as the continent's founder. (*America Not Discovered by Columbus* was the title of a popular 1874 history by a Wisconsin scholar of Danish descent.) The most renowned find, the Kensington Stone in Minnesota, bore a runic inscription that told of Goths and Norwegians who journeyed there from Vinland. Countless other runes cropped up across the heartland, as far away as Heavener, Oklahoma. How and why the seafaring Norse had traveled to landlocked states was never made clear.

Nor did any of these claims withstand close scrutiny by scholars and archaeologists. The Newport tower turned out to be a seventeenth-century windmill, and Longfellow's "Viking old" a Wampanoag Indian, buried with a colonial English kettle. The Kensington Stone was exposed as an elaborate fake, carved by the Swedish stonemason who "found" it on his farm in 1898. Other runes were determined to be Indian petroglyphs, glacial scratches, or marks left by farm tools.

It was, therefore, with considerable skepticism that scholars

VIKINGS
in the
NORTH ATLANTIC

0 — 500 Mi
0 — 800 Km

NORWAY

ARCTIC CIRCLE

FAEROE ISLANDS

ICELAND

GREENLAND

STONE SLAB LAND
(BAFFIN ISLAND)

Norse Settlements

LEIF EIRIKSSON
ca. 1000

FOREST LAND
(LABRADOR)

L'Anse aux Meadows

NEWFOUNDLAND

greeted news in 1961 of yet another discovery of Norse remains, this time by a Norwegian. Helge Ingstad, a lawyer by training and adventurer by avocation, had embarked at the age of sixty on what seemed a quixotic mission. Following vague clues in the sagas, as well as ecclesiastical records and old maps that mentioned Vinland, he set off to survey the entire northeast Atlantic coast for traces of Norse visitation a thousand years earlier. This quest eventually led him to Newfoundland, which juts so far east that it almost crosses into Greenland's time zone. If, as the sagas seemed to suggest, Leif Eiriksson sailed the far North Atlantic and then coasted south, he would have bumped into Newfoundland's northern tip.

Traveling by boat, Ingstad heard about ancient house sites near the remote fishing village of L'Anse aux Meadows. Landing at the village dock, he followed a fisherman to a grassy plateau that bore the faint imprint of vanished dwellings. Locals called this "the Indian camp," but to Ingstad the setting was reminiscent of Norse farmsteads he'd seen in Greenland.

The next summer, Ingstad and his archaeologist wife, Anne Stine, commenced excavations. Over the next eight years, they and an international team uncovered dwellings and artifacts like those found at known Viking sites. Radiocarbon dating and other tests put the remains at around A.D. 1000. And so, in 1978, UNESCO named L'Anse aux Meadows its first world heritage site, the only confirmed Norse settlement yet discovered in America. The sagas, it turned out, had been right.

THE VIKING TRAIL ran for hours along a bare coastal plain. The few settlements I passed were functional to the point of austerity: tidy unadorned houses, plain churches, and Soviet-style groceries with signs saying "Food." The only radio station I could pick up issued fisheries broadcasts from Labrador. Even the moose signs disappeared.

Exhausted and bored by the daylong drive, I started to feel sympathy for Bjarni Herjólfsson. If the coast he stumbled on looked anything like this, he could be forgiven for thinking America "worthless." Later visitors concurred in his judgment. Jacques Cartier, who coasted Newfoundland in 1534, called it "the land that God gave to Cain."

At the top of the island, the road cut east through stony rubble, peat bogs, and glacial lakes. Then the Viking Trail forked and I followed one branch to its end at a seaside cliff. Stepping from my car, I was greeted by a frigid wind and a view of sheer rock enclosing a narrow inlet: a fjord. Sheltered within it was what looked like a sinking cruise ship, huge and white and listing. It took me a moment to register "iceberg," a thing I'd never seen outside an IMAX theater.

The Viking Trail's other fork led to L'Anse aux Meadows, a name that sounds deceptively lovely and lush, like "Flanders fields." It's actually a corruption of the original French: Anse à la Médée, or Medea's Bay, after the mythological Greek murderess. I passed another iceberg and patches of snow. Then the few stunted trees vanished and the view opened up: subarctic heath rolling down to the sea. It was beautiful but bleak, and so cold even in summer that my breath clouded as I stepped from the car.

The road ended at a wharf and a dozen or so homes by the water. At a gas station an hour earlier, I'd learned that a man named Tom kept a tour boat at L'Anse's dock. This seemed a nice way to start my exploration, viewing the coast from the water, as the Vikings had done. But the only person at the dock was a man in a parked car with a cap pulled low on his brow. I tapped on his closed window and asked where I might find Tom and his boat.

"No icebergs here," the man replied, barely lowering his window.

"I don't want to see icebergs," I said.

"What do you want to see?"

"Where the Vikings came in."

"No Vikings here, never were," he said. "No sir. That's all bullshit. They'd a found a better place than this. In the winter it's not fit to live in." He rolled up his window and drove off.

Across the way, I saw an old man emerge from a small home and walk over to pet a goat. A sign in his yard said, "For Sale Wool Socks," which I realized I could use. Wandering over, I commented on the chill.

"This is a hot day, today," he answered, lifting his wool sweater to reveal a sweatshirt, flannel jersey, and T-shirt beneath. "Almost naked, I am."

The man was Job Anderson, one of the locals who'd helped the Ingstads when they started excavations in the 1960s. "Work was scarce, so I said yes," Job recalled. He mentioned that his grandfather was Norwegian, and I asked if this had given him any sense of identity with the Vikings whose homes he'd helped unearth.

"Too far back," Job replied. "I can't tell you no lies. I never ran with them. I'm old, but not that old." Then he broke into song: "Born here in the morning, quarter after two, with me hands in me pocket, and me old ragadoo." When I looked at him blankly, he said, "A ragadoo's a coat."

Job patted his goat. "She'll live till she dies, this one." I nodded, bought a pair of socks, and retreated to my car, bewildered by my first contact with Newfoundlanders. Were they having fun with me? Or were they all barking mad?

IN THE SAGAS, little is told of Leif Eiriksson after his voyage to Vinland. But his siblings took up where he left off, leading several follow-up expeditions to the Land of Wine. First, a brother named Thorvald sailed west and wintered in the camp Leif had established. During a summertime tour of the surrounding waters, Thorvald sailed up a fjord and found a forested cape with a sheltered cove. "This is an attractive spot," he declared, "and here I would like to build my farm."

Then the Norse noticed what looked like three hillocks on the beach. "Upon coming closer they saw they were hide-covered boats, with three men under each of them." The sagas devote only a few lines to this epochal moment: the first recorded encounter between Europeans and Native Americans, two branches of humanity that had been separated so long they barely recognized each other as kin.

When and how the first people reached America is a subject of keen debate, roiled by recent archaeological finds and new genetic and linguistic evidence. It's generally believed that early humans migrated out of Africa some fifty thousand years ago, with one stream eventually reaching northeast Asia, at about the same time and latitude as others settled the northwest corner of Europe. Near the end of the last Ice Age, roughly twelve thousand years ago, hunters crossed from Asia to today's Alaska before spreading across the Americas. Then another eleven thousand years passed before the family of man reunited—or, rather, collided—on a beach in eastern Canada.

In the sagas, the word for "native" is *Skraeling,* an archaic Norse term that is variously translated as "wretch," "ugly," "screecher," or some combination of the three. Natives are also described as short, dark, and "evil-looking," with coarse hair and broad cheekbones. Of course, we only hear one side of the story. To native eyes and ears, the Norse—pale, hirsute, long-faced, and speaking a strange tongue— must have seemed like ugly screeching wretches, too.

Upon discovering the Skraelings under their boats, the Norse "divided their forces and managed to capture all of them except one, who escaped with his boat. They killed the other eight." No reason is given for this slaughter. Then "a vast number of hide-covered boats came down the fjord," ready for battle. The Norse repelled the assault, but Thorvald was struck under his arm by an arrow. Realizing he was mortally wounded, he asked to be buried at the farm site he had chosen.

The next chapter of the Vinland story begins with a passage of the sort that can vex modern readers. Names in the sagas not only sound the same; sometimes they *are* the same. Another Eiriksson brother, Thorstein, decides to set sail from Greenland to reclaim Thorvald's body. But Thorstein becomes ill and dies at the home of a farmer named Thorstein. His widow, Gudrid, has an encounter with a ghostly woman, also named Gudrid. And so on.

Eventually, Gudrid remarries, to a wealthy captain named Thorfinn Karlsefni, and they sail off to Vinland with sixty men, six women, and "all sorts of livestock with them, for they intended to settle in the country if they could." Arriving at Leif's old camp, they lived well from the land's "natural bounty" of grapes, fish, game, and whale.

Then in summer, Skraelings appeared again. At first, natives were frightened off by the bellowing and snorting of a bull, a creature they'd never seen. But they returned bearing "fur pelts and sables and all kinds of skins," which they offered in exchange for weapons. This prefigured hundreds of encounters between natives and newcomers in centuries to come. Though wary at first, and unable to understand each other, the two parties quickly found a common tongue in trade.

And it rarely took long for natives to recognize the strangers' most valuable commodity: their edged steel swords and, later, their guns.

Karlsefni forbade his men from trading swords, instead "having the women bring out milk and milk products." So began another trend in relations between Europeans and natives: the lopsided deal, at least in the eyes of the newcomers. "The Skraelings carried their purchases away in their bellies, and left their packs and furs."

Karlsefni returned the next spring to Greenland, his ships laden with grapevines and skins. His visit left one other legacy. While in Vinland, Karlsefni's wife, Gudrid, gave birth. Almost six centuries would pass before the birth of the first English child in North America: Virginia Dare, a babe lavishly commemorated in marble, poetry, novels, and plays. Gudrid's infant, like so many Norse, remains unheralded outside the sagas. His name, for the record, was Snorri.

AFTER BEDDING DOWN at the Vinland Motel, I went to see the small national park enclosing the Norse settlement at L'Anse aux Meadows. Stopping first at the visitors center, I watched a film interview with the site's discoverer, Helge Ingstad, who had recently died at the age of 101. The lean, handsome Norwegian spoke of his deep admiration for Vikings, whose "lust of adventure" drove them across the ocean in open boats to "find a new country."

This romantic image stood in contrast to the humble Norse artifacts found at L'Anse and now on display at the visitors center: a rusted nail, a wooden skewer "used to hold sod in place on roofs," a ringed bronze pin for fastening cloaks, and a spindle whorl used by Norse women when spinning thread. Small, round, and cut from soapstone, the whorl looked like a flattened doughnut.

An adjoining exhibit, about Norse life on both sides of the Atlantic, also punctured my stereotype of Vikings as marauding berserkers. Technically, the term "Viking" refers only to Norsemen who went on raids. Most Norse stayed home, farming peacefully in Scandinavia. Nor did the Greenland and Vinland settlers travel in sleek, sharp-prowed "dragon ships" like those used by warriors in northern European raids. Instead, they sailed a broad-beamed workhorse known as a *knarr,* designed for toting passengers, cargo, and farm animals across open ocean.

A longship of the Viking Age, from the Bayeux Tapestry, eleventh century

Finally, lest I imagine pagan orgies in honor of the sex goddess Freya, the exhibit reported that most of the Vinland settlers were recent converts to Christianity. The overall impression was of a homey and pious bunch of pioneers who spun wool, cut timber, and caught fish: an early, somewhat chillier version of Pilgrim Plymouth.

Outside the visitors center, a boardwalk led down a gentle slope, between a peat bog and a moss bog, to the archaeological site. I stopped first at a furnace and smithy, where Norsemen used local bog iron to smelt low-grade metal, the first industrial enterprise in America. All that remained was a faint disturbance of the earth, no more conspicuous than a gopher hole.

A short way on, I came to a plateau dotted with grassy craters: the heart of the Viking settlement. The depressions outlined seven halls and huts. Slight breaks in the shin-high walls revealed where doorways had been; tiny holes denoted fire pits. Circumnavigating the plateau several times, I tried to conjure Leif and his men arriving in America. The site occupied a headland beside a shallow bay, with a brook running into it, just as the sagas described. And here were the "large houses" the Norse wintered in. It all fit, except for the weather: forty-one degrees with blowing rain, not quite the temperate, vine-rich paradise of the sagas.

I glanced at my watch. It had taken me ten minutes to tour the remains of Norse America. The story here was bigger than the place.

Purists might complain, but having traveled this far, I was glad to
find that Parks Canada had reconstructed several buildings as they
would have appeared in A.D. 1000. Set away from the archaeological
site, the buildings looked at a distance like low green mounds rising
from the coastal plain. Up close, they resembled hobbit homes, with
turf walls and sod roofs that drooped almost to the ground. Grass and
wildflowers sprouted on top. Ducking through a low doorway, I felt as
though I were plunging straight into the earth.

Darkness and warmth enveloped me as soon as I stepped inside.
When my eyes adjusted, I saw dirt floor, timber framing, and wooden
platforms draped in furs. A cauldron hung over a small fire. Beside the
pot knelt a beautiful young woman with long blond hair, her rough
brown cloak roped at the waist.

"Gothen dyen," she said. "I did not see your *knarr* arrive."

"Excuse me?"

"I said 'Good day' and asked after your vessel. Is it a large one?"

"Subcompact," I replied. "And yours? When did it arrive?"

"Sir, I have been here a thousand years and all that time a slave."
She poked in the pot. "May I offer you some blubber?"

A gruff voice bellowed from the gloom at the other end of the
longhouse. "Bera, you lazy thrall, bring me my mead!"

Bera sighed. "That is Bjorn, my master. A cruel and stupid man."
At this, a burly man appeared, with wild, shoulder-length locks and almost as much hair sprouting from his face. He wore a gray tunic over
woolen trousers and goat-skin boots. "What's this?" he growled, peering into the cauldron. "Swill, *again*?"

Bjorn turned and glared at me, gesturing at my pad and pen. "A
true *skald* needs no such tools," he said. Then he recited from a poem
called the "Hávamál," or "Sayings of the High One," which offered
homilies about proper behavior for Vikings. "Cattle die, kinsmen die,
and you yourself must likewise die," he boomed. "I know of only one
thing that never dies: the reputation of each man dead."

After fifteen minutes of this, he and Bera lapsed out of period
character. Bjorn, in real life, was a former fisherman named Mike who

had worked at the park for six years. At one time, becoming a Viking had seemed the coming thing in Newfoundland's depressed north, where the closing of the exhausted cod fishery in the 1990s threw thousands out of work. The government sponsored a program to retrain some of the unemployed as Norse reenactors, in hopes the thousandth anniversary of Leif's sail, in 2000, would spark a surge in tourism. But few travelers made it this far north and a number of laid-off fishermen now had the added distinction of being laid-off Vikings.

Bera was a former teacher, intrigued by Norse domestic life. She spent her days in the longhouse knitting, weaving, and cooking, though not the whale blubber she'd offered. The actual contents of her cauldron were beans, cabbage, turnips, carrots, and onion—cold-weather crops of the sort the Norse grew along the North Atlantic.

"We used to eat what we cooked," Bjorn said. "But it's gassy food, not the best thing when you're shut in here all day."

He showed me the rest of the longhouse, which was seventy-two feet long and nine feet wide, the exact dimensions of one of the building sites found outside. The interior details reproduced those of a Norse dwelling in Iceland that had been preserved under volcanic ash. Hanging on the wall was a pointed helmet with an iron nosepiece. This, too, was based on a historic model—and it was nothing like the horned helmets worn by cartoon Norse, or Minnesota Vikings' fans. Like so much Viking lore, the horned helmet was a romantic fiction, created in the nineteenth century by costume designers for Wagnerian operas.

While the longhouse's props were museum grade, other aspects of Norse life had proved harder to re-create. "We imagine them as primitive compared to us," Bjorn said, "except we can't do basic things they did." Venting the smoke from a fire, for instance. When the longhouse opened, Bjorn said, "Smoke was glued to the floor. We were coughing and couldn't spend a large amount of time in here."

The park installed roof hatches, but they caused sparks to rise, setting fire to the ceiling. Attempts at creating the right draft through doorways or the floor also failed. Finally, the park gave up on wood and installed propane jets and fake logs. However, once the real fire was gone, damp set in. The sheepskin sleeping sacks became soggy and bug-ridden and started to stink.

Still, longhouse life had its compensations. Whenever visitors entered, the cool and gloom drew them into a companionable circle around the fire. With no windows, and only the doorway giving a narrow glimpse of the harsh world outside, the longhouse seemed an earthen, fur-draped womb. Sprawled on a skin, listening to Bjorn tell tales from Norse mythology—dwarf craftsmen laboring underground; Valkyries scooping the souls of slain warriors from the battlefield; mighty Thor battling giants with his hammer—it seemed small wonder that the Norse created one of the world's richest troves of spoken lore. What setting is more conducive to storytelling and fantastic imaginings than a long, dark winter spent gathered in a circle of firelit faces?

It also made sense that the Norse resisted Christianity longer than any other Europeans, clinging to paganism for a thousand years after Christ. Isolation was one reason for this. But in the cold, dark, watery, and violent world the Norse inhabited, trolls and thunder gods and feasts of boar and mead, served by maidens in the Hall of the Slain, must have been hard to exchange for a belief system bred of the Middle Eastern desert.

Bjorn, for one, hadn't yet succumbed. "I got no time for Christians," he growled to a family gathered by the fire. "They go to the next life and don't take anything with them. Pagans, we go well prepared."

He brought out a spear and a broad-bladed battle-ax. "If you get a good clean smack at a Christian with this," he said, brandishing the ax at a wide-eyed boy, "he won't suffer much. Not that we care, sir, when the killing time comes." Then he showed how to thrust the spear, which Vikings twisted before pulling out. "There's nothing like the smell of intestines flying in the air of a morning."

When the visitors left, Bjorn and Bera settled into board games, another indoor pastime at which Norsemen excelled. Their favorite was *hneftafl,* a siegelike version of chess, in which one player places his king at the center and the other attacks. Bjorn was a master at this, but still a novice at another Norse pursuit. He'd spent weeks trying to carve a ship's figurehead into a fierce dragon.

"It looks like a duck," Bera said.

"No it doesn't, it's beastlike." Bjorn slashed at the creature's mouth. "See. A snarl." Bera glanced up from her knitting again. "He's going to be one ferocious duck."

I loitered in the longhouse until the park closed. Bjorn stored the weapons and shoved his dragon-duck under a fur. "I'll get the gas," Bera said, reaching beneath a rock by the fire for the propane valve.

We emerged from the longhouse into the low light of a New-foundland evening. Even so, the world seemed startlingly bright after hours in the sod enclosure. I felt pleasantly disoriented, the way one does after stepping out of a movie theater in the afternoon.

Bjorn smiled at me, familiar with the sensation. "Back to the fu-ture," he said. "Not all it's cracked up to be, eh?" Buttoning our coats, we walked through the peat bog, back to our *knarr*s in the parking lot.

THE SAGA OF the Greenlanders tells of a fourth and final voyage to Vinland. The earlier sails, by Leif, Thorvald, and Karlsefni, were evidently judged a success, as "the trip seemed to bring men both wealth and renown." So Eirik the Red's illegitimate daughter, the hot-tempered Freydis, decided to try her luck. She contracted with two brothers from Iceland to sail in convoy and share profits from the voyage. Each ship was to carry thirty "fighting men," but "Freydis broke the agreement straight away," stowing five extra warriors on her ship.

On reaching Leif's camp, Freydis demanded that only her party occupy the existing homes. So the brothers built a separate longhouse. Their suggestion that the two groups join for winter "games and entertainment" only led to more ill will, "and each group kept to its own houses."

Then, early one morning, Freydis went barefoot through the dew to ask one of the brothers to exchange ships with her, since his was larger and she wanted to go home. He agreeably assented. When she returned to bed, her cold feet woke her husband, Thorvard, who asked why she was wet. Freydis claimed she'd gone to ask about purchasing the brothers' ship and been turned down, as well as assaulted. "But you're such a coward that you will repay neither dishonor done to me nor to yourself," she said. "Unless you avenge this, I will divorce you!"

Duly shamed, Thorvard roused his men and went to seize the

brothers and their companions. When he led the bound captives outside, Freydis ordered them slain. But Thorvard's men balked at killing the five women among them.

"Hand me an ax," Freydis coolly demanded. She then dispatched the five women, and threatened to kill any of her party who told what she had done.

Freydis proved quite the Valkyrie in combat, too. During an exploratory foray, the Norse came under attack by a large force of Skraelings in canoes, wielding a strange weapon. From tall poles, they catapulted "a large round object, about the size of a sheep's gut and black in color," which "made a threatening noise when it landed." These missiles so terrified the Norse that "their only thought was to flee."

Seeing her kinsmen retreat, Freydis declared, "Had I a weapon I'm sure I could fight better than any of you." Though heavily pregnant, she joined the battle, snatching up the sword of a slain Viking. "When the Skraelings came rushing toward her she pulled one of her breasts out of her bodice and slapped it with her sword. The Skraelings were terrified at the sight of this and fled back to their boats and hastened away."

Though Freydis had warded off defeat, the settlers realized they couldn't remain in Vinland. "Despite everything the land had to offer there, they would be under constant threat of attack from its prior inhabitants. They made ready to depart for their own country."

The Norse, who had subdued so many European foes—Anglo-Saxons, Franks, Celts, Slavs—were driven off by Skraelings in skin canoes. Stray documents from as late as the mid-1300s mention expeditions to cut timber in Markland, which was probably today's Labrador. But never again would Norsemen return to explore and settle Leif's Land of Wine.

I SPENT FIVE days in L'Anse aux Meadows, trying to get to know its present-day inhabitants. Most descended from fishermen who had claimed small plots by the water in the nineteenth century. "I was born on the same spot I'm living," Clayton Colbourne said, when I met him in his yard, painting the bottom of a boat. "My mom's next door and my brother next to her."

The Colbournes occupied Beak Point, beside the shallow inlet into which the Vikings sailed. The coast of Labrador was dimly visible, thirty miles away. Clayton, a lean, ruggedly handsome man of fifty-five, with a graying reddish beard, was one of eleven children, and all had helped their father fish from an early age. In the early 1960s, when the Ingstads arrived, there was no road into L'Anse, just a footpath to the next hamlet and a half-day boat ride to the nearest town, a trip only possible during the few warm months of the year.

"You can imagine what it was like when these strangers arrived from across the sea, like Vikings, and started digging around," Clayton said. "We thought they were crazy fools." He nonetheless joined the excavation team, and later became a guide at the park, where he'd worked for several decades. "Vikings are a big part of me now, a passion," he said. "I like their courage and tenacity, to be bold enough to think they could go in an open boat across the ocean and back."

These qualities resonated in a seafaring community at the fringe of the continent. So did the Vikings' resourcefulness. "They used whatever was at hand, like us," Clayton said. "I cut my own lumber to make boats, do everything myself. You have to be tough and self-reliant." He pointed to his woodpile: one hundred loads, dragged from the woods on a sled hitched to a snowmobile. "No one lives here for the climate," he added dryly. The previous winter, the temperature had dipped to thirty below and a white-out trapped people indoors for three days.

Clayton walked me to the edge of the bay, which was only six feet deep, perfect for pulling up shallow-draft vessels like those used by Vikings and, later, by cod fishermen. The shore had ample grass for livestock; until recently, local families had grazed sheep, goats, and cows where the Vikings had a thousand years before. When Clayton was a boy, fish ran so thick in the brook by the Viking site that he could catch them with his hands.

"Everything the Vikings knew and needed was right here," he said. "My dad liked to say, 'Give a dog what he's used to.' Leif and them, they would have been out of place farther south somewhere."

Still, this was by any standard an inhospitable place. When the Ingstads arrived, L'Anse had about a hundred inhabitants—just a bit more than the Norse population in A.D. 1000. "I guess that's about all the environment here could sustain," Clayton said.

Today, it sustained even less. With the Ingstads' discovery, L'Anse had gained a paved road and a small tourist industry. But easier access to the outside world, and exposure to it through TV, hastened an exodus of young people. Only thirty-one villagers remained, many of them elderly. The saga of L'Anse aux Meadows was drawing to an end. "In another twenty years, what our families built here will fade away, like the Vikings' settlement," Clayton predicted.

With that, he resumed painting his boat, and pointed me to the small brown house of Lloyd Decker. It was Lloyd's father, George, who had first directed Helge Ingstad to the Norse site. I found Lloyd in his yard, but he said he had no time to talk. The next day, I caught him climbing into his truck. "Too busy," he said. "Need to buy nails for my boat." I asked if I could ride along to see a bit of the scenery. He shrugged and pushed open the passenger door.

Lloyd was a large, craggy-faced man of sixty-four, his hands dark brown below his shirt cuffs: the Newfoundland version of a trucker's tan. We drove to the store and back in virtual silence. By the time we returned, I'd abandoned hope of hearing his family's story. Then he shut off the ignition and said, "Come in for tea, will you?"

Inside the Deckers' immaculate house, Lloyd's wife, Madge, served us tea with cheese and crackers. Their daughter, Loretta, who worked at the national park, sat making a birchbark whistle for a program on Norse crafts. Lloyd had also worked at the park, and, before that, he'd helped the Ingstads excavate the site.

"I remember people here saying, 'Don't be fools going up there with them, they could be Russian spies.'" Lloyd laughed. "I said, 'If that's so, they're not going to find out much.'"

Loretta's experience was different; she'd grown up with the Viking dig as part of the landscape. Now a large, dark-haired woman of thirty-three, she recalled childhood summers spent sifting sand for artifacts, or using socks to stage puppet shows based on the sagas. "I wondered lots of times why the Vikings killed those natives under the canoes," she said. "Maybe it was a test, like dunking a witch. To see if they were really human. People are always scared of what they don't know."

Her own world had been widened by summers playing with archae-ologists' children. "I remember one kid telling me, 'My parents are di-vorced.' I'd never heard the word and thought it was a place. 'Where's Divorced?' When I learned what it meant, I was worried all the men here would leave if they knew they could." She paused. "Funny, it didn't occur to me the women would want to go. But they ran the households, so I thought they came with the house and couldn't leave."

Madge brought out homemade bread with gooseberry jam, and Lloyd leaned back in his chair, recounting ghost stories his father used to tell by the fire at night. The nineteenth-century settlers at L'Anse had mostly come from Ireland and Germany, and the old peo-ple's tales were filled with supernatural creatures. One story told of an old man who was murdered in his sod hut, but kept reappearing on the moor around L'Anse, wearing a brown suit. If anyone greeted him, he vanished or changed into a wolf. Villagers called him the Brown Man.

"When I first read the sagas," Loretta said, "all those shape-changers and man-beasts felt a little familiar to me." She was nostalgic for childhood nights, listening to stories, but not for the fishing that filled people's days. "I remember carrying buckets of fish guts and pouring it over the garden, flies all over me. The men had so much salt in their sleeves it'd give them boils that had to be lanced. It got so you hated to hear the word 'fish.'"

But as cod fishing faded, so had the community. Loretta was now the youngest adult in L'Anse; everyone else in their twenties and thir-ties had left to seek work on the mainland. "Vikings are about all that keeps this place going," she said.

For the first time in two hours, the talking ceased. I noticed a TV droning in the den: the room tone of modern domestic life. Thanking the Deckers, I headed out for a walk across the moor in the fading light. Lloyd saw me to the door. "Watch out for the Brown Man," he said.

BY THE END of my week in L'Anse aux Meadows, I'd met most of the hamlet's inhabitants and felt able to conjure the Norsemen who had settled the remote peninsula a millennium ago. But the Skraelings of

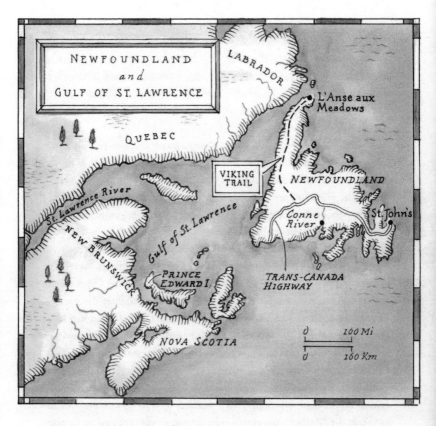

the sagas remained a spectral presence, like the Brown Man lurking at the fringes of L'Anse.

Archaeologists at the Viking site had found arrowheads and other native artifacts. However, none of this material dated from the period of Norse settlement. In A.D. 1000, the environs of L'Anse seem to have been uninhabited, one reason Leif may have chosen to settle there. Also, the Europeans who returned to Newfoundland, centuries after the Vikings, described the natives they encountered as belonging to small, reclusive bands of hunter-gatherers.

Who, then, were the myriad Skraelings, boldly attacking the Vikings with catapults and fleets of skin canoes?

The sagas provide a few clues. For one, it appears that all the

Norse contact with natives occurred during summer expeditions away from Leif's settlement. Though directions in the sagas are sketchy, excavations at L'Anse turned up pieces of butternut, a wood unknown in Newfoundland. Also, the grapes that gave Vinland its name have never grown on the island. However, both butternut and grapes can be found in New Brunswick, several hundred miles to the southwest, on the Canadian mainland.

After sifting this and other evidence, most scholars now believe that the settlement at L'Anse was a base camp or gateway to a much broader area. Vinland, in turn, may be best understood as the overall region the Norse explored. Only then do the stories about Skraelings make sense. Though scarce around L'Anse, maritime peoples lived in large numbers along the milder shores of the Gulf of St. Lawrence, coasts the Vikings could easily have reached during summer sails.

These coastal natives are silent in the sagas, except as "screeching wretches." But their descendants have a voice now. On my last day at L'Anse, I learned that Parks Canada had recently instructed employees to stop using the word "Skraeling." A native group had complained about the term's derogatory connotations. "So now we say that the Vikings met 'aboriginal people' or 'first nation people,'" Loretta Decker said.

Intrigued, I asked her where the complaint had come from. She unfolded my map of Newfoundland, which I'd squared like origami to navigate the northern peninsula. Her finger finally stopped at Conne River, a remote dot on the island's southern coast, roughly five hundred miles' drive from L'Anse, most of it on two-lane roads. "I'd give yourself two days to get there," she counseled, "on account of the moose."

CALLING AHEAD, I learned that the community at Conne River would be holding a powwow at the end of the week, a good time to learn about the tribe's culture. This also left me several days to get there without driving at dawn and dusk, when moose like to feed on roadside plants or lick salt left from winter snow and ice control.

But as soon as I departed the wind-scraped coast, I discovered a new peril. Stopping to piss in woods by the road, I'd barely unzipped my jeans before bugs assaulted every millimeter of exposed skin. Annie Proulx, the author of *The Shipping News,* once said in an interview that the ferocious blackflies of Newfoundland "can exsanguinate a human adult in 23 minutes." I escaped with a few dozen bites and my hands, neck, face, and groin covered in flecks of blood.

Swarming insects were one reason the island's moist, sheltered interior had never been heavily populated. Another reason was food, or the lack of it. Though rich in fish, Newfoundland had little game apart from caribou and beaver (moose were a nineteenth-century import). This scarcity not only limited the size of the native population, but also made it vulnerable to sudden shifts, like the one that occurred when Europeans returned to the island five hundred years after the Norse.

The first to come were fishermen—English, French, Basque, Portuguese—and then trappers who ventured inland in search of fur. They came in contact with tall natives who set feathers in their plaited hair and wore caribou hides with the fur against their skin. But the natives' most distinctive feature was the red ocher covering their faces, bodies, clothes, and possessions. The English began referring to them as "Red Indians," the first to be so called in America. Curiously, the sagas mention that natives who traded with the Norse showed a distinct preference for cloth of a certain color—red—which they tied around their heads.

The natives called themselves Beothuk, meaning "Human Beings" or "the People." Such names were characteristic of indigenous peoples across America, where nation-states and strong racial differences were absent. The fate of the Beothuk was also typical. At first, the newcomers were mostly seasonal fishermen who left behind nails, hooks, and other items that natives put to their own uses—for instance, draping their conical birchbark dwellings with discarded sails. But gradually, English traders and settlers spread across Newfoundland, competing for the fish, game, and fur on which the Beothuk relied. Small thefts by natives became an excuse for colonists to shoot them and burn their homes. By the early 1800s, the Beothuk had dwindled to a few scattered bands, roaming the mostly barren interior.

In 1823, fur trappers captured three starving Beothuk and brought them to Newfoundland's capital, St. John's. The only one to survive

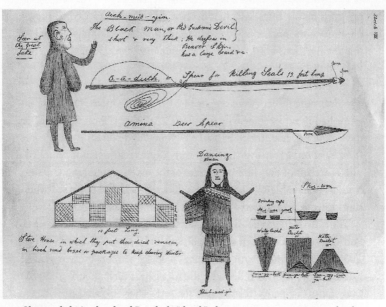

Shanawdithit's sketch of Beothuk "devil," dancing woman, spears, and other items, circa 1829

was a six-foot-tall woman in her twenties, named Shanawdithit. She learned a little English and came under the care of a Scotsman, W. E. Cormack, who had founded an institute to protect and study Newfoundland's "ill-treated first occupiers." He collected more than a hundred Beothuk words and phrases, including those for "beaver," "mosquito," "puppy," "hiccough," "kiss," and "cry."

Shanawdithit also drew pictures, always depicting Beothuk figures in red. She never explained—or Cormack didn't understand—why her people prized this color. Ocher, mixed with grease, had a practical value, as an insect repellent, and possibly as camouflage while hunting game in autumn. But the fact that Beothuk coated their possessions in red, and put packages of ocher in graves, suggests the color also had spiritual power, perhaps as a symbol of blood and life.

Shanawdithit used black lead to draw non-Beothuk figures, including a stout bearded man identified as Aich-mud-yim, or the Devil. Shanawdithit said the Beothuk "feared some powerful monster, who was to appear from the sea and punish the wicked." Beothuk also believed that they went to a "happy island" after death, but not if they consorted with white men.

After six years in captivity, Shanawdithit died of tuberculosis, bequeathing Cormack pieces of quartz and a lock of her hair. "Here ends all positive knowledge of her tribe, which she never narrated without tears," he wrote. No Beothuk were seen thereafter.

The scant artifacts of Beothuk life that survive include items buried with a boy: miniature bark canoes, toy bows and arrows, red ocher, and other equipment for his journey to the happy island. "We have traces enough left only to cause our sorrow that so peculiar and so superior a people should have disappeared from the earth like a shadow," Cormack wrote. "They are irrevocably lost to the world."

NEAR THE CENTER of Newfoundland, I turned off the Trans-Canada Highway and followed a badly paved road with a sign at the start warning, "Check Fuel: Next Service 127 km." An hour and a half later, I came to another sign, adorned with a wigwam and welcoming me to Micmac territory: a fourteen-square-mile Indian reserve on the hilly, wooded shore of the Bay D'Espoir.

Unlike the Beothuk, the Micmac are believed to have migrated to Newfoundland after the arrival of Europeans, from Nova Scotia and New Brunswick, where most of the tribe still lives. For centuries before that, ancestors of the Micmac inhabited the shores of the Gulf of St. Lawrence. This put them right in the path of Vikings who went on summer sails in search of grapes and timber. If any group today can claim descent from the Skraelings of the sagas, it is the Micmac.

In contrast to the wary and reclusive Beothuk, the Micmac engaged in a lively trade with the French who began settling eastern Canada in the early 1600s, and became early converts to Christianity, led by a chief who entered the "Wigwam of Jesus" in 1610. "They have often told me that at first we seemed to them very ugly, with hair both upon our mouths and heads," a priest wrote of the Micmac in 1611. "But gradually they have become accustomed to it, and now we are beginning to look less deformed." Another priest observed that the

Micmac "find the use of our handkerchiefs ridiculous; they mock at us and say that it is placing excrements in our pockets."

The French, for their part, were struck by Micmac respect for the animals they killed. It was customary to return the bones of beavers—"those animals almost men," the Micmac called them—to the rivers the animals came from, "so that the lodges would always be there." Micmac imagined heaven as a place where "animals allowed themselves to be hunted," and where people always had "much meat and fat and marrow. Their chins are always dripping with fat."

While French-Micmac contact was generally peaceful, it brought a scourge that would ultimately afflict native peoples across America: epidemic European diseases, to which Indians lacked immunity. "They are astonished and often complain that since the French mingle with and carry on trade with them," a priest wrote in 1612, "they are dying fast." One particularly deadly campsite became known to the Micmac as "the place of measles."

Like many other tribes, the Micmac also became caught in the long struggle between Europeans for control of the continent. The French paid and armed Micmac to attack the English, who in turn urged settlers to "annoy, distress, take or destroy the savages," offering ten guineas for every scalp. "Our nation is like a withering leaf in a summer's sun," declared a group of chiefs who petitioned the Newfoundland government for aid in 1849.

I was surprised, then, to arrive at Conne River and find a relatively thriving community, with many new houses and powerboats and Jet Skis perched in driveways and yards. At the powwow site, in a park overlooking the bay, I joined a crowd of several hundred people milling around three wigwams and craft stands selling dream catchers, moccasins, Indian dolls, and beadwork made in China. Most of the people were olive-skinned, black-haired, and heavyset, no longer the lean, athletic figures described by early Europeans.

"We're *big* people now," an old man named Michael Joe said, as we stood in line at a stall offering fried cod tongues, fried chicken, fried scallops, and French fries—a modern-day version of the Micmac's fatty heaven. The only nonfried item was mooseburger. I asked Michael what this tasted like. "Moose-ey," he said.

Michael Joe introduced me to several other people, all with the last name Joe. This was a legacy of the seventeenth century, when the Micmac converted to Christianity and swapped monikers such as Born on the Way and Make Sure You Dream of Me First for French names. Then the Micmac took their fathers' first names as surnames. Anglicized over time, the family names became John, Joe, Paul, and Louis.

Michael Joe's nephew, Missel Joe, was *saqamaw,* or chief, of the Conne River Band, which numbered about two thousand. A barrel-chested man wearing oval sunglasses and a beaded caribou jacket, Missel Joe had initiated the campaign against Parks Canada's use of the term "Skraeling." " 'Squaw' is a derogatory word," he explained. " 'Nigger' is derogatory. 'Skraeling' is, too." He raised the issue with officials and the term was dropped. "A rare victory over the white man," he said, smiling thinly.

Missel Joe also told me about a Micmac legend that recalled early contact with Europeans. "Our people thought white men looked like dried sea salt on rocks, a sort of off-white. And they had seaweed stuck to their faces—our people didn't have beards." He smiled again. "Too bad we don't know the word our people used to describe Vikings. It was probably worse than 'Skraeling.' "

We were joined by Calvin White, a longtime Indian activist. He said government aid and tribal programs had improved conditions for the Micmac, but prejudice against them lingered. "White people love the Beothuk, they're very romantic," he said. "You know why? The Beothuk are a lost tribe, like your Vikings, and easy to deal with because they're all gone. They can't file lawsuits or raise awkward questions."

AT SUNSET, A band started playing, the cue for the powwow to begin. The first song was "Heave Away," a Newfoundland shanty about a spurned suitor. This was followed by a girl banging a drum. "Thank you, Great Spirit," she intoned before launching into a traditional Micmac chant, honoring the eagle. Then she sang a pop song, "Can't Fight the Moonlight." As darkness fell, an emcee announced, "We'll have karaoke now—traditional karaoke of course. And there's a sweat lodge back near the sacred fire."

I wandered across the field to see the fire: a pile of logs tended by men slumped in lawn chairs. Curious what made it sacred, I asked one of the men, "Do you use a special wood?"

"No," he replied. "Just the wood we got." He grunted, rising from his chair to heave another log on the fire.

"Do you say a special prayer?"

The man guffawed. "Pray it doesn't rain." The others laughed and went silent again.

Nearby arose a much larger flame, tended by a lone figure named Don. He had a long face, high cheekbones, a large broad nose, and straight black hair draped forward across either side of his chest. Don looked like an Indian out of central casting, which he was, having played a warrior in films such as *The Last of the Mohicans*. After telling me this, Don fixed me with a stare so solemn and intense that I couldn't maintain eye contact.

"Hollywood loves us like that," he said, breaking into a grin. "You'd think Indians never laughed." He dragged another pole onto the fire, now a five-foot pyre with sparks shooting high into the sky. When I asked what the blaze was for, he pointed at an igloo-shaped structure nearby. It was made of bent boughs with blankets and a tarpaulin thrown on top. Rocks anchored the edges of the tarp so no air could get in, except through a heavy flap covering the entrance.

"Are you going to have a sweat?" Don asked me.

"Um, sure. I mean, if it's okay."

"It is if you haven't had any drugs or alcohol for four days. And if you want your spirit cleansed."

I hadn't had a beer for several days, so was more or less clean on that score. About my spirit I wasn't so sure. But the night had turned cold and drizzly, the same as it had been for most of my stay in Newfoundland. A nice, hot sauna sounded appealing, as did the chance to experience a more traditional aspect of Micmac culture than karaoke.

"When's the sweat start?" I asked.

"The fire's hot enough. All we need are bodies."

The first to appear was Joey Paul, the ceremony's leader, or "sweat keeper." He was tall and broad-shouldered, with blue eyes, a heavily lined face, and a New York Yankees cap over a ponytail that fell almost to his waist. "My Indian name is Rainbow Child He Who Speaks Like the White Buffalo," Joey told me. "It is a name the spirit brought to me in a vision."

Joey had grown up on a reserve in New Brunswick and been sent to a residential school at the age of six, as part of a government program to assimilate Indians. "When I returned to the reserve, at twelve, I couldn't speak my language anymore and the other kids treated me as white," he said. "They shunned me, or beat me up. So I turned to animals. Birds and bugs became my friends." He paused. "I can learn from an animal. People give you a runaround."

Joey had also apprenticed himself to a Cree medicine man in Alberta. The Micmac, like other tribes from eastern Canada and the United States, freely adopted the traditions of Plains Indians. "A lot of our songs and stories and rituals were lost," Joey said. "So we borrow from out West, where Indians were closer to their traditions. I pick up pebbles wherever I find them, any wisdom I can get."

As we talked, fifteen or so people gathered, more than enough to fill the sweat lodge. They appeared restless and self-absorbed, pacing around the fire and swilling water from plastic bottles, like tennis players before a big match. The fire had burned down to a pyramid of blazing coals. Beneath them, I now saw, lay a pile of large stones.

Joey wandered off for a moment and reappeared bare-chested, wearing only a rough skirt. The others started pulling off their shirts as well. "You'll want to take off your pants and shoes, too," Joey told me, "and also your glasses, unless you want them melted to your face."

This was the first clue that I was in for something more intense than a locker-room sauna. Also disconcerting was the exodus of prospective sweatees: most had drifted into the night, including Don, who had suggested it to me in the first place. That left Joey and his girlfriend, a willowy Frenchwoman wearing a singlet and cotton skirt, three Micmac men in boxer shorts, and me in Gap briefs.

Joey knelt by the fire, burning stalks of sweetgrass and leaves of tobacco and cupping his hands to channel the smoke onto his body. He called this "smudging," or cleansing himself in preparation for the sweat. Then he led us to the lodge.

We crawled through the heavy flap covering the low entrance.

Inside, there was only about four feet between the grass floor and bough ceiling, and just enough space for us to squat in a circle, shoulders touching. Then the flap opened and a pitchfork appeared, with several glowing rocks perched on the tines. A designated "door man" was filling the shallow pit at the center of the lodge. The flap closed and the cramped space instantly filled with dense smoke. Everyone began coughing and clearing their sinuses.

Joey, who sat just to my right, gave a long oration in Micmac, a singsongy tongue that sounded vaguely Asian to me. Then he broke into English, introducing the ritual's props: pipes, a rattle, a small drum, an eagle feather, and a birchbark bowl filled with blueberries. Each had significance, which he'd tell us about as the ceremony proceeded.

Then he shouted, "More grandfathers!" The flap opened again and another pitchfork full of hot stones spilled into the pit. Joey said the stones are called grandfathers because they're ancient and wise, and "help open us up." He dipped the eagle feather in a bucket of water and ladled it onto the rocks. The lodge filled again with the sound of hacking. Then more water, more smoke, and still more coughing, until the lodge sounded like a sanatorium.

Joey chanted, his voice rising above the coughs. "Our lodge door faces east," he said, "so we begin our prayers there, with the eagle, with spring, with vision. We pray for the eagle to bring us the gift to see beyond, to seek enlightenment."

The others answered by saying *"Te-ho,"* a Micmac assent or amen. I was hacking so hard that it took me a moment to realize my skin was on fire. The heat not only burned my face but scorched my throat and nose each time I breathed. Just when I thought I couldn't bear it anymore, I heard the sizzle of more water sprinkling on the rocks. This made it easier to breathe, but also much hotter.

"We pray for our relations," Joey went on. "In Micmac, we say *umsed nogamuch*. That means all of God's creation. Fire is the oldest life force on Mother Earth. It is a living thing and needs air to live, like us."

Te-ho, I thought, no longer able to speak. Joey splashed more water on the rocks. The coughs in the lodge now mingled with moans, including my own. The heat and smoke made my head cloud, and the two mooseburgers I'd consumed weren't sitting well, either. They seemed to be recooking inside my gut.

Joey held up a pipe and said, "The pipe represents connection. The spirit passes through the bowl, which represents the people, and then into us as we smoke. Tobacco is an offering for the ancient ones to be with us."

He intoned a prayer, sucked hard on the pipe, and passed it to me. Just what I needed: more heat and smoke in my lungs. The tobacco was strong and sweet, and seemed to offer momentary relief, or perhaps just distraction. I took several long puffs and passed the pipe to my left. By the time it returned to me, a second and third time, the smoke in the lodge was so thick I couldn't keep my eyes open. Joey sprinkled more water on the rocks. My nose hairs felt on fire. I was about to spontaneously combust.

Then, just as I'd decided to crawl over the others and flee the lodge, Joey shouted, *"Bantadegawi!"* Open up! The door man threw open the flap and a gust of oxygen flowed in. I gulped at the fresh air, relieved and elated, until I realized the ceremony had only just begun. The open flap framed the bonfire outside: a vision of hell still to come.

Joey passed around a jug of water for us to sip and said we could go out for a few minutes, women first. His girlfriend stoically shook her head. "Then you other ladies may go out if you wish," Joey said. There was a moment's pause before the man closest to the door crawled out, quickly followed by the two other men and myself. We had been inside for about forty-five minutes.

It was cold outside and drizzly. I rolled in the wet grass like a puppy. "That's a powerful sweat," said one of the other men, who introduced himself as Gary. I nodded, and confessed that Joey seemed to have a heavy hand with the water. "Don't fight the heat," Gary advised. "Go with it. Give in."

I followed him back into the lodge. "More grandfathers!" Joey shouted. The flap opened and more glowing rocks piled in, like coals shoveled into a coke oven. "Our prayers go clockwise, so the next door is south, the direction of the thunderbird," Joey began. "The season is summer. People get angry and frustrated and desperate when it's hot. Pray for them."

I tried, but could only find a prayer for myself. I loved my grandfathers, they were kind to me. But two of them had been enough.
Please, Lord, let this stop. . . .

My plea was interrupted by more water and a wave of steam so tor-
rid it seemed to blow my head off. I tried pleading in other languages.
No más. Ça suffit. Chalas!

The pipe circulated again. Sucking hard, I became even dizzier. I
thought of what Gary had said. Go with the heat. Give in. I had a momentary sensation that I'd left my body, or fantasized that I had. My
pores weren't just open; they were spigots. Sweat cascaded down my
brow and neck and sides, pooling in my lap. My head began to swim.
I was going under.

"Bantadegawi!" Joey shouted.

This time everyone crawled out. Joey came over and said, "You're
doing well. A lot of people don't make it through one prayer their first
time." He said it helped to take short rapid breaths, which didn't burn
as much. "Or you can lie down and clutch Mother Earth."

I asked if people ever passed out, as I'd felt I'd been about to.

"Oh, yes," he said. "That's when the spirit is really with someone,
so you don't want to wake them up."

We returned to the lodge for round three, which was west, autumn, the bear spirit, and prayers for healing. The hottest round,
Joey said. He passed around the bowl of blueberries: an offering to
the bear, which represents medicine. As Joey shook a rattle, Gary
blew softly on a bone whistle and used a feather to fan yet more heat
on us.

I tried the rapid short breaths Joey had suggested. This made me
hyperventilate. Finally, I stopped struggling and gave in to the torment,
entering a trancelike state, less from heightened consciousness than
from impaired body function. What spirit I had wasn't raised; it was
crushed.

At the end of the third round I felt too weak to go out. Anyway, the
earlier breaks had only made me feel worse, deepening my dread of
what was still to come. Eyes closed, I noticed for the first time the
sound of karaoke drifting across the field. Someone was singing,
"Knock, knock, knockin' on heaven's door."

Round four was north, winter, and the white buffalo—all cold images that seemed impossible to conjure while seated a few inches from a mountain of white-hot grandfathers. A sweat's intensity is measured by the number of hot rocks in the lodge. We'd reached forty-two, not quite a "bear sweat," the pinnacle of suffering, with fifty-six stones and only one break. Still, as Gary had said, a powerful sweat.

Joey talked about the spiritual wisdom of the buffalo. I tried to summon snow-laden bison charging across a wintry plain. But inappropriate images kept intruding: funeral pyres, molten lava, Joan of Arc. Then Joey told us to think of our ancestors and their suffering. Gary began mumbling in Micmac. The man to his left softly wept. They were experiencing a powerful communion with their heritage, as I was with mine—the part that perished in the ovens of Auschwitz.

When the rocks' glow became so low that we couldn't see one another, I took Joey's second piece of advice. There was just enough room to lie back in an awkward curl. Closer to the ground, the air wasn't quite so searing, and when one side of me felt cooked I contorted myself to barbecue the other. I wasn't so much clutching Mother Earth as writhing on top of her.

"The last prayer is for ourselves, but not for money or material gain," Joey said. My prayer wasn't answered; the ceremony still had some time to go. There was another pipe to smoke and more chants. Then Joey asked each of us to speak. One man told of his long battle with diabetes and said, "I wake up every day and thank the Creator I am still alive." Gary thanked his ancestors for surviving so he could be here. Joey spoke of a five-day fast followed by a bear sweat with a hundred-year-old man who said of his spiritual quest, "I am only at the beginning."

By comparison, my four hours of self-involved misery seemed banal. I said I felt ashamed that I'd thought of little during the sweat except how to endure. And then we were done. Following Joey's lead, we slapped our chests and blessed ourselves before crawling out of the lodge, into the light of the guttering bonfire. Our faces glowed like grandfathers. Streaked with sweat and dirt, hair matted, my soaked and filthy briefs clinging to my loins, I felt like one of the Irish hermits encountered by Vikings on North Atlantic islands. A mad monk, minus the spiritual insight.

Joey took me aside in the dark. He wanted to speak to the confession I'd made at the end. "If your spirit is clear," he said, "you have less to cleanse and don't suffer so much." Then, putting a hand on my sweat-slick shoulder, he added a consoling note. "It'll be a lot easier next time."

I AWOKE THE next morning at a no-star motel near the powwow site. Grass and grime still clung to my legs. An angry rash covered my torso—from the heat, or from rolling on ground carpeted in poison sumac. My throat felt as if I'd spent the night snorting ash. Staggering to the bathroom mirror, I saw a figure that looked vaguely Beothuk: red face, red eyes, and red-striped chest, to go with the swollen bug bites.

"Rough night?" a man asked, watching me drain a pitcher of orange juice in the motel breakfast room.

"First time in a sweat lodge," I mumbled.

He nodded sympathetically. "I once saw a man go into a sweat on crutches and come out running. He was that eager to get out."

This cheered me up a little, as did the orange juice. At one deranged moment the night before, I'd felt so sapped of vital fluids that I half expected blood to start spurting from my pores.

The powwow had several more days to go. But I only lasted until early that evening, when the moose meat reappeared and the emcee announced another night of karaoke and sweats by the sacred fire. Like the Norse, I made ready to depart for my own country.

During the long voyage home, and the itchy week after, I read the last chapter of the Vikings' saga in the North Atlantic. Though driven from Vinland, the Norse stayed on in Greenland for several centuries, becoming gradually more isolated from European affairs. The last news trickling out of the colony, in the early 1400s, told of a man burned at the stake for witchcraft, and the marriage of a Sigrid and Thorstein. Then, silence.

In 1721, a Lutheran missionary sailed from Norway to Greenland in search of converts (among other developments, Greenlanders would have missed the Reformation). But he found only ruins and a few tales among Inuit of white men who had vanished long before. Three centuries later, archaeologists in Greenland uncovered hundreds of Norse graves, bones of butchered dogs, and other hints of famine. A Danish anatomist concluded that the "tall Northern race" had "degenerated" in Greenland, becoming puny and weak-minded. More sober theorists have since attributed the colony's mysterious demise to a mini Ice Age, plague, pirate raids, or Inuit attacks.

But the latest trend is to blame the colonists themselves. The scientist Jared Diamond used Norse Greenland as exhibit A in his 2005 bestseller, *Collapse: How Societies Choose to Fail or Succeed*. The Norse, in Diamond's view, brought about their own extinction by clinging to Eurocentric ways that depleted scarce resources and left settlers unable to adapt as the climate and circumstances changed.

The Norse venture to Vinland is likewise remembered for its failure. Daniel Boorstin, one of America's best-known historians, offers a typical view in *The Discoverers*. "Was there ever before so long a voyage," he writes, "that made so little difference?" His short chapter on Vikings in America is titled "Dead End in Vinland."

If judged only by its legacy, Vinland was indeed a dud. The Norse achieved little, and what knowledge they gained of America died with them. There's no evidence that Europeans who set off across the Atlantic in later centuries were aware of the Norse voyages that preceded theirs.

But after visiting Newfoundland, and learning about life in A.D. 1000, I found it strange to look back at the Norse and see only failure. At the time Eirik the Red discovered Greenland, Europeans rarely sailed out of sight of their own continent. By the time they began doing so, in the fifteenth century, mariners sailed in swift and nimble caravels, steered with rudders and guided by sextant and compass. The Norse lacked these tools, yet voyaged countless times across the stormy North Atlantic.

Vinland's brief flicker was even more extraordinary. When Leif and his siblings set off, Norse Greenland was only fifteen years old, with a population of about five hundred. Vinland was a satellite of a satellite, its voyagers on the medieval equivalent of a space walk, tethered to a mother ship already at the furthest reach of European society and knowledge. Almost five centuries would pass between Leif's sail and the next attempt to so much as cross the Atlantic. What seems most surprising is not that Norse Vinland failed, but that it happened at all.

Nor was the Vikings' fate anomalous. The Europeans who resettled America after 1492 brought horses, guns, and other advantages unknown to the Norse. Yet they, too, found it hard to sustain a toehold, even in settings much gentler than subarctic Canada. Dozens of early colonies foundered in mass death or abandonment. Failure was the norm, not the exception.

According to America's national saga, English settlers ultimately triumphed because of their superior grit, idealism, and entrepreneurship. But Thomas McGovern, a leading scholar of Norse settlement, draws on the field of biogeography to make a less ennobling case. Not only humans, but all invasive species struggle to survive when colonizing new environments. Small incoming populations rarely take root. The difference between success and failure typically depends on the number of times a new group arrives, and in what strength.

The mortality rate among early settlers of Jamestown was close to 80 percent. In Plymouth, half the *Mayflower* passengers died within six months of landing. But waves of settlers kept restocking Virginia and Massachusetts. "Sheer weight of numbers and the backing of increasingly powerful mercantile states," McGovern concludes, proved critical to success.

So, too, was English colonists' ability to subdue, destroy, or displace the host population. The Norse lacked this power, at least in America. Their swords, axes, and Viking bravado made them deadly in close combat, but not against a mobile force in canoes, wielding bows and catapults. Outnumbered, on alien terrain, and at the end of a supply line fifteen hundred miles long, the invaders gave up. In the first recorded contest between Europeans and natives of America, the home team had won.

The next encounter would occur five centuries later, on very different ground, between very different players: southern peoples, meeting on hot, sandy beaches near the Tropic of Cancer. But in one respect, the saga of first contact would repeat itself. America, discovered accidentally by Bjarni Herjólfsson, would be rediscovered by a man who didn't know where he was, or what he'd done.

CHAPTER 2

1492

THE HIDDEN HALF OF THE GLOBE

> An age will come after many years when the
> Ocean will loose the chains of things, and a
> huge land lie revealed.
>
> —Seneca, *Medea*

CHRISTOPHER COLUMBUS, ADMIRAL of the Ocean Sea, commands more print than almost any man in history. There are more books devoted to his memory than to Alexander the Great, Leonardo da Vinci, or Adolf Hitler. He appears in Milton's *Paradise Lost,* Adam Smith's *Wealth of Nations,* and the Beat verse of Lawrence Ferlinghetti. Antonín Dvořák composed a symphony in his honor. Friedrich Nietzsche even penned a youthful poem, "Colombo," casting the navigator as an existential seeker who cries, "My mind is wrestling with doubts!"

Yet despite this attention—and, often, because of it—the real Columbus remains elusive. No contemporary portrait of him exists. Historians disagree on basic facts about his life: where and when he was born, married, and buried. A scan of Columbus-related titles (more than fifteen hundred in all, in many languages) includes *The Mysterious History of Columbus, The Master Puzzle of History, El Enigma de Colón,* and two books called *In Search of Columbus.*

One reason for this mystery is that Columbus invited it. He

masked his own story, even signing his name in a pyramid of symbols that has yet to be conclusively deciphered. "Like the squid," writes the Spanish historian Salvador de Madariaga, "he oozes out a cloud of ink round every hard square fact of his life."

Mystery, in turn, gave rise to myth. Several centuries after his death, Columbus was disinterred by nationalists in the newly created United States. Eager to establish an identity apart from England, they enshrined the Genoese mariner as a proto-American hero: underdog, individualist, pathfinder, and Pilgrim-like agent of Christianity. Later, Italians and other Catholic immigrants made Columbus a source of ethnic pride. He was even put forth as a candidate for sainthood.

The navigator's deification peaked with the four hundredth anniversary of his 1492 sail, a gala marked by the World's Columbian Exposition in Chicago, the raising of a statue at New York City's Columbus Circle, and parades across the land. "Columbus stood in his age as the pioneer of progress and enlightenment," President Benjamin Harrison declared.

By the five hundredth anniversary of his sail, in 1992, a very different mood prevailed; progress was out, postcolonialism in. Columbus was dug up again, this time to be damned as the first in a long line of Europeans to exploit and exterminate Native Americans. The Indian activist Russell Means set the tone for the 1992 remembrance by pouring blood on a Columbus statue and declaring that the discoverer "makes Hitler look like a juvenile delinquent."

The well of Columbian myths and countermyths is now so deep that one can extract from it any number of contradictory figures: devout Christian and closet Jew, medieval spiritualist and modern empiricist, Italian hero and imperialist villain. About the only thing on which most sources agree is that Columbus transformed the world with his sail in 1492.

ON MY RETURN from Newfoundland, I spent weeks that stretched into months navigating the Columbus literature. The first biography of him, by his son Ferdinand, seemed a good place to start—except that even Ferdinand was left in the dark. On the biography's opening page, he confides that his father "chose to leave in obscurity" all details of his early life.

After piloting through a half dozen other tomes, I turned to Columbus's own writing. This was heavy sailing, too. No two editions and translations agreed, and some of what Columbus wrote was un-translatable, at least for a lay reader. "The kingdom of Tarshis is at the end of the Orient," he scribbled in the margin of a book on geography. "Note that the king of Tarshis came to the Lord at Jerusalem, and spent a year and 13 days en route." Or this: "I saw three sirens that came very high out of the sea. They are not as beautiful as they are painted, since in some ways they have a face like a man." Before long, I realized I needed a Bible, a bestiary, and a medieval *mappa mundi* to begin making sense of the man.

Slowly, though, an outline of his thinking started to take form. And what struck me, by the time I'd called an arbitrary halt to my bi-ographical research, was how radically the historic Columbus diverged from my childhood image of America's "discoverer." The flesh-and-blood navigator wasn't just more nuanced than the storybook icon; he was its virtual opposite.

Most scholars believe Columbus was born in 1451, to a family of wool weavers in Genoa. After working in the wool trade, he went to sea and literally washed ashore in Portugal after an attack on his ship by the French. He married, only to be quickly widowed and left with a young son. First in Portugal, and then in Spain, Columbus tirelessly peddled his vision of a westward sail to Asia. By the time he finally won support from Queen Isabel and King Ferdinand, the tall, ruddy Ge-noese was forty years old and his red hair had turned white.

This synopsis of Columbus's life to 1492 fits an appealing Ameri-can trope: the up-from-nothing striver, like log-cabin Abe or the mil-lions of immigrants who crossed the Atlantic. But Columbus would have been appalled to be cast in this mold. Not only did he conceal his modest origins; he had a child by a peasant's daughter but never mar-ried her, apparently because of her lowly status. And one reason Columbus struggled to find a patron for his voyage was his excessive demand for noble titles and privileges, including "Admiral of the Ocean Sea" and "Viceroy" of the lands he found. Don Cristóbal Colón, as he became known in Spain, was a man of his feudal day: honor and status meant everything. A champion of the common man he was not.

Nor was Columbus a lonely individualist, struggling to overcome impossible odds. His native Genoa was a bustling international port, renowned for its traders and financiers. Columbus allied himself with the city's leading merchants, with influential Genoese overseas, and with powerful clerics and courtiers in Spain. He married into a family of noble descent and hereditary privileges, including a governorship in the Azores. Columbus knew how to network.

But the most persistent and misleading myth about Columbus is that he was a farsighted modern, battling medieval darkness. Learned men of the day, the story goes, opposed the mariner because they thought the earth was flat. Anyone who sailed too far west would tumble over the world's edge, like water spilling off a table. As told by Washington Irving in his 1828 biography (a source of many enduring fictions about Columbus), the "simple mariner" stood "pleading the cause of the new world" before an ignorant Old World establishment. In the end, Columbus boldly sailed off and proved his critics wrong.

It *is* true that expert councils in Spain and Portugal rejected Columbus's plan. But their reasons for doing so had nothing to do with flat-earth superstition. The Greeks had first posited the roundness of the planet some two thousand years earlier, and their writings were widely accepted in the fifteenth century. Even the medieval church, an institution unrenowned for its forward thinking, had acknowledged that the earth was round—seven hundred years before Columbus's birth, in the depths of the so-called Dark Ages. Islamic scholars concurred in this opinion.

The question confronting cosmographers in the late 1400s wasn't the shape of the earth, but its size. Ignorant of America, Europeans imagined one vast "Ocean Sea" to their west, washing against the shores of Asia. But how wide was that ocean, and could it be crossed? To answer this, Europeans studied ancients such as Ptolemy, as well as Marco Polo and other travelers whose writing held clues to the extent of Asia. The result was a tangle of calculations and conjectures based on flawed data. In this respect, Columbus was indeed a maverick. His image of the globe was the most extreme and wrongheaded of them all.

Everyone knows Columbus landed in America thinking he'd reached "the Indies" (which referred in 1492 to all of Asia east of the Indus River). But this famed mistake flowed from a much more fundamental error. To estimate how far he needed to sail, Columbus took the imperfect coordinates of earlier theorists and magnified their faults. "The end of Spain and the beginning of India are not far distant," he jotted in the margin of one book. "This sea can be crossed in a few days with a fair wind."

Columbus buttressed this vision with scriptural passages, such as one stating that six-sevenths of the world is land. In later life, the navigator wrote a manuscript called *The Book of Prophecies,* casting himself as God's agent and his westward sail as the fulfillment of a divine mission. "All the sciences," he wrote, "were of no use to me." Rather, he was propelled across the ocean by "the Lord having opened my mind to the fact that it would be possible to sail from here to the Indies." He also thought his voyage would bring about worldwide conversion to Christianity and the recapture of Jerusalem from Muslim infidels.

In short, the man so often celebrated as a bridge to the modern era was closer to a mystic knight-errant, tilting at a globe of his own imagining. Columbus sailed off believing that Asia lay about three thousand miles west. The true figure was over eleven thousand miles—not to mention that a huge continent blocked his path. The long-maligned experts in Spain and Portugal were therefore right to doubt the navigator. But he didn't heed them, and the rest is American history. Columbus changed the world not because he was right, but because he was so stubbornly wrong. Convinced the globe was small, he began the process of making it so, by bringing a new world into orbit of the old.

BUT THAT WAS, at best, only part of the story. With Columbus, even more than with most figures, it's easy to fall prey to "Great Man" history. This old-school approach sees the past as the biography of extraordinary individuals: men make the times, not the other way around. Critics of Columbus are as prone to this as his admirers, blaming him for the despoliation of the lands and peoples he discovered. Hero or villain, however, Columbus was only able to put his idiosyncratic vision into practice because he arrived at a propitious moment in Western history.

A sixteenth-century engraving of Columbus taking leave from Ferdinand and Isabel

In 1453, two years after his birth, Constantinople fell to the Ottoman Turks, cutting Europe's traditional path to the spices and other goods of the Orient. This hastened the search for alternative routes and riches, led by Portugal, which had already begun probing Africa under the leadership of Prince Henry "the Navigator." The sobriquet is misleading; Henry rarely strayed far from shore, and when he did he got seasick. But his expansionist impulses and support of overseas navigation helped turn tiny Portugal into a maritime power.

Among other innovations, the Portuguese developed a versatile, shallow-draft ship, the caravel, which Columbus would use on his 1492 voyage. They also turned long-distance ocean sailing into a rich commercial venture, by founding fortified trading posts on the West African coast and bartering finished goods for gold, spices, and slaves. When Columbus washed ashore in Portugal, in his twenties, he arrived at the perfect place to train as a navigator and colonizer.

But it was the wrong place to peddle his vision of a westward sail to Asia. Portugal was already charting a sea route to the Indies, via Africa, which Bartholomew Dias rounded in 1488. By then, Columbus had decamped to Spain—another timely arrival. The country was just emerging as a unified power, eager to compete with Portugal and to open its own trade routes. Spain was also completing its triumphant *Reconquista* of lands held by Muslims since the eighth century. Queen Isabel and King Ferdinand's eventual decision to back Columbus, in April 1492, came just months after the fall of Granada, the last Muslim outpost in Europe, and within weeks of their decree (drafted by the Grand Inquisitor Tomás de Torquemada) commanding all Jews to convert or leave Spain. Columbus was the same age as Isabel and appealed to her deep piety. He promised not only to fill Spain's war-depleted coffers but to use the proceeds toward a Holy Land crusade.

Another reason the monarchs agreed to dispatch Columbus was that they risked little in doing so. Legend depicts Isabel as selling her jewels to pay for the navigator's voyage. She didn't need to. The cost of the mission, about two million maravedis, is hard to convert into modern currency, but it was one-thirtieth the amount that Ferdinand and Isabel spent on their daughter's wedding. The Crown also had a convenient debt to collect: the use of two equipped caravels in the southern port of Palos, punishment for unspecified crimes committed by the town. The ships were called *Niña* and *Pinta,* or "Girl" and "Painted Lady." Columbus borrowed money to charter a third vessel, his flagship, the *Santa María.*

No drawings of the ships survive and little is known about them. Columbus's most eminent biographer, Samuel Eliot Morison, believes the *Pinta* was seventy feet long, with the *Niña* a bit smaller and the *Santa María* a larger and less nimble vessel. The captains of the *Niña* and *Pinta* were brothers from Palos, and most of the sailors came from the same region. The crew included four men condemned to death, one for murder and three for trying to free him from prison. They won pardons in exchange for sailing with Columbus.

Among the eighty-six or so others who embarked from Palos, the credentials of two reveal the novelty of the entire enterprise. Luis de Torres was a converso, or converted Jew, who knew Hebrew, Arabic, and Aramaic. Rodrigo de Xeres, also probably a converso, had sailed to Guinea and met an African king. It was thought that these two cosmopolitans would act as ambassadors to Oriental potentates on the far side of the Ocean Sea. The Crown also sent along a passport and a letter of introduction to the Grand Khan, written in Latin.

Columbus's ships weighed anchor in August 1492, one day after the last of the vessels carrying Jews from Spain had been ordered to depart. He spent a week reaching the Canaries, an Atlantic outpost newly colonized by the Spanish, and a month on the islands provisioning for the voyage ahead. Columbus believed the ocean crossing to Asia would take twenty-one days. But to be safe, he carried ample supplies, including olive oil, wine, dried meat and fish, and biscuits, or hardtack. Then he launched into the Atlantic.

In open water, a different Columbus emerges. Though often deluded on land, he was utterly clear-eyed at sea. "Only by looking at a cloud or by night at a star, he knew what was going to happen and whether there would be foul weather," a shipmate observed. Using simple instruments of the day—quadrant, compass, sand-filled half-hour glass—Columbus set a course due west. He may not have realized where he was headed, but he knew how best to get there: by dead reckoning along a latitude that put the prevailing winds at his back, propelling him across the ocean. These breezes, now known as the trade winds, move clockwise in a giant circle in the middle of the Atlantic; they later helped carry Columbus back to Europe.

From the time of his departure from Spain, we also have his own impressions, recorded in a daily journal. The original has been lost; what survives is an abridgment—some of it transcribed, some summarized—by others after the voyage. It is hard to determine how much these versions corrupted Columbus's words, or what was omitted. But the voice and content of the journal accord with other writings by Columbus. For the most part, it has the feel of a reliable and contemporaneous record of his thoughts and actions—including some that aren't flattering to the navigator. The first such passage appears on September 9, just after Columbus left the Canaries. "This day we completely lost sight of land, and many men sighed and wept for fear they would not see it again," he wrote. "I decided to reckon fewer leagues than we actually made. I did this that they might not think themselves so great a distance from Spain as they actually were." The next day, the ships sailed 180 miles, but "I recorded only 144 miles in order not to alarm the sailors if the voyage is lengthy."

For a few weeks the journey was uneventful, except for the Sargasso Sea, a vast area of ocean covered in dense weed: a strange sight to the crew, but no impediment to sailing. Columbus, an acute and sensuous observer, noted the ocean's smoothness and color and the air's "sweet and balmy" feel, "so fragrant that it is a pleasure to breathe it." As the voyage progressed, he saw signs everywhere that land was near. Whales, weeds, bird flocks—all became for the navigator "a sure sign of land," the constant refrain of his voyage.

His crew wasn't so sanguine. Reaching the northern edge of the trade winds, the ships lost speed, slowing from 165 miles one day to 75 the next, and then only 24. As the wind weakened and shifted, so did the sailors' morale. "The crew is agitated, thinking that no winds blow in these parts that will return them to Spain," Columbus wrote on September 22. "I am having serious trouble with the crew," he added two days later. "They have said that it is insanity and suicidal on their part to risk their lives following the madness of a foreigner."

Columbus also sensed that the *Pinta*'s captain, Martín Alonso Pinzón, "cannot be trusted." Pinzón sailed ahead, and Columbus suspected he did this so he could be first to sight land and claim "the rewards and honors of this enterprise for himself."

At sunset on September 25, Pinzón shouted from the *Pinta* that he'd sighted shore. Sailors on the *Niña* climbed the rigging and seconded the claim. In the morning, however, Columbus saw it "was nothing more than squall clouds." Eleven days later, the *Niña* fired its cannon and raised a flag to signal that land had appeared. This, too, "was only an illusion." Columbus adjusted course to the southwest, following a flock of birds in hopes they would fly toward shore.

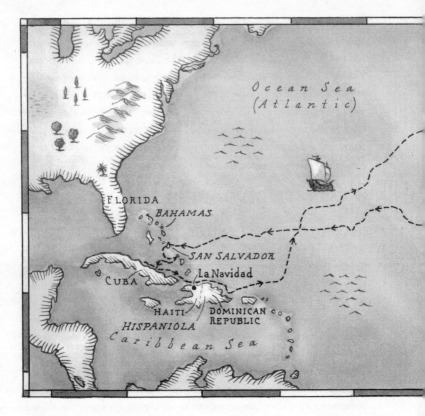

By then, the ships had sailed for four weeks since last sighting land. This was double "all previous records for ocean navigation," writes Samuel Eliot Morison. The ships were also well past the point by which Columbus had expected to reach Asia. The hourglass on his men's patience had run out.

"They could stand it no longer," Columbus wrote on October 10. He reproached the sailors for their lack of spirit, and made it plain their complaints were useless. "I had started out to find the Indies," he told them, "and would continue until I had accomplished that mission, with the help of Our Lord."

The next day, he saw green reeds and a stick in the water "that looks man-made." He doubled the number of lookouts and reminded

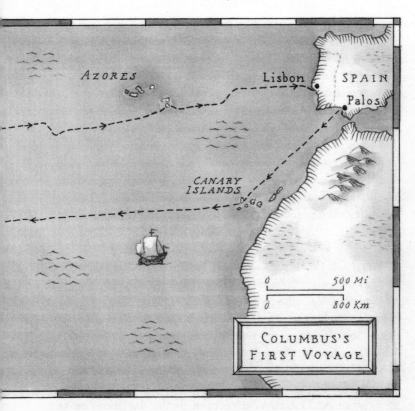

COLUMBUS'S
FIRST VOYAGE

them that the first to make a confirmed sighting of land would receive a large cash prize from the Crown and a silk doublet from him. Late that night, Columbus thought he saw a light to the west, "like a little wax candle bobbing up and down." He summoned two other men; one saw the light, the other did not. "It was such an uncertain thing that I did not feel it was adequate proof of land."

Four hours later, the *Pinta* fired one of its guns. A lookout named Rodrigo de Triana had sighted land, about six miles to the west. Columbus reconsidered his doubts from the night before. "I now believe that the light I saw earlier was a sign from God and that it was truly the first positive indication of land."

Scholars and naval officers have concluded that Columbus

couldn't have seen a fire or any other light the night before, when his ship lay about thirty-five miles offshore. Overwrought and exhausted, he may have imagined a light where there was none. But Columbus claimed the honor of discovery, and the reward. Of Rodrigo de Triana we hear no more in the navigator's journal.

The morning of October 12 brought Columbus his first clear view of the coast. "At dawn we saw naked people, and I went ashore in the ship's boat," he wrote. He raised banners emblazoned with a green cross and the initials of Spain's monarchs, claiming the land in their name. Columbus called it San Salvador, or Holy Savior. According to one account, he and his men then knelt to kiss the sand, "thanking God who had requited them after a voyage so long and strange."

I FIRST READ Columbus's account of his landing in a writing studio forty miles from my hometown, Washington, D.C., short for "District of Columbia"—a feminized version of "Columbus." Two state capitals and some forty other U.S. cities, towns, and counties also bear his name. So do countless institutions, including Columbia University, which I'd attended. His landing date, of course, is a national holiday.

Like most Americans, I'd never given any of this a second thought—until I tracked Columbus's path on a nautical chart pinned to my office wall. Only then did it occur to me that the nation's capital and a host of other sites across the land are named for a man who never set foot on this continent.

Just to be sure, I skipped ahead, tracing the rest of his voyage and three later sails he made across the Atlantic. Columbus hopscotched all over the Americas between 1492 and 1504, and was the first European to land at a score of modern nations. Not once did he see or touch anything that later became U.S. soil.

I returned to his first landing, at the island he called San Salvador. The literature on this alone could fill a bookshelf. A painting of the scene adorns the U.S. Capitol Rotunda. Yet, as with so much about Columbus, a key detail remains mysterious. Where, exactly, was he?

As best as mariners and scholars can determine, Columbus made landfall at the eastern edge of the Bahamas, some four hundred miles southeast of Florida. But the Bahamas are an archipelago of seven hundred islands, plus three times that number of the sand-and-coral islets called cays. Elaborate cases have been made for at least nine different islands and cays, including one named Watlings that helpfully rechristened itself San Salvador in 1926. But no conclusive trace of Columbus's Bahamian visit has yet been found.

The mystery of his landing site is all the more tantalizing because of what he wrote about it. The journal entries for the week he spent touring San Salvador and nearby isles read like postcards from paradise. "The water is very clear and you can see the bottom during the daylight hours. . . . Here the fishes are so unlike ours that it is amazing . . . colored in a thousand ways; and so bright that anyone would marvel." He observed strange plants with equal relish. "You can even smell the flowers as you approach this coast; it is the most fragrant thing on earth." Though animal life was sparse, Columbus and his men sampled a local delicacy, a six-foot "serpent" that was probably an iguana. "Tastes like chicken," Columbus observed.

He also marveled at the naked islanders who greeted him on the beach, describing them as tall, "well-proportioned," and "the color of sunburned peasants," with "very pretty" eyes and straight hair worn short in front and long in back. Columbus, believing he had reached islands off the Orient, called the natives *Indios,* or Indians. In a roundabout way, he was right; Columbus hadn't reached Asia, but he had stumbled onto people of Asian stock. The islanders, like the natives encountered by Vikings, were distantly descended from migrants who had crossed from Asia to America thousands of years before.

Columbus's perspective was also influenced by his earlier travels in the Old World. Islanders lived in tall, airy structures that resembled "Moorish tents," and traveled in "boats fashioned in one piece from the trunks of trees," which he called *almadias,* the Portuguese term for African dugouts. Only later would he learn the native word: *canoa.* He also noted swinging beds made from "nets of cotton," which islanders called *hamaca.* Like canoes, hammocks would quickly become part of the European lexicon, and a convenience adopted by sailors.

Communication, at this point, was limited to gestures. So it's hard to know how Columbus learned that the native name for San Salvador

An Indian paddling a canoe, from a 1535 Spanish history of the Indies

was Guanahani (which may have been a word for iguana). Even more dubious were his attempts at divining native beliefs. "By the signs they made I think they are asking if we came from Heaven," he wrote, adding that they shouted to one another, "Come see the men from Heaven." He would repeat this claim at other islands, and later visitors to America took up the self-serving belief that awestruck natives thought Europeans fell from the sky.

Columbus also helped implant the image of Indians as childlike innocents. "I cannot get over the fact of how docile these people are," he wrote. Later, he called them "tractable." The first evidence of this came on the beach at San Salvador, where Columbus distributed trinkets that had been market-tested in Africa: red caps, glass beads, and small, tinkling hawks' bells. Natives "took great pleasure in this," and offered all they owned in exchange, including parrots and balls of cotton. Columbus's men, like the Vikings before them, couldn't believe their luck, and started swapping broken glass and crockery for spears tipped with fish teeth.

The islanders were accommodating in other ways, too. "Some brought us water; others, things to eat," Columbus wrote. "Others, seeing that I did not care to go ashore, jumped into the sea and swam out to us." On another island, natives showed crewmen where to find fresh water and carried full casks to the boats.

It's impossible to know whether natives behaved this way out of instinctive hospitality, for fear of Spanish swords, or in hopes of extracting more bells and beads. But Columbus's response says much about his mind-set and the legacy of his voyage. After just a few hours ashore, he wrote of islanders: "They ought to make good and skilled servants." Two days later, having departed San Salvador with seven captives to bring to the king and queen, he added: "After they learn our language I shall return them, unless Your Highnesses order that the entire population be taken to Castile, or held captive here. With 50 men you could subject everyone and make them do what you wished."

As callous as this sentiment appears, Columbus didn't conjure it out of nowhere. He'd voyaged to slave ports in Africa; to the Atlantic island of Madeira, where the Portuguese imported slaves to work on sugar plantations; and to the Canaries, where the Spanish were completing the conquest and enslavement of the native Guanches. Europeans also enslaved Muslims captured in battle, and, in earlier times, had done the same to Slavs: the origin of the word "slave." Columbus's tragic contribution was to be the first European to see the potential for forced labor in the New World.

Another enduring affliction also traces back to that first, seemingly innocent encounter at San Salvador. Among the goods that natives offered sailors was "a kind of dry leaf that they hold in great esteem." This mysterious plant reappeared on other islands, where Columbus finally recognized its use. Men and women carried "a half-burnt weed in their hands, being the herbs they are accustomed to smoke." The herbs were rolled inside a leaf to form tubes the natives called *tabaco*s. Before long, tobacco would hook Europeans and become one of America's most profitable exports.

In 1492, however, Columbus was fixated on a more familiar commodity. He noticed a piece of gold hanging from an islander's nose and learned "by signs" that a sail to the south would lead him to a king who "has great containers of it." Back at sea, the natives he'd seized directed him to an island where they said people wore gold bracelets. Columbus suspected they "made up the tale in order to get me to put ashore so they could escape." But he landed anyway, staying just long enough to establish that there wasn't any gold. Then he headed off for yet another island, rumored to be even richer. Thus began the frantic

Indians smoking cigar-like rolls of tobacco, from a sixteenth-century French account of the New World

chase after precious metal that would drive the Spanish all over the Americas in the fifty years to follow.

After finding no gold in the Bahamas, Columbus embarked for an island his captives called Cuba, the rare native place name in the Caribbean that survives to this day. Indians told him the island "has much commerce; gold, spices, ships, and merchants." This report, and Columbus's "globes and world maps," he wrote, convinced the navigator that Cuba and Japan "are one and the same."

Reaching Cuba's north coast, he declared the island "the most beautiful I have seen," mountainous, fecund, and mild. But the promised riches were nowhere in sight. Nor did the island match Marco Polo's tales of "Cipango," as he called Japan. The Venetian had described gold-plated palaces and wondrous pink pearls. Columbus found only palm huts and "tasteless snails."

Rather than be discouraged by this, Columbus displayed his exceptional talent for wishful thinking. If Cuba wasn't Japan, then it must be the Asian mainland. The Great Khan of China couldn't be far off!

To find him, Columbus dispatched his converso emissaries, Rodrigo de Xerez and Luis de Torres, carrying trade beads, their Latin letter from the Crown, and samples of cinnamon and pepper, "so that they would recognize the same if they came across them." Columbus remained with his ship; throughout the voyage, he rarely ventured ashore for long.

The diplomats and their Indian guides returned several days later, having traveled thirty-six miles inland to a large settlement. The emissaries were lodged, fed, carried on villagers' shoulders, and enthroned on chairs shaped like "a short-legged animal," with the tail lifted up to form the seat's back. Women surrounded them, "kissing their hands and feet, trying to see if they were of flesh and bone like themselves."

The scene sounds like a classic of first contact. But Columbus tells us little else, except that Indians studied the cinnamon and pepper, of which they themselves had none. Evidently eager to please, they "told by signs that there were many such spices nearby to the SE"—or so the diplomats understood. Torres's Hebrew, Arabic, and Aramaic weren't of much use. "Having seen that there were no rich cities," Columbus tersely concludes, "my men returned."

Still, the navigator was undaunted. While the envoys were away, he, too, had heard about spices to the southeast, as well as gold. So he coasted Cuba until he came to its eastern edge, within sight of an island called Bohio. The Indians on board were terrified of Bohio's people, who they said had the faces of dogs and one eye in the middle of their foreheads. In fact, such monsters had been imagined by the medieval writer John Mandeville, whose fanciful travelogue was extremely popular in Columbus's day. Indians evidently picked up on sailors' belief in such creatures, and also warned of warriors on Bohio who ate other humans (Mandeville had written of this, too). Natives called these man-eaters Canibales, thus introducing yet another word to the Western lexicon.

Columbus, as usual, put a positive spin on this report. He guessed that the Canibales had taken captives in Cuba and were therefore "more astute and intelligent" than the Indians he'd met so far. To Columbus, this could only signify one thing: Canibales belonged "to the domain of

Dog-headed cannibals butcher and prepare humans for eating, from a German book on Columbus's discoveries, 1525

the Great Khan." And so he headed out to sea again, steering for Bohio.

The new island was even more beautiful than Cuba, with wide plains that reminded Columbus of Castile. He called it La Isla Española, "the Spanish Island." And instead of Canibales—or Caribs, as the man-eaters were also called—he met coastal natives "so liberal in giving, and so timid, that they strip themselves of everything to give all that they have to us." At one point, he claimed, a thousand people paddled canoes out to greet the Spanish ships, holding up their goods and crying, "Take, take."

Better still, they told of vast gold deposits in the island's interior, at a place called Cibao. To Columbus, the name "Cibao" sounded enough like "Cipango" to convince him that he'd finally reached Japan. And the gold was there for the taking, or so he surmised. Meeting a cacique, or hereditary ruler, Columbus confessed that the two parties comprehended nothing of what the other said. "Nevertheless, I understood he told me that if anything here would please me, the whole island was at my command."

But the seas and shoals were not. On Christmas Eve, a "young ship's boy" was carelessly left at the helm of the *Santa María,* perhaps because the rest of the crew was sleeping off their holiday drinking. Currents carried the ship onto a reef, where it became stuck and took on water. Columbus and his crew had to abandon ship and board the *Niña*. Indians came out in canoes to unload the *Santa María* so that its provisions were saved.

Columbus had lost his flagship, yet even this misfortune seemed to him providential. "Our Lord miraculously ordered that the *Santa María* should remain here because it is the best place on the islands to make a settlement, and it is near the gold mines." He used wood from the *Santa María* to build a small fort and left thirty-nine men with enough bread and wine for a year, as well as seeds. Columbus named the outpost Villa de la Navidad, City of the Nativity, since it was founded on Christmas.

The navigator commanded the Spanish settlers to respect island chiefs, commit no injuries or insults (particularly toward women), and stay together at La Navidad, unless guided by Indians to gold mines. Sailing off, he felt sure he would return from Spain to find that his men had discovered riches "in such quantities that within three years the Sovereigns will prepare for and undertake the conquest of the Holy Land."

THE HEROIC VERSION of Columbus's story, taught to generations of American schoolchildren, is radically abridged. It dwells on the difficult lead-up to his voyage and climaxes with his dramatic "discovery" in 1492. All but forgotten are Columbus's three later sails to America and his checkered career as a colonial administrator. Modern critics of Columbus reverse the traditional narrative. They focus on his troubled later voyages, and the horrors that followed in his wake, to cast the Genoese as a genocidal figure. Columbus didn't discover America; he destroyed it.

But the more I read of the navigator's story, the less he seemed to fit either paradigm. After leaving the thirty-nine settlers at La Navidad, Columbus followed the coast of La Isla Española to the island's eastern edge, where he met natives very different from those he'd encountered so far. Their faces were smeared with charcoal, they wore parrot-feather headdresses, and they carried bows and heavy clubs. Sailors who tried to trade with them quickly became afraid and launched an attack, slashing one man in the buttocks and wounding another in the chest before the natives took flight.

Columbus, characteristically, stayed on board his ship during the fight. But after hearing the report of his men, he wrote, "The people here are evil, and I believe they are from the island of Caribe, and that they eat men." Of the violence, he added, "In one way it troubled me and in another it did not, in that now they might be afraid of us."

The encounter at what Columbus called the Gulf of Arrows marked the only recorded bloodshed during his first voyage. This may have been due to the pacific character of most islanders he met, and the weakness of their arms. But the absence of carnage is nonetheless striking. Vikings had slain the first natives they met, without provocation, and many of the Europeans who followed Columbus to America began killing almost from the moment they hit the beach.

On his first voyage, at least, Columbus didn't instinctively resort to violence. Nor did he regard natives as subhuman Skraelings. Rather, he saw them as children and potential converts, albeit in servitude to Europeans. Only the Caribs, as alleged cannibals, were beyond redemption. That Columbus felt troubled at all by violence against them was unusual in an era that lionized crusaders and the spilling of "infidel" blood.

He was also determined to find the island he believed the Canibales came from. But by the time he left the Gulf of Arrows, Columbus's caravel was leaking, his sailors were restive, and he feared that the captain of the *Pinta,* the troublesome Martín Alonso Pinzón, would sail ahead to Europe and claim the glory of discovery. So when a strong wind "blew very favorably for going to Spain," Columbus abandoned his plans for further exploration and headed home.

He almost didn't make it. Near the Azores, the ships hit a winter storm so fierce that huge waves crashed from opposite directions, breaking over the *Niña,* while the *Pinta* "disappeared from sight." Even Columbus's habitual confidence was shaken. "All were resigned to being lost," he wrote. Fearing that news of his discovery would never reach Spain, he put a wax-sealed manuscript telling of his voyage in a barrel and had it thrown overboard. He and his men also drew lots—actually, chickpeas from a cap—to determine who would make a religious pilgrimage if the crew survived.

The next day the sky cleared, and soon after the *Niña* took refuge in the Azores. But when Columbus resumed sailing, he hit another storm that shredded the ship's sails and brought out the chickpeas again. When the gale abated, Columbus found he was off Lisbon, and brought his crippled ship to shore. During his short stay, he was received "with great honor" by Portugal's king, who had turned down the chance to sponsor the voyage: for the spurned mariner, a delicious vindication.

Finally, on March 15, 1493, Columbus anchored near Palos, in Spain, thirty-two weeks after his departure from the town. His journal ends that day, on a told-you-so note. "The remarkable miracles which occurred during this voyage and for me," Columbus wrote the king and queen, came despite the opposition "of so many of the principal persons of your household, who were all against me and treated this undertaking as folly." As for his other nemesis, the *Pinta*'s captain, Columbus had reached Palos just ahead of him. Pinzón performed an additional favor by dropping dead soon after coming ashore.

Nothing, it now seemed, stood between Columbus and the glory and honors he so avidly sought. The mariner began a triumphant procession to the royal court in Barcelona, bearing Indians, parrots, sweet potatoes, and other novelties as presents for the queen. "Eternal God our Lord," Columbus wrote, in a letter that quickly circulated across Europe, "gives to all those who walk His Way, victory over things which seem impossible."

GLASSY-EYED FROM STUDYING logs and letters and nautical charts, it dawned on me one afternoon that Columbus Day loomed a few weeks off. This seemed an appropriate moment to revisit one of the navigator's discoveries. The question was, Which one?

His first landing, on Columbus Day in 1492, seemed the logical choice. But as I'd already learned, no one knew for certain where in the Bahamas he arrived. Nor did anything in the former British colony recall his visit, except a stone cross on San Salvador and Club Med's "Columbus Isle" resort.

The navigator's next stop, Cuba, struck me as difficult to tour on short notice. And I rather doubted that Castro's *república* observed Columbus Day, except as an opportunity to denounce imperialism. In any case, Columbus didn't penetrate beyond Cuba's coast.

That left the neighboring island he'd named La Isla Española, which today is known as Hispaniola and is divided between Haiti and the Dominican Republic. It was on Hispaniola that Columbus planted the first European outpost in America, after Vinland. The Spanish later founded the first permanent European settlement in America, at Santo Domingo, now the capital of the Dominican Republic. Columbus's bones allegedly resided there, too.

This was all I knew of the Dominican Republic, past or present, apart from its roster of baseball stars. In fact, I'd never visited any country in Latin America. But ignorance, in this instance, seemed appropriate. Columbus dead-reckoned his way to the Indies, and improvised once he got there. Booking a ticket to Santo Domingo, I figured I would do the same.

DURING THE WEEKS before my departure, I boned up on Columbus's return to Hispaniola, in 1493. This was a very different affair from the modest expedition of three ships and ninety men that the navigator had steered across the Ocean Sea a year before. Columbus was now a Spanish noble and Capitán General de la Armada, commanding a fleet of seventeen vessels and twelve hundred passengers, including several hundred gentlemen seeking fortune and adventure in the Indies. Horses, sheep, cows, and pigs also crowded aboard. "No European nation," Samuel Eliot Morison observes, "had ever undertaken an overseas colonizing expedition on anything approaching this scale."

The big-budget sequel Columbus had negotiated with the Crown had two ambitious plot lines: extracting Hispaniola's riches (one-eighth of which would go to the Capitán) and Christianizing its inhabitants. Gold and God, conquest and conversion—the incompatible twins of Spanish policy in America for decades to come.

After a smooth Atlantic passage, Columbus island-hopped across the Caribbean, bestowing names still familiar to tropical vacationers: Dominica, Guadalupe, the Virgin Islands. At St. Croix, the Spanish skirmished with natives, killing several and taking many captive. Columbus gave one prisoner, "a very beautiful Carib," to an Italian nobleman and friend, Michele de Cuneo, who took her to his cabin.

"She being naked according to their custom, I conceived a desire to take pleasure," Cuneo wrote. "I wanted to put my desire into execution but she did not want it and treated me with her finger nails in such a manner that I wished I had never begun." But Cuneo persisted. "I took a rope and thrashed her well, for which she raised such unheard-of screams that you would not have believed your ears." Eventually, his victim succumbed. The first recorded sex between a European and American was rape.

Such behavior had already caused trouble in Hispaniola, where Columbus arrived to find the fort he'd established at La Navidad in ruins. Decomposing bodies littered the coast. From Indians who had survived the round-trip to Spain and now served as translators, Columbus learned that La Navidad's settlers had enraged islanders when each of them seized "five women to minister to his pleasure." Then, heading inland in search of fresh plunder, settlers encountered a fierce cacique named Caonabo. He and coastal Indians killed the Spanish and laid waste to La Navidad—and to the notion that *los Indios* were, in Columbus's earlier words, "cowardly beyond help."

Sailing east along the coast of Hispaniola, from today's Haiti to the Dominican Republic, Columbus selected a new site for settlement, which he named La Isabela, in honor of the queen. The coast was low, pestilential, and badly watered. But Columbus picked the spot because it lay close to the rumored gold mines of the inland region called Cibao, which he was impatient to find. Just four days after founding La Isabela, he dispatched reconnaissance parties to the interior.

The outriders returned with gold nuggets and other samples from streambeds. "All of us made merry," wrote Cuneo, whose greed matched his lust, "not caring any longer about any sort of spicery but only for this blessed gold." Columbus had originally planned to model La Isabela on Portuguese trading posts along the African coast. Now, fired by gold, he marched inland at the head of a large force to establish forts and secure the mountains and valleys of Cibao.

Columbus, however, had no talent for the role of conqueror and colonizer. Among his many shortcomings was his poor judgment about those to whom he gave authority. As lieutenant and scout, he chose Alonso de Hojeda, a man described by a contemporary as "always the first to draw blood wherever there was a war or a quarrel." When Hojeda captured several Indians accused of minor theft, he cut off the ears of one and sent the rest in chains to La Isabela. Columbus ordered that they be decapitated in the town plaza. Though others prevailed on him to lift the sentence, the relatively peaceful relations he had maintained with Indians until then had ended. In the future there would be little except mistrust and violence.

Columbus also failed as a colonial administrator because he never really wanted the job. He was a seaman, not a landsman: a fish out of water whenever he went ashore. Rather than deal with the troubles brewing in Hispaniola, he decided to sail off and make new discoveries, leaving in charge a council headed by his hapless brother Diego. By the time Columbus returned from Cuba and Jamaica, five months later, the fledging colony on Hispaniola was near collapse. Crops planted at La Isabela had withered; no one wanted to tend chickpeas when they could search for gold. Parties sent inland to find riches had run amok, killing and raping and stealing food from natives. A mutinous Spanish faction had seized three ships and sailed home.

Worst of all for Columbus, the vast mines of Cibao hadn't been found. Islanders' jewelry and other gold items had misled the Spanish; these riches weren't the tip of a vast buried treasure but rather a modest store hoarded and crafted over generations. Most of the raw gold that existed on Hispaniola had to be painstakingly sifted from streambeds.

To get it, Columbus enacted a cruel tribute system, requiring each adult Indian to produce a set amount of gold dust. If there was none to be found, natives had to deliver other products, such as hammocks, hatchets, and cotton skirts. Columbus also made a commodity of natives themselves. Previously, he'd enslaved small numbers of Indians, and only those known as Canibales or Caribs. As alleged man-eaters, and as prisoners captured in a "just" war, they could be sold as chattel. Or so went the logic of the day.

Now, however, Columbus rounded up several thousand natives of Hispaniola, loading some 550 of the "best males and females" for shipment to Spain. About two hundred died during the ocean crossing and were thrown into the sea. Many more perished soon after being put on the block in Spain. "They are not very profitable," a cleric who witnessed the sale noted, "since almost all died, for the country did not agree with them."

Their own land did not agree with the Spanish, either. By late 1495, a visitor to La Isabela reported, the sick and hungry colonists were so discontented that they swore only one oath: "God take me to Castile." Instead, soon after Columbus sailed home in 1496, colonists relocated to a harbor on Hispaniola's south coast. At first, it was known as Isabela Nueva. But as the settlement grew, it acquired a name of its own: Santo Domingo, the first European city in the New World.

SANTO DOMINGO

THE COLUMBUS JINX

> In a museum in Havana there are two skulls
> of Christopher Columbus, one when he was
> a boy and one when he was a man.
> —Mark Twain, *The Adventures of Thomas
> Jefferson Snodgrass*

A T THE AEROPUERTO Internacional Las Américas, I was welcomed with a paper cup of rum and a power blackout. Outside the darkened terminal, men surrounded me, shouting "Taxi!" One burst from the pack, grabbed my wrist, and escorted me to a cab. He wasn't the driver, just a middleman. "Welcome to the D.R.," he said, holding out his hand. "I work for tips."

A few minutes from the airport, the taxi approached a tollbooth with no clear driving lanes, just motorists nosing between other cars in a honking mêlée. After the toll, we trailed a truckful of bananas, the azure Caribbean on one side and a cement-block shantytown on the other. Then the road arced over the Ozama River and into Santo Domingo's Zona Colonial, the heart of the original Spanish city.

In contrast to cursed La Isabela, Santo Domingo had been well sited, on a fine harbor surrounded by fertile land. Enriched by sugar plantations, the outpost also became the hub for Spain's conquest of South and Central America. Within a few decades of its founding in 1496, Santo Domingo grew into a settlement of four hundred houses and two thousand people, with a town crier, an aqueduct, and a university.

Five centuries later, the Zona Colonial still had a pleasant Old World feel. It stretched for roughly ten square blocks, a carefully plotted grid of streets and plazas that reflected the sixteenth-century Spanish love of symmetry. Handsome, flat-fronted stone buildings opened into courtyards with fountains and Moorish arches. Every avenue seemed to boast at least one *"primada de America"*: the first cathedral, the first convent, the first hospital, the first fortress, the first courtroom. Though many of these structures were now picturesque ruins, the Zona was a reminder of how substantial the Spanish presence in America had been a full century before the first English settlers built huts in Virginia and Massachusetts.

The Zona's elegance was also a reminder of how far Spanish America had fallen since. Outside the small cocoon of the colonial district, and at many points within it, Santo Domingo resembled capitals across the developing world: a desperate and chaotic mess. About a quarter of the D.R.'s nine million people crowded in and around the city, many of them occupying slums like those I'd passed while driving from the airport. Guards with shotguns stood before every bank. Anger over power blackouts and soaring prices periodically erupted in general strikes, street protests, and barricades of burning tires.

This state of near collapse made Santo Domingo a challenging place to operate. So did the weather. Though the temperature didn't budge much either side of eighty-six degrees, the humidity was more oppressive than the wet season in Tahiti or a heat wave in the bayous of Louisiana. The chicken-broth air felt as if it would break into a downpour at any moment, but never did. Pens melted in my hand and pocket. Even my wristwatch and glasses became intolerable. Within minutes of stepping outside, I was a sodden, ink-stained wreck.

In other tropical locales, the solution was to strip down to shorts and T-shirt. But in Santo Domingo this was unthinkable. Almost no one wore shorts; even short sleeves seemed taboo. Instead, men strolled past in dress shirts and slacks, and women in form-fitting blouses and the tightest skirts and jeans I'd ever seen. Yet they somehow stayed perfectly groomed and dry. This struck me as a dazzling

sort of performance art, and a way to maintain private dignity amid
public squalor. Bags disgorged trash over every sidewalk, and honking
vehicles clotted every street. But individual Dominicans looked *great*.

Which made me feel all the more pathetic—an alien who moved
too fast, sweated too much, and had skin too pink for the tropical sun.
Worse still, if Dominicans cared so much about their own appearance,
what did they make of mine? Hair plastered to skull, cheap shirt stuck
to chest, khakis stained with ink and sweat, fogged glasses sliding
down my nose. Only the dogs, flat on the sidewalk as if slain by the
heat, seemed fit company for a wretched and panting Americano.

Not that I had anyone else to talk to. My original plan had been to
contact journalists, professors, and museum curators who might get
me started on Columbus's trail. But simply consummating a phone call
in Santo Domingo proved a chore. My Berlitz Spanish and the meager
English of most operators and receptionists made communication difficult. Almost no one answered office phones, anyway, probably because they were rarely in the office. Most Dominicans, I learned,
devoted their time to second jobs that paid better than their official
posts. Cell phones couldn't be counted on, either: the frequent blackouts made them hard to keep powered.

The few appointments I managed to arrange also turned out to be
highly provisional. Among the first Dominican words I learned was
ahorita, akin to *mañana* or the Arabic *insha'allah. Ahora* is Spanish for
"now." *Ahorita,* when used in the D.R., means roughly, "between now
and never."

So my first few days followed a dispiriting routine. My hotel room
in the Zona fronted on a narrow street where buses with pneumatic
horns set off car alarms, jolting me awake at dawn. I'd take a cold
shower, chill-dry myself before a wheezing air conditioner, spray-
paint my entire torso with Arrid Extra Dry, and go downstairs to
sweat into a strong cup of *café con leche.* Then I'd start working the
hotel's crackly phone line. If I was lucky enough to reach someone,
I'd hop in a taxi and sit in heavy traffic, haggling over the fare until I
reached an office where the person I'd come to see wasn't there. Then
I'd take a taxi back to the Zona, drink more *café con leche,* and walk
around until the caffeine and my sweat glands gave out. By eleven

A.M., I'd surrendered hope of interviewing anyone. By noon, I no longer cared. And by my third day, I realized that without a superhuman expenditure of will and pesos, I'd accomplish nothing at all during my entire stay.

The one source of solace was an outdoor café, El Conde, where I whiled away my evenings over Presidente beer and dishes such as *mangoo* (mashed plantains with eggs and onion) and *chivo guisado* (translated on the menu as "fricasse kid"). The café was reasonably peaceful, apart from the beggars, shoeshine men, money changers, blaring merengue music, and a tour guide named Hector, who kept hectoring me in a raspy smoker's voice to pay $10 for a tour I'd already taken with another guide. To fend him off one night, I struck up a conversation with a Scotsman at the next table.

"Three bad days and you're moaning?" he said, when I shared my reporting woes. "I've been here five months and haven't had a good day yet."

George Houston was an engineer who had come to the D.R. on a government contract, to fix a traffic bridge over the Ozama River. Although the bridge was about to collapse, his company had yet to be paid, or even given the go-ahead to start work.

George didn't take this personally. The government wasn't paying its foreign creditors either, or many of its employees, or its power generators (hence the blackouts). Inflation ran at 50 percent a year, and the value of the peso against the dollar had plunged 120 percent in just the past nine months. Along with *ahorita,* I'd picked up an expressive Dominican phrase: *Estamos jodidos,* meaning "We're fucked." How's the economy? *Estamos jodidos.* What do you think of the government? *Estamos jodidos.*

George was just hoping his firm in Glasgow would call him home before the bridge and the whole country fell down around him. "In the meantime I get a lot of reading done," he said, hefting a fat novel, "when there's light."

IN 1496, AS Santo Domingo arose on the banks of the Ozama, Columbus was back in Spain, struggling to secure support for a return to the

Indies. The failures of his second voyage had badly dented his reputation, and his third sail, in 1498, would do nothing to restore it. Though Columbus ventured much farther than he had before, he showed signs of losing his grip on the sea and sky—and, possibly, on his own mind.

At one point, faulty stargazing led Columbus to conclude that he had sailed uphill. This caused him to reconsider the shape of the globe. He compared it to a round pear with a stalk, "like a woman's nipple." At the tip of this nipple resided "the earthly Paradise." In other words, Columbus thought he was sailing up the breast of the world to the Garden of Eden. His actual location was present-day Venezuela, making the South American continent yet another of his unwitting discoveries.

Columbus and his brothers also continued to bungle their management of Hispaniola, which was riven by mutiny and Indian rebellion. When word of the chaos reached Spain, the Crown sent a judge to investigate. He promptly arrested Columbus and shipped him home, in chains, on trumped-up charges of abusing colonists.

The Admiral was soon freed, but he no longer commanded much trust or backing in Spain. He'd shown himself an incompetent administrator, and had failed to deliver on his promise of great riches in Hispaniola. His advocacy of the slave trade—at one point, he proposed the trafficking of four thousand natives yearly—also discomfited Spain's monarchs. The Crown's contradictory policy toward Indians called for conversion and "benign subjection." While sanctioning the enslavement of alleged cannibals, the Crown freed and returned home some of the Hispaniola natives whom Columbus sent for sale in Spain.

The monarchs also began chipping away at the Admiral's many privileges. They suspended his governorship of Hispaniola and allowed others to embark on voyages of their own, breaking Columbus's monopoly on trade and discovery. When, after much hesitation, they authorized another voyage by Columbus, it was to explore only; the Admiral was barred from returning to Hispaniola.

Columbus's fourth and final voyage, in 1500, ended in calamity. After reaching Central America—which he believed was the site of King Solomon's mines—his worm-eaten ships took on so much water that he had to run them aground in Jamaica. He was marooned there for a year, until rescued by several men who succeeded in canoeing to

Hispaniola and securing another vessel. By then, the Admiral of the Ocean Sea had lost all four of his ships, a quarter of his sailors, and what little remained of his reputation.

Columbus made it back to Spain in 1504, just a few weeks before the death of his longtime patron, Queen Isabel. He was now past fifty and crippled by arthritis, yet he trailed the peripatetic royal court on muleback, vainly pleading for the privileges and riches he felt were still owed him. One of his last surviving letters, asking the monarchs for "restitution of my honor and losses," captures the self-pitying despair of his final years. "I am ruined," he wrote, "alone, desolate, infirm, daily expecting death. . . . Weep for me, whoever has charity, truth and justice!"

In May 1506, still on the Crown's trail, Columbus died, "much afflicted," wrote his son Ferdinand, "by grief at seeing himself fallen from his high estate, as well as by other ills." Columbus's descendants ultimately lost all but a few of his hereditary titles.

In a final insult, the most enduring honor of all went to a fellow Italian who had befriended Columbus in his last years. "He is a very honorable man and always desirous of pleasing me," wrote Columbus, ever a poor judge of character, "and is determined to do everything possible for me." The man's name was Amerigo Vespucci.

A well-connected Florentine merchant and a scion of the Medicis, Vespucci moved to Seville and outfitted fleets crossing the Atlantic. He sailed to the Indies several times between 1499 and 1502, under both Spanish and Portuguese auspices, and claimed to be a great navigator. But his true genius was for hype and self-promotion.

"I hope to be famous for many an age," he wrote, in one of the embellished accounts he gave of his voyages. Vespucci invented some episodes and lifted others from Columbus's writing. Unlike the Admiral, though, he showed great flair for lubricious tales designed to titillate his European audience.

Native women, he claimed, were giantesses—"taller kneeling than I am standing"—and impervious to age and childbearing, with taut wombs and breasts that never sagged. "Being very lustful," Vespucci wrote, the women used exotic devices and insect venom to "make their husbands' members swell" to fantastic size. Best of all, they were "very desirous to copulate with us Christians," and native men regarded it as

Amazons, or women warriors, from a Dutch edition (ca. 1507) of
Vespucci's account of his voyage to South America

a "great token of friendship" to give the Christians one of their daughters, "even when she is a young virgin." Not surprisingly, Vespucci's
account became an instant bestseller.

Vespucci also claimed to have reached South America in 1497, a
year before Columbus arrived there on his third voyage. Vespucci referred to the region as "a new world," unknown to "our ancestors."
Though little is known about his travels, scholars have determined that
he couldn't have reached South America until 1499, after Columbus
did. Nor is it clear that Vespucci regarded the "new world" as separate
from Asia. Columbus also called South America "an other world," and
a "very large continent which until now has remained unknown"—
while still believing he was somewhere in the Far East.

But some scholars in Europe had come to doubt that these lands
were part of Asia, and they found support for this belief in Vespucci's account. In 1507, a year after Columbus's death, the German geographer

Martin Waldseemüller published a text and map adding a "fourth part" to the known world of Europe, Asia, and Africa. "I see no reason why one should justly object to calling this part Amerige," Waldseemüller wrote, "or America, after Amerigo, its discoverer, a man of great ability." His revised world map had "America" engraved next to a landmass roughly resembling Brazil.

Waldseemüller later changed his mind and dropped the name from a subsequent edition. But "America" was reprised in 1538 by the great cartographer Gerard Mercator, who applied it to continents both north and south.

"Strange," lamented Ralph Waldo Emerson, "that broad America must wear the name of a thief. Amerigo Vespucci, the pickledealer at Seville, who . . . managed in this lying world to supplant Columbus and baptize half the earth with his own dishonest name."

AFTER SEVERAL DAYS in Santo Domingo, I met a museum guide named Carlos who taught English as his second job and agreed to take on a third, as my translator. Lean and handsome, with close-cropped black hair, Carlos had a firmly set jaw that emphasized his glumness. The only time he smiled was when I told him about my fruitless phone calls and failed appointments.

"El fucu de Colón," he said.

"*El* what?"

"*Fucu*. That means curse or jinx." Most Dominicans, he explained, believed Columbus brought bad luck. Even mentioning his name risked misfortune. Few businesses were named for the navigator, and the ones that were had gone bust. "Of course, our luck in the D.R. is bad to begin with," Carlos said. "But with Columbus it is worse."

"So that's why no one will meet with me?"

"Probably not. To see anyone, you must know someone who knows someone. Or you must pay."

Carlos didn't know anyone, except other ill-paid guides around the Zona Colonial. But he was willing, for a modest wage, to risk assisting my cursed pursuit of Columbus.

We began where the navigator's story ends, at the alleged resting places of his remains: El Faro a Colón, the Columbus Lighthouse. The Faro occupied a vast park on the other side of the Ozama River from the colonial district. The massive scale and layout of the grounds—a rectilinear expanse decked with flags, pavilions, and artificial ponds—reminded me at first of the Mall in Washington, D.C. Except that the Faro was a memorial space devoted to a single shrine: an enormous concrete cross laid on the ground.

"Monumental" seemed too minimalist a word to describe it. The Faro was almost seven hundred feet long and sloped upward, with the top of the cross reaching a height of ten stories. The Faro was also equipped with 150 powerful searchlights, and a beacon designed to project a crucifix into the night sky that was visible in Puerto Rico, two hundred miles away. I hadn't seen a monument so grandiose, and so at odds with its environs, since visiting Saddam Hussein's Iraq.

But even the mammoth Faro was subject to the Columbus jinx. Conceived during a pan-American conference in 1923, the project lay dormant for lack of funds until the late 1980s, when the Dominican strongman, President Joaquín Balaguer, rushed to build the monument in time for the five hundredth anniversary of Columbus's sail. He ordered the razing of a shantytown on the site, forcibly relocating thousands of residents, and channeled almost all the poor nation's cement and about $100 million of its scarce funds into erecting the lighthouse.

Then the *fucu* struck. Tests of the beacon caused city-wide blackouts and protests by Dominicans. Balaguer's sister dropped dead within hours of visiting the Faro. The pope, scheduled to inaugurate the monument, was diagnosed with cancer. He also came down with political doubts about aligning himself with the structure, which had become a symbol of the nation's corrupt, dictatorial, and oligarchic rule. Before long, the searchlights and beacon had to be shut down; the 300,000-watt light show was an insult to the thousands of city dwellers who lacked power.

So there it stood: a lighthouse without light. In fact, nothing about the Faro fit its name. It didn't soar. It squatted, blocky and gray and streaked with grime, like a neglected public housing project. Carlos walked me to the edge of the park surrounding the supine cross, and pointed at a six-foot coral and concrete barrier topped with barbed wire. "We call this *el muro de la vergüenza,*" he said, "the wall of shame." The barrier had been built to shield visitors to the Faro from the impoverished neighborhood beside it.

Returning to the lighthouse, we entered through a slit in one of its massive walls. The Faro was as cheerless within as it was forbidding without. The arms of the cross formed narrow corridors between towering walls of concrete. The Faro's architect had designed these claustrophobic "canyons," he wrote, to convey "the gloom, confinement and superstition of Columbus's own time." The beacon atop the Faro was meant to contrast with the interior and symbolize modern progress.

This may have sounded inspired on paper. In practice, with the beacon shut off, there was only the gloom and confinement. The design also diminished Columbus's mausoleum, which sat in the space where the two arms of the cross met. Ornately carved from Carrara marble, with steps leading up to an arched door, the crypt looked like a toy cathedral deposited on the floor of a prison block. A guard leaned on a rifle before the tomb. He was the only person in sight.

Behind him, inside the crypt, lay the bones of the Great Discoverer. Or possibly not. Columbus was maddeningly elusive, even in death. In 1506, he'd been buried without fanfare in the Spanish town of Valladolid, and was moved three years later to a monastery in Seville. The body of his son Diego joined him there in 1526. Then, in about 1541, Diego's widow arranged for father and son to be shipped to Hispaniola, where Columbus had stated he wished to be buried. Christopher and Diego were interred beside the altar of Santo Domingo's cathedral. But the stone or inscription marking the spot was covered up, to protect the remains from the pirates who frequently looted the city.

In 1795, Spain ceded its colony in Hispaniola to Napoleon. So that the navigator's remains would not fall into the hands of the perfidious French, a box believed to contain Columbus's bones was removed to Spanish-held Havana. At the end of the nineteenth century, Spain lost Cuba, too, and Columbus's peripatetic remains went to sea again, returning across the Atlantic to the soaring Gothic cathedral in Seville.

In 1877, however, workmen at the Santo Domingo cathedral had unearthed a lead box with bones inside and an inscription that read, "Illustrious and esteemed gentleman, Don Cristóbal Colón." This raised the possibility that the wrong remains—those of Diego—had been sent to Cuba and later to Spain. Dominicans certainly believed so, and had built the grand mausoleum before me to hold what was left of the navigator.

Spanish researchers had long disputed the Dominican claim, casting doubt on the coffer's inscription and other evidence. Just before my visit, forensic geneticists in Spain had reignited the controversy by announcing plans to DNA-test the bones inside the Seville crypt. Despite repeated requests over the years, the D.R. refused to allow study of the Faro's bones. This raised suspicions that Dominicans preferred that their claim on Columbus not be subject to scientific analysis. The Faro was a big enough albatross without its centerpiece turning out to be the wrong man's dust.

"It is Columbus, absolutely," said a guide named Leopoldo, who materialized out of the Faro's gloom and joined us by the crypt. "Spain wants to take our tourists."

If so, there weren't many to steal. At the moment, Carlos and I were the only visitors. "But come," Leopoldo said, "let me show you the museum."

He led us down one of the long corridors, our footfalls echoing in the empty concrete canyon. Then we turned through a doorway and into a large room with a painting of Columbus, copies of books he'd read, the marriage certificate of Ferdinand and Isabel, and other displays. I barely had time to study this exhibit before Leopoldo took my arm. "Come, come. We have sixty-four more rooms to visit."

"Museum" didn't capture the Faro's interior, just as "lighthouse" misrepresented its exterior. Tucked within the monument's walls was a collection that covered a city block. The Faro had been intended to honor not only Columbus, but also the global network he helped create: a monument, its builders proclaimed, to world peace. So Dominicans had set aside space—immensities of space—for countries from around the world to put up national displays, rather in the manner of an old-time world exposition.

The first room we'd visited was Spain's. Next was Japan's, which displayed samurai armor and a picture of a golden pagoda. Most nations followed this model, exhibiting proud emblems of their history and culture. China: calligraphy and Ming vases. Russia: a samovar and a set of Matryoshka nesting dolls. And so on through the continents until we reached the Americas. Guatemala displayed a Mayan vase, Ecuador a set of twenty-five-hundred-year-old bowls that Leopoldo said were worth millions of dollars. As we toured room after room, I began to wonder how my own country would present itself in this ersatz United Nations.

We went through another door and there it was, spanning two walls. On one hung a few small photographs of July 4 celebrations: fireworks and flag-waving. The other wall, much more prominent, was covered in poster-sized blowups of newspaper front pages. All were dated September 12, 2001, and bore images of the previous day's attack on New York's Twin Towers.

"DAY OF TERROR," read the hugely enlarged headline from the New Hampshire *Concord Monitor*.

"HOW MANY DEAD?" (*Arkansas Democrat-Gazette*).

"OUR NATION SAW EVIL" (*Raleigh News and Observer*).

"WAR AT HOME" (*Dallas Morning News*).

No other items were displayed. Registering the shock on my face, Leopoldo shook his head sympathetically. "I am so sorry," he said. "You must think of it every day."

What I felt at that moment wasn't sorrow for the 9/11 victims, but mortification. Tiny Ecuador gave precious pottery as a token of its heritage. My nation, the hemisphere's richest, offered only this: Share our fear and feel our pain. In a venue designed to promote global amity and understanding, the United States chose to emphasize how divided and troubled the world remained. It was a minor thing, really, a display in a little-visited Dominican museum. But still, the exhibit rankled: my own small wall of shame.

"I leave you to visit the rest on your own," Leopoldo said, accepting a tip before melting back into the gloom. "The rest" was several more floors, with odd displays of Dominican history: rusted cannons, old coins, the skeleton of a soldier with a bullet in his ribs. The higher Carlos and I went, the dimmer and emptier the display cases became, until there was nothing to observe but dozing guards. The Faro was the largest and strangest museum I'd ever visited.

Descending to the ground floor, we became lost in a warren of dark offices. Stumbling into one, we found a man in a suit with a scale model of the Faro on his desk. This turned out to be the Faro's administrator, Teódulo Mercedes, one of the many people I'd phoned repeatedly without success. He seemed as startled to see us as we were to find him: an official caught in the act of doing his official job.

Worried he might somehow dematerialize, I jumped straight to the object of my quest. Who, I asked, was buried in Columbus's tomb?

Teódulo chuckled. "It is Columbus, this is certain," he said, without specifying Christopher or Diego. "But let us talk of other things."

The Faro's 45,850 cubic yards of concrete, for instance, and 125 bathrooms. Incredibly, the original design had called for the building to be a third larger. An engineer by training, Teódulo went on for half an hour, cataloguing the Faro's immensity. "It is like the Eiffel Tower in France," he concluded, "a symbol of our country."

This was true: the D.R. was in trouble, and so was the monument. Apart from school groups, Teódulo acknowledged, the Faro attracted few visitors. And there was the embarrassing problem of the darkened searchlights, which the D.R. couldn't afford to turn on.

Encouraged by his frankness, I steered us back to Columbus's remains. Teódulo sighed. "The Spanish made a mistake, they took the wrong bones. Now they must protect their claim. This is understandable."

If the Spanish were wrong, why not let them test the remains here?

"The method they use is not certain," he replied. "Why disturb the bones for nothing? We know we are right. This will all be revealed on Sunday."

Sunday was October 12, Columbus's landing date, commemorated each year at the Faro with a formal ceremony attended by Dominican dignitaries. Teódulo said a churchman would open the locked coffin so those in attendance could view the great man's remains. I felt a flutter in my chest, as Columbus must have whenever he heard fresh news of gold. Very few outsiders had ever glimpsed the bones. The elusive Admiral, or what was left of him, lay almost within my sight.

I asked Teódulo if there was any chance an American writer, a great admirer of Columbus and of the Dominican Republic, could be on hand to document this glorious event. The engineer smiled. "Yes, you may come," he said, "and if I am right, for you I will have a very big surprise."

I SPENT THE few days until the twelfth learning about the people Columbus called *los Indios*. In the D.R., they are known as Taino, a native word that apparently meant "good" and was used by islanders to distinguish themselves from their enemies, the Caribs. The Taino descended from natives who had migrated from the South American mainland over two millennia earlier. While there were variations in dialect and custom, the islanders Columbus encountered across the Caribbean belonged to the same linguistic and cultural family.

Estimates of Hispaniola's population in 1492 range as high as several million, though most scholars put the figure closer to 500,000. A third perished within a decade of Spanish settlement, from war, disease, overwork, and the devastation of native agriculture, due in part to the arrival of European livestock. "People continue to die daily as do cattle in time of pest," a Spanish chronicler wrote of a famine in the 1490s. Some Taino committed mass suicide, poisoning themselves rather than submit to Spanish rule.

In Santo Domingo's curiously named "Museum of Dominican Man," I gazed at dioramas of the Taino lying in hammocks, and exhibits displaying *zemi*s, small wood or stone idols representing deities and ancestral spirits. Carved with huge eye sockets, gaping mouths, and enormous genitals, the *zemi*s had platters perched atop their heads. These were designed to hold *cohoba,* a hallucinogenic powder made from crushed seeds. Taino communicated with *zemi*s by sticking wooden spatulas down their own throats, to induce vomiting, and then snorting *cohoba* through forked canes.

Most of what's known about Taino culture comes from the writings of their Spanish subjugators. A cleric on Columbus's second voyage, Father Ramón Pane, lived among the Taino for several years

Indians mining gold from a stream, from a Spanish history of the Indies, 1535

and learned some of their language. His brief account represents the first attempt in the New World at what would now be called anthropology.

According to Pane, Taino believed the dead came out at night and could be distinguished from the living by their lack of navels. He also told of a prophecy communicated by a *zemi* to a leading cacique. Whoever succeeded the chief, Pane wrote, would rule for only a short time "because there would come to his country a people wearing clothes who would conquer and kill the Indians." At first, Pane added, the Taino thought this prophecy referred to the dreaded Caribs. "They now believe that the idol prophesied the coming of the Admiral and the people who came with him."

While Pane is forgotten, another Spanish friar in Hispaniola is renowned to this day as "Defender of the Indians." Bartolomé de Las Casas arrived in Santo Domingo in 1502, at the age of eighteen, and prospered from the sweat of Taino awarded him through the *encomienda* system, which made settlers the overseers of natives living on grants of Crown land. In theory, this feudal institution meant that natives became vassals, working in exchange for the protection and Christian instruction of their masters. In practice, the system led to enslavement.

In 1511, a priest shocked his audience at a Santo Domingo church by condemning "such cruel and horrible" servitude. "Are they not men?" he asked of Indians. "Are you not obliged to love them as you love yourselves?" The sermon stuck with Las Casas, who later renounced his *encomienda* and became a Dominican friar. He spent the rest of his long life writing about Indians, petitioning the monarchy to treat them humanely, and attempting to found peaceful colonies in America that accorded with Christian belief.

In a stinging work titled *A Short Account of the Destruction of the Indies,* Las Casas sought to break what he called the "conspiracy of silence" surrounding the brutality of Spanish conquest. The *Account* is a country-by-country survey of torture and genocide; it reads like an Amnesty International report on Spain's first decades in the New World. In Hispaniola, Las Casas described the Spanish slow-cooking Taino on grills, or laying wagers on "whether they could manage to slice a man in two at a stroke." Those Taino who weren't slaughtered outright were starved and worked to death: digging for gold, cutting sugarcane, carrying loads for hundreds of miles.

Las Casas also edited Columbus's journal. He tended to absolve the Admiral, instead blaming the "cruel, grasping and wicked" settlers he believed had betrayed the navigator's evangelizing mission. Las Casas, even more than Columbus, also idealized and infantilized natives, describing them as "innocent and pure in mind," "like gentle lambs," "without malice or guile"—in short, Man in a blessed state of nature, before the Fall. This prelapsarian image helped give rise to the myth of the Noble Savage, which would endure in the Western imagination for centuries.

Las Casas's adoration of Indians contributed to another, harsher legacy. One way to protect natives, he believed, was to replace their labor with that of African slaves. By the second decade of the sixteenth century, large numbers of Africans were being shipped to Hispaniola, to replace the dwindling Taino and islanders imported from elsewhere in the Caribbean.

This set a pattern that would repeat itself across the Americas. As Indian laborers died off, or escaped to areas outside colonial control, African slaves filled the breach. In the three centuries after the first direct shipment of slaves to Hispaniola, in 1518, some twelve million Africans would be taken by force across the Atlantic—five times the number of white Europeans who migrated to America during the same period.

Contrary to Las Casas's hopes, the importation of Africans did nothing to save the Taino. In 1514, when the Crown ordered a careful census of Hispaniola natives, to determine the surviving labor force, it found only 22,726 islanders of working age. In many villages, "there were found no children among the people." Within a few decades, the Taino of Hispaniola had ceased to exist as a distinct people. Natives of neighboring islands suffered a similar fate.

THOUGH THE TAINO were the first natives of America driven into extinction by Europeans, they were also the first to have sustained contact with the West. As such, they left a lasting imprint on European thought, language, and lifestyle. The long list of Taino words adopted and adapted by Europeans includes not only *hamaca* and *canoa,* but also *huracán* (hurricane), *barbacoa* (barbecue), and *savanna.* Along with tobacco, a host of Taino crops became European and African staples: *maize* (Indian corn), *casabe* (cassava), *batata* (sweet potato), peppers, peanuts, and pineapples. As explorers fanned out across America, they often saw natives through the prism of Columbus's early encounters with *los Indios.*

The Taino also exacted an enduring, if unintended, revenge on their conquerors. It is generally believed that sailors returning from Hispaniola after Columbus's second voyage, or Indian captives on board their ships, carried with them an awful disease. The affliction first appeared in epidemic form in Europe following a French army's march to Naples in 1495. It caused high fever, a skin pox, and often death. Italians termed the unfamiliar ailment "the French disease," while the French called it "the Neapolitan disease." There were also reports of cases in Spain, including some among men who had been to Hispaniola. A Spanish historian said the illness should therefore be called "the disease of the Indies."

Still another name was coined by an Italian physician, Girolamo Fracastoro. He wrote a poem in 1530 about an unnamed "hero" who sailed west from Spain and discovered a land of scabby natives. They said their affliction was given to them by the Sun God, as punishment for blasphemy by a shepherd named Syphilus. And so the disease has been known ever since.

OCTOBER 12 DAWNED hot and insufferable, worse than any day since my arrival in Santo Domingo. I'd revisited the Columbus Lighthouse twice to confirm that the ceremony would begin at eleven A.M., and also to make a modest contribution to the Faro's upkeep. Each time, the administrator, Teódulo, had reiterated his promise of "a great surprise" to be revealed that Sunday. I'd arranged for both Carlos and Leopoldo to meet me at the Faro to translate, in case one didn't show, and bought a tape recorder in case neither did. I also had my camera and a wallet stuffed with pesos, should a last-minute "tip" be required. Only heatstroke could prevent me from carefully documenting the surprise, whatever it was.

Clad in a coat and tie, I arrived at the Faro already drenched in sweat to find the normally silent monument abuzz. Women in white dresses set out crystal glasses for the reception to follow the ceremony. Naval cadets drilled in pressed white uniforms. Girls in brightly colored costumes paraded around the monument. "Today you will see all," Teódulo exclaimed, clapping me on the back.

An hour passed with no sign of Carlos or Leopoldo, or of the ceremony's start. But a small crowd formed, mostly elegant women dressed in white, and distinguished-looking men in dark suits and military uniforms. I made several trips to one of the Faro's 125 *baños* to splash water on my face and pat my torso with paper towels. To conceal my sodden shirt, I buttoned my jacket, which only made me hotter. The ceremony hadn't yet begun and I was starting to feel faint.

Trolling the crowd, I met a ribbon-bedecked man, César Lavandier, who was president of a group called the Naval League and a veteran of several sea battles in World War II. "What Columbus did, without any modern instruments, it is unimaginable today, an inspiration," he said. "Of course, many people hate him now. They need someone to blame their problems on, and we have many problems." He glanced at his watch. It was almost two hours past the ceremony's scheduled start of eleven A.M. César smiled and said, "Maybe they meant Greenwich Mean Time."

I went to the *baño* again but hurried out at the sound of a drumroll. An honor guard circled the mausoleum, rifles shouldered, and stood at attention. I finally spotted both Carlos and Leopoldo, who had turned up two hours after we'd arranged: right on time. They took

turns translating as an emcee introduced generals, government minis-
ters, Spain's ambassador, and other notables. Then an assistant to the
cardinal of the Dominican Republic mounted the mausoleum steps
and stuck an enormous key into the lid of the crypt.

The lock wouldn't open. The priest fiddled and twisted and banged
the lock with his palm. "Columbus, don't do this to me," he muttered,
to chuckles from the crowd. *El fucu de Colón* had struck again.

After five more minutes of struggle, the priest was joined by another man, who twisted the key hard and yanked. Finally the latch
sprang and the crowd broke into relieved applause. Then the band
struck up, and the assembled dignitaries approached the mausoleum
with bouquets. I edged behind them to try and get a glimpse inside the
tomb. All I could see was a glass plate laid over the lead coffer containing the remains. I raised my camera from behind the wreath-layers
and clicked. Nothing happened. The camera had jammed, or the bat-
tery had died, probably from the heat and humidity.

"You will see the bones with your own eyes," Leopoldo assured
me, "as soon as the speeches are over." At which point, the national cultural heritage minister began a florid oration. "What we celebrate today, ladies and gentlemen, is a journey as unpredictable as the sea in
front of the New World's unknown lands . . . an endless journey that
the Admiral began and that still goes on . . . a journey of discovery . . ."

I was barely listening by the time he concluded to weary applause.
Girls in costumes representing America's many nations promenaded
around the mausoleum, and then the dignitaries lined up to view the Admiral's remains. I positioned myself as close to the front of the queue as
seemed decent. We edged forward to the base of the mausoleum steps.

"Mr. Tony!" exclaimed the Faro's director, Teódulo, grasping my
sleeve. "The minister of cultural heritage would like to speak to you."

"I'd like to speak to him, too. After the reception?"

"No, now. He must leave. Please, in my office. It is air-
conditioned."

Talking to the minister seemed the polite thing to do, and I might
never get another chance to interview a senior Dominican official.
Besides, Teódulo had told me the previous day that the crypt would
remain open all afternoon. So I let him tug me gently from the line.

The minister was very obliging. I asked him a single question, about the significance of Columbus, and he launched into an answer as prolix as the speech he'd just delivered. "Columbus is the adventure, the journey of our national and cultural voyage . . ."

When he finally finished, I thanked him for his time and stood up. I was anxious to glimpse the remains—and to get at the pitchers of lemonade I'd seen laid out for the reception. But the door was blocked by Teódulo and a gray-suited man, trailed by a camera crew. "May I present the governor of the city and owner of the television station here today," Teódulo said.

He motioned us back into his office. I struggled for a fresh question. What did Columbus mean to modern Santo Domingo?

"Because of him, the whole world appreciates the importance of this city," the governor began, before talking for twenty minutes about tourism's contribution to the economy. Again, I resisted a follow-up question. As soon as the governor departed, I tried to do the same.

"Sit down, sit down," Teódulo insisted. "It is time to reveal the surprise."

Teódulo melodramatically searched in his desk drawer, leaving me to guess at its contents. DNA evidence proving that Columbus's bones resided in the Faro? A long-lost document?

Finally, he produced a piece of paper and summarized its contents. The monument was inaugurated in 1992. Since then, Spain's ambassador had only appeared once on October 12, a decade ago. He looked up at me triumphantly.

"So what's the surprise?" I asked.

"That the Spanish ambassador came this year! She would not do this without the approval of her superiors. The Spanish are saying, 'We see the truth.' It is a diplomatic way to recognize that Columbus's remains are here."

"That's it?"

"That is it."

I checked my watch. It was almost an hour since the ceremony had ended. Perhaps there was still a drop of lemonade left. I hurried into the corridor. A few men were folding up tables. All the dignitaries and girls in bright costumes and soldiers in uniform had fled the stifling

Faro. The canyons were empty again. I rushed over to the mausoleum and skipped up the steps. The crypt was closed.

I sprinted back to Teódulo's office and cried, "You said it would be open all day!"

"There must be some mistake," he replied. We went in search of the Faro's caretaker, touring a dozen deserted offices before finding him. The caretaker looked at Teódulo and shrugged. The crypt was locked. The cardinal's office kept the only key. There was nothing to be done.

"That's impossible!" I shouted, unable to contain myself any longer. "I came all the way from Virginia to see those bones!"

My face was on fire and I felt my depleted sweat glands empty the last of their contents into my sopping shirt. The Dominicans couldn't contain themselves either. They convulsed with laughter. *El americano patético* has lost it!

"I am so sorry," Teódulo said. "Can you come again next year?"

I turned and walked out of the Faro, with as much dignity as I could muster in a full-body wetsuit. I felt like Columbus, led on by islanders in his deranged search for gold. If there was any to be found here, one small nugget of hard information about Columbus, the natives weren't sharing it. The D.R.'s comedy of incompetence had turned into a joke on me, the bullying, buck-waving Yankee.

That night, rehydrating with Presidente beer at El Conde café, I told the story of my day to a disconsolate Dutchman who had lived in the D.R. for decades. He was sympathetic but unsurprised. "It is the way of Dominicans," he said. "We foreigners kicked their asses around for centuries. So if they can kick our asses, they never miss a chance."

THE NEXT DAY, I rose early to watch the seven A.M. TV news, which I'd been told would show the ceremony at the Faro. Perhaps, for my toils, I could still catch a glimpse of the bones. But a few minutes before seven, the hotel's power died. Still unwilling to capitulate, I caught a cab to the TV station. Flashing the business card given me by the station's owner, the governor of Santo Domingo, whom I'd interviewed at the Faro, I was shown in to see a producer. He said the station hadn't broadcast the ceremony, but he offered to show me the raw footage his camera crew had taken.

So I sat in a studio and watched an hour of tape, replaying the struggle to open the tomb, the long speech by the minister, the officials lining up to pay their respects to the Admiral. I waited expectantly for the money shot: a nice clear image of Colón's exposed bones. Instead, the picture abruptly switched to the familiar gloom of Teódulo's office, where the governor sat talking to a sweaty, distraught figure I recognized as myself. The camera stayed with us for twenty excruciating minutes before the tape ended.

As dismaying as this was, one moment in the tape offered a faint lead. It showed the Spanish ambassador saying something to the camera about Columbus, what exactly I couldn't make out. Was it possible Teódulo had told me the truth? Did the ambassador's presence mean that Spain acknowledged the Dominican claim? Did I have anything else to do with the long day ahead?

Catching a cab to the Spanish embassy, I pleaded with a secretary, and after a long wait was granted an audience with the ambassador, María Jesús Figa López-Palop, an elegant brown-eyed woman with streaked blond hair. Not wanting to waste her time, I dived right in, asking what she'd said to the TV crew the day before.

"They wanted to know, of course, if my being there meant Spain admits that these are Columbus's remains," she said. "I told them the truth. Normally we celebrate the Spanish National Day on October twelfth and host a large party, so I cannot go to the Faro. But the twelfth fell on a Sunday this year, not a good day for a party. So we had our party on Saturday. I was free on Sunday, it is a courtesy, so I go. That is all."

She laughed. "Who cares about these bones? Some things are best left as myths or curiosities. My God, if we started opening tombs of all those kings and queens in Spain, who knows what we would find."

I told her some Dominicans feared that tests on the bones would hurt tourism. This made her laugh again. "How many tourists go to the Faro? It has no architectural interest at all, no real history. I suppose the numbers are ridiculous. No one who has visited me has ever asked to go to the Faro. No one goes to Seville to see Colón's remains there, either."

If the debate over the Admiral's bones seemed silly to the ambassador, honoring Columbus on October 12 did not. "It is a reminder of the connection between Spain and America, and we are very proud of this part of our story." She acknowledged that crimes were committed against natives, but felt Spain received more blame than it deserved. "I defend our colonization. We weren't the worst. Normally we melded with the cultures in America, we stayed here, we spread our language and culture and religion."

This was true, to a degree. Other European colonizers were brutal, too, and the English were far less inclined than the Spanish to live among Indians, or to make them a part of colonial society. Still, as I listened to this regal Iberian, her business card embossed with Spain's crown-topped coat of arms and the words "*plus ultra*" ("further beyond," a reference to Spain's once-vast empire), I was struck by the prideful echo of bygone imperialism. "Columbus is a symbol of what Spain has been and still is," she said. "A symbol of our influence in the world."

Fixated for days on Columbus's bones, I'd lost sight of the navigator's larger legacy in Santo Domingo. His voyages launched an empire that burst out from this very city, across the Americas, until Spain's domain reached from Canada to southern Chile. I was sitting near ground zero of one of the greatest colonial explosions in history, with aftershocks that resounded to this day.

"You know, there are now more Spanish-speaking people in the United States than in Spain," the ambassador observed, seeing me to the door. "The future of all the Americas is Spain, and that story begins in 1492. It is your story, too."

DOMINICAN REPUBLIC

YOU THINK THERE ARE STILL INDIANS?

> Aborigines, n.: Persons of little worth found
> cumbering the soil of a newly discovered
> country. They soon cease to cumber; they
> fertilize.
> —Ambrose Bierce, *The Devil's Dictionary*

THE *FUCU* FINALLY lifted the afternoon after my fiasco at the lighthouse. Wandering back from the embassy, I stopped to buy a newspaper and see whether the local press had covered the Columbus ceremony. If not, deciphering the news with my pocket Spanish dictionary would pass the time while I waited out the heat. When I asked the shopkeeper, *"¿Cuanto es esto?"* he gestured at the newspaper and said, "Brother, don't bother with that. It's all bullshit."

The merchant's slang and American-accented English startled me. So did his appearance. A wiry, mocha-colored man of about forty, with short frizzy hair, he wore baggy blue jean shorts and a loose T-shirt—more American street than Dominican chic. I stuck out my hand and asked his name.

"Caonabo," he said, proffering the name of the great Taino cacique who had slaughtered the first Spanish settlers at La Navidad. I figured he was pulling my leg.

"And I'm Christopher Columbus," I said.

The shopkeeper smiled and slapped my shoulder. "Brother, it's about time. I've been waiting five hundred years to kill you, too."

Caonabo explained that his father had been a *bohemio,* a rebel and jazz musician who named all his children after Taino chiefs. Caonabo had taken his own name to heart. "I feel Taino inside," he said. "It's a way to deny the Spanish part of me."

An architect by training, he'd worked for many years in New York and Miami; hence his colloquial English. Now, in addition to selling newspapers, he designed handbags adorned with swirling Taino motifs like those I'd seen in Santo Domingo museums. Women sewed the bags in a room behind his airless shop.

The attic above served as Caonabo's painting studio. Following him up a rickety ladder, I was greeted by a huge, brightly colored canvas of Spanish ships arriving in Hispaniola. The foreground showed a Christ-like figure nailed to a palm tree.

"The painting represents the martyrdom of the Taino," Caonabo said. It had been inspired by a Pablo Neruda poem. "Basically, it says natives were sons of God before 1492, but the Spanish used the cross to beat them into dead Indians."

We were interrupted by a bill collector. Caonabo had inherited an enormous water bill from the shop's previous owner. Each month, he had to give the collector a hundred-peso bribe to go away. He also had to contend with electricity prices, which had just spiked by 25 percent. "A technician is coming over to 'fix' my electricity meter so I can do some cheating," Caonabo said. "Free enterprise, brother."

I told him about my chase after the Admiral, and the vague plan I'd formed to get out of Santo Domingo and visit Columbus-related sites elsewhere on the island.

"You must see the Hoyo Santo," he said.

"What's that?"

"The Holy Hole. I'll close the shop on Wednesday and we'll go."

THAT NIGHT, I reread the Spanish accounts telling of the original Caonabo. He was first mentioned in 1493, when Columbus returned to Hispaniola to find that the settlers he'd left at La Navidad had perished.

The cacique was said to have attacked them with a small portion of the fifty thousand warriors he commanded in gold-rich Cibao. The Spanish described Caonabo as "lord of the mountains" and a chief who "outdid all others in strength, majesty of bearing and court ceremonial."

In 1495, after many small attacks on colonists, Columbus marched from his base at La Isabela with two hundred soldiers to subdue the Taino of Cibao. Five centuries before, when Europeans and Americans first met in open battle, native weaponry had rivaled that of the outmanned Norse. In late-fifteenth-century Hispaniola, natives still had the advantage of numbers, but European weapons radically shifted the balance of power.

The Taino, carrying clubs and bows, faced off against soldiers armed with crossbows, swords, lances, and a newly invented firearm, the harquebus. Though the guns were clumsy and inaccurate, their detonations caused Indians to panic and break ranks. Then the Spanish assaulted with cavalry, an unfamiliar and terrifying force to Indians, "who imagined that man and horse were one animal." The Spanish also deployed attack dogs, another strange sight to the Taino, whose own dogs were so mild that they didn't even bark. The battle became a bloody rout, the first of many lopsided victories by small Spanish armies in America.

Caonabo, however, continued to elude and threaten the Spanish. So Columbus sent his ruthless lieutenant Alonso de Hojeda to capture him. Hojeda lured Caonabo to La Isabela with the promise that the chief would be given a brass church bell. En route, Hojeda produced manacles and claimed they were bracelets of the sort worn by the Spanish king during royal processions. Caonabo fell for the ruse and was taken to La Isabela with his feet and hands shackled.

Columbus took Caonabo and thirty other captives with him when he sailed home in 1496. The cacique perished during the ocean crossing; one account says he died from grief, another that he hanged himself. His brother survived and was paraded across Spain wearing a heavy gold collar.

Caonabo's widow, Anacaona, later became Hispaniola's leading chief. She tried to accommodate the Spanish and was famed for her beauty, once meeting colonists clad only in a garland of flowers. In

1503, Anacaona called together eighty of her principal subjects to entertain Hispaniola's Spanish governor. After three days of dancing, feasting, and games, he ordered his men to surround a building where the Taino leaders had gathered. The governor had heard rumors of an impending revolt, and was determined to crush Taino resistance once and for all. The Spanish set fire to the place, burning alive everyone inside.

Caonabo's comely widow was spared the inferno. "As a mark of respect and out of deference to her rank," Bartolomé de Las Casas wrote, "Queen Anacaona was hanged."

THOUGH THE LAST Taino perished in the sixteenth century, they had a long half-life in the Dominican imagination. With the importation of African slaves, blacks quickly came to outnumber Europeans on Hispaniola. This was particularly so in the island's western third, which was better suited to plantation agriculture; in 1804, following a slave rebellion against French rule, it became the black nation of Haiti. The rest of Hispaniola slowly emerged as the Dominican Republic, following a long struggle against both Haitian and Spanish control that lasted into the 1860s.

While the D.R. was overwhelmingly mulatto, lingering hostility toward Haiti, and old hierarchies linked to skin tone, led many Dominicans to deny the African part of their heritage. The tenth or so of the population that appeared Caucasian identified itself as Hispanic, while Dominicans of color considered themselves Indian, even though no such population had existed for centuries and native blood constituted, at most, an infinitesimal remnant of the gene pool.

This racial reinvention reached its apogee under the D.R.'s twentieth-century dictator Rafael Trujillo, who styled himself generalissimo and "Father of the New Fatherland," renamed Santo Domingo after himself, and entered the *Guinness Book of World Records* as the world leader with the most monuments erected in his own honor. In the 1930s, he launched an ethnic cleansing campaign that led to the massacre of tens of thousands of Haitians living in the D.R.

The dark-hued Trujillo, whose own grandmother was Haitian,

wore makeup to lighten his skin. He also tried to purge the country's African heritage from textbooks and official memory, and cast himself as the savior of Spanish and Catholic Hispaniola. Elevating Columbus, the first bearer of European culture and religion, was a natural part of this enterprise.

Assassins gunned down Trujillo in 1961, as he drove along a coastal road in Santo Domingo. The spot is now marked with a memorial to the victims of his brutal rule, and he and his henchmen are execrated in today's D.R. But the racism and *antihaitianismo* of his long reign endures.

At El Conde café one night, the Scot engineer, George Houston, introduced me to a Dominican who worked in his office, a young woman named Alba Hernández. She explained that Dominicans refer to *pelo bueno* ("good hair") and *pelo malo* ("bad hair") depending on how kinky it is. Someone with body odor is said to "smell like a Haitian." Alba showed me her national identity card, on which the government identified Dominicans as "B," for *Blanco;* "N," for *Negro;* or "I," for *Indio.* Alba, a brown-skinned beauty, was *Indio.*

"Unless someone is black as night they won't put an 'N' next to their name," she said. Dominicans also described one another according to a complex scale of skin tones, such as *moreno* (brunet), *Indio claro* (light Indian), and *Indio canela* (cinnamon-colored Indian). "If you care about a person," Alba said, "you call them any shade but black."

CAONABO'S CAR WASN'T fit for long drives, so I reserved one at a rental agency for seven A.M., in hopes of an early start. After ten days in the D.R., I should have known better. We spent an hour filling out rental forms, and another doing the "damage report" on a Hyundai that looked as though it had just run the Paris-to-Dakar rally. Finally, at nine A.M., Caonabo climbed in and turned the key. The engine barely turned over. The air conditioner wheezed once and died.

"Welcome to the D.R., brother," he sighed. "The only attitude you can have is 'I don't fucking care.'" He slumped back in the driver's seat. "But I *do* care about air-conditioning. Without it we will die."

The rental agency claimed it had another car on the way, so we began the paperwork all over again. An hour and a half passed. No car appeared. Caonabo asked the agent when he thought it would arrive.

"*Ahorita,*" he said. Between now and never.

"*Estamos jodidos,*" Caonabo replied. We're fucked.

It was late morning: the familiar heat and apathy had set in. Caonabo suggested we try again tomorrow. But I couldn't face another day of defeat in Santo Domingo. So I asked the agent whether he knew of any other place we could rent a car. He pointed us down the street to a tiny storefront with an unreassuring logo: "STOP Rent a Car," enclosed within an octagonal stop sign.

After another hour of paperwork, we climbed inside an ultra-compact model called a Daihatsu Move. "We'll see if it does," Caonabo said, turning the key. The engine and air conditioner worked, though little else did. I signed the last of a dozen forms and we pulled out of the parking lot and straight into a *tapón,* a traffic jam. It was noon, we were sweaty and exhausted, and hadn't yet traversed one block of our long drive.

"Believe me," Caonabo said, "we are making good time."

As we crawled out of Santo Domingo, Caonabo briefed me on the driving rules for the Dominican Republic—or, as he put it, the d.r. for the D.R. "Rule number one, defensive driving," he said, accelerating as we approached a busy intersection. "Never stop at a red light, because the guy behind you won't, and he'll rear-end you."

"What about drivers coming the other way?" I asked.

"Their light's green, so they know to stop and then go very cautiously. Yellow's the easiest. You step on the gas." He paused. "Of course, a lot of the time the stoplights aren't working. Then the rule doesn't apply."

Caonabo leaned on the horn and accelerator, darting between lanes as we passed through the *cinturones de miseria,* the "misery belt" of barrios ringing Santo Domingo. Most of the people who dwelled there were recent migrants from the countryside and many drove unlicensed motorbike taxis, called *motorconchos,* adding to the traffic chaos. "They have no respect for the rules," Caonabo said, dodging around a motorbike, plunging through a red light, and going the wrong way up an exit ramp to enter the main highway connecting Santo Domingo to the island's interior.

Reaching the hilly countryside beyond the capital, we encountered another hazard. Vendors crowded both sides of the road, creating a Dominican strip mall of sweet-potato stands, rabbit cages, children dangling crabs from strings, and women holding signs offering goat *vivo y matado*—alive or killed. It was impossible to focus on the road, which was even more critical now, because drivers kept veering across lanes at high speed to stop and make purchases. Run-over dogs littered the roadside.

Before long, we had to fill up with gas; STOP had given us only enough to get out of town. As soon as we left the station, the Move started sputtering. Caonabo said that gas in the D.R. is often diluted with heating oil, which is cheaper than petroleum. This led him to driving rule number two.

"See that cop?" he asked, pointing at an officer standing by his patrol car, aiming a radar gun at oncoming traffic. "That means speed up." Caonabo hit the pedal, pushing the Move to its limit of seventy miles per hour. Cars to either side of us did the same.

"Are you mad?" I shouted, glancing over my shoulder for a red light and siren. At El Conde, I'd been warned by expatriates to avoid run-ins with Dominican police, who were famously corrupt. This was precisely why Caonabo sped up.

"The police are very badly paid," he said, "so they're only given one gallon of gas at a time. Otherwise, they'll siphon it off for themselves. That cop won't waste his gallon chasing us, as long as we have a head start. Even if he does, we have a full tank and can probably outlast him."

A few miles past the speed trap, Caonabo eased back to fifty-five. "It's when you're going too slowly that the police grab you." No infraction was required, and tickets were rarely issued. A hundred pesos was the standard bribe. "After that, they're very polite and say, 'Have a nice trip, Doctor.' Cops always give you an advanced degree once you've tipped them."

I stopped monitoring Caonabo's driving and tried to distract myself by gazing out at hazy fields and ramshackle towns and villages. At the edge of every settlement appeared a curious sign saying, in English, "Disco Car Wash." Caonabo said the name came from Dominicans who had lived in New York City in the 1970s, returned to the D.R.,

and opened car washes. Gradually, these businesses evolved into road-side taverns offering cold beer, sports TV, and bar girls, who rented rooms in cheap motels nearby. "The main thing they wash clean is your wallet," he said.

Casual sex, paid for or not, came with the territory in the D.R. Since arriving in the country, I'd been struck by women's revealing attire, and by the flirtation that accompanied almost all contact between the sexes. Viagra was advertised at every pharmacy, and markets hawked a drink called Mama Juana, a mix of roots, coffee beans, and turtle penis alleged to increase potency.

"Most Dominicans live day by day," Caonabo said. "It's hard to feel great about the future. So you don't believe in anything, and try not to care. The attitude is 'Have a fuck whenever you can. Live for today.'"

At least, men lived that way, married or single. Wives who played around were asking for trouble. "It's the machismo culture, men are from the street and can do what they want, ladies are for the house," Caonabo said. "It's unfair, but that's how we're raised." AIDS, I later learned, was the leading cause of death for Dominican women of childbearing age.

Two hours from Santo Domingo, we reached La Vega, a rice-growing center choked with motorbikes and fumes. Caonabo skirted the town and climbed a steep, winding road lined with religious statues. It ended at a village called Santo Cerro, or Holy Hill. "Now you are going to hear about a virgin, a very rare thing in the D.R.," Caonabo said.

He parked beside a pale yellow church crowning the hilltop. Beneath us spread the broad, fertile valley of Cibao, which Columbus had named the Vega Real, or Royal Plain. At a shop selling religious trinkets we bought a booklet on Santo Cerro, and Caonabo translated its contents while we rested in the shade and munched on *roqueta,* a ring-shaped snack made of corn and cassava that tasted like well-salted sawdust.

The booklet told of the great battle in 1495 that I'd read about the night before. But this version didn't say much about the role played by guns and horses. According to the booklet, Columbus positioned part of his army on this hill and erected a cross at its center. Then, in the valley, he saw an Indian army that stretched to the horizon and numbered in the tens of thousands. "The Spaniards were so small in number that a miracle was needed to stop the force of such a crowd."

The Indians attacked, drove the Spanish from the hill, and tried to burn the cross, "which they supposed to be a magical power that supported their enemies' courage." But the cross refused to burn. Natives tried to pull it down with vines. When this, too, failed, they chopped at it with stone axes, which broke against the wood.

Then another miracle occurred. The Virgin, with a babe in her arms, appeared above the cross. The Indians pelted her with arrows; the missiles bounced back and struck them instead. When the Spanish counterattacked, the Indians fell by the thousands, the survivors fleeing to every corner of the Vega Real.

The miracle at Santo Cerro had made the hilltop a pilgrimage site, the first Christian shrine in America. The wide, spreading tree shading us was a tropical plant called *nispero,* the same type from which Columbus allegedly cut the cross. Pieces of the cross had circulated to cathedrals across Hispaniola.

But the holiest link to the miracle lay inside Santo Cerro's hilltop church. Caonabo led me across the chapel's tiled floor to a dim alcove with a grate set in the floor. Beneath it was the Hoyo Santo, the Holy Hole. "In this very place," said a sign above the grate, "according to a very old tradition, Christopher Columbus on March 25, 1495, planted a tall cross."

As sacred sites went, the Holy Hole wasn't much to look at. Crouching on our knees, we peered through the grate at a shallow cavity in the ground. Dirt, a stone, and above the hole, a slotted box marked "offerings and promises." Votive candles and a small statue of the Virgin perched nearby.

In the church office, we found a rotund cleric clutching rosary beads. This was Antonio Camilo, bishop of the local diocese. He said eighty thousand pilgrims came to the Holy Hole each year, usually to give thanks for healing. "We even have prisoners who come when they get out of jail," he said, "to thank the Virgin for their freedom." The grate had been installed some fifty years ago, he said, because people took too much soil out of the hole, sometimes eating the dirt. "It became a health and safety problem," he said.

I asked him if the annihilation of the Taino was a source of any discomfort for those who flocked to the shrine. "For me, Columbus is a sympathetic figure," he said. "A visionary, even if he was a poor administrator. He didn't intend to wipe out the Indians. Disease did that. But now he is blamed, because there is some kind of aversion to anything that represents Spain." The bishop shrugged. "If Columbus hadn't come, someone else would have."

The bishop had a service to conduct, but he directed us to another Columbus site, just down the hill. Around the time of the 1495 battle, Columbus established a fortified settlement, Concepción de la Vega, and Hispaniola's first monastery. Following the bishop's directions, we drove in circles for half an hour before spotting a battered, barely legible sign reading "National Historic Park." It pointed us to an empty ticket booth that looked as though it had been splintered by a shotgun blast.

Climbing through a hole in the surrounding fence, we toured what had been, in the early 1500s, the first boom town in Spanish America, enriched by Cibao's modest deposits of gold. Archaeologists had un-

covered an aqueduct and luxury items such as Venetian glass. Destroyed by an earthquake in 1562, Concepción de la Vega was now a
ruin of crumbled walls and rusted signs.

Even less remained of the monastery, located on a rutted road a
few miles off. There were no signs at all, just piles of stones in a field
ringed by palm trees. We were climbing over a fence to take a closer
look when two young men appeared. They said it cost seventy pesos to
enter, a price that included a guided tour.

Caonabo looked at the rocky field and laughed. "And see what?"
he asked.

"The dead," one of the men said.

We paid and followed him as he walked among the stones, pointing to the outline of a chapel, classroom, cloister, and library. Then he
walked us across the blazing hot field to an area littered with large
canopies of corrugated metal. With the help of his friend, he lifted one
of the metal shields.

Beneath lay an open grave and skeleton. "This one is Spanish," he
said. The body had been buried on its back, arms crossed on its chest.
He lifted another piece of metal to reveal a skeleton in fetal position.
This was how the Taino were buried. Another difference: the Taino
were buried with wooden plates, shells, and other items, apparently to
equip them for the next life. Ramón Pane, the Spanish friar who lived
with the Taino, wrote that they believed the dead came out at night to
eat guava and "have festivities" with the living, even sex.

The guide lifted another shield. "The papa, the mama, and the
baby," he said of three skeletons, packed close together. And so on
through the rest of the graves: flat Spaniards, fetal Indians. He wanted
us to get our seventy pesos' worth.

Depressed by the scene, and depleted by the baking heat, we cut
the tour short and went to chat in the shade. The guide, Juan Carlos,
said he lived on a nearby farm where he and his family grew yucca and
sweet potato, using a horse and plow. The government paid him a
small fee to look after the fort and monastery. We were the first visitors
in many months.

I asked Juan Carlos whether his job had given him any appreciation of Columbus. He answered with a guffaw and a Dominican

phrase I hadn't yet heard: *"¿Tú crees que todavía hay indios?"* Caonabo said the literal translation was "You think there are still Indians?" It referred to the innocence of the Taino, who had been tricked by the Spanish with hawks' bells and other trinkets into surrendering their wealth and freedom. In modern parlance, the phrase meant, "Do you take me for a fool?"

Columbus, Juan Carlos went on, was a *"hijo de puta,"* a son of a whore. "This was a rich island. He took away all the gold and other goods and ever since we've been poor." Five hundred years later, he added, "the Spanish are still fucking us," this time with their corporations, including a hated power company. "So nothing has changed. Except that we don't pay energy bills, as a protest." He spat in the dust. "The people of this island are not fools anymore. We won't let them cheat us again."

CAONABO AND I climbed back in the Move and puttered out to the highway. I was tired and low, and the prospect of retreating to Santo Domingo depressed me. Studying the map, I located La Isabela, the wretched outpost Columbus had established on the north coast of Hispaniola. It looked to be about sixty miles to the northwest, half the distance we'd already traveled. That left us plenty of time to get there before dark, or so I thought.

Half an hour later we reached the outskirts of Santiago, the D.R.'s second-largest city. The traffic on our side of the highway slowed to a crawl. "Driving rule number three," Caonabo announced, "head for daylight, wherever you can find it." He edged the car onto the road's shoulder. When that lane filled, he put two wheels up on the sidewalk and steered around the traffic. Motorists in the left lane jumped a low median strip and drove the wrong way down the oncoming lanes. As we nosed forward, it became apparent that cars coming the other way had done the same. So all four traffic lanes, as well as the shoulder and sidewalks, were now tangled like intertwined fingers.

We came to a halt when the Move's front bumper pressed against the front bumper of a car coming down the sidewalk the other way.

Everyone honked madly, to no purpose. After an hour, rain started pelting down and darkness fell on the logjam. Caonabo cut off the engine and lit a cigarette.

"Estamos jodidos," he said. Exhaling, he offered the last driving tip for the day: "If everyone follows the rules, it leads in the end to chaos."

LATE THAT NIGHT, we reached the coastal city of Puerto Plata, so named because Columbus called a nearby peak Monte de Plata, or Silver Mountain. When he wasn't seeing gold, he saw silver.

We couldn't see a thing because of a blackout. Edging along the waterfront we found one place with a generator and a sign that identified it as the Puerto Plata Beach Resort and Casino. Caonabo suggested we bed down there for the night.

"I don't know. Sounds expensive."

Caonabo chuckled. "Not anymore." The place had gone bust several years before and recently reopened as a resort hotel, minus the resort. In the dimly lit lobby, we woke a young clerk who offered us rooms for the equivalent of $17, less than one-tenth the resort's previous rate. We walked past the closed swimming pool, its surface coated in dead bugs, and entered cavernous rooms stripped of everything except beds.

I was ready to fall into mine, but not Caonabo. He had an old girlfriend in town and wanted to catch up. "You must see some Dominican nightlife," he said. So we headed off to collect his friend, a brown-eyed woman named Filbia, who wore a cross dangling from her throat. Then Caonabo drove us down the coast to Playa Dorada, or Golden Beach, a gated resort with an eighteen-hole golf course, a mall with designer shops, and a bar called Hemingway's. There were no Dominicans here, except for young women on the arms of elderly American and European men.

While stuck in traffic in Santiago, Caonabo had told me he'd stopped drinking eighteen years ago, after waking up one morning on the street and learning from friends that he'd been dancing in a trash can the night before. But as soon as we reached the bar, he ordered rum. Caonabo downed his drink and ordered a different brand, called Brugal Viejo. "Very old and very strong," he said. "There is a saying, 'When you drink Brugal, you either fight or fuck.' Or both."

I wasn't keen to rescue him from a trash can, or have to take the driver's seat and navigate the darkened streets of Puerto Plata. Besides, I was obviously a third wheel. Before Caonabo could order another drink, I suggested that he and Filbia drop me near our hotel so I could grab a bite and walk back. They left me across from a neon-lit nightclub. "Filbia says you might enjoy yourself there," Caonabo said, driving off into the dark.

I poked my nose into the club, which had a sign saying "Karaoke Erotica." There was no sign of karaoke, only tables of German men bellowing at bare-breasted, pole-dancing women. The bouncer said I could have a "private dance," upstairs, for $75 an hour. Sex tourism had replaced gold as the draw for European males in Hispaniola.

I retreated to an outdoor restaurant across the street, only to be besieged by teenaged girls muttering *"Puta."* I walked on, until I saw a man on the sidewalk hacking at something with a cleaver and piling it onto paper plates. Having eaten little all day, I ordered a serving of the mystery meat. On my plate, in the dark, it looked like burned ear. I took a tentative bite; the meat was smoky, hard to chew, and very greasy. Tasty in a revolting sort of way. So I ordered another plate before returning to the hotel.

The next morning I woke to find my bed vibrating. At first I thought Caonabo was trying to shake me awake. By the time I'd spilled onto the floor and realized that this was my first earthquake, the tremor had stopped. Outside, a dozen people stood nervously in the parking lot. One of them said that a few weeks before, a powerful quake had knocked down hundreds of homes in Puerto Plata. This must be an aftershock.

Caonabo emerged from his room looking rumpled and bleary. I asked how his night had been. "Don't remember," he said, holding his head. "Yours?"

"Ate some street food. Not sure I should have."

Caonabo looked alarmed. "What was it called?"

"Don't know. Chimichanga, or something."

"*Chicharrones?*"

"That's it. Chewy and greasy."

Caonabo shook his head. "This is very bad." *Chicharrones,* he said, were deep-fried pork skins with gristly flesh and fat attached, flavored with road fumes and flies. Though popular among Dominicans, the dish was famously lethal to foreigners. "Eat just a little bit and you regret it for the rest of your life, which isn't long," Caonabo said.

"I ate two plates."

Caonabo glanced at his watch. "You may have a few more hours before the symptoms appear. We better hit the road."

La Isabela lay an hour's drive west, along a small coastal road between mountains and the sea. The sky was cobalt, clear of the humid haze I'd become accustomed to in the D.R. Sugarcane rose like high, wide-bladed grass beside the road, and we passed wood houses roofed with palm fronds, much like those the Spanish described. Columbus wrote that the fields and hills along this coast were "the best and most lovely lands in the world." For the first time, I felt able to grasp his awe at the beauty of this tropical isle.

Near La Isabela, a herd of cows crowded the road. "Another *tapón,*" Caonabo said, honking and nosing his way through the bovine jam. Then we reached the national park enclosing the original Spanish settlement. In contrast to Concepción de la Vega, this one was well-kept and staffed, with a museum on Taino and Spanish life.

Founded in 1494 as a settlement of two hundred wood and thatch houses, La Isabela had been troubled from its start. A third of Columbus's men quickly fell ill, though no one knows from what. The causes may have included spoiled rations, parasites, insect-borne disease, and syphilis. Adding to Columbus's woes was the presence of minor noblemen, "for whom having to work with their hands was equivalent to death, especially on an empty stomach." Columbus had to quell one mutiny by hanging several ringleaders.

Resupply fleets kept the settlement afloat, but just barely. A new arrival from Spain in late 1495 reported that colonists were subsisting on small quantities of wheat, rancid bacon, and rotten cheese. Deserted soon after, in favor of Santo Domingo, La Isabela became a literal ghost town. Those who visited in the 1500s were frightened off by *caballeros fantasmas,* phantom knights who, when removing their hats in greeting, lifted off their heads as well.

The ruins of La Isabela remained relatively undisturbed until the nineteenth century, when a revival of interest in Columbus led treasure hunters to dig up relics and cart away chunks of stone buildings. Then, in 1945, the Dominican dictator Trujillo ordered local officials to "clean up" the site in time for a tour by international archaeologists and politicians. When the visitors arrived, they found nothing left above ground. Local officials, misunderstanding Trujillo's order and terrified of failing to carry it out, had sent in workmen with bulldozers.

"They flattened all the trees and what was left of the buildings," a park guide named Bernardino told us. Later, when the D.R.'s north coast became a landing point for anti-Trujillo forces, the dictator sent in heavy equipment again, to grade the site for military drills.

Remarkably, archaeologists in the 1980s and 1990s had nonetheless unearthed a number of relics and the remains of five buildings, including Columbus's fortified house. Originally a two-story structure with plaster walls and a watchtower, the casa was built on a point of land with an expansive view of the aquamarine bay. The prevailing breeze made it the most comfortable spot in La Isabela.

A nobleman on Columbus's second voyage wrote in 1494 that "the Admiral's residence is called the royal palace," in expectation that Spain's sovereigns would one day stay there while visiting "this well favored land." Another document listed items needed for the Admiral and his household, including mattresses made "of fine Brittany linen," silk cloth, "tapestries depicting trees," brass candlesticks, and "twelve boxes of quince-preserve."

Five centuries later, the palace consisted of several crumbled walls, none higher than my thigh—a memorial in fallen stone to the unfulfilled dreams of the man who built it. Just outside the palace walls stood rock piles and small white crosses. Hundreds of Spaniards, and untold numbers of Taino, had died in and around La Isabela during its brief existence.

"Muchos muertos," Bernardino said, walking us to holes in the ground covered in wire mesh. Here, again, lay exposed skeletons:

Spaniards with arms crossed, Taino in fetal curls. In Santo Domingo, I'd been desperate to glimpse bones. Now I'd seen quite enough of them.

I was also growing weary of "firsts," which seemed to be awarded very promiscuously in the D.R. As Bernardino showed us another rectangle of stones, site of "the first church and the first mass in the first city in America," I realized I'd heard much the same claim made in La Vega and Santo Domingo. Peevishly, I asked about La Navidad, the outpost Columbus built from the wood of the *Santa María,* and technically the first Spanish settlement in America.

"It is in Haiti," Bernardino replied, as if that made it unworthy of consideration. "And it was just a fort."

At least that's the translation Caonabo gave me. Worn out from the heat and his lingering hangover, he'd taken off his T-shirt and tied it around his head as a shield against the sun. When Bernardino talked at length about the contents of an excavated storehouse, Caonabo offered this abridgment: "He says, 'Columbus brought animals and seeds and stuff.' "

We tipped Bernardino, bought a reproduction *zemi* at the gift shop, and retreated to the car. Studying the map again, I plotted a return drive along small roads that followed the route Columbus had taken as he crossed the mountains and rivers to reach Cibao. It looked as though we'd see some nice scenery, and skirt Santiago, site of the hideous traffic jam we'd hit the day before.

Caonabo was doubtful—"Driving rule number five: never trust a Dominican map"—but too exhausted to argue. So we set off in the direction of a bridge over the Yaque River, the gateway to Cibao.

Before long, we became hopelessly lost, winding down back roads that carried us deeper into the countryside. Barefoot, shirtless kids waved to us from atop mules loaded with thatch. Men carried machetes and bags of bananas on their heads. Whenever we stopped to ask the way to the bridge over the Yaque, passersby consulted one another, pointed in opposite directions, and then shouted gaily after us, "*¡Vaya bien!*" Good traveling!

After an hour of clueless meandering, we found ourselves on a narrow track that turned from gravel to dirt, tunneling between woods draped in Spanish moss. Then the road dead-ended at a bluff by a wide muddy river. We'd finally stumbled on the Yaque.

I followed Canoabo down to the river, through heavy brush, in hopes of peeling off my sweaty clothes and taking a plunge. But the riverbank was a dump, piled with trash hurled from the bluff above. The garbage stank and buzzed with insects. Gazing down the river in both directions, we couldn't see any sign of a bridge. The only way out was to backtrack through the labyrinth we'd just traveled.

"Fine navigating, Admiral," Caonabo said, swatting away flies. "I doubt even Columbus got this lost." He slumped on the sand and held his aching head. "I give up. The Spanish, I forgive them. You, no. This has been a fuck of a road trip."

AS CAONABO NAPPED with his head under a bush, I went to dip my toe in the fetid Yaque. It was along this river, in 1493, that the Spanish saw their first raw gold in America. Grains "the size of lentil seeds" sparkled in the sand, Columbus wrote, and caught in the hoops of water casks. He named the waterway El Río del Oro. The name hadn't stuck, but for once Columbus was right; the river *did* carry traces of gold as it ran down from the mountains of Cibao.

But the sparkling Yaque—the first tangible evidence of all the rumors he'd chased since arriving in the Indies—led to Columbus's undoing. The Admiral never needed much to inflate his imagination. He later wrote Isabel and Ferdinand that the Spanish had found "rivers of gold" in Hispaniola, a claim he could never make good on.

It was this propensity for magical thinking that seemed, in the end, to define Columbus. A bookish man, he read widely, but rarely in search of new knowledge; instead, he sought confirmation of his preexisting fantasy, about an Orient that lay almost on Europe's doorstep. This dream drove him across the Ocean Sea, where he saw and heard things already in his own head: sirens, cannibals, subjects of the Great Khan, even an island off Hispaniola inhabited by Amazons.

Other men of his day had clearer vision. "The hidden half of the globe is brought to light," Peter Martyr, an Italian historian in the

Spanish court, wrote upon Columbus's return from his first voyage, in 1493. The next year, Martyr became the first European to refer to the Indies as *ab orbe novo*—the new world.

Yet Columbus never grasped the immensity of what he'd done. The more he saw, the less he learned. Mysticism and dreams of the Orient kept overwhelming the evidence of his own senses. Upon reaching the South American continent in 1498, Columbus realized he'd come upon an enormous landmass—then concluded he was at "the end of the East," where the sun first rose on Eden. Five years later, on his final voyage, he was still chasing after Asian gold and spice, and believed while in Costa Rica that he was just ten days' travel from the Ganges.

"The world is but small," he wrote near the end, reiterating his old belief. "Experience has now proved it." He went to his deathbed still convinced he'd reached the Orient.

In the space of just twelve years, Columbus had introduced Europe to a hemisphere that held 28 percent of the world's landmass and millions of unknown people. But the Admiral found only what he'd gone looking for in the first place. He never discovered America.

BY THE TIME Caonabo and I found our way back to Santo Domingo, it was after dark. Returning the Move required as much paperwork as renting it. *"Problema,"* the STOP agent finally announced. My credit card had been rejected.

"That's probably because the people who took an imprint of it yesterday are now on a spending spree," Caonabo told me. Between us we had just enough pesos to pay the bill, leaving nothing for a taxi to carry us the several miles back to the Zona Colonial.

We hiked in weary silence and parted beneath a dead street lamp near Caonabo's shop. In the morning I'd be flying out of Hispaniola, to start following the conquistadors who reached the continent Columbus never touched. "Wanna come?" I asked.

Caonabo looked at me incredulously. "You think there are still Indians?"

He lit his last cigarette and offered a final piece of advice. "If the *chicharrones* strike tonight, do not even think of going to the hospital. Believe me, it is better to die on the street. Or find someone who does voodoo." He slapped my shoulder and headed off into the dark. "*Vaya bien,* brother," he shouted. "*Vaya* fucking *bien.*"

PART II
CONQUEST

The frontispiece of a sixteenth-century manual for conquistadors, showing a Spanish captain holding dividers and a sword hilt. The couplet translates: "With the compass and the sword / More and more and more and more."

CHAPTER 5

THE GULF COAST

NAKED IN THE NEW WORLD

We Spaniards know a sickness of the heart
that only gold can cure.
— Hernán Cortés, conqueror of Mexico

OR FIFTEEN YEARS after Columbus built a fort from the timbers of the *Santa María,* Spain's conquest of America was confined to Hispaniola. Not until 1508 did colonists start exploiting nearby islands the Admiral had found—Puerto Rico, Jamaica, Cuba—where they repeated the grim cycle of subjugating natives and importing Africans when Indian labor gave out.

Then, beginning in 1513, Spain's small realm exploded out of the Caribbean. Vasco Núñez de Balboa reached the Pacific; Ferdinand Magellan crossed it, after rounding South America. Hernán Cortés conquered the Aztec of Mexico, Francisco Pizarro the Inca of Peru. By 1542, the fiftieth anniversary of Columbus's first sail, Spain had laid claim—and often laid waste—to an empire larger than Rome's at its peak.

One engine behind this extraordinary conquest was Spain's crusading zeal. The vanquishing of Muslim armies at home had infused Iberians with a confidence and fervor that spilled over to America. "As Christians," Cortés told his men in the midst of battle against the

Aztec, "we were obliged to make war against enemies of our faith." This was militant Christianity in the literal sense.

Convinced of their superiority, and the rightness of their conquest, Spaniards also felt entitled to the spoils. In the vanguard of plunder were men from the lowest ranks of Spain's nobility, called hidalgos— literally, sons of somebody—and caballeros, or gentlemen. Unlike peasants, these minor nobles had the means to sail for America, seeking riches and status unavailable to them in hierarchical Spain.

Behind them stood a Spanish Crown that needed funds for its ceaseless military campaigns in Europe, and for the lavish life of its court. The Crown kept pressing for the conversion of Indians, and passed laws to protect them, but its overriding interest was the extraction of mineral wealth. Charles I, who succeeded Ferdinand in 1516 and was crowned Holy Roman Emperor in 1519, made his first public reference to Spain's American domain the following year. He called it the "gold-bearing world."

While colonists had culled a modest amount of gold from the Caribbean, the first great lode was discovered by Cortés. A former Latin student and notary, Cortés landed four hundred men on the coast of Mexico in 1519, for what was intended as an exploratory probe. But upon learning of a fabulously rich empire to the interior, he marched to Tenochtitlan, an island metropolis of more than 100,000 people, comparable to the largest European cities of that era.

The Aztec ruler, Moctezuma, greeted the Spaniards with gifts of gold. Cortés nonetheless seized him, laid siege to Tenochtitlan, and ultimately destroyed it, toppling a warrior empire that ruled some ten million people from central Mexico to Guatemala.

Historians have often cast this stunning conquest as a clash of civilizations: European reason and military technology versus Aztec sunworship and spiked clubs. Less recognized, until recently, was the critical role played by Cortés's native allies, Indians who resented the Aztec and swelled the small Spanish army by the tens of thousands. Also, a smallpox epidemic swept Tenochtitlan during the battle for the city, enfeebling the Aztec and killing many more natives than Spanish arms.

But little of this was apparent to Cortés's contemporaries. To them, his exploits seemed straight from the chivalric romance *Amadis*

Human sacrifice by the Aztec, who believed in nourishing the sun with hearts. From a sixteenth-century Mexican codex illustrated by native artists.

de Gaula, one of the most popular books of the sixteenth century (and a favorite of Don Quixote's). Amadis is a wandering knight who beds maidens, slays monsters, finds enchanted isles, and kills 100,000 foes single-handed. Cortés, likewise a man who took many mistresses, outdid Amadis: he brought down a heathen empire that practiced human sacrifice, and he looted gold on a scale that made him one of the wealthiest men in the New World.

His conquest also deepened Spaniards' sense of themselves as invincible Christian warriors, and provided them a potent model. The riches of the Aztec exceeded the wildest rumors that had circulated since Columbus's landing in America. With a small but determined force, led by a hidalgo as bold and ruthless as Cortés, what fortunes remained to be found in lands the Spanish had not yet conquered?

LIKE MOST AMERICANS, I'd learned a little about Cortés in grade school, along with his most famous successor, Francisco Pizarro, the illiterate pig farmer who became conqueror of Peru. As a teenager, I listened to Neil Young wail "Cortez the Killer" and watched my loinclothed brother play a guard to the Inca emperor Atahualpa in *The Royal Hunt of the Sun*. But "conquistador" was a term I associated with Mexico and Peru. It wasn't until I began my reeducation campaign that I realized how much of North America the Spanish had invaded, too.

Their first incursion was also very early, preceding Cortés to Mexico by six years and the Pilgrims to America by more than a century. In 1513, Juan Ponce de León, a veteran of Columbus's second voyage, set off for a land rumored to lie north of the Caribbean isles already in Spanish hands. Sailing from Puerto Rico, he reached a lushly wooded shore at Easter time, a season celebrated in Spain as the "Feast of Flowers." Because of the date, and the beauty of the place, he called the coast La Florida.

Ponce de León's arrival, near Daytona Beach, marked the first recorded landing by a European on what is now U.S. soil. He was also the first to observe a current "more powerful than the wind" drawing his ship out to sea: the Gulf Stream. By the logic of naming lands after their European discoverers, the future American nation should have been called the United States of Juan, or Ponce de Leónia.

But the conquistador suffered from bad fortune, and worse publicity. On a return trip to colonize La Florida, he was wounded by an arrow and soon after died. Adding insult to fatal injury, a Spanish historian later claimed that Ponce de León had sailed in 1513 to find a mythic spring, as a cure for his impotence.

Ponce de León was thirty-nine at the time, and had fathered four children. Moreover, his charter from the Crown made no mention of a "fountain of youth," only a more familiar grail: gold. But the legend of his quest endured. And so, Ponce de León went down in history as a wistful graybeard, seeking eternal youth, like so many Floridians today.

WHILE THE NAME Ponce de León was at least dimly familiar to me before I researched his voyages, the same wasn't true of the hundreds of Spaniards who soon followed in his wake. In fact, as I scanned the roster of expeditions, I recognized a total of two men, De Soto and Coronado, best known to many Americans as the names of bygone automobiles.

Discovering the depths of my own ignorance no longer came as a shock to me. What *did* was the astounding journey made by one of these little-known Spaniards. Between 1528 and 1536, Alvar Núñez Cabeza de Vaca took a cross-country trek that made Lewis and Clark's expedition, three centuries later, look like a Cub Scout outing by comparison. His desperate crossing, which transformed him from armed invader to native healer, also demolished my image of Spanish conquest as a relentless steamrolling of America and its people.

"I wandered lost and naked through many and very strange lands," Cabeza de Vaca wrote in a chronicle of his journey, the *Account*. Of his story, he adds, "this is the only thing that a man who returned naked could bring back."

Cabeza de Vaca had set off a decade before as a fairly typical Spaniard on the make in America. He came from military stock, including a grandfather who led Spain's brutal conquest of Grand Canary and sold its natives into slavery. Cabeza de Vaca fought in several campaigns in Europe before joining an expedition to La Florida. "I preferred to risk my life than have my honor questioned," he writes early in his account, sounding very much the haughty caballero.

In the years following Ponce de León's brief probe, "La Florida" had come to designate a vast, vague territory stretching roughly from the Atlantic to Mexico. Somewhere in this uncharted expanse, Spaniards hoped to repeat their pillage of the Aztec. But the man commanding the La Florida expedition, Pánfilo de Narváez, was no Cortés. Upon landing near present-day Tampa in the spring of 1528, he sent his five ships and a quarter of his men to sail off in search of a harbor. This instantly severed Narváez's land force of three hundred men and forty-two horses from transport or resupply.

Ill-provisioned and overclad, the Spaniards spent a wretched summer slogging through Florida's swamps and dense woods. Reaching the site of today's Tallahassee, they came under attack by Indian archers and fled to the nearby coast, in hopes of rescue by their ships. But the vessels had searched for Narváez's army in vain and sailed off.

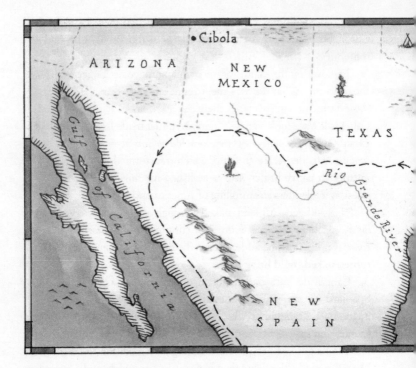

Abandoned in "that awful country," Cabeza de Vaca wrote, the Spaniards built crude boats, fashioning spurs into nails, horse manes into rigging, and shirts into sails. Then, after eating the last of their horses, the 242 survivors crowded onto five rafts and launched out to sea, "without having anyone with us who knew the art of navigation."

Floating west, along the shore of the Gulf of Mexico, they ran out of fresh water and drank from the sea, poisoning men with salt. Then, reaching "a very large river" that "emptied into the sea in a torrent"— this was the Mississippi—the flotilla was pushed from shore and began to separate. Rowing hard, Cabeza de Vaca and his exhausted crew tried to keep up with Narváez's raft, which "had the healthiest and strongest men." Cabeza de Vaca called out to his commander for a rope so the boats could stay together.

"He answered me that it was no longer time for one man to rule

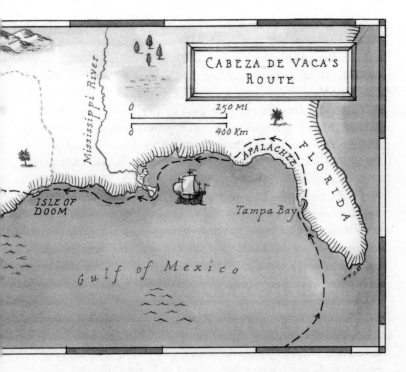

another," Cabeza de Vaca wrote. "Each one should do whatever seemed best to him in order to save his own life." With that, Narváez "veered away with his raft," never to be seen again.

Adrift, in hurricane season near present-day New Orleans, Cabeza de Vaca's craft was blown back toward shore by a fierce storm. "Near land," he wrote, "a great wave took us and cast the boat out of the water as far as a horseshoe can be tossed." Coastal natives, their nipples and lips pierced with cane reeds, approached the Spaniards. "We were so scared that they seemed to us to be giants."

The Spanish tried to relaunch their craft, only to have it capsize and then sink in heavy surf, taking down several men and the remains of their gear. "Those of us who survived were as naked as the day we were born and had lost everything we had," Cabeza de Vaca wrote. "Although the few things we had were of little value, they meant a lot to us." The weather turned cold, and the men had eaten little except parched corn since boarding their boat two months before. "We were closer to death than to life."

It was at this moment, when he was stranded and stripped, that Cabeza de Vaca's metamorphosis began. The Indians "sat down with us," he wrote. "They felt such great pain and pity at seeing us in such a state that they all began to cry." Taking the castaways to simple lodges, natives warmed them by fires while dancing through the night. The Spanish feared they were about to be sacrificed. Instead, the Indians fed their guests and treated them well.

In all, several rafts and some eighty Spaniards washed ashore at what Cabeza de Vaca called the Isle of Doom, today's Galveston Island, Texas. This was more men than the island and its natives could support. Over the winter, many of the Spaniards died from hunger, and from a "stomach ailment" that also killed half their hosts. Natives thought the newcomers were the cause (as they may well have been) and decided to kill the fifteen Spaniards still alive.

The men were spared at the last moment, but denied food unless they healed the sick. Native practices included blowing on sufferers "where the pain is." So the Spaniards, who lacked even the poor medical tools and training then current in Europe, blended what they'd seen of native ritual with a bit of Catholic theater. "We did our healing," Cabeza de Vaca wrote, "by making the sign of the cross on the sick persons, breathing on them, saying the Lord's Prayer and a Hail Mary."

Miraculously, the sick recovered. Grateful Indians fed the Spaniards and clothed them in hides. Cabeza de Vaca's regard for his hosts also grew. "These people love their children more and treat them better than any other people on earth," he wrote. And they shared everything they had.

But the natives possessed very little, and in spring they put the Spanish to work picking berries and pulling cane from the water. Half-starved, and covered in cuts from the cane, Cabeza de Vaca fled to another tribe on the nearby mainland. A resourceful and adaptable man, he found a new role, as a trader carrying sea snails, flint, and other goods between coastal Indians and their enemies in the interior. He kept at this for more than four years.

"I liked this trade, because it gave me the freedom to go wherever I wanted," he wrote. "I was obligated to nothing and was not a slave." There are stirrings in this passage, and elsewhere in the *Account,* of the future American story: living free, in a wide land, by one's own wit and enterprise.

BUT CABEZA DE Vaca couldn't leave the Old World behind. Each year, he returned to the Isle of Doom to plead with a fellow Spaniard to flee with him toward "the land of the Christians," in Mexico. When he finally prevailed, the two traveled a short way before learning that the land ahead was barren. Cabeza de Vaca's companion, who had gone more native than he, returned to his Indian family.

Pressing on alone, Cabeza de Vaca found the only other survivors of Narváez's three-hundred-man force: two Spaniards, and a "black Arab" who had come to La Florida as one of their slaves. They were all slaves now, to an Indian tribe, and Cabeza de Vaca became one, too. This was the low point of his journey, an unceasing round of forced labor and scarce food. The Indians were so hungry that they ate spiders, worms, powdered fish bones, dirt, even deer dung. Worst of all were the mosquitoes, which left everyone so bitten that they looked to Cabeza de Vaca like lepers. "I can affirm that no other affliction suffered in the world can equal this."

He also wrote of native customs that shocked him, including what he called drunkenness, likely the result of smoking peyote or consuming it as tea. Women and the elderly, "the people they least esteem," carried all loads. Fathers sometimes buried their young sons alive, in obedience to dreams, and fed newborn daughters to their dogs. They did this rather than let the girls be taken by the other tribes with whom they were constantly at war. "If their enemies were to marry their daughters, they would multiply so much that they would conquer them and take them as slaves."

Cabeza de Vaca relates this dispassionately, and on the next page describes these same natives as "very merry people." His writing about Indians is rarely judgmental, but nor is it romantic. Though many people today imagine early America as a gentle and bountiful paradise, Cabeza de Vaca depicts the lands he passed through as an impoverished and Hobbesian world, where all struggled against all for survival.

After more than a year of bondage, Cabeza de Vaca and the other three survivors escaped and fled west, subsisting on the juice of a cactus fruit (the prickly pear), until they encountered another Indian clan. The natives, having heard of bearded strangers who possessed the power to heal, came to one of the Spaniards, "telling him that their heads hurt a great deal, and begging him to cure them." He prayed and made the sign of the cross, and "they immediately said that all their pain was gone." The wanderers were rewarded with more venison than they could eat or carry.

Cabeza de Vaca, the most confident of the Spaniards, became the lead physician. He performed surgery, using a knife to remove an arrowhead from an Indian's chest and sewing up the wound with a bone needle and deer sinew, and he even restored to health a man who had no pulse and appeared dead.

He attributed his medical success to divine mercy. But natives had their own beliefs about illness and healing. After resurrecting the "dead" man, Cabeza de Vaca recorded Indians' fear and awe of "Mr. Bad Thing," a small, bearded figure who lived in the ground and never ate. Periodically, he rushed into lodges and drove a sharp flint into random victims, then pulled out their entrails; or he slashed and broke arms. Afterward he reset the bones and laid his hands on the wounds, instantly closing them. Indians may have associated the bearded Mr. Bad Thing with the strange men who had come among them.

As the Spaniards traveled on, passing from tribe to tribe as celebrated medicine men, the *Account* becomes gradually more mystical and surreal. Naked as the natives, the nomads broiled under the desert sun. "Since we were not used to this, we shed our skins twice a year like serpents." Covered in sores, and pricked by thorns, Cabeza de Vaca consoled himself with thoughts of Christ's much greater suffering. The Spaniards also adopted an ascetic air, to awe

Indians. "They were astonished to see how little we ate. They never saw us get tired, and really we were so used to hardship that we did not feel tired."

To amplify their aura of mystery and power, the Spaniards carried gourds given them by native shamans, and rarely talked to Indians. Instead, the black slave, Estevanico, acted as scout and intermediary: it was he who "always spoke to [natives] and informed himself about the roads we wished to travel and the villages that there were and about other things that we wanted to know."

Gradually, an entourage of several thousand Indians began trailing the four men, reverently asking them to blow on and bless food and drink. These followers may have been using the Spaniards, too. At each settlement the Spaniards approached, their native escorts warned people that the bearded men were fearsome creatures, capable of bestowing life or death. Then the escorts sacked the village. The looted, in turn, joined the looters in pillaging the next place. Heralds ran ahead to announce the approach of this ecstatic, marauding procession.

Where it was headed isn't clear. "We wanted to go towards the sunset," Cabeza de Vaca wrote, offering a rare directional detail; his descriptions of the landscape and Indian customs also provide clues. But it's impossible to reconstruct the Spaniards' route with any precision. The best guess is that they walked across Texas and parts of the Southwest, and crossed into northern Mexico before reaching the Gulf of California.

Turning south along the coast, Cabeza de Vaca entered settled farmland and learned that "bearded men like us, with horses, lances and swords," had terrorized natives and carried them off in chains. Though gladdened to hear "news of Christians," he observed the desolation they'd wrought: burned villages, abandoned fields, natives living on tree bark.

Then, scouting ahead with Estevanico and a party of natives, Cabeza de Vaca encountered "four Christians on horseback." The riders "were quite perturbed to see me so strangely dressed and in the company of Indians," he wrote. "They looked at me for a long time, so astonished that they were not able to speak or ask me questions."

After eight years and several thousand miles of wandering, Cabeza de Vaca was barely recognizable to the riders as a fellow countryman. Nor could natives "be persuaded to believe that we were the same as the other Christians."

In a sense, they no longer were. The horsemen were slave raiders who wanted to seize the Indians trailing behind Cabeza de Vaca. He negotiated their safety before sending them home to their villages. But he later learned that the slave raiders had come back and attacked. "We wanted freedom for the Indians, and when we thought we had secured it, quite the opposite happened."

So began Cabeza de Vaca's return to a civilization that now felt foreign to him. He was given clothing but couldn't wear it for many days, and was only able to sleep on the ground. Sailing home to Spain, he took up his pen in defense of the Indians he'd set out to conquer. "All these people, in order to be attracted to becoming Christians and subjects of your Imperial Majesty, need to be treated well," he wrote. "This is a very sure way to accomplish this; indeed, there is no other way."

THE *ACCOUNT* IS a curious document that can be read on many levels: as a travel adventure, a manifesto, a castaway story, a captivity narrative. It is also a spiritual memoir that echoes Paul's conversion on the road to Damascus. At other points, the *Account* seems a precursor of classic American journeys into and across the continent. Like Huck Finn and Jim, the Spaniards and Estevanico wander a wilderness where "sivilized" rules no longer apply. Like the self-reliant heroes of Hollywood Westerns, Cabeza de Vaca often journeys alone through the vast empty spaces of America. The *Account* even evokes a psychedelic sixties road trip: four naked, shaggy guys, adrift in a desert of peyote-smoking shamans.

A British writer, Richard Grant, eloquently captures these resonances in his own nomadic travelogue, *Ghost Riders*. The *Account* feels "characteristically American," he writes, because its author "had become an American by the time he wrote it. He had been through an odyssey that was not possible in Europe, and by the end of it he no longer thought or behaved like a European. In a sense, he had been conquered by America."

IF THAT WERE the end of Cabeza de Vaca's saga, it would represent an uplifting tale of two worlds, commingling rather than colliding. But his journey had a cruel coda, for both Cabeza de Vaca and his vision of peaceful coexistence. After writing the *Account,* he sailed from Spain to become governor of a troubled colony in South America. Landing in Brazil, Cabeza de Vaca decided to travel the rest of the way overland, embarking on another epic trek, this time through jungle.

Reaching his post in present-day Paraguay, he enacted reforms to protect Indians and the poor. But the colonists, accustomed to enslaving and looting natives, rose in revolt and arrested him. They charged him with assorted crimes, such as raising his family banner rather than the king's, and sent him in chains to Spain, where authorities ordered him banished to a penal colony in North Africa. Though the sentence was later lifted, Cabeza de Vaca died in obscurity, at a time and place unknown.

His plea for kind treatment of the natives he'd encountered in North America was likewise betrayed. Soon after he and his fellow survivors reached Mexico in 1536, they gave a report to Spanish officials that previewed Cabeza de Vaca's published account. What caught the attention of officials, however, wasn't the generosity of poor natives: it was hints the travelers gave of riches in the land they'd wandered.

For instance, the nomads had been given a brass or copper bell, which, they were led to believe, came from a wealthy society to the north that smelted and cast metal. They were also given stones that Cabeza de Vaca called emeralds, brought from a mountainous region where "there were villages of many people and very large houses." The stones were probably turquoise, and the populous villages the high-walled pueblos of the American Southwest.

This was enough to inflame the fevered imagination of settlers in New Spain, as colonized Mexico was known. Though Cabeza de Vaca sailed home in 1537, the viceroy of New Spain recruited one of his fellow castaways, Andrés Dorantes, to head back north and "learn the secret of those regions." This agreement collapsed, but not before the viceroy had bought Dorantes's slave, Estevanico. It was he, rather than Cabeza de Vaca, who would have a lasting impact on the history of North America.

WHILE READING THE *Account,* I'd highlighted every mention of Estevanico, and tracked footnotes in search of any scrap about him. In the annals of early America, it is extremely rare to find a slave described as an individual, or even named. I was also intrigued by the parallel between Estevanico and the American slave York, who played a crucial yet neglected part in the Lewis and Clark expedition.

According to the *Account,* Estevanico was a native of Morocco, presumably a Muslim who had converted to Christianity (Spain didn't send infidels to the New World, at least not officially). His original name is unknown: Estevanico is a diminutive of Estevan, the Spanish rendering of Stephen. Some documents call him Estevanico de Dorantes—"Dorantes's little Stephen," or "Stevie." At other times he's referred to by his skin color only, as *el negro.*

Estevanico's role in the *Account,* as interpreter and scout, suggests he was a skilled linguist and intermediary who moved easily between the worlds of Spaniards and Indians. Like Cabeza de Vaca, he also must have been a man of exceptional strength and stoicism to survive the eight-year ordeal. His new owner, the viceroy of New Spain, seems at least to have recognized these traits. In 1538, he sent Estevanico as guide on a mission to probe the unexplored region north of Mexico that had become known as Tierra Nueva: the New Land.

As leader of the reconnaissance party, the viceroy chose Fray Marcos de Niza, so called because he was from Nice, in southern France. The friar had traveled to Peru following Pizarro's conquest of the Incas. Apparently, this qualified him as an expert who would recognize any other rich kingdom that existed in the mountains of Tierra Nueva.

In the viceroy's written instructions to Marcos, he assured the friar that Estevanico had been ordered to obey the friar absolutely, as he would his own master. But soon after the expedition departed for the north, Estevanico raced ahead with a group of natives. Marcos, in a report he later gave to the viceroy, claimed that he'd dispatched "the Black" as an advance scout.

Other Spanish accounts tell a different story. According to one, Estevanico offended Marcos by "taking the women the Indians gave him, collecting turquoises, and amassing a quantity of both." Also, the Indians "understood the Black better, because they had already seen him before." As he proceeded north, Estevanico gathered an entourage of some three hundred natives and began carrying a gourd hung with bells and feathers, reinhabiting the role that Cabeza de Vaca's troupe had played several years before. Now, Estevanico had the part to himself.

Before leaving Marcos, however, he agreed to keep the friar informed by sending back messengers bearing crosses. The size of the cross would signify the importance of what lay ahead. Soon after Estevanico's departure, a messenger returned with a cross "the height of a man," Marcos said. The courier told him that Estevanico had heard "a report of the greatest thing in the world"—seven great cities, their multistoried dwellings adorned with precious stones. The city dwellers were also "well dressed" in long cotton shirts, hides, and belts. This was significant, because Europeans associated clothes with civilization, and Indians' frequent nakedness with the absence of it.

Soon after, another large cross arrived with a message urging Marcos to hurry; Estevanico was speeding toward the seven cities, which he called Cibola. As Marcos followed, he, too, met Indians who told of Cibola's streets, plazas, and very tall buildings. The friar innocently asked whether "the men of that land had wings so they could climb to those upper stories. They laughed and pantomimed a ladder to me."

The next message Marcos received wasn't a cross but the arrival of bloodstained refugees from Estevanico's party. A day before reaching the first of Cibola's cities, they said, Estevanico had sent heralds ahead with his customary calling card: his ceremonial gourd and a message "that he was coming in order to make peace and heal them."

In response, one of Cibola's leaders angrily flung the gourd to the ground and declared that anyone coming to the city would be killed.

Estevanico ignored this warning, only to be stripped of his turquoise and imprisoned in a building outside the walled city. When he and his native escorts tried to flee, the Cibolans attacked. One of the Indians who escaped said he'd seen no more of Estevanico. "We believe they shot him with arrows."

Though frightened by this report, Fray Marcos nonetheless pressed ahead to see Cibola for himself, or so he later claimed. His report on the last leg of his journey is brief and lacking in fresh detail. Marcos said he reached a hill "within sight of Cibola" and glimpsed exactly what the Indians had described: a large settlement of tall, flat-roofed buildings, grander even than Mexico City. According to his native guides, it was also the least magnificent of the seven cities. Having confirmed Cibola's existence, Fray Marcos turned and raced back to Mexico, "with all the speed I could."

Like the fountain of youth, the legend of seven enchanted cities ran deep in European belief. According to medieval lore, seven bishops had fled west from Portugal in the eighth century, to escape invading Moors, and had founded Antilia, also known as the Isle of the Seven Cities. In later centuries, sailors periodically claimed to have glimpsed Antilia, and the isle migrated around maps of the Ocean Sea: a floating fable. Some Europeans thought Columbus had found Antilia and nearby islands: hence the Antilles, still the name of a Caribbean archipelago.

Now the elusive Seven Cities had surfaced again, in Tierra Nueva. On the face of it, this made no sense: Cibola wasn't an island. But in a world where marvels such as Mexico and Peru had only just been discovered, anything seemed possible. And the more Marcos talked, the more wondrous Cibola became. An irrepressible storyteller, he told his barber that Cibolans wore necklaces and belts of gold—a detail he hadn't reported before and couldn't have seen from his distant glimpse of the city. Marcos also told of camels, elephants, and creatures with a single horn that extended to their feet and forced them to eat while lying on their sides.

The viceroy, meanwhile, had wasted little time in acting on Marcos's official report. He quickly organized a major expedition, spending 85,000 silver pesos of his own money. Early in 1540, just months after Marcos's return, the friar was headed north again, as part of the largest army of conquest the Spanish had yet assembled in America.

MEN WHO TOOK part in this expedition would later write, in passing, about Estevanico. While retracing his route, they learned from Indians that he had outraged the people of Cibola by demanding turquoise and women. Also, "it seemed nonsense to [Cibolans] to say that the land he was coming from was one of white people who had sent him, when he was black." They concluded he was a "spy or guide for some people who were trying to come to conquer them," which was essentially the case.

Nowhere in the half dozen Spanish accounts of Estevanico's journey is there any expression of regret over his death, or appreciation of his service. "He thought he could get all the reputation and honor himself," one Spaniard wrote of the slave's race ahead of Marcos, "and be considered bold and courageous." But lust and greed undid him. Natives saw "he was a bad man and not like the Christians," another Spaniard claimed. "He was touching their women, whom the Indians love more than themselves. Therefore they decided to kill him."

Even if these reports were accurate, they described classic conquistador attributes: initiative, courage, and a hunger for glory and spoils, including women. Cortés was lionized for the same traits; for a black slave, they brought only censure and obscurity.

Estevanico's trek with Cabeza de Vaca, and his discovery of Cibola, set in train the Spanish conquest of the southwestern United States. Yet this remarkable man—African, Arab, European slave, American healer, interlocutor between three continents and cultures—is barely remembered today, except at a small park named for him, in a barrio at the edge of Tucson.

THE SOUTHWEST

TO THE SEVEN CITIES OF STONE

> God knows that I wish I had better news to
> write Your Lordship, but I must give you the
> truth.
>
> —Francisco Vásquez de Coronado, to the
> viceroy of New Spain, 1540

I N 1893, DURING the Columbian quadricentennial, Frederick
Jackson Turner delivered a paper entitled "The Significance of
the Frontier in American History." Turner argued that America's
steady push west had forged the country's character. "Stand at Cumberland Gap and watch the procession of civilization," he declared of
the pioneer pass through the Appalachians. "Winning a wilderness,"
over and over again, tore settlers from their European roots and created "a new product that is American."

Turner's frontier thesis isn't as popular today as it was in the heyday
of American expansion. But his geographic framing of the national
story endures. The narrative of America flows east to west: Atlantic,
Appalachians, Plains, Rockies, Pacific. Pilgrims, Pathfinders, Pioneers.
Go West, Young Man. Get Your Kicks on Route 66. Which I'd done, as
a Kerouac-addled teenager, hitchhiking from Maryland to California.
To make the same trip in reverse would have been unthinkable, like
watching a film from finish to start.

So it felt strange, three decades later, to find myself tracing a very

different path, one that was truer to the story of the continent's opening. Turner's gateway to the "Great West" was the Cumberland Gap;
mine would be the arid, dust-blown borderland between present-day
Arizona and Mexico.

In 1540, Francisco Vásquez de Coronado journeyed this way at the
head of the only European army ever to invade the U.S. continent by
land. The stock image of Spanish conquest is a glittering pageant of armored knights, and Coronado and his officers fit this stereotype. Each
set off from Mexico with multiple horses, breastplates, chain mail,
swords, crossbows, and harquebuses. Coronado wore a plumed helmet and gilded armor.

But the mass of his army was less resplendent. Fray Marcos de
Niza's report on Cibola had sparked a frenzy in Mexico, arousing fears
that the colony would lose precious manpower in the rush to Tierra
Nueva. To allay these concerns, the viceroy held a hearing at which
prominent citizens testified about the character of those joining Coronado. Witness after witness declared the expedition a blessing to Mexico, because most of the emigrants were "single and licentious" men
without employment or prospects at home.

This rough legion was also raggedly equipped. According to the
expedition's muster roll, the great majority of Spanish soldiers brought
only a single mount and "native arms and armor," such as quilted cotton tunics, clubs, and bows and arrows. Nor were these Spaniards the
true body of the army. Accompanying them were thirteen hundred *indios amigos,* Indians in Mexico who had submitted to Spanish rule and
now served as allied warriors. They outnumbered the European soldiers by almost four to one.

Coronado, then, led a force that was more New World than Old:
mostly Indians or Indian-equipped Spaniards, commanded by a small
corps of metal-clad caballeros. This ersatz army also included civilians—
black slaves and native servants, soldiers' wives, five friars (Marcos
among them), even two painters—as well as 550 horses and innumerable
livestock. In all, some two thousand people and approximately as many
animals trod north across the arid frontier. Their passage must have
created a mushroom cloud of dust.

The man chosen by the viceroy to lead this *entrada,* or journey to the interior, was only twenty-eight. Four years before, Coronado had wed the twelve-year-old daughter of a former royal treasurer of Mexico; her considerable dowry helped finance the expedition. Coronado's other qualifications for the job weren't as obvious. He had little experience in the field, apart from suppressing a miners' rebellion in Mexico by drawing and quartering the alleged ringleaders. For the most part, he'd served as a colonial administrator, a functionary who faithfully performed his superiors' bidding and signed his letters to the viceroy "Your Majesty's humble vassal and servant, who kisses your royal feet and hands."

Even as the expedition set off from the northernmost Spanish settlement in Mexico, banners flying, some of Coronado's men wondered if this callow crony of the viceroy's possessed the fire of a true conquistador. Coronado, one horseman later wrote, was leaving behind "estates and a pretty wife, a noble and excellent lady." These circumstances, he added, "were not the least causes of what was to happen."

I CAUGHT UP with Coronado several hundred miles into his march, in the Mexican state of Sonora. Compared to Santo Domingo, Sonora's capital city, Hermosillo, seemed orderly and tame: a bland commercial and administrative center for the surrounding ranchland. At a concrete tower called the Edificio Sonora, I found the state tourism office and asked a receptionist whether anyone could advise me on tracking Coronado.

"Sí," she replied. "El Nazi."

This turned out to be a 350-pound man whose German godfather had christened him Adolfo; hence his nickname. Educated at a Catholic school in Vermont, Adolfo spoke fluent English and knew all about Coronado. Unfortunately, he said few other Mexicans cared about the conquistador. "We have Cortés to hate—he did much more damage in Mexico. Coronado is *your* sad story, not ours."

In Adolfo's view, Coronado performed a small service to Mexico by conquering lands north of today's border that would eventually earn the country a few pesos. As part of the 1848 treaty ending the Mexican-American War, the United States paid $15 million for the vast territory it annexed, and later added $10 million for another strip of borderland. "If we hadn't sold it, the Americans would have taken that, too," Adolfo said.

El Nazi sent me off with a satchel of tourist literature and a road map to guide me north with Coronado. As soon as I passed the rodeo at the edge of the city, the landscape turned arid and empty. Hermosillo lies near the southern fringe of the Sonoran Desert, which stretches hundreds of miles across northern Mexico and southern Arizona. Apart from bunches of brilliant *chiles colorados* draped on roadside stalls, the color scheme was a wash of khaki and olive. Low, gnarly creosote shrubs and spiny mesquite trees dotted the parched landscape, interspersed with organ pipe cactus and the towering saguaro, its branches upraised as if in prayer. Saguaros that hadn't sprouted limbs stood like giant cucumbers on the dry brown plain.

By the time Coronado's expedition had reached this point, having marched for two months and several hundred miles, the army was already struggling. Overburdened and inexperienced men quickly shed their gear. The army's camp master died after being shot in the eye by an arrow; several Indians were hanged in reprisal. Horses collapsed from exhaustion and sheep lost their hooves on the rough terrain. Hungry, overworked slaves ran away at the earliest chance.

Worst of all, scouts reported that the territory ahead remained rugged and barren, despite Fray Marcos's promise of a gentle and fertile land. "Everything the friar had said was found to be the opposite," Coronado sourly wrote the viceroy. Fears spread through the dispirited army that other promises the friar had made would turn out to be empty as well.

Fifty or so miles northeast of today's Hermosillo, Coronado entered the valley of Los Corazones, the Hearts, so named because Cabeza de Vaca and his fellow wanderers were given six hundred deer hearts there by Indians. Corazones is believed to correspond to modern-day Ures, a sun-struck town centered on a white plaster church and shady plaza. I parked beside a horse hitched to a post; a vaquero in jeans and boots snoozed on a bench nearby. Inside the church I met a priest named Father Coronado, and asked what he knew about the conquistador who shared his name. He looked at me blankly and said, "*Nada*. He is not a relative of mine."

The only echo of the sixteenth-century Spanish passage was a market selling *tuna,* the fruit of the prickly pear, which Cabeza de Vaca virtually lived on and Coronado's hungry men often ate as well. Yellow-green on the outside, the fruit had a seedy, whitish, and faintly sweet pulp, a bit like honeydew melon. However, as its name suggests, the prickly pear has tiny thorns. My fingers stung for an hour after handling it, as did my throat from a lunch of well-spiced chili con carne.

For miles, the road north was almost empty, except for policemen made of plywood, standing guard before somnolent towns. By the time I reached Sonora's northern edge, a long day's drive from Hermosillo, the only thing keeping me awake was chili reflux and a fiery radio show from north of the border: *Gun Talk,* which peppered its chat about high-powered weapons with this bracing refrain: "The only person who can protect you is *you.*"

Self-defense of a different sort was on vivid display at the border town of Naco. On the Mexican side, the main street ran past a car graveyard selling "*Yunque Americano*" and pharmacies peddling cut-price drugs before reaching the U.S. line. No stream or ridge or other natural feature divided Mexico from the United States, only a striking man-made boundary: a fifteen-foot-high wall of corrugated metal topped with surveillance cameras and stadium lights. The road dog-legged through a U.S. border post and then returned me to the wide main street I'd left in Mexico, twenty yards behind. Except that a battered sign now told me I was in Naco, *Arizona,* elevation 4,615 feet. The sign didn't mention population and none was in evidence, apart from a dog sleeping before a row of abandoned storefronts.

The one open business was a mission-style bar. Inside, men chatted in Spanish while playing pool beneath a ceiling fan: a mirror image of a bar I'd just visited on the Mexican side. While sipping beer, I learned that the town's name was a combination of the last two letters of "ArizoNA" and "MexiCO." The Arizona side had eight hundred residents, compared with eight thousand on the Mexican side, many of them engaged in the business of illegal border crossing. Coyotes, or people smugglers, cut doors in the border wall, tunneled under it, or climbed through the barbed-wire fence that extended from either side of the metal barrier.

On the Arizona side, the wide, treeless plain hummed with motion sensors, drone aircraft, and cameras mounted on mobile cherry pickers. Each day after dark, U.S. Border Patrol agents wearing night vision goggles scooped up hundreds of illegal entrants and transported them back to the Mexican side. Most of those caught simply tried again the next day.

"It's loco," said the bar's owner, Leonel Urcadez, a second-generation Mexican-American. He was the first person I'd met since El Nazi who had heard of Coronado. Leonel led me outside and pointed along the border wall to an old stone obelisk that marked the boundary established after the Mexican-American War. In a round-about way, Coronado's march had set in motion the long, cross-border drama that was still playing itself out around Naco.

"The Spanish are invading again, eh?" Leonel said. "Back in Coronado's day, they came for gold. Now it's jobs—same thing, really. Indians didn't want the Spanish here. Most Americans today don't want them, either. History, all over again."

THE ATMOSPHERE HADN'T always been so tense. In 1941, during the four hundredth anniversary of Coronado's expedition, Congress approved the creation of a park that would straddle the border and commemorate links between the two countries. But World War II and other obstacles intervened, including Mexico's ambivalence about the park. The country had won its independence after a bloody struggle with Spain and come to embrace its Indian rather than its European heritage. So Congress went ahead without Mexico and located the Coronado National Memorial just on the U.S. side of the border.

The park site, on a mountainous slope west of Naco, overlooked the San Pedro River and the broad plain surrounding it. There were no cars but mine on the road winding up to the park, except for Border Patrol vehicles. A small visitors center was also vacant. "This is not a typical park," explained Thane Weigand, the site's lean, brush-cut chief ranger. On average, only about twenty tourists a day stopped at the visitors center. Each night, almost twenty times that number crept across the park's three-mile border with Mexico, drawn by the cover of the park's brushy slopes. "A lot are repeat visitors," Thane said.

This annual influx of roughly 120,000 illegals had radically altered the park's mission. In earlier decades, the park hosted a "Borderlands Festival" that brought together students and artists from the United States and Mexico. But as the border tightened in the late 1980s, the festival ended. Only two rangers still performed traditional park functions. The five others did law enforcement, not only rounding up migrants but also chasing drug smugglers, and sometimes exchanging gunfire with them. A park that began as a monument to cross-border amity had become its opposite: a symbol of tension between the two countries.

"I used to talk about the history and nature here," Thane said. "Now all I know about is UDAs and OTMs." "UDA" stood for "undocumented alien," "OTM" for "other than Mexican."

Thane gave me a park map and recommended I hike to a mountain lookout called Coronado Peak. Midway along the short, steep foot trail, I stopped to catch my breath: the altitude approached seven thousand feet. A tiny roadrunner skittered past me, mocking my pace. Thorny shrubs and stunted trees clung to the dry rocky soil. Finally reaching the top, I was rewarded with a panorama that stretched south for roughly a hundred miles, to the Sierra Madres in Mexico.

Three thousand feet below me, the San Pedro trickled along the valley floor, nourishing a thin green line of foliage across the brown expanse. According to my map, I was scanning thirty miles or so of the river's course as it ribboned north from Mexico and disappeared behind mountains on the Arizona side. The Coronado expedition would have spent two days crawling across my sight line: a time and distance that represented less than one percent of its eventual journey.

The previous day, while I was speeding across the Sonoran Desert, the landscape had struck me as stark but unthreatening, at least in autumn, when the temperature topped out at 90 degrees. Now, reading a park booklet, I grasped just how punishing the desert can be. In summer, when Coronado and his men crossed, the heat often exceeds 120 degrees. Rain is scarce: sometimes none falls for two years. The best-adapted Sonoran creature, the kangaroo rat, survives without drinking water at all. Its organs extract fluid from plants and seeds, even from the rat's own feces.

Other desert fauna include tarantulas, scorpions, rattlesnakes, a

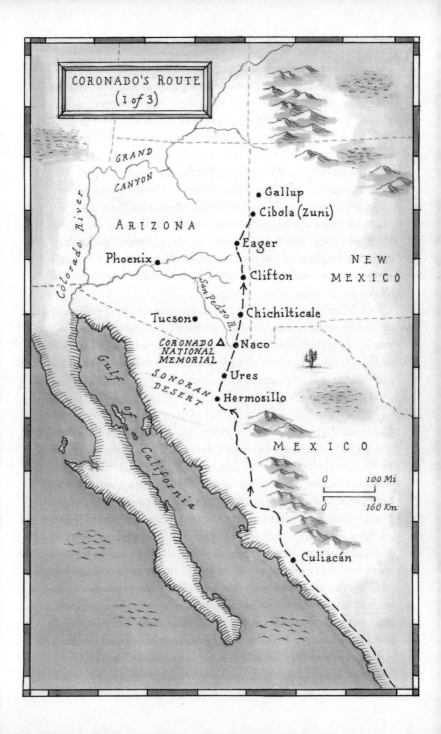

CORONADO'S ROUTE
(1 of 3)

GRAND CANYON

ARIZONA

Colorado River

Phoenix

San Pedro R.

Tucson

CORONADO
NATIONAL
MEMORIAL

SONORAN
DESERT

Gulf of California

Gallup

Cibola (Zuni)

Eager

Clifton

NEW
MEXICO

Chichilticale

Naco

Ures

Hermosillo

MEXICO

0   100 Mi

0   160 Km

Culiacán

poisonous giant centipede, and the Gila monster, which latches onto prey with small teeth and "grinds its jaws so that the venom, mixed with saliva, can enter the wound." Even the picturesque flora was hazardous. The cute, furry-looking teddy-bear cholla, which I'd stopped several times to photograph, has spines that "easily impale clothing or flesh."

I'd read little about these hazards in the Spanish accounts. Typical was Coronado's terse observation about his passage across Sonora: "The route is rough and long." But hunger was a constant theme. Fray Marcos had led the Spanish to believe that the route to Cibola ran close to the sea, meaning the army could be reprovisioned by ships from Mexico. Instead, on reaching today's United States, Coronado realized he was heading deeper inland. Indians said the sea was several weeks' march in the opposite direction.

On learning this, Coronado confided to the viceroy, "We all experienced great distress and confusion." Yet the expedition pressed on, into a rugged *despoblado,* an uninhabited wilderness, devoid of food or fodder. Conquistadors, whatever their many faults, were a tough and daring bunch of hombres.

CORONADO'S ROUTE NORTH of today's border crossed the arid valleys and rugged mountains of southeast Arizona. Fray Marcos had promised Coronado that he could feed his men and horses at an Indian stronghold called Chichilticale. But when the Spanish arrived, they found an abandoned clay fortress and a few scattered Indian camps. This desolate sight, wrote one of the Spaniards, "grieved everyone."

Even traversed by car, almost five centuries later, southeast Arizona had a scale and vacancy that felt unsettling, at least to an easterner. I spent three days exploring small roads on Coronado's trail through Arizona without leaving Cochise County, a jurisdiction larger than Connecticut. Heading off one morning at sunrise, I reckoned I could breakfast at a crossroads marked on my road map. Two hours later I came to my intended rest stop: a cattle guard, an abandoned shop named Frontier Relics, a fence with sun-blanched cow skulls stuck on each post, and a "Beware of Dog" sign. No dog, or other life of any kind, was in sight. After another hour without passing so much as a car, I started scanning the roadside scrub for a prickly pear to suck on.

The Spanish described Chichilticale as a once powerful bastion set in a mountain pass between hot desert and high alpine terrain. Though the army's horses were "worn out," Coronado wrote, he rested for only two days: food was too short for the Spanish to linger longer. So they plunged ahead, into the worst terrain they'd yet encountered, a mountainous *despoblado* where horses dropped dead from hunger and exhaustion, as did some of the *indios amigos*. A Spaniard and two Moors died after ravenously devouring a poisonous plant.

Then, after two weeks in this wilderness, the Spanish reached a gentler region of streams and trees. For the first time, they encountered Indians from the seven cities of Cibola, who had come "to tell us we were welcome." Coronado gave them a cross and rosary beads, and told them they should not be afraid, "since I was coming in His Majesty's name only to protect and help them."

Neither side was sincere. The next night, Coronado's advance guard found Indians waiting in ambush. Though the warriors quickly retreated, they appeared well-disciplined, sounding trumpets to assemble their force and sending up "smoke clouds, which were answered from a distance with as much coordination as we would have known how to do ourselves," Coronado wrote.

His own men were anything but battle ready. During the foiled ambush, one Spaniard wrote, inexperienced soldiers "became so flustered that there were some who put their saddles on backwards." But Coronado had no choice other than to advance quickly toward Cibola. "With such a shortage of food," he wrote, "I was worried that if we had to delay one more day, we would all be dead of hunger." After almost three months of hard travel from the last Spanish outpost in Mexico, Coronado's force wasn't so much a conquering army as a desperate mob of starving men and animals.

The next day, the Spanish finally glimpsed the destination they'd dreamed of for so long. When they saw the first of Cibola's cities, one soldier wrote, "such were the curses that some of them hurled at Fray Marcos that may God not allow them to reach his ears." The friar had told of a settlement more impressive than Mexico City, "the grandest and best" yet found in America. What the Spanish beheld, the soldier wrote, was "a small pueblo crowded together and spilling down a cliff." In Mexico, he added, there were ranch settlements "which from a distance have a better appearance."

Coronado didn't record his first impression of Cibola. Instead, he described a curious ritual the Spanish performed outside the pueblo's walls. Coronado sent several soldiers, a friar, and an Indian interpreter ahead to deliver the edict called the Requerimiento, or Summons. Drafted three decades earlier by a Spanish jurist, the document was part of the Crown's tortured attempt to define "just war" against Indians: a sort of sixteenth-century Geneva Convention. Conquistadors carried copies of the Requerimiento all over the Americas and were commanded to read it to Indians before commencing battle.

The proclamation opened with an abridged history of the world: God's creation of heaven and earth; Adam and Eve; St. Peter and the papacy. It also explained that the pontiff in Rome had authorized Spain's claim to the New World, a grant recorded in various documents. "These you may view, if you wish," the Requerimiento assured its Indian audience. Then came the summons. Natives who peacefully accepted the Spanish Crown as "king and lord" would be welcomed "with complete affection and charity," and extended many privileges. Indians should pause to consider this generous offer, taking as much time as "is reasonable."

However, if they delayed, or refused to submit, the consequences would be immediate and awful. "I assure you that, with the help of God, I will attack you mightily. I will make war against you everywhere and in every way. . . . I will take your wives and children, and I will make them slaves. . . . I will take your property. I will do all the harm and damage to you that I can." And further: "I declare that the deaths and injuries that occur as a result of this would be your fault and not His Majesty's, nor ours."

The document concluded with the chilling legalism of Spanish conquest; a notary, required to be present at the scene, signed an affidavit attesting that the edict had been pronounced. In modern terms, the Spanish thereby affirmed that natives had been read their Miranda rights. In practice, the Requerimiento was more akin to last rites—a death sentence delivered in language Indians couldn't possibly comprehend, in the name of forces they couldn't possibly imagine. Who was "God, Our Lord"? The "Pope"? The "exalted and powerful monarch" of a place called Castile and Leon?

As if the Requerimiento wasn't a bald enough sanction for slaughter, it was often read without an interpreter present, or was delivered from a distance of several miles, or uttered at night while Indians slept, unaware of an impending attack. The Dominican friar Bartolomé de Las Casas declared that he didn't know "whether to laugh or to cry" at the absurdity of the document.

The Indians gathered before Cibola had a different response. "Being arrogant people," Coronado wrote, "they showed it little respect." So little, in fact, that one warrior shot an arrow through the robe of the friar attending the reading. After a brief skirmish, the natives retreated inside their well-fortified pueblo.

Attacking a walled city customarily required a siege. But desperation, once again, dictated the Spanish strategy. Because the pueblo "was where the foodstuffs were that we needed so sorely," Coronado wrote, he dismounted and prepared his men for a frontal assault. The first pitched battle between Europeans and Indians in the American Southwest would be waged, not for God or gold or glory, but "because the hunger we were suffering did not permit delay."

Coronado ordered his crossbowmen and harquebusiers to fire at warriors guarding the pueblo's narrow entrance. But the crossbowmen quickly broke their strings, and the musketeers "were so weak and debilitated that they could hardly stay on their feet." Meanwhile, Indians were hurling large stones from atop the pueblo's rooftops. Coronado, in his plumed helmet and gilded armor, presented a conspicuous target. Twice, stones knocked him to the ground. He was carried off the field, having sustained two face wounds, many blows to his arms and legs, and an arrow in the foot.

The Spanish nonetheless succeeded in fighting their way inside the pueblo. Prior to the battle, the Cibolans had evacuated women, children, and old people, leaving only warriors. After a short fight, they too abandoned the pueblo. The Spanish didn't pursue them, instead falling on the spoils of victory.

"We found what we needed more than gold and silver," one soldier wrote. "Corn and beans and fowls, better than those of New Spain, and salt, the best and whitest that I have seen in all my life."

THE ROUTE FROM Chichilticale to Cibola, a passage Coronado described as *tristissimo,* appeared just as bleak today. Descending Apache Pass, I sped past arid scrub, a bare mountain branded with a ranch trademark, and a sign warning "State Prison: Don't Stop for Hitchhikers." Then I entered Greenlee County, the least populous in Arizona: only five people per square mile, one-sixteenth the national average.

Reaching the county seat of Clifton, an old mining town at the foot of a mountain road called the Coronado Trail, I stopped at the office of the local newspaper, *The Copper Era.* Its editor, Walter Mares, sat smoking and gulping coffee at a desk so cluttered he could barely find space to set down his mug. Heavyset, with graying hair and mustache, Walter had spent much of his twenty-three-year tenure covering labor strikes, copper price collapses, and floods in the deep canyon enclosing Clifton. But he also wrote features about the Coronado Trail, which gave beleaguered Clifton its town motto—"Where the Trail Begins"— and a small point of tourist interest to promote at civic events and state fairs.

As part of this, Walter sometimes donned a conquistador's helmet and gave talks about Coronado. "Kids always ask me, 'Who are you supposed to be—Columbus?' " he said. "They have no idea about their own history." This had prompted Walter to become a serious student of Coronado, and, rarer still, a great admirer of conquistadors.

"Americans today get tired walking to and from their cars," he said. "These guys were marching miles and miles with no idea who or what they'd meet. The Oregon Trail, the Santa Fe Trail—those were *trails*! Coronado didn't have one until Arizona paved the road here and named it after him."

Strictly speaking, this wasn't so. Coronado, like other early Europeans, generally followed Indian trails. But as I tried to compose a diplomatic correction, Walter raced ahead.

"Our whole sense of history is twisted," he said. "The Pilgrims, they were boat people. Johnny-come-latelies. Intolerant sons of bitches who came to America so they could persecute people in a way they couldn't back home." Walter tossed his cigarette in his coffee. "I hate the whole Thanksgiving story. We should be eating chili, not turkey. But no one wants to recognize the Spanish because it would mean admitting that they got here decades before the English."

Walter traced his own lineage to the Spanish colonists who followed in Coronado's wake, settling northern New Mexico in the late 1500s and early 1600s. He'd grown up a few miles from the New Mexico line, in the Colorado town of Romeo, an unromantic burg where his family lived without running water. "In history class, all we heard about was the Forty-niners and mountain men and Pike's fucking Peak," Walter said. "Anglos called us 'chili eaters' and looked down on us as newcomers, even though we'd been there three hundred years before the so-called pioneers came west."

Walter didn't like being lumped with Mexicans in the Southwest, either. Most were recent arrivals; even their language was different from that of the colonists who had come centuries before. "I'm *Spanish*," he said. "Mexico only had control of the Southwest for about twenty-five years, after becoming independent from Spain and before losing this land to the U.S."

Walter paused to search his desk for a fresh cigarette, giving me a chance to pose the obvious question: what about conquistadors' brutal treatment of Indians?

"Okay, the Spanish were butchers," he acknowledged. "So was everyone then. At least the Spanish debated violence and slavery, and made policies towards Indians based on morality as they saw it. Also, their butchery lasted about fifty years. If you start with the Anglos, and all the others who joined them, you're looking at centuries of killing and oppression of Indians, not to mention blacks. So who are the true bad guys here?"

Spanish burning Indians at the stake, from a sixteenth-century German book—typical of "Black Legend" images popular in northern Europe at the time

This struck me as a depressing sort of calculus: ranking European-Americans from bad to worse. But Walter had a point. In my reading on the conquistadors, I'd learned about *la leyenda negra*—the black legend—which first took root amid the religious strife and imperial rivalries of sixteenth-century Europe. Inspired by hatred of Catholic Spain, and by the reports of Las Casas and others about atrocities against Indians, Protestants in northern Europe published grisly engravings and lurid tracts that portrayed Spain's conquest of America as uniquely barbarous: the Inquisition writ large.

Nineteenth-century jingoists in the United States revived and improved the black legend, to justify annexation of Spanish and Mexican land. Added to the catalogue of Spain's ancient faults—cruelty, greed, indolence, fanaticism, authoritarianism—was the mixed population of its colonies. This was evidence, to white Americans, of degeneracy. Texas's fight with Mexico, Stephen Austin declared, pitted a "mongrel Spanish-Indian and Negro race against civilization and the Anglo-American race." It was the manifest destiny of white Americans to seize and civilize the benighted Spanish lands, just as it was to take the territory of Indian savages.

The black legend had faded in the twentieth century, but traces of the old bias were now resurfacing. Since crossing the border, I'd heard little on my car radio except angry debate about the "invasion" of Hispanic "aliens," and the threat they posed to the nation's education, economy, and identity.

"Every time I hear that stuff about English-first in schools, English only, English everything," Walter said, "I want to shout, 'Hey, the *Spanish* were here first!' Not counting the Indians, of course."

Closing his office for the day, Walter took me for a tour of Clifton, driving along Coronado Boulevard, past the Coronado Beauty Parlor and a ruined building that once housed the Coronado Inn. Then we climbed out of the canyon and parked beside a modern open-pit mine.

This wasn't so much a pit as a stripped and decapitated mountain: a man-made mesa, five miles across. Tank-sized shovels dumped ore onto the biggest trucks I'd ever seen, with tires twice my height. A conveyor belt snaked through the crater, past orange-red cavities and mountainous slag heaps tinted blue by malachite. The mine produced more copper than any site in North America. One of its largest lodes was called the Coronado Pit.

"People think the conquistadors were mad and greedy, always searching for pay dirt," Walter said, over the clank and crush of machinery. "Well, here we are, still digging." He took a long drag on his cigarette. "Those evil Spaniards weren't aliens, they were us. Get rich quick—that's the American dream, isn't it?"

IN 1540, THE Spanish dream of easy riches dissolved as soon as Coronado's men fought their way into Cibola. "So as not to beat around the bush," Coronado wrote the viceroy, "I can say truthfully that he [Fray Marcos] has not spoken the truth in anything he said." The glittering cities turned out to be "small towns" of stone. The only mineral of any value was turquoise, which Cibolans used to decorate their multistory houses. "I think they have turquoise in quantity," Coronado wrote, but "by the time I arrived, this had disappeared, along with the rest of their possessions." There was nothing to loot, except corn.

Several days after the battle for Cibola, a native delegation appeared, offering "some turquoises and poor, little *mantas,*" or cloaks. Coronado reiterated his claim that he'd come to Cibola so Indians could "know the true God for their Lord, and His Majesty for their king and earthly lord." Again, natives were unimpressed. Briefly returning to their homes, they "fled to the hills, leaving their towns deserted."

Though Spanish contact with Cibolans was cursory, it left a strong impression on the invaders. "I have not seen one important house here, from which the superiority of any person over another might be distinguished," Coronado wrote. Instead, Cibola was governed by a council of elders. Priests also held great sway, orating like town criers from the rooftops of houses. Overall, the conquistador judged Cibolans "intelligent," "very well brought up," and exceptionally skillful at needlework and other crafts.

But none of this compensated for the absence of riches. Coronado ended his letter to the viceroy by listing the native items he was sending back to Mexico, including baskets, turquoise pendants, and a "cow skin," undoubtedly the hide of a buffalo, a creature the Spanish had not yet seen. Fray Marcos was also sent home, probably to protect him from the wrath of disappointed soldiers.

"There does not appear to me to be any prospect of obtaining gold and silver," Coronado concluded, "but I trust in God that if it exists here we will obtain it."

I FOUND A sign for the Coronado Scenic Trail beside a slag heap at the edge of the open-pit mine near Clifton. The trail was better known as the Devil's Highway, because of its high fatality rate and the route number it bore on road maps—666, which is linked in the Book of Revelation to the Antichrist. After lobbying by religious groups, Arizona had renumbered the highway, to Route 191. But the road still had a devilish cast. It commenced with a steep climb and panoramic views of the red and hellish mine pit. Then came endless hairpin curves, more than five hundred in all, and vertiginous glimpses of the three-thousand-foot plunge awaiting careless motorists.

After winding along the road for several hours, I reached a log lodge perched at 9,100 feet. It was here, in 1926, that the Coronado Trail had been inaugurated with barbecued bear, a rodeo, and a "devil dance" by Apaches. None of this had much to do with Coronado's passage; nor, it turned out, did the road itself. According to the lodge's literature, Coronado probably stuck to lower ground rather than risk "the rocky and waterless terrain of the Coronado Trail." Few tourists came this way, either. The 120-mile trail was less traveled than any other federal highway in the continental United States.

The mountains, at least, offered relief from the heat. In the course of my drive, the temperature had dipped to fifty degrees, forty degrees lower than in the high desert I'd crossed the day before. But descending the trail to the town of Eager and driving on toward New Mexico, I entered yet another baked plain, treeless and sandy, with parched riverbeds and signs warning "Blowing Dust Area." The only scenery was a creaking windmill and a gate marked "Slim Pickin's Ranch." Like Coronado and his men, I was weary of *despoblado* and desperate to reach the Seven Cities, or any place, really.

CIBOLA, IN 1540, wasn't a collection of seven "cities" but rather a cluster of well-spaced pueblos, possibly numbering only six. Nor were any of these settlements called Cibola by their inhabitants, the Zuni people. Curiously, the Zuni term for the Spanish—*tsibolo'wa*—may itself be derived from "Cibola," the unfamiliar sound they kept hearing the bearded white strangers repeat.

A century and a half after Coronado's arrival, the Zuni gathered within a single pueblo, and their descendants still live in the town that has grown up around it. This gives the Zuni people a rare distinction among North American tribes: though hit by the first wave of Spanish conquest, they nonetheless occupy the same territory they did when Europeans encountered them over 450 years ago.

The Zuni, to a much greater degree than most U.S. tribes, have also retained their own language and religion. All this enticed me—as did the tribe's exotic name, its reputation for fine jewelry, and the prospect of visiting a laddered and walled pueblo, a sight I'd never seen. After a thousand miles of hot and dusty driving, Zuni loomed in my imagination as an enchanted land, if not of gold then of silver and turquoise and tradition.

Just past the New Mexico line I came to a sign saying, "You Are Entering Zuni-Land, Welcome." Then another arid plain, a scattering of trailers and small houses, and Zuni's commercial district, mostly jewelry shops strung along the highway. Following a sign to the local museum, I stepped from my car and was greeted by a stiff wind that buffeted my face with dust. Everything around me—vehicles, buildings, street—wore a coat the color of dun and rust, as if the earth were rising, or drawing the town back into the ground.

This earthiness infused Zuni belief as well. According to the tribe's creation story, the world's first people climbed ladders from deep underground before emerging through a great crevasse, sometimes identified as today's Grand Canyon. They then wandered in search of a promised land called the middle place, guided by a giant water bug that stretched its legs to the far corners of the world. Just beneath the bug's heart was a spot equidistant from all these points. Zuni called this Halona Idiwan'a, the Middle Anthill of the World, and they had lived there ever since.

At least, that's what I gleaned from the museum, and from the many books and articles I later read. The Zuni cosmos, like the Dreamtime of Australian Aborigines, doesn't translate easily into Western language and concepts. The Zuni, for instance, divide the world into two realms, the "raw" and the "cooked." Humans are cooked, while the earth, wind, and man-made objects are raw. Simply rendering Zuni language in written form requires a thicket of esoteric symbols to denote glottal stops, voiceless lateral fricatives, and other sounds. The result looks like *t?ek?ohanan:e,* or *onaya:nak^ä a:'ci'wan:i.* Linguists classify Zuni as one of the world's few "language isolates," bearing no apparent kinship to any other tongue.

Like Aboriginal ritual and belief, Zuni religion is also wreathed in secrecy and taboo. I studied a wall panel at the museum telling of

Frank Hamilton Cushing, a Smithsonian anthropologist who lived among the Zuni in the late nineteenth century. Cushing went so native that he was inducted into one of the tribe's priesthoods, and returned from a battle carrying an enemy scalp. He was embraced by the Zuni—until he published his findings, which disclosed ritual details the tribe regarded as "private information."

Worse still, his writings had brought a flood of inquisitive anthropologists to Zuni ever since. The museum quoted a tribal councilor, who complained, "We have been studied to death. We don't need that—we know who we are!"

When I tried to chat up a young Zuni at the front desk, he smiled politely but gave no answer to my questions. Instead, he directed me to the tribal headquarters, where I was ushered into an unusual office. Zuni's eight-member elected leadership occupied a single room, their desks in a tight semicircle. The arrangement wasn't a space-saving measure; it reflected Zuni's communal governance, on which the Spanish had remarked 455 years before my arrival.

"This way, our decisions have to be made together," explained the lieutenant governor, Carmelita Sanchez, a mocha-skinned woman in a brown pantsuit. She led me to a conference table facing the semicircle of desks. "Are you an anthropologist?"

When I said no, she appeared visibly relieved. But Coronado, like Cushing, was an unpopular subject in Zuni. His invasion in 1540 led to the Spanish colonization of New Mexico and the establishment of missions across the state. This, in turn, sparked a widespread pueblo revolt in 1680, which led to harsh reprisals by the Spanish and the abandonment of five of the six original pueblos around Zuni.

"The conquistadors brought only bad things, violence and theft and missionaries," one of the councilors interjected, when I asked about memory of Coronado. "Why remember them?"

Carmelita took a somewhat gentler view; Spanish influence wasn't *entirely* bad. Two things people often associated with pueblo life, silverwork and adobe brick, were Spanish imports. Before, Indians made their jewelry from turquoise and shells, and built their multistory dwellings from stone, or earth and straw. The Spanish also brought crops and livestock, including sheep, a mainstay of the Zuni economy ever since.

"The Spanish weren't worse than Cushing and the others like him who invaded us later," Carmelita said. "Now, people want to DNA-test us and prove we migrated from Asia. We originated *here*. That's our belief. Maybe people in Asia came from the Southwest."

This ran counter to the conventional wisdom of scientists and archaeologists. But what struck me about Carmelita's comment was the emphasis she placed on religion. The Spanish might have encroached on Zuni sovereignty. But anthropologists committed a graver sin, by trespassing on Zuni belief.

On this subject, Carmelita spoke only in general terms: religion "is a way of life" for today's 9,500 Zuni, and "sustains the people." The tribe functioned, in essence, as a theocracy; religious leaders, including several of the councilors, were consulted on almost all matters. Though many Zuni observed Christian rituals and holidays, they did so as a complement to traditional religion. If the two conflicted, it was Zuni practice that prevailed. Christmas, for instance, coincided with Zuni observance of the winter solstice, an occasion marked by fasting and a ban on noise or showy displays. This meant no caroling or Christmas lights.

Carmelita also explained a ritual referred to by the early Spanish. At Cibola and other pueblos, warriors met Coronado's men by drawing lines on the ground and telling the intruders not to cross. When the Spanish did, fighting erupted. Carmelita said the lines were drawn with cornmeal, a sacred symbol of life to the Zuni and a way of demarcating boundaries. In a sense, the cornmeal line represented a Zuni Requerimiento, one that fell on deaf ears, just as the Spaniards' summons had done.

"We are accepting of other people," Carmelita said, seeing me to the door, polite but unsmiling, as she'd been throughout. "But there are lines one does not cross."

Leaving the office, I went for a walk around the rest of Zuni. The once vertical settlement had gone horizontal, becoming a low-rise sprawl of trailers and modest houses radiating from the town's original center. What remained of the old pueblo appeared shrunken and semi-abandoned: a lived-in ruin of two-story stone houses, dirt alleys, and dusty plazas. As I toured it at dusk, the only people outside were teenagers in baggy jeans, shooting hoops, and an alcoholic-looking man who whispered hoarsely, "Want to buy a wolf fetish?"

Retreating to the main road through town, I dined at Zuni's lone restaurant, a pizzeria, and checked into its only accommodation: a pueblo-style inn with a flat roof, adobe walls, and cozy, close-packed rooms. This was pleasing—until I tried to sleep, only to be kept awake by a crying baby and a bathroom in constant use. Finally dropping off, I woke before dawn to heavy footfalls in the room just above. Pueblo life might be picturesque to tourists, but it was easy to understand why the Zuni themselves had opted for a little elbow room.

THOUGH DEFLATED, LIKE the Spanish, by my first encounter with Fray Marcos's gilded city, I had one promising lead to pursue. At the museum the day before, I'd learned of a ruined pueblo outside town, where archaeologists had recently found evidence of Coronado's inaugural assault on Cibola. The Zuni resented outsiders digging into traditional belief, but encouraged respectful study of their physical history. So in the morning, I went to the tribe's archaeological office, and met its director, Jonathan Damp, a pale, middle-aged man with wire-rimmed glasses. He was one of the few Anglos living in Zuni, and all the more exotic for having grown up in the echt-Yankee environs of northern New Hampshire.

"In school," he said, as we climbed into his four-wheel drive to visit the archaeological site, "I got the whole nine yards of New England history, and not much else. It was as if nothing happened in this country until the Pilgrims landed." He slowed as we passed Zuni's new high school. "When they started construction over there, a three-thousand-year-old irrigation canal turned up. That's King Tut's time. A little before the *Mayflower*."

A few miles outside Zuni, the road turned from asphalt to gravel to dirt. Jonathan departed even this faint track, veering straight across the plain. Then, pointing at a low hill, he said, "That's Hawikuh."

Hawikuh was the Zuni name for the first of the pueblos reached by Coronado. As we drew nearer, I was reminded of the disappointed Spaniard who observed on first approach, "It is a small pueblo crowded

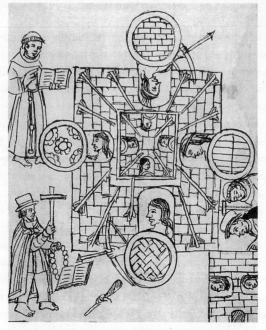

*A fanciful image of the battle for Cibola, from a
sixteenth-century Mexican manuscript on Spanish conquest*

together and spilling down a cliff." Now, with the houses gone and the
slope eroded, it was even less: a lonely mound, no more than a bump on
the otherwise featureless terrain.

Parking by the base of the hillock, Jonathan walked me to the top,
which was littered with shards and animal bones. "*OH'ku* glazeware,"
he said, nonchalantly picking up and casting away an ancient piece of
black, orange, and white pottery. "Site's full of this stuff."

Unfortunately, Hawikuh had first been excavated over a century
ago, when archaeology was relatively primitive. Apart from tumbling
walls, outlining the pueblo's small, square rooms, little remained. But
fresh probes of the ground circling the pueblo had uncovered a number of Spanish artifacts. By carefully mapping their location, Jonathan
felt able to reconstruct the battle that occurred at Hawikuh on a hot
summer day in 1540.

"Sometimes you have to read between the lines of the written record," he said, descending to the pueblo's base. Spanish accounts made it seem that the bedraggled soldiers had triumphed through sheer grit and superior combat skills. Jonathan believed the story was more complex. "Swords and crossbows are sexy, but archaeology has a way of revealing humbler things."

Horseshoe nails, for instance, which had turned up at a rocky spot just beside the pueblo, where they'd probably been thrown when the animals' hooves hit rough ground. Harness bells had been found there, too. On another flank of the pueblo, archaeologists uncovered pitted, large-caliber lead balls like those the Spanish shot from their muskets. Ballistic tests revealed the bullets hadn't hit anything except sand. But their impact, like that of the horses, may still have been felt.

"People today talk about terrorist tactics, or 'shock and awe' on the battlefield," Jonathan said. "Well, think about the Zuni in 1540. They've never seen soldiers on horses, or heard and seen a gun fired. Coronado must have known that cavalry and guns would terrorize his foe, even if they weren't directly effective in taking the pueblo."

There's no record of how the Zuni reacted to guns, but horses clearly made an impression. When Coronado later sent a lieutenant to a Hopi pueblo in Arizona, the officer learned that its inhabitants "had heard that Cibola had been captured by very fierce people, who traveled on animals who ate people." (Horses had similarly terrified the Aztec, who described them as snorting stags with loud bells, foaming mouths, and hoofs that scarred the ground.)

Archaeologists had also found obsidian arrowheads at Hawikuh, possibly from arrows shot by the *indios amigos* who accompanied Coronado from Mexico. The Spanish, who were eager to highlight their own bravado, made no mention of their native allies in accounts of the battle. But the presence of hundreds of Indian warriors may explain how the small Spanish force was able to quickly seize the well-defended pueblo.

Jonathan also suspected that the Zuni chose to flee rather than put up a strong fight. As we drove back from Hawikuh, he pointed at a steep, thousand-foot-tall mesa, a sacred site known as Dowa Yalanne, or Corn Mountain. "Whenever the Zuni came under threat," he said, "they retreated up there." They did so after killing two Spanish friars in 1632, after an attack by the Apache forty years later, and after the great pueblo revolt of 1680. When Coronado wrote that the Zuni "fled to the hills," he probably meant Corn Mountain.

In a sense, the Zuni had stuck to a strategy of tactical retreat in the centuries since. After 1680, they never took up arms against whites again. More bellicose tribes suffered tremendously, losing their lands and lives, while the Zuni kept to themselves and clung to their diminished but relatively intact society.

Jonathan said the Zuni continued to keep their distance today, not only from whites but also from other tribes, such as the Navajo, who lived on nearby land and in the closest city, Gallup. After ten years in Zuni, Jonathan still felt he'd barely penetrated the place, beyond the surface soil on archaeological sites.

This resident-alien status was a source of confusion to his six-year-old son, who had lived in Zuni his entire life. "He knows I'm not Zuni, and he's been to the Wal-Mart in Gallup, so he knows I'm not Navajo either," Jonathan said. "And I don't look like his mother, who's from Ecuador. So one day he said to me, 'Dad, I've figured out what you are. You must be a Hopi!'"

CORONADO SPENT THE summer and fall of 1540 in Cibola and obsequiously renamed the largest of its pueblos Granada, the hometown of his patron, the viceroy. He also dispatched scouts to reconnoiter other parts of Tierra Nueva. One party traveled west until reaching a river gorge so vast that the Spanish thought it ten miles "through the air to the opposite edge." Three of the most agile men tried to descend to the river, and were "lost from sight." They returned at day's end having made it only a third of the way down.

"Those who stayed above had estimated that some huge rocks on the sides of the cliffs seemed to be about as tall as a man," one Spaniard wrote, "but those who went down swore that when they reached these rocks they were bigger than the great tower of Seville"—a 250-foot-tall campanile. This wondrous testimony is the first European description of the Grand Canyon.

That same summer, another Spanish party had its own adventure while exploring Arizona, by water. Soon after Coronado's departure from New Spain, the viceroy had sent two ships from the west coast of Mexico to resupply the army, mistakenly believing that Cibola lay close to the coast. The convoy's commander, Hernando de Alarcón, ran out of sea at the head of the Gulf of California, where he found the mouth of "a very powerful river," today's Colorado. He took twenty men and two boats upstream, pulled by a towrope, to see if he could reach Cibola.

Though he failed, Alarcón left an unusually sensitive account of first contact with Indians. Upon encountering natives with bows and arrows, he threw down his sword and shield, "stepping my feet on them, making them understand by this and other signs that I did not wish to make war." He also lowered his boat's banner and ordered his men to sit down. For a moment the natives seemed uncertain, murmuring among themselves. "Suddenly, one came out from among them with a rod that bore some shells," Alarcón wrote. "I embraced him and gave him in exchange some beads and other things."

Thereafter, he traveled peacefully through several hundred miles of well-populated country, fed and fêted by Indians who wore waist cords adorned with feathers, "which hang behind them like a tail." Natives, in turn, marveled at the Spaniards, combing their beards and patting the wrinkles from their clothing.

But this mutual discovery required a great deal of effort. Conversation, even with an Indian interpreter from Mexico, was halting and poorly understood. Most communication had to be done with gestures, gifts, pantomime, drawings, even crude carpentry. "With some sticks and paper I had some crosses made," Alarcón wrote. "I made it clear to them that they were things I esteemed most."

One native, who understood some of the interpreter's language, asked Alarcón if the Spanish "came from beneath the water or from the earth or had fallen from the sky." Alarcón replied with a stock conquistador line: "I was sent by the sun." But the Indian persisted, "asking me how the sun had sent me, since it traveled on high but did not stop."

Also, why hadn't the sun sent anyone before? And why couldn't children of the sun understand everyone?

"I began to wear myself out," Alarcón wrote of his attempts to persuade his inquisitor. "I told him that God abided in heaven and that he was called Jesus Christ. I was careful not to stretch myself further into theology with him." Later, in apparent mockery of his claim to have come from above, Indians "took corn and other seeds in their mouths and sprayed me with them, saying that was the kind of offering they made to the sun."

Natives were as exhausted by Alarcón's constant questions as he was by theirs. When Alarcón invited an Indian elder to sleep on board the Spanish boat, "he replied to me that he did not want to come, because I would tire him out asking him about so many things."

Farther upriver, Alarcón heard of a pueblo that had been visited by a bearded black man who wore bells and feathers on his arms and legs. He'd been killed, Indians said, so he couldn't take news of the pueblo to other strangers. This was undoubtedly a reference to Estevanico's visit to Cibola, which Alarcón learned was just ten days' travel away. But the river narrowed between high mountains and he could go no farther. Outriders from Coronado's army later found a tree etched with the words "Alarcón reached this point."

Like so many of the Spaniards who wandered early North America, Hernando de Alarcón is little remembered today. But his brief account gave me a glimpse of an alternate history embedded in the saga of European conquest. With hindsight, it's tempting to see the exploration and settlement of America as grimly mechanistic: the inexorable grinding down of one world by another. Individuals seem to matter little, except as agents of distant empires, or as their inevitable victims.

But what happened in America wasn't foreordained, particularly during the fluid period of early contact. Nor did all newcomers, or all natives, behave the same. Those Europeans who reached across the canyon of language and culture, as curious fellow humans rather than as combatants, almost always discovered Indians willing to respond in kind.

The list of such men is short, and most, like Alarcón and Cabeza de Vaca, were vulnerable wanderers who might have acted differently if they'd had more men and arms. Still, it was refreshing to encounter

the rare Spaniard who didn't reach for his sword and recite the Requerimiento at the earliest chance.

I SPENT FIVE days in Zuni, trying to glimpse what lay behind the
pleasant but impassive mask the town presented to outsiders. Each
night, I compared notes with the innkeeper, a Frenchman who had
lived in Zuni for thirty years. "I still don't know what's going on here,"
he confessed. "A Frenchman goes to church for an hour on Sunday
and is saved. Here, not. The ritual is constant, a ceremonial cycle that
keeps drawing people back into the loop of their culture." He
laughed. "I'm not in the loop."

As a blow-through, I had even less hope of understanding. But on
my last day in town, I decided to try again with the most forthcoming
Zuni I'd met, a young man named Wells Mahkee. Heavyset, with
close-cropped hair, Wells had studied English at a college in New
Mexico and now edited and produced reports at Zuni's archaeological
office. He'd also grown up in the old pueblo, and still lived there with
his family. When I first met him, Wells promised to show me around.
But each time I'd returned to his office, he said he was too busy; perhaps he was regretting his earlier offer.

When I appeared yet again, just as the office was closing for the
week, Wells shut off his computer and walked me to a wall photo of
Zuni in 1890. The picture showed tall, tightly packed houses, ladders,
and rooftops crowded with earthen ovens. "People lived literally on
top of each other," he said.

The twentieth century had brought an end to Apache and
Navajo raids; Zuni no longer needed to live so defensively. Eventually,
the pueblo's top stories had crumbled or been dismantled to build
new houses. The Zuni also began to adopt American notions of
space and privacy. When Wells was a child, the houses still had interior doors between them, so that one room opened into a neighbor's
home.

"We didn't even knock before going in," he said. Over time,
though, Wells's family had piled clutter on their side. Then their neighbor renovated and put Sheetrock over the door. "I didn't really think

Zuni Pueblo in 1882

about it at the time, but I miss that sense of doors everywhere, of everyone's lives opening into each other's."

Wells's grandmother had barely spoken English. She washed her long braided hair with yucca root, combing it with broom stalks. "She always smelled of earth," he said. His father began each day by facing east and saying a prayer while offering cornmeal to the rising sun. "Unfortunately, I didn't learn his prayers, and now he's gone."

Wells wasn't alone; many young Zuni had drifted from traditional religion. The priesthood and roles in Zuni's ceremonial societies required a lifelong commitment, rigid adherence to observances and taboos, and periodic abstinence from sex, sleep, commerce, and certain foods. Zuni who worked off the reservation found that employers weren't always willing to allow weeks away from the job for ritual purposes. Television, consumerism, drugs, and other temptations had also encroached on Zuni life.

But a strong current of traditionalism still ran beneath the town's modern surface. As we drove to the old pueblo, known locally as the middle village, Wells pointed to the bland new houses and trailers along the main road. "See how they're clustered? Those are family groupings, and inside most of those homes live several generations. People have left the middle village but they've created new nests outside it."

Marriage also differed from the American norm. Traditionally, families simply exchanged corn and other gifts as a way of confirming a union. That custom had ended, but few Zuni held Christian or court-house weddings. "If you're together for six months, you're considered married," Wells said. After five years, a couple could go to the tribal headquarters on Valentine's Day to have their common-law union formally recognized. This was as much ritual as most spouses observed.

Wells parked in a dirt alley beside an adobe and pine-beamed mission church near the center of Idiwan'a, the Middle Place. The mission had first been constructed by the Spanish in 1629, right on top of Zuni kivas, or ceremonial chambers, which one of Coronado's men described as semi-subterranean lodges, "like the baths which they have in Europe." European colonists, the world over, often erected churches atop natives' sacred ground, to displace their practices and enhance Christianity.

But in Zuni the transplant hadn't taken. An early Spanish missionary complained that it was almost impossible to convert natives, "due to the repugnance that they show for the Divine Law." Services at the mission church had stopped years ago. The interior walls were now painted with vivid murals of Zuni ceremonial figures, such as "mud-heads" wearing grotesque bulbous masks. Christ also appeared, clad in a blanket and wide pants and carrying a cornmeal pouch.

"We've outlasted the Spanish and Zuni-fied what they left," Wells said. In the mission graveyard, crosses intermingled with bowls holding cornmeal, a traditional offering to the dead. The church was also ringed by restored kivas: square blocks of adobe with ladders leading to a ceiling hatch.

Wells lived just behind the mission, in a house built of purplish stone and wooden beams. He walked me to the door but didn't invite me in. We stood outside in the dwindling light, watching boys skateboard across the pueblo's flat rooftops and past beehive ovens used to cook bread, squash, and mutton stew.

"I always see our young people as being figuratively at Idiwan'a, the Middle Place," Wells said. "We're trying to be in the traditional world and the outside world at the same time. I work with computers, with Anglos, speaking English, and then come home and speak Zuni and try to keep our family's ranch going, which is hard when you have another job." He shrugged. "I'm trying to lead a simple life. But it can be a struggle to keep it that way."

I thanked Wells and wandered the pueblo until dark, ending up back at the mission graveyard. As soon as I came out its gate, a boy rode up on a bicycle. "When you leave a graveyard, you have to put dust on yourself," he said.

"Where on myself?"

"All over."

I scooped up a handful of dust and sprinkled it on my head and clothes. "Why?" I asked.

"It's the law of the grave," the boy replied, cycling off into the dark.

Dusty and bewildered, I walked to my pueblo-cum-inn for another night of fitful sleep before leaving Zuni to the Zuni, like so many visitors before me.

CHAPTER 7

THE PLAINS

SEA OF GRASS

> I arrived at some plains so without land-
> marks that it was as if we were in the middle
> of the sea.
>
> —Coronado, letter to the viceroy
> of New Spain, 1541

L ATE IN THE summer of 1540, a peace delegation arrived at
Zuni from a distant pueblo. Its leaders brought tanned
hides, and one of the Indians bore a tattoo on his body of the
creatures the skins came from. These "seemed to be cows," a soldier
wrote, "although from the hides this did not seem possible, because
the hair was woolly and snarled."

Twenty of Coronado's men went to visit the pueblo, called Cicuique, and returned with an Indian slave from a "level country" far to
the east, where the strange cows roamed. The Spanish called the slave
El Turco, because he was "very dark" and "personable," qualities they
associated with Turks. He said his homeland had large towns and so
many riches that the lord of the realm napped beneath a tree hung
with golden bells. This enchanted land was called Quivira.

Coronado, one of his men wrote, "felt no slight joy at such good
news." He was likewise heartened by El Turco's claim that he had proof
of Quivira's riches: gold bracelets that his pueblo masters had seized
upon taking him captive. When the people of Cicuique denied this,

the Spanish took several of their leaders away in chains, including the head of the peace delegation that had come to Zuni. They later set dogs on the prisoners, badly maiming them.

"This began," a soldier wrote, "the want of confidence in the word of the Spaniards whenever there was talk of peace from that time on."

Coronado's men also aroused fury when they decamped from Zuni and established winter quarters in pueblos along the Rio Grande, near present-day Albuquerque. At first, the inhabitants welcomed the intruders peacefully. And the Spanish wrote admiringly of native men spinning and weaving cloth, women grinding corn while singing to flute music, and native pottery of "extraordinary labor and workmanship."

But none of this prevented the cold and hungry Spanish from looting food and blankets, and molesting native women. When Indians retaliated by killing Spanish horses, Coronado ordered his men to "make an example" of the pueblo where the rebels took refuge. A hundred or more Indians were burned at the stake.

All along the Rio Grande, natives rose in revolt and fought through the snowy winter. Many hundreds died, and at least a dozen pueblos were destroyed before Coronado achieved what he called *la conquista y pacificación* of the region. It was a victory so savage that some of his men began to turn against him. By betraying and brutalizing the peaceful pueblo people, one soldier observed, Coronado had made potential allies into vengeful enemies, "as will be seen by what happened afterward."

THE DRIVE EAST from Zuni carried me through a landscape where the scenery and culture changed by the hour. I passed from Zuni ranchland to a Mormon farm town, its streets shaded by poplars and ringed by fields of rye and alfalfa. Beyond the town stretched a Navajo reservation dotted with log-and-mud hogans. Then the road climbed hills of juniper and piñon pine to the Continental Divide, which was marked by a ridge of black ash: the cinder cone of an extinct volcano. Early Spanish travelers called this El Mal País, the Bad Land, because the jagged lava fields made walking painful.

The Spanish also noted a huge stone headland just east of the divide, which they named El Morro: the Bluff. Visible for miles, with a shaded catch pool at its base, El Morro was a natural oasis along the rough, dry trail between Zuni and the Rio Grande. A sandstone cliff beside the pool also afforded an inviting canvas to resting travelers, and centuries of carvings survive to this day.

The oldest artwork, done by Indians about seven hundred years ago, depicts birds, lizards, bighorn sheep, and stick-figure humans. The meaning of these works aren't known, and the artists are anonymous. Not so the Spanish, who extolled themselves in large, looping script, like subway graffitists. One official etched a verse that loses its rhyme in translation but not its grandiosity. "Here passed I, the Governor Francisco Manuel de Silva Nieto, Who has done the impossible, by his invincible arm and valor, with the wagons of the King our Master, a thing he alone put into effect August 5, 1629, that one may pass to Zuni and carry the faith."

The first Anglo names don't appear until 1849, when U.S. soldiers arrived after the Mexican-American War. Later inscriptions record the passage of wagon trains, railroad surveyors, and members of an experimental camel caravan. The American carvings are less florid than the Spanish, often just a name or initials enclosed in a tightly etched box. By the time El Morro became a national monument, in 1906, the centuries of carvings covered almost an acre of rock.

Lingering in the cliff's shady cool, I tried to decipher the inscriptions and the impulse that prompted so many travelers to carve them. The surrounding landscape lent itself to feelings of isolation and insignificance. In this arid vastness, scratching one's name or "Here passed I" seemed a small act of bluster, like shouting into a canyon to hear your own echo. Or, perhaps, a gesture of brotherhood with other lonesome travelers. Whatever the urge, El Morro was a stele of bygone America, not yet homogenized by strip malls and mass culture. Here, carved in weather-worn sandstone, the Southwest's rich heritage remained on display: Indian, Spanish, Mexican, and, belatedly, Anglo-American.

ANOTHER HOUR'S DRIVE, another culture: Acoma Pueblo, also known as Sky City because of its perch atop a 370-foot mesa. When Coronado's men arrived, the only way to reach the pueblo was by climbing single file, using steep stairs and handholds cut into the rock. Near the top, they had to wedge their hands and feet into a cleft and claw their way onto the summit, like mountaineers. It was, a captain wrote, "such a rough ascent that we repented having gone up."

Atop the mesa, the climbers found a settlement of tall houses with cisterns and gardens. While the Spanish had only been able to reach the summit by passing their weapons up to one another, natives nimbly ascended bearing jars of water and loads of food on their heads. The rock-top aerie struck one Spaniard as "the strongest place ever seen in the world."

Acoma appears just as imposing today. The mesa rises like a huge loaf of rock from the surrounding plain, with a crown of stone houses crenellating its flat top. In front of the mesa stand towering slabs of stone, as if keeping guard. From a distance, Acoma evokes another ancient desert citadel, Masada, to whose history the pueblo's bears a tragic resemblance.

In the half century after Coronado's men visited, Acoma was a peaceful way station for the occasional Spaniard traveling between Zuni and the Rio Grande. Then, in 1598, a conquistador named Juan de Oñate led four hundred soldiers and settlers north from Mexico to colonize the pueblo country. When Oñate's nephew visited Acoma at the head of a small party, Indians killed thirteen of them, including one who died while leaping off the mesa.

Oñate—a hard-handed man, even by conquistador standards— sent a force led by his slain nephew's brother to exact revenge. Oñate's orders were explicit: "Leave no stone on stone, so that the Indians may never be able again to inhabit it as an impregnable fortress." The soldiers killed some eight hundred Acomas, a Spaniard wrote, and "the pueblo was completely laid waste and burned."

About six hundred survivors were rounded up and brought before Oñate, who put them on trial, granting them an attorney and the right to testify. Five did so, stating that Oñate's nephew and his men were killed because of their excessive demands for food and blankets. The Spanish defense attorney asked Oñate to show mercy on the Acomas, "in view of the fact that they are barbarous"—an ironic characterization, given the conquistador's verdict.

"Males who are over twenty-five years of age," Oñate ruled, "I sentence to have one foot cut off and to twenty years of personal servitude"—enslavement to Spanish soldiers. Males between the ages of twelve and twenty-five, and females over twelve, were also enslaved for twenty years. Two Hopis who had joined in the fighting were sentenced to have their right hands cut off and then to be set free, "in order that they may convey to their land the news of this punishment." As a further warning to natives, the amputations of hands and feet were carried out in public, on different days and at different pueblos.

Oñate would later be tried himself, by Spanish authorities in Mexico, for his cruelty to both Indians and settlers, and he was banished for life from the colony he'd founded. But the conquistador left his mark on New Mexico—literally so, near the base of El Morro. He inscribed the cliff on his way back from a vain search for riches that carried him to the Gulf of California. The engraving reads: "Here passed by the Governor-General Don Juan de Oñate, from the discovery of the South Sea, the 16th of April, 1605."

Oñate's is the oldest Spanish inscription at El Morro; he could have carved almost anywhere on the empty sandstone. Instead, the conquistador chose to etch his grand words directly on top of an Indian petroglyph.

MAIMED, ENSLAVED, AND dispersed, the Acomas nonetheless returned and rebuilt their pueblo within a few decades of Oñate's assault. They have clung to the rock-top ever since: an isolated aerie of pueblo life. Unlike the Zuni, though, Acomas now court visitors, with a Sky City Casino by the interstate and a well-oiled tour business at the mesa's base. The only way to see the pueblo was to buy a ticket and board a bus for the disappointingly easy climb to the top of the once impregnable mesa.

"You can blame John Wayne," said our guide, a stout Acoma woman named Dale Sanchez. During production of one of the actor's Westerns, in the 1960s, a paved road was built, winding up to the pueblo. "After that, we decided we could use it to make money from all of you."

In recent decades, most Acomas had moved off the rock and into federal housing on the plain below. Thirty people still lived full-time on the mesa top, without electricity or running water. But the pueblo was a hybrid of ancient and modern. On stone foundations, some of which dated to the twelfth century, Acomas had piled upper floors built of cinder block or prefabricated adobe brick from Home Depot. Some families ran TVs off car batteries and installed Porta-Johns beside mud-plaster houses trimmed with turquoise: a traditional talisman against the evil eye.

As we walked down narrow dirt lanes, inhabitants peered from behind curtains and popped out to tend pottery stands. Acomas are famed for their light and delicate pots, decorated with black and white geometric patterns. As soon as we passed, the vendors vanished back inside their homes.

Dale showed us a seventeenth-century mission church, but otherwise said nothing of the Spanish. When I asked about their impact on Acoma, she glared at me, as if warding off the evil eye. "You mean Oñate?" she hissed.

Each year, Dale said, Acomas carried a figure of the martyred St. Stephen through the pueblo's streets to bless the ground where Indians fell. They also kept an open grave in the mission cemetery, awaiting the returning souls of Acomas killed or enslaved by the Spanish.

"If you want to know more, go to Alcalde," Dale said, circling a small town on my map of New Mexico. When I asked why, she smiled enigmatically and turned to greet a fresh group of tourists.

ALCALDE STRADDLED THE highway between Santa Fe and Taos, near the center of an old Spanish region first settled by colonists who came with Oñate in 1598. Occupying the northernmost frontier of Spanish America, and isolated in later centuries from the mainstream of American life, the people of El Norte had never fully assimilated. Theirs was a proud, private subculture, a remnant of colonial Spain in the rural backwater of northern New Mexico.

During a stopover in Santa Fe, I met a professor from one of El Norte's old families. He said the region not only retained an antiquated Spanish dialect, but also an attachment to *limpieza de sangre,* or purity of blood. In Inquisition-era Spain, this had signified lineage untainted by Muslims or Jews. In El Norte, it meant genes that had never crossed with natives.

"You can tell by looking at me and most other people that there are plenty of Indians in our family tree," the professor said. "But the view is 'We're pure, we're Spanish, and not half-breeds like the dirty Mexicans.'"

At first glance, Alcalde seemed an unremarkable farming town, ringed by fields. Then, at its northern edge, I came to an arresting statue perched right beside the highway: a twelve-foot-tall bronze of a helmeted figure astride a muscled steed. A marker identified the heroic-looking horseman as "El Adelantado Don Juan de Oñate." Set

on a high platform, so motorists had to gaze upward at the conquistador, the towering bronze was modeled on the equestrian statue of
Marcus Aurelius in Rome.

An adjoining "Oñate Monument Center" was closed, so I went
across the road to a shed with a sign announcing vegetables for sale.
Inside, an old man named Max Martinez sat stringing chilies. When I
asked about the statue, he said, in heavily accented English, "Did you
look at it closely?"

"Not really. Why?"

He walked me back to the statue and pointed at one of the conquistador's spurred boots. In 1998, on the four hundredth anniversary
of Oñate's expedition to New Mexico, the foot disappeared. "Someone came in the night and cut it off," Max said. "Sliced clean through
the bronze. Must have used a power grinder." The job had also required considerable stealth, since a state trooper lived in a trailer beside the monument.

The statue's sculptor had since attached a new foot, and the repair
was barely visible. But the original foot had never been found. Nor
were the persons who severed it, though they'd sent an anonymous letter to newspapers, claiming the amputation "on behalf of our brothers
and sisters of Acoma."

Max walked me back to his shed and opened us each a beer. The
descendant of a pioneer family, he hadn't learned to speak English until he went to school. "We're not as isolated anymore, but some things
we keep," he said. "Words and accents from the old time. Strong family ties. An easygoing lifestyle—relations are more important than
money. And the church is still central, of course."

Also distinctive were the Penitentes, who performed self-
punishment as a mark of devotion and contrition. Their practices, similar to those of medieval flagellants, may have come to El Norte with
the first Spanish. In Max's childhood, Penitentes held processions,
gashing and whipping themselves as they dragged heavy crosses into
the hills. The ceremony ended with a man being tied to a cross. There
were unconfirmed reports that nails were sometimes used, and even
that men had died while reenacting the crucifixion. "Years ago," Max
said, "they used to go all the way."

The Penitentes had since dwindled in number and now kept their rituals private. One of their meeting places, a *morada,* stood just down the road. It was an austere building with a cross in front and an out-house behind. Max said it was used only for funerals and at Easter. "Eventually, the Penitentes will fade away and all the Spanish here will blend in," Max said. "No one will notice us anymore—except for Oñate up there on his horse. He's hard to miss."

Max didn't care one way or the other about the statue. But he knew someone who did: Emilio Naranjo, the driving force behind the memorial and known as El Patrón, the political boss of the valley. On my way to see him, I noticed a sign for San Juan pueblo, the site of Oñate's first headquarters in 1598. It was now a reservation, centered on a cluster of adobe buildings and a crafts cooperative, where I met the tribe's histo-rian, Herman Agoyo. He wore a cap advertising the tribal casino, on the nearby interstate, and appreciated the irony of his headgear. Euro-peans first came to New Mexico to loot pueblos of their riches; now In-dians were getting back their share, with roulette and blackjack. One pueblo casino was named, appropriately, Cities of Gold.

"The conquistadors were gamblers, they took big risks, and I ad-mire that," Herman said. But he resented the Oñate statue, particu-larly the "in your face" placement, which forced Indians to look at the conquistador each time they drove past. "If you want to recognize con-quistadors, remember the bad with the good," he said. "The Spanish here don't want to do that. They make pure heroes of these men."

Pueblo tribes had waged a countercampaign to honor a controver-sial hero of their own: Po'pay, a San Juan Indian who led the great Pueblo Revolt in 1680, which killed hundreds of Spaniards and drove colonists from New Mexico for twelve years. A statue of Po'pay was set to go up in the U.S. Capitol Building, as a representative figure of New Mexico history. "Of course, some Spanish people hate that—they think Po'pay was a murderer," Herman said. "Which is just how we feel about Oñate."

When I told him I was on my way to see the man behind the Oñate statue, Herman went to a shelf at the craft cooperative and handed me a rawhide necklace. Dangling from the string was a small clay foot, cleanly severed at the ankle. "You might want to take him this," he said.

EMILIO NARANJO LIVED in a ranch house with a cross in the yard and an American flag on his truck. In person, El Patrón didn't look like the feared political boss I'd heard about. He was in his eighties, quite deaf, and seemed in poor health. But he kept active in local affairs, from a home office lined with signed photographs of U.S. presidents, senators, and governors.

"I've been everything," he said, ticking off his many posts, including head of the local Democratic Party for fifty years. He paused before a picture of himself beside the Oñate statue, the proudest of his many accomplishments. "This was my idea, it came into existence because of *me*. My forefathers came with Oñate. He should be honored here just like the Pilgrims in the East, who got to America much later."

As he talked about the region's history, and his efforts to commemorate conquistadors, I felt as though I was back at El Morro's cliff face, reading the imperious Spanish inscriptions. "I have the guts to do things, and I get them done," Emilio said. "I owe it all to my Lord. My own time and money went into the statue, I made it possible and people gave thanks."

"Even Indians?" I interjected.

"Why shouldn't they? My God, Oñate made this place. He introduced cabbages, chili, tomatoes, and what not. He created an irrigation system. Oñate did many things for Indians."

Including, I pointed out, killing and maiming Acomas. "That's a lot of bullshit!" Emilio shouted. "When his nephew was killed, naturally he sent an expedition to pacify the Indians. That story about him cutting off feet, I don't believe that. It's propaganda by people who didn't like him."

This wasn't true; the Spanish, like more recent European perpetrators, kept careful records of their atrocities. But it was impossible to break into El Patrón's monologue: about how well Indians were treated, how they'd gotten rich from casinos and government aid, how ungrateful it was of them to resent Oñate. "People have just been told to hate him," he concluded. "There's no reason they should."

I'd often heard an eerily similar refrain while traveling the American South. To die-hard defenders of the Confederacy, Dixie was a gentle land of kindly whites and happy blacks; Confederate leaders were unblemished heroes; it was just a few "troublemakers" who agitated over displays of the rebel flag. In New Mexico, as in the South, the bloodshed had ended long ago. But the combatants still lived side by side and continued fighting, with statues and symbolically severed feet rather than with swords and arrows.

El Patrón, for one, was used to ideological slugfests; his armor was as thick as his hero's. "I know why they cut off Oñate's foot. It was payback." He smiled thinly. "But you know what? I don't think it hurt very much."

COMPARED WITH OÑATE, Coronado was little remembered in New Mexico, even at the Coronado State Monument. Created to mark the four hundredth anniversary of the expedition, the park lay near the Spaniards' winter camp, at a pueblo outside Albuquerque. I found the turnoff on a busy interstate spur, between a gas station and outlet store. All that remained of the pueblo were low walls outlining a checkerboard of house sites. A trail led to the Rio Grande, slow and brown and only fifty feet across, but nonetheless grand after all the trickles I'd crossed since Hermosillo.

The park museum had a few Spanish artifacts. Still, considering this monument was named for Coronado, the conquistador seemed strangely absent. "There was supposed to be more, but it didn't pan out," a ranger explained. He showed me a sketch for a two-hundred-foot-tall statue of Coronado, with a pavilion and walkway stretching down to the river. Conceived during the Depression, the grandiose design had proved too costly.

Also overblown was a speech by Spain's ambassador to the United States at the park's dedication in 1940. He likened Coronado's expedition to Spain's expulsion of the Moors, and to the country's recent civil war, when "Spain shed the blood of her sons to defend our Christian world against a new menace from the Orient—the menace of Communism." This seemed an expansive use of "Orient," and put Coronado in league with the fascist dictator Francisco Franco. Every era found its own meaning in the exploits of conquistadors.

"Personally, I think we should rename this place for the Indians who lived here, and leave Coronado out of it," the ranger said. "Anyway, this isn't even the site of his winter camp." Excavations had revealed that the camp actually lay at another ruined pueblo a few miles downriver. Following the ranger's directions, I passed a Home Depot and Wendy's and Walgreen's until I saw a roadside marker for Coronado's nearby camp. The historic site was impossible to reach or even glimpse. A four-lane highway moated off access; behind it stood a subdivision of starter castles.

Pueblo is Spanish for "town," a word that accurately described the settlement pattern in native Arizona and New Mexico: compact, high-rise communities, surrounded by open country. Spanish colonists, who equated urban living with civilization, built their own well-ordered towns, in accordance with planning ordinances that dictated the precise layout of streets and plazas. Now, in most of the Southwest, the footprint of both Indian and Spanish settlement lay buried beneath an avalanche of sprawl.

THE NEGLECT OF Coronado in New Mexico was matched by a scarcity of recent scholarship. The most readily available translation of documents relating to Coronado's expedition dates to 1896; the standard biography, Herbert Bolton's *Coronado: Knight of Pueblos and Plains,* was published in 1949. Since then, the conquistador has fallen out of favor, certainly as compared with other explorers.

In my reading, though, I'd kept coming across the names Richard and Shirley Flint. They'd published a new translation of Coronado-related documents and countless articles on the *entrada.* Much of their research focused on reconstructing Coronado's route, or the army's members and equipment. From this arcane research, and the Flints' address in backcountry New Mexico, near Coronado's route, I'd formed a vague impression of fusty local historians, the sort often active in antiquarian and genealogical societies.

"We're six miles off the main road and nine from the nearest neighbor," Richard Flint said, when I phoned to ask if I could visit. He told me to turn at a green gate on a rural route lacking other landmarks. When I did, the rutted dirt road quickly became impassable. I abandoned my car and hiked a mile before meeting Richard, who had come the other way to find me.

A lean, graying man with a mustache and large round glasses, Richard led me to his four-wheel drive and drove to a small stone-and-beam house. A windmill-driven well provided water, solar panels the only power. Inside, Shirley Flint stood by a wood stove, cooking garbanzo beans. Deeply tanned, with pale blue eyes and a long blond braid, and wearing an embroidered blouse, she looked very much a child of the sixties. She and Richard had met at St. John's College in Santa Fe during the Vietnam War.

"I objected to killing human beings, and still do," Richard said. In 1969, the couple moved to Sweden and then Canada. On returning to the United States, Richard applied for conscientious objector status. With the help of a draft resisters' group and a sympathetic legislator, his induction was deferred. After that, the Flints bought fifty-five acres of high, scrubby plain for $7,500 and built an adobe cottage on it with their own hands.

"We were just subsisting, really," Shirley said. Then, from a bookmobile volume on Coronado, the Flints learned that the conquistador had traveled by their property. They began researching his route, initially as a hobby and then as an obsession. Richard went back to school for a master's degree in archaeology and a Ph.D. in Latin American history (Shirley already had a master's in history). In the two decades since, they'd turned their remote house into a cottage Coronado industry, churning out books and articles and securing a Fulbright and other grants for research trips to Spain and Mexico.

After a dinner of cheese, apple slices, bread, and soup, Shirley showed me the document she was currently translating. "It's a bit like reading Shakespearean English," she said. In the 1500s, spelling and grammar weren't standardized, and written Spanish was evolving from Gothic script to modern cursive. Also, authors employed their own shorthand and abbreviations of Spanish and Latin words. So Shirley had compiled an *abecedario,* or key, for each scribe whose writing she deciphered.

"Some letters take weeks to crack," she said. As the Flints hunched over their shared desk in the dim light of a low-wattage lamp, debating a line of Castilian legalese, I felt as though I'd been transported to a medieval monastery where clerics transcribed ancient manuscripts.

But this wasn't how the Flints saw themselves. " 'Question authority,' that was our generation's motto, and that's what we're still doing," Shirley said. "Once you start poking at the received wisdom, it unravels pretty quickly."

The orthodoxy, in this case, was the Bolton school, named for Herbert Bolton, a renowned California professor and president of the American Historical Association in the first half of the twentieth century. Bolton championed the Spanish and their role in the hemisphere. In his eagerness to dispel the "black legend," he created a "white legend" that romanticized conquistadors as heroic and civilizing "knights." The many students Bolton trained in his long career helped perpetuate this image.

Richard admired the sense of mission Bolton displayed at a time when Hispanics and their history were ignored or reviled by Anglo-Americans. "But he swung the pendulum so far the other way that he obscured the truth."

Bolton, for instance, glossed over some of the brutalities inflicted in Tierra Nueva and wrote that Coronado possessed a "finer sense of the rights and dignity of human beings" than other Spaniards. Richard showed me one of his own books, *Great Cruelties Have Been Reported,* an anthology of documents from a 1544 Spanish investigation of Coronado's *entrada.* In those documents, members of the expedition described in flat detail the many atrocities committed against Indians: massacres, sexual assaults, torture, burning at the stake. "Here's the rebuttal to Bolton," Richard said, "in the Spaniards' own words."

The Flints also questioned contemporary scholarship about early America. The trendy new orthodoxy emphasized the role of European-borne disease in destroying native societies. Records from sixteenth-century Mexico and the Caribbean, telling of horrific epidemics, buttressed this thesis. But no such evidence existed in the many documents relating to Coronado. Nor had Spaniards who followed him a generation later noted a population decline among Indians.

"Germs were clearly a factor in many places Europeans invaded—a lot of natives died," Richard said. "But a lot of people were murdered; that's in the records, too." By focusing on disease, he said, scholars risked sanitizing conquest and absolving the invaders, just as Bolton had done. "The message of the new scholarship is 'Europeans did awful damage to natives, but most of it was unintended and inevitable.'"

Richard returned to his documents to illustrate his point. As he walked me through still more carnage and plunder, I began to see the Flints as latter-day Las Casases: bearing witness, like the Dominican friar, to crimes against natives and Spain's betrayal of the Christian ethos.

When I mentioned this, Richard and Shirley surprised me again. They didn't want to resurrect the black legend, which tarred Spaniards as heedless butchers. The fact that Coronado and many other conquistadors were prosecuted for their cruelties gave evidence of Spain's moral struggle over conquest. Nor did the Flints bear any animus toward Coronado as an individual. "He was a prominent cog in the imperial bureaucracy," Shirley said, "not a forward- or independent-thinking person."

The real issue, as the Flints saw it, was the very enterprise of one society imposing its will on another. "There are so many parallels between that era and our own," Richard said.

Shirley finished his thought. "Arrogance and empire, Spain's and now America's. It never works, but the damage that's done lasts for centuries."

CORONADO LEFT THE pueblo country in late April 1541, guided by several Indians, including El Turco, the captive who had promised to lead the Spanish to his wealthy homeland of Quivira. After ten days of travel, Coronado wrote, "I reached some plains so extensive that wherever I traveled on them I did not find their end."

The Spanish had entered the vast grassland that once covered a quarter of the continent. Few travelers today regard this landscape as wondrous. But to sixteenth-century Spanish eyes, the endless Plains were a world truly new, stranger and more striking than the arid and mountainous Southwest—which, after all, bore a passing resemblance to parts of their homeland.

"The country is like a bowl, so that when a man sits down, the horizon surrounds him all around," one horseman marveled. Also astonishing was the grass, which "straightened up again as soon as it had been trodden down." Coronado's immense legion left "no more trace where they passed than if nothing had been there—nothing."

Even more astounding were the "cows" pounding across the plain in herds so vast "that to count them is impossible." As yet, the Spanish had no word but *vaca* for the American bison (commonly called buffalo), a huge, horned, and aggressive creature that frightened both the metal-clad conquistadors and their mounts.

"There was not one of the horses that did not take flight when he saw them first, for they have a narrow, short face," one rider wrote. "They have long beards, like goats, and when they are running they throw their heads back with the beard dragging on the ground." Another Spaniard thought them "the most monstrous thing in the way of animals which has ever been seen and read about. . . . There is such a quantity of them that I do not know what to compare them with, except with fish in the sea."

Several weeks after entering the Plains, the Spanish also met Indians unlike any they'd yet encountered: tall, "well-built" nomads with painted faces, who followed the buffalo herds and lived entirely off their prey. They ate buffalo meat raw or half roasted over fires of buffalo dung; drank buffalo blood from sacks made of buffalo gut; used buffalo hides for their clothing, shoes, and conelike "tents," and buffalo sinew, wool, and bone to make thread, rope, and awls. "They were very intelligent," one of Coronado's men wrote. "Although they conversed by means of signs they made themselves understood so well that there was no need of an interpreter."

At first glance, the Spaniards' admiring description of Plains Indians sounds strikingly familiar. The natives' statuesque bearing, hide teepees, and incomparable skill with bow and arrow were qualities

Early Spanish image of a buffalo, 1553

that would later strike Americans in the nineteenth-century West. But one critical detail was different. In the sixteenth century, Plains natives had no horses. Instead, they harnessed dogs and loaded them with teepee poles and other possessions.

"When the load gets disarranged," one Spaniard observed, "the dogs howl, calling someone to fix them right." Unfortunately, the Spanish didn't record the natives' first impression of the animal that would transform them from foot-bound nomads into mounted warriors, the most formidable native fighters on the continent.

CONTINUING EAST, THE Spanish reached the plainest of the Plains, a dead-level expanse of grass. Even the army's Indian guides became lost, Coronado wrote, since "there was not a stone, nor a bit of rising ground, nor a tree, nor a shrub, nor anything to go by." He sent ten mounted scouts "to go at full speed towards the sunrise for two days." They couldn't find their way back, or be tracked, because of the unbending grass. When the outriders were finally discovered, they reported having traveled for sixty miles and "seen nothing but cows and sky."

After that, scouts made piles of buffalo dung for the army to follow, like Hansel and Gretel, trailing manure instead of breadcrumbs. The Spaniards also gave one man the duty of measuring and counting his steps to calculate how far the army traveled, on average about fifteen to twenty miles a day. Later, the Spanish learned a trick from the Plains Indians. "In the morning they notice where the sun rises and observe the direction they are going to take, and then shoot an arrow in this direction. Before reaching this they shoot another over it, and in this way they go all day."

A month after leaving the pueblo country, Coronado encountered Indians who knew of his destination, Quivira. However, their description was very different from El Turco's. Quivira's houses were rude dwellings of thatch, not multistoried stone, and there was no gold, only corn. The Indians also said Quivira lay to the north, another forty days' travel away. Thus far, El Turco had led the army east and south.

"With this news I received the utmost pain," Coronado wrote, "seeing myself in those tiresome, endless plains, where I had an extreme need of water." The army's supply of corn had also run out. (El Turco had told the Spanish to carry few provisions so they could reach Quivira quickly and be able to tote back gold.) Under questioning, El Turco insisted he had told the truth about his large, rich homeland. But Coronado decided to send the mass of his army back to New Mexico and continue on toward Quivira with only thirty of his best horsemen, as well as El Turco, who "was taken along in chains."

PICKING UP THE interstate soon after leaving the Flints, I sped east, gradually descending through mesa land to Tucumcari, where the distant line of flat-topped hills finally vanished. As I crossed into Texas, the time zone changed, from Mountain to Central, and so did the landscape. I crested an escarpment to see the Plains before me, a brown carpet patched with green, stretching to the horizon.

As I navigated small roads through Deaf Smith County, the terrain turned even more level. There were no trees, no traffic, and no dwellings,

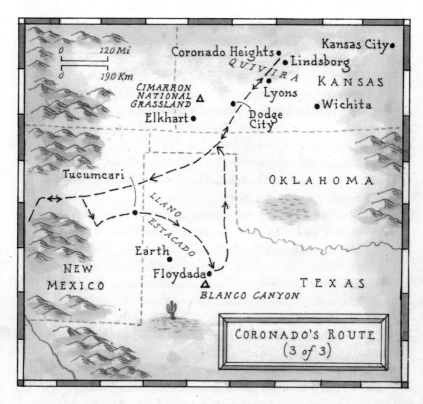

just endless crew-cut fields. The roads ran dead straight for miles, then made perfect ninety-degree turns, as if drawn with an Etch-a-Sketch. I felt as though I were motoring across the world's largest pool table.

Deaf Smith County, named for a Texas scout, formed one edge of the territory Coronado described as "so without landmarks that it was as if we were in the middle of the sea." Later Spanish travelers named this tableland El Llano Estacado—the Staked Plain—possibly because they planted stakes to mark their way across the featureless terrain. The Llano was a geological oddity, a deposit of silt and stone that had washed down from the Rockies millions of years ago and baked hard and flat—"a pancake plopped down in a skillet," one Texas writer called it. Elsewhere in the Plains, there are rivers and undulations. In the Llano, the land barely changes for 32,000 square miles: a parched, almost perfectly flat surface larger than Maine.

On my second day of driving through this numbing landscape, I was roused by a startling sign: "Welcome to Earth." Then came shuttered shops, a broken stoplight, and a defunct movie theater whose marquee touted its final show: *The Blob.* I passed a church, "Mission Earth"; a gas pump, "Earth Station"; a closed newspaper office, *The Earth News*; and a sign saying "Try Earth First" beside what looked like a former bank. Earth might not have much life, but it seemed to possess a fertile sense of humor.

Spotting a lone car by an insurance agency, I went in to ask about the origin of the town's name. The agency's owner, Fran, a big-haired woman with red fingernails, shook her head and said, "I've lived here my whole life and have no idea." An older woman, Lavelle, didn't know either, but said the town's name was a cross to bear for its inhabitants.

"You tell folks where you're from and they always say something like, 'I'm from Earth too' or 'Really? I'm from Mars.' It gets old." Lavelle sighed. "Some folks here call themselves Earthlings. That doesn't help."

"It should be called Flat Earth, really," Fran added. "When I get into the hills and woods of east Texas, it bothers me, I can't see anything. I feel crowded. Guess this is just what I'm used to."

As Fran told me about the 1980s farm crisis that had killed commerce in Earth, Lavelle went to the hairdresser to ask if anyone knew the history of the town's name. She called to report that it dated to the opening of the first post office in 1925. The postmaster submitted several names, but they'd already been taken by other Texas towns. He went for a walk around and all he could see was soil, so he chose the name Earth.

"I guess it could have been worse," Fran said. "Can you imagine saying, 'I'm from Dirt'?"

I DROVE ON, through Halfway and Plainview and on to Floydada, where the welcome sign said, "Pumpkin Capital USA." Floydada looked as flat as Earth, but just a few miles from town the tableland suddenly cracked, revealing a broad ravine about half a mile across and a hundred feet deep—the first natural break in the landscape since I'd entered the Llano.

The Spanish had been startled by the ravine, too, describing it as a *barranca grande,* or great canyon. While the army was camped in the gorge, a fierce hailstorm erupted, showering the Spaniards with stones "as big as bowls" and "as thick as raindrops." Men held up shields against the hail while trying to control their horses, which tried to climb out of the gorge. If the storm had caught the army in the open plain, a soldier wrote, the horses would have run off and imperiled the expedition. As it was, the hail tore tents, dented helmets, and smashed all the crockery.

Four centuries after that summer hailstorm, a farmer named Burl Daniel was digging a drainage ditch just outside Floydada, at the edge of Blanco Canyon, when his plow hit metal. Burl thought it was a wad of chicken wire, and tossed it in his truck with other junk. Then he noticed the metal was hand-shaped, with the last two fingers missing. So he sent it to a museum at the University of Texas, which identified it as an early Spanish gauntlet, or chain-mail glove.

No one paid the discovery much notice until twenty-five years later, in 1991, when Nancy Marble was going through old newspapers at the Floyd County Historical Museum. "I just wondered how that Spanish glove ended up here," Nancy said, when I met her at the museum, on Floydada's town square. So she tracked down Burl Daniel and convinced him to sell the glove to Floydada's museum for $500.

She also told a local relic hunter to keep an eye out for metal around Blanco Canyon. He did, returning with what looked to Nancy "like a crushed pen." She contacted the Coronado experts Richard and Shirley Flint, who identified the metal as the bolt of a crossbow, a weapon used by Coronado's men but not on later Spanish expeditions. When the relic hunter uncovered more bolts, a professional archaeological team came to survey the canyon. Excavations have since uncovered horseshoes, nails, crockery, and more chain mail—by far the largest trove of Coronado artifacts ever found.

Most of it now resided in a jeweler's case at the Floydada museum. "This is a young county, it didn't organize until 1890," Nancy said, showing me the museum's pioneer displays, including a sod house. "But now that we know Coronado was here, I feel like we're ancient."

I circled back to Blanco Canyon, just south of town on the road to Cone. It was easy to see why the Spanish had chosen the canyon as a campsite. A stream shaded by cottonwood trees ran along the gorge's wide flat bottom, and the canyon offered shelter from the Llano's relentless wind, if not from the hail. The Spanish later camped at two other canyons nearby, using one as a base for hunting buffalo and preparing jerked beef.

"Many fellows were lost at this time who went out hunting," one soldier wrote, "wandering about the country as if they were crazy." Each night, the army tried to draw the lost hunters back to the ravine camp by firing guns, blowing trumpets, beating drums, and building bonfires. Even so, some of the riders never returned. It was a haunting image: well-armed horsemen who had survived the long voyage from Spain and even longer trek from Mexico, only to vanish in a sea of grass.

SERENADED BY GRAIN reports and Christian radio, I followed Coronado north as he and his advance party of thirty horsemen rode on toward Quivira, through what is now the panhandle of Texas and Oklahoma, and then into the southwest corner of Kansas. This tri-state territory was the epicenter of the 1930s Dust Bowl, a disaster that Coronado and his men might have predicted. The Spanish regarded the southern Plains as a sandy-soiled, windblown, semiarid "desert," suited only to buffalo, nomads, and tough short grass. But the homesteaders who poured in during the late nineteenth century brought modern tools and can-do American optimism. Within just a few decades, their plows and tractors and grazing cattle tore up the native grass that had held the soil in place and protected it from frequent drought and lacerating winds.

When the rain stopped and the winds gusted during the "Dirty Thirties," the unanchored topsoil simply blew away. At the Kansas line, I entered Morton County, the worst affected of any in the Dust

Bowl; over three-quarters of its acreage had been seriously eroded by wind. Almost half the population fled, and the county still has fewer people than it did in 1930.

This exodus, however, proved a boon to environmental preservation, which was why I stopped in Morton County. In the wake of the dust storms, the federal government bought vast stretches of "submarginal" land from ravaged farmers who wanted out. Removed from agricultural use, and reseeded with grass, these tracts gradually healed. One of the largest such plots became the Cimarron National Grassland: over 100,000 acres that had returned to something approaching their appearance in Coronado's day.

At the ranger station in the Morton County seat of Elkhart, I picked up a promising-sounding tour map labeled "Sea of Grass." Driving as far as I could into the grassland, I got out of my car and started walking. For the first time since I'd entered the Plains, the landscape was completely free of barbed wire, telephone poles, the redolence of fertilizer, or other man-made intrusions. Knee-high grass swished against my jeans as I hiked for several miles in as straight a line as I could. With the late-day sun beating on my shoulder, it wasn't hard to keep my sense of direction. But the bit of horizon I'd chosen as a guide-on didn't get any closer. I seemed to be traveling without moving forward, as if on a grassy treadmill, tilted slightly up. Or, as one of Coronado's men put it, as if I were in a vast, shallow bowl.

Viewed from my car, the Plains had seemed flat and featureless. But on foot, I began to see subtle variations: gentle swales and dips, and in the distance, a stony outcrop that rose seventy or so feet above the grass. According to my map, this rocky "bluff" was the third highest point in Kansas, and had served as a lookout for pioneers on the Santa Fe Trail. In a landscape this level, even a bump seemed Himalayan.

Life of any kind also loomed large. At sunset, quail and grouse darted through the dun-colored grass. I saw a box turtle and the burrows of prairie dogs—"animals like squirrels," the Spanish called them. A rattlesnake darted its tongue in my direction before uncoiling and slithering off.

One creature, though, was conspicuously absent. As late as the early nineteenth century, some thirty million buffalo roamed the Plains. "In terms of kilograms of matter belonging to one species," observes the biologist Tim Flannery, America's bison herds "formed the greatest aggregation of living things ever recorded." Yet this massive population had barely survived the second half of the nineteenth century, when hunters with repeating rifles killed herds en masse: for hides, for tongues, for sport—and for the U.S. Army, which sought to drive Indians off the Plains by exterminating the buffalo on which they relied. The last wild buffalo in Kansas was killed in 1879, near where I now walked. By 1900, fewer than a thousand buffalo remained in all of North America.

Careful breeding and preservation had since boosted the population to several hundred thousand. But despite constant queries, the only buffalo I'd heard about since entering the Plains were a few at a Texas state park. A ranger there told me not to waste my time. The buffalo could be seen only with a high-powered telescope from a viewing platform, and then only rarely. Creatures once so multitudinous that Coronado wrote "to count them is impossible" were now so scarce that they had to be stalked at remote sanctuaries, like rhinos on the Serengeti.

I'd almost given up hope when I learned over a steak-and-egg breakfast in Elkhart that a retired farmer kept a few buffalo outside town. Keith Jarvis lived off a dirt road fifteen miles from Elkhart and more than a mile from his own mailbox. A burly man in blue jeans and a Kansas State Wildcats cap, he seemed amused when I pulled up by his tractor and explained my quest.

"You're welcome to look, and buy 'em, too, as far as I'm concerned," he said. Keith walked me to a fence—"It's hot," he warned; "buffalo respect electricity"—and pointed to a clump of humped creatures, heads down as they grazed about seventy-five yards off. At this distance, they did resemble cows. But Keith knew different.

"I'll tell you about buffalo," he said. "Try to corral or crowd them or force them in any way and they get all on edge. Cattle don't do that." He gazed at the herd. "People get all soft and fuzzy about buffalo, but they're wild animals, they'll never be your friend. They tolerate me because I feed them. But they'd just as soon gore me as not."

Keith unhooked the electric fence and we walked over for a closer look. We'd only walked a few yards when one of the buffalo raised its head and loped off with an awkward, bouncing gait. The others quickly followed. "They're strictly herd animals," Keith said. "Find one and you find 'em all."

As we hiked back to get his truck, I asked Keith how he'd come to raise buffalo. "Just the novelty of it, I guess. Picked one up for a thousand bucks—top of the market, which is when I always get into things." He laughed. "Thought it would give me a little income, too. But I can't hardly give the hides away, no one wants 'em. Grind the buffalo up usually, for hamburger."

Climbing in his pickup, we drove through a field of olive-gray sagebrush and into the middle of the herd. Unlike Coronado, I had a clear image in my head of what the creatures would look like, from pictures and from buffalo-head nickels I'd collected as a child. Still, it was easy to see why the Spanish found them so strange and amusing. Even Juan de Oñate, not a man I imagined as prone to merriment, became droll on the subject of buffalo: "No one could be so melancholy that if he were to see it a hundred times a day he could keep from laughing heartily as many times."

Up close, what seemed most comical was the buffalo's front-loaded physique. Its weight and reddish-brown hair bunch around the shoulders and neck, with the torso tapering down to an improbably small bottom and skinny, piglike tail. The huge head is so shaggy that the wool almost covers the buffalo's horns and small, sleepy eyes. And the legs, particularly the short, small-hoofed forelegs, look much too delicate to support so much bulk.

"They may look funny," Keith said, "but it's no laughing matter when they pivot on those little feet and go over you or through you." Still, he sometimes found his herd amusing, too. "The beard's what I've never figured out. When they drink, it goes in the water, and when they run, it drags along the ground. Can't imagine what good it does."

After I'd gawked for a while, Keith showed me the rest of his property, mostly fields of brown autumn wheat. "I wasn't a good farmer," he said. "Had these fields in hock more times than I can recall." When I told him about Coronado searching for gold in these plains, he laughed. "Yeah, just like folks thought they could get rich quick growing crops out here. Dust Bowl cured that. Then folks started hunting oil and gas, not that I've ever found any." Keith smiled. "Finally found my niche, though, which is doing nothing. Just glad to still have the house and land."

We circled back to the small house Keith had built from scrap lumber. As his wife, Beulah, silently sorted green tomatoes in the kitchen, Keith prepared me a plate heaped with slabs of grayish-brown meat. "It's a day old, and not as tender as beef. Gotta cut it in small pieces."

I was still recovering from my sclerotic breakfast in Elkhart, and not entirely sure I wanted to eat part of the herd I'd just admired. But it seemed impolite to say no. Fortunately, the buffalo steak tasted very much as Keith described, a bit chewy and tough, like slightly overdone beef, but not bad.

"It's delicious," I said, tamping the last piece down my gullet. At this, Keith went to the freezer and loaded a large plastic cooler with what looked like an entire haunch. "For the road," he said, helping me haul it to the car. "In this country, never know when you'll find your-self short."

AFTER LEAVING HIS army behind in Texas, Coronado and his horse-men rode through the summer of 1541, across hundreds of miles of desolate plain. They lived like Indians, subsisting solely on buffalo they killed and cooked on fires of buffalo dung. On many days, the Spanish went without water. Then, in what is now central Kansas, the horsemen halted. "It pleased Our Lord," Coronado wrote the viceroy, "that at the end of having traveled seventy-seven days through those empty lands, I reached the province they call Quivira."

This relief, however, instantly gave way to disenchantment. In the next line of his letter, Coronado began listing "the things of great mag-nificence" he'd been told of by El Turco and contrasted this to what he actually found. Rather than tall stone buildings, even grander than the pueblos, Coronado saw only round thatch huts. The inhabitants wore buffalo hides and ate raw meat; no sign of cotton or golden platters.

The only metal they possessed was a single piece of copper hanging from a chief's neck.

"The people are as uncivilized as all those I have seen and passed until now," Coronado wrote. In short, the golden land of Quivira was even more of a mirage than the seven glittering cities the Spanish had expected to find at Cibola the summer before.

Coronado stayed in Quivira for almost a month, while combing the countryside for evidence of the rich and populous society he'd been promised. He found "nothing but villages" and homes of "skins and sticks." Nor did his scouts hear news of settled communities anywhere in the region, except those in Quivira, "which are a very insignificant thing."

Insignificant, perhaps, in terms of mineral wealth or prosperous natives from whom to extract tribute. But Quivira was rich in other ways. "The land itself," Coronado observed, was "fat and black and well-watered" by streams and springs. The natives raised corn; walnuts, plums, grapes, and mulberries grew wild. "This country presents a very fine appearance," wrote one horseman. "I have not seen better in all our Spain nor Italy nor a part of France." He thought the region very well suited to both crops and livestock.

But Coronado hadn't come this far to till the soil or husband cows. While others praised Quivira, his own dispatch to the viceroy was sour and self-pitying throughout. "I have suffered. . . . The report given me was false. . . . I have done everything I possibly could."

The conquistador had gambled his fortune, and that of his patron, on hopes of finding fame and riches in Tierra Nueva. Instead, after almost two years of hard travel since leaving his wife and home in Mexico, he found himself in the middle of a vast continent, cut off from his army, with winter approaching. And for the second time on his journey, he'd been duped; first by the fanciful Fray Marcos and now by a crafty Indian guide.

One night, Coronado ordered El Turco taken from the tent where the Spanish held him prisoner. Under interrogation, the Indian finally confessed to having deceived the Spanish. He'd spun golden lies about Quivira in hopes of going home and rejoining his wife. Also, his pueblo masters had told him to misdirect the Spanish through the Plains, so the army would perish from hunger or thirst, or return so weakened that Indians could easily "take revenge for what had been done to them."

Instead, it was the Spanish who took revenge—on El Turco. "Without waiting for further talk, or counter-arguments," a soldier "put a cord around the Indian's neck from behind and tightened it with a stick. That strangled him, and then they buried him next to the tent."

Coronado raised a cross to mark the farthest spot that his expedition had reached in Tierra Nueva. Then, provisioned with dried corn, and led by fresh Indian guides, the conquistador and his thirty horsemen turned and rode west along buffalo paths, back to the land of the "flat-roofed houses."

BLOATED WITH BUFFALO meat, and bleary from too much driving, I barely registered the scenery as I drove east from Elkhart, piloting from silo to silo, the great pueblos of grain marking every town. The farther I went into Kansas, the more incredible it seemed that Coronado had kept going—seventy-seven days on the Plains!—through a landscape that offered so little relief, not only to Spanish stomachs but also to their spirits.

At earlier points in my trip, crossing the Sonoran Desert and mesa land and the Llano Estacado, I'd often felt awed by the Spaniards' resilience. Hunger, heat, harsh winters, a steady diet of buffalo meat— none of this deterred them from their mission. But as my odometer ticked over the three-thousand-mile mark since Hermosillo, I started to wonder if the Spaniards weren't so much dogged as possessed. Greed and desperation I could grasp, up to a point. But to plunge this deep into a sea of grass, on a quest so doubtful, seemed evidence of a tenacity that bordered on derangement.

From almost the start of Coronado's long journey to Quivira, he had ample reason to doubt El Turco, just as he'd had cause to doubt Fray Marcos. El Turco's pueblo masters, a second Quiviran guide on the expedition, the nomads Coronado met in the Plains—all of them contradicted El Turco's tales of great riches far in the interior. Yet still the Spanish rode on, and on, and on.

This willfulness spoke to a late-medieval imagination that I couldn't wrap my modern mind around. Seven Cities of Gold, the Isle of the Amazons, El Dorado—these weren't wild fantasies to the Spanish, they were vivid realities, just waiting to be found. Europeans often wrote disdainfully of Indian "superstition"—while marching through jungles and mountains in pursuit of their own potent myths. Natives clearly sensed the power that legend had over Spaniards. Despite the linguistic and cultural divide between them, El Turco immediately surmised that he could inflame these gullible strangers with visions of golden platters and trees hung with golden bells.

By the time I reached Lyons, Kansas ("Land of Quivira," according to its welcome sign), my own dream was a tall cold beer. The town announced itself with a sixty-foot marble cross honoring Juan Padilla, a friar who accompanied Coronado to Quivira and returned there a year later to bring Christianity to the natives. He was promptly killed, apparently by Indians who coveted his vestments and other goods. This made Father Padilla, in the eyes of his admirers, the first Christian martyr in the future United States.

Lyons also had an excellent museum with displays on the Spanish and on the Indians of Quivira. They're believed to have been ancestors of the Wichita, who lived in conical pole-and-grass homes like those described by Coronado. I lingered until closing and asked the museum's director whether there was anything else to see around Lyons related to the conquistador.

"Not really," she said, "unless you count Coronado Heights." This was a hill in the next county, topped by a monument to the conquistador. "Folks there like to say *that* was Coronado's last stop." She obviously didn't agree, though she confessed there was no hard evidence that Lyons had a better claim. "The best we can say is that Coronado's journey ended 'near here.'"

This was a bit disappointing, as was downtown Lyons, where I'd planned to celebrate the end of my own journey. The only nightlife in sight was a dingy tavern called Bill's, filled with patrons who looked as if they'd been there since lunchtime. When I asked a man beside me at the bar what he thought of Coronado, he slurred, "Dunno. Buy me a beer and I might remember him." Instead, I decided to ignore the museum director's caveat and raced the fading light to try and reach Coronado Heights.

Earlier in the day, while driving from western to central Kansas, I'd watched the landscape gradually soften, from high dry plain to midwestern prairie. East of Lyons, it began to gently roll, with dark plowed earth and lush fields of sunflower and corn. Quivira might not have been the gilded paradise Coronado imagined, but it looked heavenly—golden, even, at sunset—after the hundreds of miles that had preceded it.

Zigzagging on rural roads, I made a wrong turn and didn't find a sign for Coronado Heights until nightfall. Rather than scale the elevation in the dark, I headed for the lights of the nearest town, a few miles off, and trolled the main street until I came to a bar. The tavern was called Öl Stüga, with "Välkommen" written on the window.

Stepping inside, I ran straight into a bearish, bearded man who looked as though he'd just disembarked from a longship. Almost everyone in the pub seemed a clone of him: tall, fair, and broad-shouldered. A horned helmet perched over the tavern's TV. I fought my way to a stool at the bar, next to a handsome man with blue eyes and long blond hair.

"This may sound stupid," I said, "But is this a Viking convention or something?"

He smiled. "I take it you've never been to Lindsborg?" When I shook my head, he thrust out his hand. "Well, then, welcome to Little Sweden. I'm Nels Peterson. Can I buy you an aquavit?"

Lindsborg, Kansas, it turned out, was one of the largest Swedish communities in the nation. Most of its 3,300 residents descended from pietistic Lutherans who settled in the nineteenth century, and they still held Swedish festivals, decorated their homes with painted wood Dala horses, and called their sports teams Vikings and Terrible Swedes. I'd trailed the Spanish from Mexico to Kansas only to land in a nest of latter-day Norsemen.

"No one here cares much about Coronado," Nels said. "Even if the Spanish did get here, so what? The Vikings beat them to America by five hundred years."

Nels's family had farmed the land around Coronado Heights for

132 years, and he offered to give me a guided tour. I bedded down at the Viking Motel, and then drove with Nels the next morning to the top of the three-hundred-foot bluff. "Kansas is hillier than people think," he said.

The bluff was the tallest of a small chain of buttes called the Smoky Hills, overlooking a river and prairie. The setting corresponded with the description of one of Coronado's horsemen, who wrote that Quivira was a land of "hills, plains, and beautiful-looking rivers and streams." Another Spaniard went so far as to write, "At that place there begin to be some mountain ranges."

Since there were no other rises nearby, the Spanish were probably referring to the Smoky Hills. It also seems likely that they would have scaled one of the hills to survey the surrounding landscape. In any event, this—along with a scrap of chain mail uncovered nearby—was evidence enough for local boosters to claim the hill as the farthest point reached by Coronado. In 1920, they christened it Coronado Heights, later crowning the broad top with a stone castle and a simple stone monument, etched with Coronado's name and the words "A Place to Share."

"People have taken that message rather literally over the years," Nels said. "I'd guess at least three thousand people have lost their virginity up here. Major party spot."

He led me inside the lichen-covered castle, a gloomy, mock-feudal fortress with a crenellated top and arrow slits in the walls. The interior had a great hall with a beamed ceiling and giant hearth. "This place is meant to honor Coronado," Nels said, "but since we're Scandinavians, we don't have a clue about the Spanish. So we built a little Elsinore."

As it happened, the Lindsborg boosters who conceived the memorial weren't really admirers of Coronado at all. Quite the opposite. I later found a 1922 speech by the leading promoter of the Heights, who described "Coronado puffing his way up this hill in his cast-iron suit," and contrasted him to the Swedish immigrants who "settled in the shadow of this majestic landmark and found the gold that Coronado missed." These "frugal sons of the north had learned the lesson that the hot-blooded, adventurous Spaniards never learned," he went on.

"Only the wealth which comes from patient toil and the health that comes from the simple open life survives."

Coronado Heights, in other words, celebrated the superiority of Lutheran Swedes over Catholic Spaniards. The sweeping view, at least, bore this out. From the rampart of the castle we gazed out at a manicured checkerboard of wheat and alfalfa. To the south soared the church spires of Lindsborg. Not far to the north lay the exact geographic center of the U.S. continent. The territory Coronado had spurned was now America's heartland, one of the most productive agricultural districts in the world.

Still, Nels felt some sympathy for the conquistador. "He came all this way and looked out and saw grass and more grass—nowhere going on forever. I can see a weary spirit being broken by that view."

We climbed down from the castle and drove back to Lindsborg for a Sunday lunch of Swedish meatballs, pickled herring, and dill potatoes. A Lutheran pastor in a starched collar circulated between tables, greeting congregants. "Swedes are very close to the vest, very *Prairie Home Companion*," Nels confided. "To tell you the truth, I hate this place."

Nels worked as a landscaper, but at heart he was a Beat poet. The night before, while chain-smoking and swigging aquavit, he'd recited entire poems by Allen Ginsberg. After lunch, when I dropped him at his trailer, he went inside and returned with his most prized possession, a signed first edition of William Burroughs's debauched classic, *Naked Lunch*.

"I lived in New York for a while and found it weird that people still have this Wizard of Oz image of Kansans—they think we're shorthand for clean, honest living," he said. "I hope I changed some people's stereotypes, at least about the clean-living part."

Nels lit a final cigarette. "You know, in a way it's too bad that Coronado cut and ran. If those mad Spaniards had stuck around, Kansas would be a lot more fun."

UPON RETURNING FROM Kansas to New Mexico, Coronado hunkered down with his army for a last hard winter by the Rio Grande.

Badly clothed, beset by lice, and surrounded by restive Indians, the Spanish were also divided among themselves. Many wanted to go back and settle Quivira, while others had "set their prow" toward home. "There began to be grumblings and sourness," a soldier wrote.

Then, during a horse race, Coronado's saddle cinch broke and he fell beneath his competitor's mount, taking a kick to the head. Confined to his bed and convinced he was dying, Coronado expressed a "desire to return and die where he had a wife and children." Or so his army was told. Some soldiers suspected that Coronado's doctors and captains conspired to make his injury seem worse than it was, to justify the retreat to Mexico.

And so, in the spring of 1542, the demoralized army straggled back the way it had come two years before, from the pueblos to the desert to Mexico. As soon as the army reached Spanish-held land, men began peeling off, until the once mighty force had disintegrated. Coronado reached Mexico City leading fewer than a hundred men. The viceroy "did not receive him very graciously," a soldier wrote. "His reputation was gone from this time on."

When Coronado returned empty-handed, prominent colonists who had invested heavily in the expedition found themselves in financial straits. His return also coincided with the passage of new laws in Spain, designed to curtail abuses against Indians. Coronado's expedition became a test case, with Crown lawyers charging that the torture of natives and burning of pueblos were unwarranted.

Coronado was ultimately exonerated (his field commander was blamed instead, and lightly punished). But the conquistador lost his governorship of a northern province, his estates, and the fortune he'd invested in the expedition. "I was left in debt and am so now," Coronado stated in a legal petition, in 1553. He died soon after, at the age of about forty-four.

A decade later, one member of Coronado's expedition sat down to write an account of what he'd seen in Tierra Nueva. Pedro de Castañeda had ridden with Coronado all the way to Quivira, and felt he'd glimpsed "the marrow of the land in these western parts." In retrospect, Castañeda wished he had settled its fertile expanse. But "it was God's pleasure," he wistfully concluded, "that we who had been there should content ourselves with saying that we were the first who discovered it."

In passing, Castañeda also related the incredible saga of a "tattooed Indian woman." A captive of the Pueblo people, she was purchased from them by a Spanish captain and taken on the expedition to the Plains. When the army reached Texas, the woman recognized she was nearing her homeland and hid in a canyon before escaping the Spanish. She then fled east across Texas, only to be seized again, by another group of bearded Spanish speakers. The Indian woman told her new captors that "she had run away from men like them," and gave the names of Coronado's captains as proof.

Castañeda learned all this upon his return to Mexico, where he met members of the Spanish party that had recaptured the woman. The men were survivors of another major expedition, this one led by Hernando de Soto, who had set off from Florida at almost the same time Coronado left Mexico. Several years later, the paths of the conquistadors' armies—one wandering east, the other straggling west—had almost intersected in the middle of the continent.

Of the tattooed woman who witnessed the two greatest expeditions of conquest in North America, and became captive to both, nothing more is known.

THE SOUTH

DE SOTO DOES DIXIE

> Knights errant are exempt from all jurisdic-
> tional authority . . . their law is their sword,
> their edicts their courage, their statutes their
> will.
>
> —Miguel de Cervantes, *Don Quixote*

ERNANDO DE SOTO was a self-made conquistador, the first to spend more of his life in the New World than the Old. Born in Extremadura, the rugged Spanish province that also spawned Cortés and Pizarro, De Soto sailed to America at the age of fourteen and arrived with only a sword and buckler. He went straight to work, fighting Indians in Panama, and quickly won renown as a ruthless warrior: the go-to guy for brutal raids against natives. Contemporaries described him as dark, handsome, hotheaded (*apasion-ado*), "hard and dry of word," and "very busy in hunting Indians."

He was also a shrewd businessman, amassing a diversified portfolio of plundered gold, grants of Indian labor, and stakes in mining and shipping. De Soto sealed his fortune by joining in the conquest of Peru, where Pizarro dispatched him as an emissary to Atahualpa. With characteristic bravura, De Soto rode straight into the Incan camp and reared his foaming steed before the emperor. When the Spanish later garroted Atahualpa and looted Peru's gold and silver, De Soto's cut came to more than $10 million in today's dollars.

The hidalgo who had left Spain as a teenager returned home in his mid-thirties as one of the country's wealthiest men. He bought a palace in Seville, acquired pages, footmen, an equerry, and a majordomo, adorned himself in velvet and satin, and married into a distinguished noble family. Capping this astonishing rise was his induction by the king into the Order of Santiago, Spain's loftiest chivalric society.

But De Soto had no intention of settling down. In 1537, a year after his return to Spain, he won a charter from the Crown to conquer and colonize La Florida. In the sixteenth century, conquest remained a private enterprise. The Crown granted licenses to explore and exploit new lands—retaining its royal fifth of the booty—but didn't bankroll expeditions or send soldiers. Conquistadors were, in essence, armed entrepreneurs, who assembled their own force and assumed the risk.

In La Florida, the risk was considerable. Ponce de León had died trying to colonize it, and the follow-up mission by Pánfilo de Narváez had ended in the disaster that only Cabeza de Vaca and a few others survived. Several other expeditions had foundered along the coast. Undaunted, De Soto spent his entire fortune and went into debt assembling an invasion force of nine ships, six hundred men (including hardened veterans of Peru), 220 horses, a herd of pigs, and *perros bravos*—dogs trained to track and tear apart humans. In late May 1539, having established a base in Cuba, the armada arrived on the west coast of present-day Florida. The territory De Soto had contracted to conquer was vast, vaguely defined, and still virtually unknown to Europeans. Under the terms of the Crown's grant, he had four years to make good on his audacious gamble.

THOUGH THE PRECISE site of De Soto's landing in Florida isn't known, Bradenton has long claimed the honor for itself. The city is home to the De Soto National Memorial and the De Soto Historical Society. Its main bridge is named for the conquistador, as are a speedway, mall, mobile-home park, Laundromat, and animal clinic. A De Soto–themed weekend is the city's premier social event.

Bradenton is also the base camp for a rare band of conquistador reenactors, called Calderon's Company in honor of a captain in De

Soto's army. Though I'd dabbled in Civil War reenacting near my home in Virginia, the existence of weekend conquistadors surprised me. Playing Johnny Reb and Billy Yank was one thing; portraying metal-clad Spaniards who slaughtered thousands of Indians seemed quite another.

After discovering Calderon's Company on the Web, I phoned the bearded, helmeted figure pictured on the group's home page: Tim Burke, a Bradenton land surveyor with a voice like poured gravel. He said a few members of the company were about to attend a history fest in Naples, Florida, and I was welcome to join them, even try on conquistador gear if I liked.

"What should I bring?" I asked.

"A nasty attitude," Tim said.

THE HISTORY FEST was held at a small park between a Wal-Mart and a county jail. Arriving at twilight, I followed a trail into the palm grove shading the reenactors' camp. The fest was a "Timeline" event, meaning that every era was represented, other than the present. I passed the tent of a Confederate doctor studying a jar of leeches, and another occupied by Revolutionary Minutemen. A World War II G.I. strode past, griping to a pirate about the difficulty of getting decommissioned grenades through airport security. Then I spotted a brawny, bearded man in a rough jersey, hacking at something by a low fire.

"Are you by any chance a conquistador?" I asked.

"No, sorry." He held up a piece of flint he was honing. "I'm a paleo. The Spaniards are over near the Seminoles, I think."

I finally found Calderon's Company sipping wine from period goblets, though not yet in conquistador attire. Tim Burke turned out to be an amiable middle-aged man with gentle eyes and a quick smile. His *compadre,* Larry May, tall, lean, and soft-spoken, was a hospital technician who ran a vineyard on the side. Larry had brought along his wife and children, all of them blond and blue-eyed. As a group, Calderon's Company looked about as fierce and Iberian as the Brady Bunch.

"Larry and I met years ago, doing medieval combat with wooden swords," Tim said.

"I gave him a few blows and lopped off his head," Larry recalled, sipping Shiraz. "Then we became friends."

The two had since traveled forward in time, from Chaucerian days to the Age of Conquest, mainly to fill a void in the reenacting scene. "Medieval, Civil War, Wild West—everyone wants to do that," Tim said. "Not many people want to be conquistadors. There's a shortage of masochists in Florida."

I UNDERSTOOD WHAT he meant the next morning, as I watched Larry and Tim unpack armor they'd made by beating sheet metal with auto-repair hammers. Larry strapped heavy plates over Tim's chest, back, legs, and arms. A gorget went around his neck, beneath the high-crested helmet called a morion. "This is my light summer suit," Tim quipped. Normally, he wore metal gloves and plates over his feet and ankles. Even without them, his outfit weighed sixty pounds.

Larry's attire was much lighter but just as eye-catching: green wool jacket with braided buttons, green striped breeches, a green floppy hat, and knee-high black boots. He looked like a giant leprechaun. Larry's outfit, like Tim's, had been painstakingly researched and was modeled on the flashy camp attire of sixteenth-century Spaniards.

Tim flung a filthy white sack at my feet. "*Your* uniform, Don Antonio." Reaching inside, I extracted a pair of baggy woolen breeches that reached only to my knees, with a cod flap sized for a porn star. Next I pulled out a ruffled muslin blouse that looked like a nightgown. At the bottom of the bag lay a pair of leather buskins. Donning the blouse, knee pants and slippers, I confessed to Tim that I'd anticipated a rather manlier ensemble.

"Not done yet," he said, handing me a quilted wool doublet, just the thing for a hot autumn day in Florida. "And now, your *cota de mallas*." Tim had crafted the coat of mail from flattened, interlocked rings of heavy wire, exactly like the museum pieces I'd seen in the Southwest. As he hoisted the mesh shirt, allowing me to slide in my head and arms, I felt as though I were climbing inside a chain-link fence. The mail weighed over thirty pounds, and that was before Tim strapped on a belt, scabbard, and sword. On my head, he planted a visored helmet with flaps that covered my neck and ears. All told, I was wearing fifty pounds of steel.

Staggering a few feet, I knocked over a camp table and slumped awkwardly onto a tree stump. The chain mail bunched over my belt, giving me a Gothic German beer belly. "What now?" I asked. The words echoed inside the cavern of my helmet.

"Take it slow and drink lots of water," Tim said. "And resist the urge to use your sword on people who ask stupid questions."

A few minutes later the crowds arrived, clad in the costume of twenty-first-century Floridians: shorts, flipflops, and T-shirts. They meandered from camp to camp, like window shoppers at the Mall of Time, snapping pictures of Indians weaving palm leaves, or pioneer women scouring pots. By comparison, our camp offered little drama: two steel-clad figures standing in the sun, and a leprechaun polishing armor.

"What period is this?" a woman asked, consulting her Timeline brochure.

"Sixteenth-century Spanish," I muttered through my visor.

"Oh. Looks miserable." She moved on to the Seminole camp.

Then a man stopped to study my chain mail. "If you look inside your toaster," he said, "you'll see metal bits that look just like what you're wearing."

Others were less inventive.

"That your shark suit?"

"Need some oil?"

"Hot?"

As Tim had warned, I felt like running them through with my sword. Instead, I offered samples of the hardtack biscuits Larry had put on display. Earlier in the day, I'd tried one and almost chipped a tooth. Larry showed me the recipe: flour, water, and salt, baked "until golden brown and rock hard," then left to cool in the oven, "a process similar to case hardening in blacksmithing." In Mexico, Moctezuma sampled Spanish hardtack and declared it indistinguishable from limestone.

By midmorning I was drenched in sweat. In theory, chain mail offered ventilation—De Soto's men even used it for sifting flour—but the heavy doublet I wore underneath trapped the heat and moisture. Tim's plate armor allowed air in the sides and seemed to command respect, at least compared with the gawks and laughter my chain mail evoked. So at midday I asked whether we could swap outfits.

"Be my guest," he said, stifling a smile.

The plate armor not only weighed more than chain mail; it had all the flexibility of a back brace, and poked into my kidneys, collarbones, and groin. The gorget was unbearable, like an iron collar. And the armor was even hotter than mail. After ten minutes in the midday sun, the plate on my chest felt like the hood of a parked car on the Fourth of July.

"The Spanish didn't really wear this," I moaned. "They couldn't have."

In answer, Tim hurled a piece of hardtack at my chest. The biscuit crumbled on impact. Then he gave me a sharp blow with the butt of his musket. I was conscious of having been struck, but only just, as when someone taps your car bumper in traffic. Tim explained that chain mail was effective at blunting sword slashes, but it didn't offer defense against the fire-hardened arrows of Florida Indians. In battle, you wanted the sixteenth-century equivalent of Kevlar.

De Soto's men, however, didn't just fight; they marched, typically fifteen miles a day, across the entire South. When I took a sample stroll around the park with Tim, I lurched and creaked like the Tin Man. My sword, protruding tail-like behind me, kept catching on bushes and the wide skirts of pioneer women. As we approached a narrow bridge over a pond, Tim took firm grip of my arm. "If you fall in you'll go down like a sinker," he said. Small wonder that several of De Soto's men drowned while crossing the South's many rivers.

Clunking back to camp, with passersby affording me a wide berth, I sensed that Americans' neglect of conquistadors was partly due to their attire. Unlike others represented at the history fest, knights in armor seemed utterly misplaced on the U.S. continent. They belonged in the Crusades, or at the battle of Agincourt, not tramping through the woods and swamps of Florida.

I also felt a stab of period envy, jealousy of reenactors from other eras who appeared much more sensibly clad: bare-chested Indians,

Highlanders in kilts, even the "paleo" I'd met the night before, who was still wearing his sleeveless jersey and hacking at his flint.

"What's your technique?" I asked, stopping to watch him.

"Basically, beating a rock into submission," he grunted.

I also paused to chat with a fellow "Spaniard," a bearded man in sandals and hooded cassock who played an early missionary, Juan Rogel. The historic Father Rogel found it impossible to convert the Calusa Indians of southwest Florida, who believed that humans possessed three souls: one inside the body, another in the pupil of the eye, and a third in each person's shadow. The present-day Father Rogel faced a different challenge. "People keep asking if I'll hear their confession," he said. "I have to tell them, 'No, I'm Jewish.' "

A Bronx-born teacher, Larry Litt had agreed to the role because the event's organizers needed a friar, and he looked the part. Larry also played Santa Claus at his school. "*I'm* the one who needs forgiving," he said, as another penitent approached. "A bar mitzvah boy, and look what's become of me."

When I returned to the conquistador camp, Tim was busily priming his harquebus, or musket, for the day's climactic event: the Timeline Shooters, a demonstration of weapons from every era, in chronological order. The show opened with an Indian using an atlatl to fling a spear. Then came Tim, who asked me to stand beside him, holding up a shield. Early Spanish firearms were extremely clumsy, almost five feet long and so heavy that soldiers rested them on tripods. Harquebusiers also had to carry their own ignition, a piece of slow-burning rope called a match cord.

Tim poured black powder into a flash pan, pretended to ram a bullet down the muzzle, and cocked the trigger. "I'm being shot at with arrows all this time," he told the audience. That's where I came in: as an expendable, shielding the harquebusier. Finally, Tim touched the burning wick to the powder and yelled, *"¡Fuego!"* Fire flashed from the barrel and an imaginary lead ball crashed into the palms.

We exited to polite applause and stayed to watch the others: Brits in bearskin hats, firing flintlocks; Johnny Rebs shooting muskets; a cowboy emptying a Remington; and, as a crowd-pleasing finale, World War II Marines rattling off hundreds of blanks from a mounted machine gun. Taken together, the Timeline Shooters was a fireworks display in which we'd played the part of sparklers. Which made me wonder yet again: why choose to reenact a conquistador?

When I posed the question that night, Larry stared into his goblet. "Maybe it's because modern life can be so soft and boring," he said.

Larry had served with the Special Forces in Vietnam and the Middle East. He said modern soldiers carried as much weight as the Spanish did, "and maintaining your gear is still crucial." But he was struck by how much more intimate and horrible warfare must have been in the sixteenth century, when the killing occurred at close range, rather than from tanks, planes, or missile batteries.

"We can't condone what the Spaniards did; it seems barbaric to us," Larry said. "But I admire their tenacity, giving up everything familiar to come here. It would have been like traveling to the moon today."

Tim agreed. "Unless you reenact Mother Teresa, you're going to run into problems if you judge people by today's moral standards."

Also, whatever one thought of De Soto, the man had *cojones*. He'd made a fortune several times over before turning forty. But rather than live out his days as an idle aristocrat, he'd risked everything on the chance of making the biggest score yet, in La Florida.

"Probably a drug kingpin is the closest you could get to him today," Tim said. "Like one of those Colombian cartel leaders who can never get enough of the action, and can't quit when they're on top."

SOON AFTER LANDING in Florida, De Soto had an extraordinary stroke of luck. Near shore, mounted Spaniards came upon Indians with bows and arrows. One of the horsemen was about to charge with his lance when his intended target, a naked man with tattooed arms, cried out in Spanish. The tattooed man's name was Juan Ortiz. He'd come to Florida on an expedition eleven years before, only to be captured by Indians. He said his native captors had bound and laid him on a grill, and were about to kindle a fire under him when the chief's daughter intervened, begging that the Spaniard be spared.

This story bears a striking resemblance to that of John Smith's rescue by Pocahontas, which occurred eighty years later, near Jamestown.

A portrait of De Soto from a Spanish history of the Indies

It's possible that Indians in both Florida and Virginia practiced a similar ritual, threatening to execute captives before adopting them. It's also possible that John Smith lifted his romantic story from published accounts of Juan Ortiz's earlier rescue. The Spaniard was saved a second time by the Indian princess, who warned that he was about to be sacrificed to appease an Indian spirit. He fled to another tribe, which alerted him to the arrival of De Soto's ships. So Ortiz had come in search of the Spanish, only to narrowly escape their lances.

"He knew little of our language, since he had forgotten it," wrote one of De Soto's men. "He remembered how to call to Our Lady, and by this he was recognized to be a Christian." For several days he could barely communicate, "since upon saying one word in Spanish, he would say another four or five in the language of the Indians."

Ortiz's fluency in the language and customs of Florida Indians made him invaluable to De Soto as an interpreter and intermediary.

Without Ortiz, De Soto wrote soon after landing, "I know not what would become of us."

De Soto possessed another great advantage over his predecessors: several decades of experience in hostile lands, from the jungles of Panama to the mountains of Peru. The qualities he'd honed in Central and South America—daring, deception, utter ruthlessness—quickly came to the fore in Florida. De Soto left a hundred men at a base camp by the coast and marched his army inland, taking few provisions. Upon reaching native settlements, the Spanish looted storehouses of maize and seized Indians as guides and porters, chaining them together at the neck so they couldn't escape.

Those who tried to flee, or who misled the Spanish, were burned at the stake or thrown to attack dogs. De Soto's favorite, an Irish greyhound named Bruto, once chased down a fleeing chief and dragged him to the ground. In his initiative and ferocity, Bruto matched his master. Before battle, one Spaniard wrote of De Soto, "He was always the first or the second to come out armed, and never the third."

His men weren't quite so avid. Early on in their march, they realized De Soto was leading them to Apalachee, the warlike Indian province where Narváez's expedition had unraveled, causing the desperate flight by sea that few of the three-hundred-man force survived. As De Soto's men struggled through woods and swamps in summer heat, fending off hit-and-run attacks by native archers, they buried horseshoes and other supplies to dig up during what they felt sure would be the army's eventual retreat.

De Soto not only pressed ahead; he went on the attack. Warned by Juan Ortiz of an impending ambush, he laid a trap of his own, luring four hundred Indians into open ground and launching a cavalry assault. Those warriors who weren't lanced fled into shallow ponds, hiding beneath water lilies as Spaniards shot at them with muskets and crossbows. Fatigue finally forced the two hundred or so survivors to surrender. Most were quickly massacred. The rest, apart from "the youngest boys," were fastened to stakes and shot with arrows by Indians of another tribe, whom the Spanish had previously captured.

Torture, slaughter, and the terrorizing of natives were familiar tactics of Spanish conquest. But few conquistadors deployed them as routinely and as unapologetically as De Soto. Other men, such as Coronado, acted under the faint constraint of Spanish law and custom, and tried to justify their ruthlessness. Coronado was also a young bureaucrat whose *entrada* was linked by land to Spanish-held Mexico, allowing his superiors to keep distant watch on his actions and progress.

De Soto had no such oversight. He quickly severed contact with his base in Cuba, and seems even to have dispensed with the Requerimiento, the official "summons" to Indians. There is no record of its being read before battle in Florida. The friars on his expedition were evidently too cowed or acquiescent to raise objections.

Nor did De Soto pay much heed to his officers. "After he had voiced his own opinion," one of his men wrote, "he did not like to be contradicted and always did what seemed best to him." Let loose in the wilds of La Florida, De Soto could be as mobile and deadly as his war dogs.

AT THE END of the history fest, I bade *adiós* to the conquistadors and *shalom* to Father Rogel, then drove north to follow De Soto's path through present-day Florida. Reaching Bradenton, I immediately became lost in a maze of interstate spurs and access roads clotted with big-box malls. Walking wasn't an option: the sun-struck, car-spaced sprawl of modern Florida is as inhospitable to foot traffic as the state's swamps had been to the Spanish. Development hadn't been kind to Florida's history, either. At Bradenton's museum, I learned that most of the mounds and shell middens that once marked Indian settlements had been bulldozed for use as road fill.

Beside the museum stood the De Soto Historical Society, housed in a handsome Spanish-style manor. De Soto's coat of arms decorated the entrance and a statue of him stood nearby. Fittingly, though, given Florida's habit of burying its history, the De Soto Historical Society had little connection to the real De Soto. It was a civic and charitable group that held Spanish-themed parades, elected an honorary "Hernando" and De Soto "Queen," and celebrated the anniversary of the conquistador's landing with a monthlong bash.

When I asked the society's director what she thought of the group's namesake, she seemed caught off guard. "I guess you could say he had a lot of tenacity and took risks. Is that any different from a businessman who goes out to ruthlessly make a fortune today?" Before I could reply, she walked me to a wall lined with photos of former De Soto Queens. "Aren't they lovely girls?"

The reigning Queen and the society's honorary Hernando were scheduled to appear at Bradenton's upcoming Veterans' Day parade a few days later. I went to meet them at the parade staging ground by the De Soto Bridge. The society's float was easy to spot: an enormous mock caravel built onto the frame of a school bus. The motorized vessel had a tall mast, captain's wheel, and portholes, as well as "Crewe of Hernando de Soto" emblazoned on the side.

"Come aboard!" the driver shouted, lowering a gangplank. Revelers crowded the deck, mostly bearded men wearing tights, bright pantaloons, and chrome-plated helmets. At the wheel stood Hernando, or "Hern" as the others called him, a white-bearded man in a brass helmet and breastplate. "She's a smooth sailer," he joked, gazing up the mast, "but I think we'll run on engine power today."

His cell phone rang. The Queen was stuck in traffic on the De Soto Bridge. At the last minute she sprinted aboard, a well-coiffed brunette in a tiara, miniskirt, and tight black top. I asked why she didn't wear faux-Spanish attire like the others.

"For a girl, it's nothing special to wear tights and ruffles and high boots," she said. "But the boys really get into it."

As the caravel lurched forward to join the parade, the Queen waved while the Crewe cracked beers and hurled strings of plastic beads and brass doubloons at onlookers in lawn chairs. Hern cranked up the boat's sound system, blaring "The Boys Are Back in Town." What this Mardi Gras–style cavalcade had to do with De Soto, or Veterans' Day, wasn't clear.

"De Soto was a rowdy guy who came through Florida giving out a lot of beads to natives," opined one Crewe member.

"The guy was a butcher, a fucking cutlass," his rail-mate interjected. "But it wasn't us doing the killing. We're just here to party in his name. No harm given, or intended."

Not everyone agreed. In the 1990s, protestors from the American Indian Movement had pelted the Crewe with fish guts. They also disrupted the annual reenactment of De Soto's landing, at which historical society members clad as Spaniards rushed onto the beach and slaughtered "Indians," mostly members' children, wearing loincloths and face paint. The demonstrators shouted "Go home!" and "Genocide!" and burned De Soto in effigy. The reenactment had since been abandoned and the name of the anniversary changed from the De Soto Celebration to the Florida Heritage Festival.

"You've got to be sensitive, I guess," Hern said, as the caravel reached the end of the parade route. "But we're not trying to rewrite history. De Soto was a conqueror. That was his job. This is ours." He threw a last string of beads at an elderly couple in motorized carts. "What's wrong with a little fun?"

DE SOTO'S PITILESS methods would have been devastating anywhere in America, but they were particularly so in the territory he traversed. In contrast to the Southwest and the Plains, where natives lived nomadically or dispersed across dozens of pueblos, the Southeast's population was dense and concentrated in large city-states. Rather than steer around these powerful centers, De Soto headed straight for them, hoping to find huge stores of gold and silver like those discovered in the capitals of Mexico and Peru. Failing that, he could seize food, clothing, and porters for the onward journey.

These tactics inevitably provoked bloody conflict. But the many Indians killed by Spanish arms were only the first and most obvious casualties of De Soto's march. The arrival of his army, which often camped for weeks amid large and settled populations, turned the South into a breeding ground for epidemic disease. De Soto compounded this danger by dragooning thousands of Indians as guides, cooks, concubines, and porters, who were forced to live among the Spanish for long periods. Natives who survived this ordeal and straggled home became traveling agents of infection.

Grim evidence of both Spanish germs and Spanish steel turned up in the 1980s at an Indian site along De Soto's path, northeast of

Bradenton. Archaeologists found armor and glass trade beads like those the Spanish carried. More telling, though, were human arm bones, severed cleanly at the shoulder by a sharp metal weapon: a wound consistent with a downward sword blow. Other bodies lay piled in a mass grave, probably the aftermath of a sudden outbreak of disease. Soon after De Soto's passage, all signs of habitation at the settlement abruptly ceased.

The site wasn't marked on road maps, but at a small museum in the town of Inverness I got directions, which sent me winding along a country lane that ended at the Withlacoochee River. Beside the wide, tea-colored river was a fishing camp decorated with rebel flags, and a bar with a sign warning, "Unattended Children and Dogs Will Be Used For Gator Bait."

Inside, I found men in duckbill caps drinking cans of beer and talking about bass and crappie. A wall menu offered fried okra, boiled peanuts, and honey BBQ wings. Somewhere in the hundred or so miles since leaving Bradenton, I'd crossed from retiree and snowbird Florida to the state's Southern heartland.

When I asked whether anyone knew of an Indian site nearby, a drinker directed me to a wooded trail, which led to an ancient mound. "I reckon those Spaniards in their armor must've rusted up fast around here," he said. "They didn't have WD-40 back then." As I reached the door, another man called after me, "Watch for water moccasins, and don't put your hand anyplace you can't see."

This was undoubtedly sound advice, but almost impossible to follow. The trail turned out to be a narrow path through man-high saw palmettos. I could barely see the ground for all the underbrush, and quickly felt my feet sinking into muck. Groping to keep my balance, I stuck my hand into a three-foot-tall anthill. Overhead, arching live oaks, draped in Spanish moss, blotted out the sky. This shade would have been welcome on a sunny day, but on an overcast and oppressively humid afternoon, the canopy of trees closed over me like a coffin lid. Mosquitoes swarmed every inch of exposed flesh.

After a mile or so, I slumped on a rotted log and tried to imagine how alien and claustrophobic this landscape must have seemed to De Soto's men, most of them natives of Spain's arid, open backcountry.

Even in autumn, dressed in a T-shirt and khakis, I was soaked in sweat and half-mad from insects. To have trudged through this in summer, in fifty pounds of armor, with Indians raining down arrows from the jungle on all sides, seemed even more unimaginable than to have been among Coronado's men crossing the baked Sonoran Desert and the endless Plains.

I forced myself to soldier on until I reached a barbed-wire fence enclosing a hillock, apparently all that remained of the Indian settlement. Pushing aside huge, fanlike palm leaves, I went in for a closer look, and instantly sank knee-deep in stagnant black water. Invisible creatures rustled in the dense brush. Wretched and uneasy, I fled the mire and retreated to the fishing camp as fast as I could. No conquistador, I.

MUCH EASIER TO reach is the town that De Soto seized, in late 1539, for his winter encampment: Anhaica, capital of the bellicose Apalachee nation. Rather than confront Spanish horsemen in open battle, the Apalachee retreated to hideouts from which they staged guerrilla attacks. De Soto's army occupied Anhaica's clay and palm homes, looted its stores of food, and settled in for an uneasy stay of five months.

Almost 450 years later, in Tallahassee, a veteran Florida archaeologist, Calvin Jones, was taking his lunch break when he noticed bulldozers clearing a site for development. Jones took a shovel from the back of his truck and dug a few test holes, unearthing a piece of Spanish olive jar. Returning with a metal detector, he turned up nails and chain mail.

The developers halted work while archaeologists excavated the site. They found a large Indian settlement and hundreds of Spanish artifacts, including beads, buckles, gaming pieces, and sixteenth-century coins. But the discovery that confirmed the presence of De Soto's army was the jawbone of a pig—a creature unknown on the continent before De Soto brought a small herd as emergency provisions for his expedition.

I went to see the pig mandible in a basement repository near Florida's capitol, a towering shaft flanked by gonadlike domes and known to locals as "the Big Dick." Down the road, behind a Motel 6, I found the small office park that now occupies the archaeological site. Except for a plaque in the parking lot, and a patch of scrub preserved by the state, nothing marked the site as the onetime Apalachee capital and the only confirmed De Soto encampment in the United States.

The conquistador's swine had left a more enduring mark. Some ran off or were traded to Indians; fast-breeding, intelligent, and adaptable, the species *Sus scrofa* thrived in the wild, becoming a major player in the region's ecology and a staple of its diet. Millions of feral hogs still roam the South, wreaking havoc on crops, golf courses, and the food and habitat of other wild animals. Moving in packs of ten or twenty, the long-snouted omnivores can strip an acre of land a day.

"They make it look like a cottonpickin' dozer has been through," said Danny Joyner, a state ranger at the Anhaica site. "Anything that's edible, and a lot that's not, they'll just chew and root it up."

Weighing up to five hundred pounds, not counting tusks, mature hogs also charge humans when wounded or threatened. "If you corner them, they can be fierce, yes sir," Danny said. "They'll rip you from asshole to appetite. And slobber all over you, too. Not real attractive creatures, when you get right down to it."

But Danny liked the taste of their meat, which he described as musky. "This isn't a beer belly, it's a pork belly," he said, slapping his ample waist. "I reckon most Southerners don't realize we have the Spanish to thank for barbecue."

The Apalachee Indians had less to be thankful for. Estimates of their sixteenth-century population range as high as thirty thousand. Despite their early battles with the Spanish, the Apalachee later asked that friars be sent to their towns, perhaps hoping this would offer protection from both the Spanish and Indian enemies. The Spanish established a large agricultural mission in Tallahassee, soldiers intermarried with the Apalachee, and thousands of Indians were baptized.

Christianity brought an end to native rituals, including a game that was akin to soccer and basketball. Teams scored points by kicking deerskin balls against goal posts, or into nets atop the poles. The game, dedicated to the rain gods, was preceded by fasting, free love, and consumption of a highly caffeinated purgative made from the leaves of a holly, *Ilex vomitoria*. Spanish missionaries, appalled by the "devilish" game and its rituals, ordered the goal posts torn down and crosses erected in their stead.

But Christianity was no defense against epidemic disease, or attacks by English colonists and their Creek allies in the Carolinas. These led to the mission's burning in 1704, and the dispersal and enslavement of the surviving Indians. The once-mighty Apalachee nation vanished—except in name. Early European mapmakers had believed the Florida tribe so large and powerful that they drew its domain to include a distant mountain range, known ever since as the Appalachians.

WHEN DE SOTO arrived at Anhaica late in 1539, he brought a chain gang of native baggage carriers he'd captured while marching through Florida. By the time the army decamped five months later, the Spanish had to carry their gear themselves. "Most of the Indians whom they had to serve them," wrote one of De Soto's men, "being naked and in chains, died because of the hard life they suffered during that winter."

Among the survivors was an Indian youth who had come to Florida from a distant land. He told the Spanish it was ruled by a woman and rich in gold and other goods. The youth's story bedazzled De Soto, much as El Turco's tales of Quivira entranced Coronado. Originally having planned to follow the Gulf coast, so he could meet supply ships from Cuba, De Soto changed course. On leaving Anhaica in March 1540, he swung his army inland, toward the land the youth had told of. It would be three years before his men saw the sea again.

Entering present-day Georgia, they negotiated an obstacle course of deep woods and wide, swift rivers. To cross these, the Spanish built bridges and rafts, once even linking the chains they'd brought to shackle Indians so they could pull boats across. At other times, they formed a chain of men and beasts, with soldiers clutching the tails or lances of horses and men ahead of them.

They also fashioned a cumbersome linguistic chain to communicate with Georgia tribes. First, the Spanish had to find natives who

understood the youth guiding De Soto. The guide then translated the locals' words into the language of Florida Indians, which Juan Ortiz understood. Ortiz then relayed the message in Spanish, to De Soto.

As recorded by expedition scribes, these dialogues seem to have lost something in all the translation. One chief, receiving the gift of a feather, allegedly gushed: "This your feather that you give me, I can eat with it; I will go forth to war with it; I will sleep with my wife with it."

De Soto's own words were rarely recorded, but his actions spoke clearly enough. During a typical encounter, he announced his arrival at an Indian settlement by seizing hostages and informing the local chief that he "was going through this land and seeking the greatest lord and the richest province in it." The chief claimed that a "great lord lived on ahead," and provided a guide and interpreter in exchange for De Soto's captives. Chiefs of the next two settlements were even more obliging, giving the Spanish food, clothing, and hundreds of porters.

These transactions weren't entirely one-sided. Though Georgia chiefs undoubtedly aided De Soto so as to rid themselves of his rapacious army, they also did so with the expressed wish that he make war on the natives' great enemy, the female ruler of the rich province the Spanish sought.

Nor was De Soto's army an altogether awesome presence, despite its guns and horses. Spaniards lacked the mobility and know-how to track the region's abundant game, and marveled at Indians' skill at hunting deer, rabbits, and birds. Desperate for meat, soldiers fell hungrily on the one source they could catch: Indian dogs.

When even those were lacking, De Soto tapped his pig supply, which had swelled to three hundred from an original herd of only thirteen. He issued each soldier a pound of pork. This first recorded pig feast in the American South, in April 1540, sounds distinctly unappetizing. "We ate it," a Spaniard wrote, "boiled in water without salt or anything else."

THE MODERN TRAVELER runs little risk of starving in the land De Soto crossed. Following small roads through southwest Georgia, I passed pine woods and pecan orchards and fields of soggy cotton bolls the pickers had missed. Machines did most of the farmwork now, leaving derelict towns with shuttered shops and sagging verandas: the economic roadkill of the rural South. Even so, most crossroads still sustained diners, with names such as Kountry Fokes and Krispy Chik, serving meals hearty enough to fuel an entire day of field labor.

Stopping at one, I paid six dollars to load my tray from a buffet of fried chicken, fried catfish, cornbread, green beans, black-eyed peas, turnip greens, butter beans, and mashed potatoes, washed down with a pitcher of sweet iced tea. From my window seat, I faced the town's Confederate monument, its lean Johnny Reb staring back at me reproachfully as I finished off a piece of red velvet cake. Waddling back to my car, I passed a church sign that said, "Sinners Wanted!" and another shouting, "Repent!" Gluttony and guilt: constant bedfellows in the Bible Belt South.

I headed for a hamlet called De Soto and found more of the same. The town's name derived from a local legend that the Spanish had camped nearby. But it was better known as home to the "De Soto Nut House," renowned for its pecan logs and other nutty confections. Sadly, the nut house had closed, its premises now occupied by an evangelical church. A sign in front bore a biblical proverb that De Soto would have done well to heed: "How Much Better It Is to Get Wisdom Than Gold!"

In central Georgia, the landscape shifted, from swampy plain to gently rolling hills and stately antebellum towns, their streets lined with historic plaques telling of Sherman's March in 1864. Part of the Union general's route through Georgia paralleled De Soto's, as did Sherman's scorched-earth tactics. Both men led invading armies that lived off the land and terrorized natives. Few Georgians, though, were aware of the Spanish precedent. The Civil War loomed so large in Southern memory that the region's history had been telescoped into the four long years between Fort Sumter and Appomattox.

"De Soto did a lot more damage than Sherman," Charles Hudson told me, "but he wasn't a Yankee so no one here cares." We were sitting at a café in Athens, beside the University of Georgia campus where Hudson had taught for thirty-six years. "It's not just De Soto that's forgotten in the South," he said. "It's the colonial period and almost everything else before 1861."

I'd come to see the Georgia professor because the path I'd been following since Bradenton was known, in his honor, as the Hudson Route. The story of how Charles Hudson came to chart De Soto's march was as tortuous as the ten-state trail he'd mapped across the South. For starters, his academic field wasn't geography or Spanish history: it was anthropology, a specialty he traced to his upbringing on a Kentucky tobacco farm at the tail end of the Depression.

"It was a very small, very homogenous world. I never met anyone different—not even a Republican, for Chrissakes, until I was well along." Charles chuckled. "*That's* changed, of course."

Now in his seventies, he still looked the part of a Kentucky farmer: long white hair, silver mustache, wide-brimmed felt hat, denim vest and jeans. But he'd fled his modest rural roots at an early age, in rather the same manner as De Soto: by enlisting as a teenager to serve overseas, in Japan during the Korean War.

"Japan bumfuzzled me," Charles said. "I was unable to make sense of the fact that people could be so different, and have so much history. In Owen County, Kentucky, we thought we'd just come out of the ground, like the crops." So when he returned home, Charles used the G.I. Bill to attend college and went on to earn a Ph.D. in anthropology.

After a stint among the Inuit, Charles focused his fieldwork on Indians of the southeastern United States. He was quickly struck by a lacuna in their history. Archaeologists had documented the existence of large, agricultural societies that thrived for centuries before Europeans first arrived. Yet these centralized empires bore little resemblance to the scattered tribes that English colonists later encountered. The period between, from about 1500 to 1700, was what Charles called a "dark age," little studied or understood.

This led him to Spanish accounts of De Soto's expedition, known collectively as *The De Soto Chronicles*, which contain many details about native life. To mine them for anthropological insight, Charles needed to know where exactly De Soto traveled and what societies he encountered. So he started mapping De Soto's route, thinking this would be a short-term project. Instead, it consumed twenty years of his career and drew him into a contentious public fight.

The first hurdle was the comparative absence of physical markers in the territory De Soto traveled. It's relatively easy to spot the Grand Canyon or Rio Grande in the writings of Coronado's men, much harder to tell if a wide, slow river crossed by De Soto in Florida was the Suwannee, Aucilla, or Waccasassa. Also, while much of the Southwest's *despoblado* remains empty today, the Southeast's landscape has been radically reconfigured by dams, farms, logging, and sprawl.

The human landscape offered Charles even fewer historic clues. In contrast to the pueblo people, few southeastern tribes occupy the same land as their distant ancestors. De Soto's march displaced and destroyed many native societies, and the U.S. government completed the job in the 1830s, when the Indian Removal Act forced most surviving tribes to move west of the Mississippi.

As Charles grappled with these problems, his search for De Soto's route took on elements of the conquistador's own obsessive quest. With a team of academic lieutenants, he sifted documents and archaeological data for traces of gold: a bead, a nail, a village name—anything that might lead to De Soto. He pored over topographical maps, which helped strip the landscape of its modern, man-made clutter. When Charles scored a hit, identifying a site he felt confident De Soto had visited, he pinned a red flag to an aeronautical chart on his office wall.

He also took reconnaissance trips, accompanied by his wife, Joyce, who joined us at the café in Athens. "I remember one time, the landscape didn't fit and Charlie decided he had the whole route wrong," she said. "He went out that night and got drunk."

Charles also found himself battling the ghost of John Swanton, a Smithsonian scholar commissioned by the U.S. government in the 1930s to study De Soto's route. Swanton's work led to historic markers going up across the South, allegedly tracing the army's path. But much of his data had since been discredited by archaeological finds and other evidence. When the National Park Service unveiled a proposal in 1990 for a new De Soto Trail based on the Hudson Route, it bypassed many towns that had long taken pride in their connection to the conquistador.

This sparked a firestorm of local protests, and put pressure on politicians to deny the project funding or to get Hudson allies fired from state jobs. Typical of the vitriol was a submission to the Park Service by an elderly Mississippian. "What the hell does some Dr. Phuddy-Duddy Ph.D. from Georgia," he fumed, "know about the fine details of Coahoma County topography, archaeology, and history?"

In the end, the Park Service recognized "a scholarly consensus" backing the Hudson Route, but decided there was insufficient agreement to establish a national De Soto Trail. Florida and Alabama erected new markers, along the path Charles had laid out, but other states left Swanton's flawed route intact.

"I riled up the natives, like De Soto I guess," Charles said. "When you tell folks, 'Sorry, what your third-grade teacher told you and what's on your signs isn't true,' that gets people upset."

Joyce, a native of rural Georgia, sensed a deeper regional instinct. "Southerners have a strong sense of place, and it's often a place where they and their kin have always been," she said. "It's their territory. So when you go messing with the history of their place, you're messing with their identity, you're messing with *them*. It's the Civil War all over again."

Charles had since retired from the fray. But he still poked at the mystery that drew him to De Soto in the first place: whom did the Spanish meet, and what happened to them? As part of this quest, he'd written a novel imagining the thoughts of a sixteenth-century Indian priest in Georgia.

"Sometimes that's the best we can do with history," he said, as we parted in the rain. "Make an educated guess."

DRIVING FROM ATHENS to Sparta, I picked up the Hudson Route again and followed it east across the Savannah River. To ford the wide, swift Savannah, the Spanish had to tie themselves together. A number of pigs were carried off by the current. Trudging on, through a damp and trackless wilderness, the exhausted and hungry Spanish began to doubt the young Indian guide who had promised to lead them to his wealthy, woman-ruled homeland of Cofitachequi.

Then, in present-day South Carolina, the army came to yet another river and a settled bluff on the other side. For the first and almost the last time on De Soto's long journey, the encounter that followed was peaceful and enchanting. Indians came down to the river carrying a litter veiled in thin white linen. Inside sat a beautiful young woman: the "lady of Cofitachequi," as the Spanish called her.

Crossing the river in a cushioned, awning-draped canoe, she stepped ashore, removed a string of pearls, and placed it around De Soto's neck. She also provided canoes to ferry the army to her settlement, where the weary soldiers were given sable blankets and jerked venison. "That land was very pleasing and fertile," wrote one of De Soto's men, "and had excellent fields along the rivers, the forests being clear and having many walnuts and mulberries."

Cofitachequi also had a large mortuary temple, which De Soto promptly looted. Unwrapping burial shrouds, he found bodies bedecked with freshwater pearls, some two hundred pounds in all, as well as ornaments made of copper—possibly the "gold" the Indian guide had promised. The graves also held glass beads and axes, evidence of a Spanish attempt to settle the Atlantic coast a decade before. The goods had been traded or carried inland, along with another European import. Much of Cofitachequi was depopulated and overgrown, the result, Indians said, of a devastating "plague."

Even so, the province seemed heavenly to the Spanish, who had spent a year marching on short rations through mostly hostile territory. "All the men were of the opinion that we should settle that land," one wrote. Peaceful, fertile, and rich in pearls, Cofitachequi was only a few days' march from the coast—a potentially profitable base for servicing ships sailing between the New World and Spain.

De Soto's men had reason to hope their commander might concur in their wish to stay. His contract with the Crown gave him the right to choose over five hundred miles of coastline as his personal domain, to colonize and govern "for all the days of your life," with a generous annual salary. But at Cofitachequi it became clear that De Soto had his eyes on a much greater prize. "Since the governor's purpose was to seek another treasure like that of Atahualpa, the lord of Peru," wrote one of his men, "he had no wish to content himself with good land or with pearls."

And so, after a stay of eleven days, the army turned its back on the sea and marched toward yet another land rumored to have "a great lord." De Soto took along his looted pearls—and also the lady of Cofitachequi. He held the ruler hostage to guarantee safe passage through her land, and to assure he could collect corn and porters from her subjects. Accustomed to traveling in a litter, with a large retinue, the lady of Cofitachequi now had to cross her realm on foot, accompanied by a single servant.

SPEEDING DOWN THE Strom Thurmond Freeway into South Carolina, I phoned an archaeologist who had excavated an Indian settlement believed to have been Cofitachequi. The archaeologist gave me directions to the site, near Camden, S.C., but said there wasn't much to see. "It's just a bump in a field." Also, the site was on private land, owned by a family that didn't welcome visitors. "If you ask the supervisor of the plantation, he might let you have a look," she said, ringing off to go teach a class.

By now, I'd seen enough archaeological sites to know they rarely amounted to much. But the mention of a plantation intrigued me. It also seemed a pity to bypass one of the pleasantest stops on De Soto's route. So I followed the archaeologist's directions, exiting the interstate by the Wateree River and navigating a small road until I reached a tree-lined avenue leading into a plantation.

Finding the supervisor's house empty, I drove on to a brick cottage, set fifty yards in front of a columned mansion. A handsome middle-aged woman appeared at the door of the cottage and inquired, rather coolly, "Can I help you?"

Caught by surprise, I burbled something about following De Soto's route and being entranced by the story of Cofitachequi.

"Which part of the story?" she asked.

"The lady with the pearls going in a canoe to meet De Soto."

A smile crept across the woman's face, as if I'd guessed the secret password. "Well, then," she said, "perhaps I can show you around."

Marty Daniels belonged to the extended family that owned Mulberry Plantation. Her forebears had been drawn there by the rich soil and river access that Indians, centuries earlier, had recognized as well suited to settlement. Where natives sowed beans and corn, Marty's ancestors had planted indigo and cotton, seeding a plantation that grew to twenty thousand acres, worked by hundreds of slaves.

Climbing into Marty's four-wheel drive, we drove through a pine grove to a cleared bluff overlooking the Wateree, a slow brown river about a hundred yards across. At the center of the clearing rose a grassy knoll, no more than six feet high. "That's Cofitachequi, or what's left of it," Marty said.

Excavations of the surrounding land had revealed a large settlement dating back to the thirteenth century, including a workshop for mica, the shiny, thinly layered white rock that natives showed De Soto when he asked about silver. English travelers, arriving in 1670, described Cofitachequi as a still-powerful province, ruled by "an emperor." But by the early 1700s, its people had mysteriously vanished, possibly having moved west and melded with other tribes.

They left behind a dozen mounds, which incoming planters used as perches for their buildings. In the nineteenth century, an overseer's cottage crowned the tallest mound; slave quarters covered the others. The mounds had since been leveled for landfill and eroded by floods, exposing bones, pottery, and other artifacts, which Marty had enjoyed collecting as a child. But what she'd loved best was hearing relatives' stories about the Indian "queen" who greeted De Soto wearing nothing but pearls.

"For those of us born before the women's movement, the story of this chieftainess had special power," Marty said, stopping on the drive back to feed her horses. "She was a gracious hostess, a real Southern lady. But she was also this accomplished, independent woman."

Best of all, the queen eventually succeeded in outwitting De Soto. After being taken hostage and marched across her realm, she entered the woods, claiming she had to relieve herself; instead, she hid, then ran off with her servant and a cane box of pearls. "Whenever we got to the part of the story where she takes the pearls and steals away," Marty said, "all the girls in our family would go, 'Yes.'"

De Soto later learned that his escaped prisoner had met several deserters from his expedition, including a runaway Indian. He and the escaped queen "held communication as husband and wife," wrote one

of De Soto's men, "and made up their minds to go to Cofitachequi."
No more is known of the lady and her lover.

Curiously, Cofitachequi later became home to another renowned
woman: Marty's great-great-grandmother, Mary Chesnut, whose diary
of the Confederate home front is a classic of Southern literature. Chesnut chafed at her "useless existence" as a Mulberry plantation wife, attended by twenty-five house slaves. It was, she wrote, "a pleasant,
empty, easy going life. But people are not like pigs; they cannot be put
up and fattened. So here I pine and fret."

Like Cofitachequi, Mary Chesnut's coddled world came under attack, and then collapsed; after the Civil War, the plantation was abandoned, as the Indian capital had been centuries before. Marty's
grandfather later restored the Chesnut mansion to its antebellum
grandeur: formal drawing room, spiral staircase, busts of Scipio and
Caesar, shelves filled with books such as *Cotton Is King*.

Marty lived more modestly, "back of the big house" in a renovated
slave cottage. On her mantel perched an ambrotype of Mary Chesnut
in a formal gown, black hair pulled back. Marty, with her fair, un-
coiffed hair and muddy jeans, didn't take after her forebear. Though
taught by a plantation tutor before attending boarding school and
Sarah Lawrence College, she'd spent most of her adult life outdoors:
rock climbing, wrangling horses, and roaming the country in a beat-up
camper van, banding hawks.

"I guess I identify with the natives here more than with my Mulberry ancestors," she said, showing me another picture, this one of a
striking longhaired man at an American Indian rally. This was Marty's
boyfriend, Val Green, who belonged to the Catawba, the tribe that
came to occupy Cofitachequi after its original inhabitants fled.

Val was due to visit that evening and Marty invited me to join them
for dinner. The man who drove up at sunset in his pickup truck was a
combination of Indian and backcountry Carolinian: dark brow, long
black ponytail, flannel shirt and jeans, deep Southern drawl, and
"Catawba" written on the front of his baseball cap. Settling by the fire,
Val told me that he saw a natural kinship between his Indian and
Southern bloodlines.

"If you read the early English accounts, they describe how the Indian men hunted in the morning and evening and hung around like hogs in the day," he said. "Just like good ol' boys today. Indians loved their ball games, too. And their beans and corn and barbecue and tobacco. There's a lot of Indian in Southern culture."

There was a lot of Southern in Indian culture, too. While pueblo people had been partly Hispanicized, adopting Catholicism and Spanish surnames, Indians in the Southeast took on the language and customs of English and Scotch-Irish settlers. Most became Baptists, though the Catawba were predominantly Mormon, owing to the arrival of missionaries in the nineteenth century. During the Civil War, every Catawba of military age served in the Confederate Army. Most tribal members now lived on a reservation an hour north of Mulberry and worked on farms or in textile mills, much like their non-Indian neighbors.

In Val's case, the cultural fusion extended to politics. Each year, he donned a black armband to protest Columbus Day, and at election time he cast write-in votes for Geronimo. But he was also a Southern nationalist, who believed the region should secede again. To him, the Indian cause and the Lost Cause were the same.

"Both are fiercely antigovernment," he explained. "Indians are basically conservative people—they want to be left alone with their land and traditions, same as Southerners. There's no way to preserve what we have without getting out from under the Union."

I'd heard the neo-Confederate dogma many times before, but never from a ponytailed Indian who was also a fervent environmentalist. Val had recently returned to his Catawba family land, and was trying to restore it to a pre-European state. "Selective burning, planting native species, restoring full wildlife diversity," he said, sounding like a Sierra Club spokesman. "Undoing all the damage that's been done over the past four or five centuries."

Marty, who had been listening quietly, wondered what it would be like if Cofitachequi could be magically restored, too. "I think the Lady knew her culture was waning, like Mary Chesnut," she mused, walking me outside. The moon had risen, casting a yellow glow across the boxwood garden and avenue of live oaks. "Beautiful but doomed, in one era and then another. That's always the Southern story, isn't it?"

LEAVING COFITACHEQUI, DE SOTO marched northwest, across the piedmont of present-day North Carolina, and then into "very rough and lofty" mountains. To pioneers in later centuries, the Appalachians presented a formidable barrier. But De Soto, who had scaled the much taller Andes, wasn't deterred by mountains; he was drawn to them. Since skyscraping Peru had yielded a fortune in gold and silver, the Spanish equated mountains with mineral riches. Indians along De Soto's route had fed this belief, telling of mines in the hills that produced a mixture of copper and gold.

Approached from the east, the mountains of North Carolina unfold in a series of ranges: first the gentle, azure Blue Ridge, and then the Smokies, their midsection wreathed in haze. If the Spanish found beauty in this vista, they didn't say so in their writing, which told instead of exhaustion and hunger. The men could find little food apart from wild turkeys, and their horses became so weak that "they were unable to carry their owners."

Reading these lean accounts over a heart-stopping lunch at Hillbilly Barbecue and Steaks, I resolved to get off the road and do some serious walking. Rather than stick to the Hudson Route, which led along a major tourist highway through the mountains, I plotted a short detour, heading for the rare patch of ground where it seemed possible to glimpse the landscape as it might have appeared in De Soto's day.

Most of the old-growth forest that once blanketed the Appalachians was logged long ago. But deep in the Nantahala Wilderness, in the southwest corner of North Carolina, a timber company went bankrupt during the Depression before cutting all the land it owned. Purchased by the government, the remote plot became the Joyce Kilmer Memorial Forest, named for the author of the poem "Trees." Seventy years later, the park encloses one of the last stands of virgin hardwood forest in the eastern United States.

The park felt different as soon as I hiked into it. Kept as a primitive wilderness area, its paths were unmarked and dead trees lay where they fell: moss-slick giants slowly rotting into the forest floor. One tree, severed midway up, stood as a simple monument to Kilmer, who was cut down during combat in World War I, at the age of thirty-one.

In much of the modern South, the woods are a monotonous expanse of "plantation pine," sown in croplike rows, so they can be easily harvested as soon as the trees mature. The Kilmer forest, by contrast, blended oak, hemlock, beech, birch, ash, and other species. The oldest trees dated almost to the time of De Soto's expedition.

Towering over all of them were the tulip poplars, 150 feet tall and ten feet in diameter. Often growing in pairs or triplets, they sprang straight up, with no branches for the first fifty feet. The effect, as I walked beneath their dizzying loft, was of touring an outdoor cathedral. A fitting tribute to the man who wrote: "Poems are made by fools like me, / But only God can make a tree."

After hiking a few miles, I reclined on a poplar root as big as a chaise lounge. The woods were hushed in late-autumn silence, except for a lone woodpecker and the distant rush of a mountain stream. During my brief tramps in the arid Southwest and the stifling swamps of Florida, I'd pitied the Spanish, and felt glad to live in an era of bug repellent, ice cubes, and climate-controlled cars. Now, for a moment at least, I envied their long-ago trek, across a continent as yet unconquered by chain saws and interstates.

THE MISSISSIPPI

CONQUISTADOR'S LAST STAND

> . . . the river
> Is a strong brown god—sullen, untamed and
> intractable
> —T. S. Eliot, "The Dry Salvages"

BY THE TIME De Soto's men arrived at the far side of the Appalachians, one Spaniard wrote, "the horses were tired and thin, and the Christians likewise fatigued." Reaching a peaceful settlement in present-day Tennessee, the army feasted on native cuisine: corn porridge sweetened with honey, "butter" made of bear grease, and oil extracted from acorns and walnuts, which was nourishing but caused "some flatulence."

For two weeks the Spanish farted and frolicked with the Indians, even swimming with them in a river by the settlement. Then De Soto pushed his army's R & R too far. He asked his hosts to provide thirty women. When the Indians failed to comply, De Soto burned their corn fields, took their chief hostage, and pressed five hundred of his subjects into service as baggage carriers.

At the next town, soldiers in the lead began looting storehouses of food, "as was their custom." This time, natives responded with force, beating the looters with clubs and gathering up bows and arrows.

When De Soto arrived, "carelessly and unarmed," he found himself surrounded by a crowd of bellicose natives.

Always at his best in a tight spot, De Soto feigned fury at his men, grabbing an Indian club and joining the natives in thrashing the looters. Then he mollified the local chief, leading him by the hand, away from the town and toward the approaching army. Once out of danger, De Soto put the chief and his retainers in chains, "and told them they could not go until giving him a guide and Indians for carrying."

During his stay in Tennessee, De Soto sent scouts in search of the gold he'd hoped to find in the mountains. But after discovering nothing, he swung his army south, toward Coosa, a wealthy Indian nation centered in north Georgia. Coosa's ruler greeted De Soto "in a carrying chair borne on the shoulders of his principal men, seated on a cushion, and covered with a robe of marten skins." His realm was rich with corn and beans and with orchards of apples and plums—"one of the best and most abundant" lands in La Florida, a soldier wrote.

But De Soto treated this hospitable chiefdom as he had Cofitachequi. After resting and refueling his army, he seized Coosa's ruler and enchained many of his people for the onward journey. He then marched southwest, toward the Gulf coast, where he'd earlier arranged to meet supply ships from Cuba.

Though De Soto had yet to find gold, his expedition to this point was a modest success, certainly as compared with earlier forays in La Florida. In just over a year, the conquistador had reconnoitered a thousand miles of territory, found pearls and promising lands for settlement, and lost only a handful of men to death or desertion.

His army was now well fed, well rested, and well served by hundreds of native porters, servants, and concubines. The Spanish were marching in late summer through a gentle and bountiful land. They were probably more content than at any time during their long journey, and utterly unprepared for the disaster about to befall them.

ROLLING DOWN THROUGH the hills of east Tennessee, I followed a highway marked "scenic," which it might have been if viewed from a

DE SOTO'S ROUTE
(2 of 3)

double-decker bus affording a glimpse of the distant Smokies. At
sedan level, all I could see was a continuum of trailer parks, self-
storage units, and furniture and fireworks factories. The roadside
scenery in north Georgia was drabber still: mostly low, windowless
carpet mills. Checking into a motel with a flyswatter on the pillow and
trains rumbling by in the night, I awoke to heavy rain and a dispiriting
search for Coosa's capital. My quest ended at a park beside a hydro-
electric dam, where I asked a ranger for directions to the former Indian town.

"It's at the bottom of the reregulation pool," he said, pointing at a
reservoir. "Got a scuba suit?"

Many other riverside settlements visited by De Soto in Tennessee
and Georgia had suffered a similar fate. But one survived, spectacularly so. A few days after leaving Coosa's capital, the Spanish reached
"a large town alongside a good river, and there they bartered for some
Indian women," in exchange for mirrors and knives. The Spanish
called the town Itaba, or Ytaua, close to the name recorded by a missionary to the Cherokee who came upon Etowah 274 years later.

"Through the thick forest trees, a stupendous pile met the eye,"
the Reverend Elias Cornelius wrote. He described several "artificial
mounds" and, using a vine, measured one at over a thousand feet in
circumference. His Indian guides knew nothing of the mounds' origins, telling Cornelius, "They were never put up by our people."

Other mysterious mounds turned up across the American frontier
as settlers pushed west from the original thirteen colonies. Pioneers
found earthworks shaped like cones, or truncated pyramids, or giant animals, including the quarter-mile-long "Great Serpent Mound," which
slithers across southern Ohio. Indians dwelling nearby, like those at
Etowah, claimed no connection to the mounds. Nor, in the view of
whites, were Indian "savages" capable of such monumental architecture. "It seems probable," Cornelius wrote of Etowah's mounds, that
"they were erected by another race, who once inhabited the country."

Unmasking the identity of this "lost race" became an early American obsession, captivating men such as Thomas Jefferson, as well as
fanciful thinkers who believed the mound builders were ancient émigrés from the Old World. The list of candidates came to include

Phoenicians, Canaanites, Hindus, Vikings, medieval Welsh—even refugees from the lost continent of Atlantis. In the Book of Mormon, Joseph Smith ascribed the mounds' construction to an ancient Near East band called the Nephites, who had been sent by God to settle America.

Not until the late nineteenth century did archaeologists conclude that the mound builders were, in fact, Native Americans, albeit ones who lived quite differently from the dispersed tribes encountered by pioneers. Constructed centuries and in some cases millennia before Europeans arrived, mounds were the work of wealthy agricultural societies that possessed the manpower to construct huge edifices from baskets of dirt. The largest mound complex on the continent, at Cahokia, near St. Louis, covered five square miles, with a central plaza a thousand feet long. At its peak, in the twelfth century, Cahokia had a population estimated at fifteen thousand—larger than medieval London or Paris, or any city north of Mexico until Philadelphia surpassed it in the late 1700s.

By the time De Soto arrived, the greatest of the mound complexes in the Midwest and South had been abandoned or gone into decline, possibly because they'd become too big, exhausting the readily accessible supply of wood, soil, and game. But the underlying structure of mound culture remained. From Florida to the Carolinas to the Mississippi Valley, De Soto's men described city-states centered on the cultivation of corn, and ceremonial mounds that towered above the South's river plains.

Today, the mound complexes that survive aren't quite so conspicuous. To reach Etowah, I exited an interstate just north of Atlanta's exurban fringe, and wound between a chemical plant and a Glad Wrap factory before following a small road to the Bow and Arrow Mobile Home Park. I was about to pull in and ask for directions when I noticed a steep, sawed-off hill looming just behind the trailer park's stunted skyline.

On a wet weekday in early winter, I was the only visitor to the small park enclosing Etowah. A trail led me across a ditch ten feet deep, the remains of a moat that once guarded the town, and into a field: formerly, a plaza leading up to the largest mound. Three acres at its base, the sixty-three-foot mound had a ramp snaking up to a wide, flat top. This served as a platform for the dwellings of priests and chiefs, the penthouse dwellers of early America.

The summit was now bare, except for grass. But standing atop Etowah's earthen throne, it was easy to imagine a bygone ruler surveying his domain. On one side of the mound ran a swift green river, filled with V-shaped rock dams: the remains of ancient weirs used by Indians to trap fish. The cane still growing beside the river had provided raw material for baskets, mats, spears, and arrows. Beyond the river spread fertile bottomland, filled now with cows but formerly with maize. Only the mobile home park intruded on my time travel. From this vantage, the trailers looked like tiny boxes, a transient camp beside Etowah's thousand-year-old dome.

Retreating down the hill, I visited the park's small museum, which displayed artifacts unearthed at Etowah's mortuary mound. One pair of marble effigies depicted a chiefly couple: the man seated lotus style, his small-breasted mate resting on her knees, legs elegantly tucked beneath skirted buttocks. Highly stylized, the figures had flat foreheads, full lips, and pupil-less almond eyes, as striking and beautiful as Modigliani sculptures.

Other relics revealed not only the artistry of mound culture, but its geographic breadth. Centuries before railroads, canals, or interstates, Etowah's artisans tapped a trade network that brought copper from the Great Lakes, sharks' teeth and sea turtle shell from south Florida, and mica from the Appalachians. Mound architecture was even more widely spread; earthworks had been found from Florida to Oklahoma to south Ontario. Touring the museum, as haunting flute music played on the sound system, I felt the same envy I had while wandering the Joyce Kilmer Forest. The Spanish were the first and last Europeans to glimpse an astonishing culture that most Americans had never known existed.

My reverie was interrupted by chortles in the hall. I stepped out to find two paunchy middle-aged men, clad in the green pants and khaki shirts of park employees. Their matched appearance and drawling banter made them seem twinned, like the museum's mortuary figures. When I asked what sort of visitors Etowah attracted, the two men broke into chiming guffaws, finishing each other's sentences.

"There's your Satanists, your witches, your Druids—"

Marble effigies at Etowah Indian Mounds Historic Site, Cartersville, Georgia

"New Agers, Nuwaubians, nutcases—"

"You name it, we get it here."

Ken Atkins was Etowah's site manager; his sidekick, Steve McCarty, a veteran ranger. Despite their jocular manner, the two men weren't pulling my leg with their catalogue of park visitors. Etowah and other mounds had become magnets for modern-day seekers—heirs, in a sense, to the nineteenth-century fantasists who attributed mounds' construction to Atlanteans or the Lost Tribes of Israel.

New Age visitors buried crystals by the mounds, to "reenergize them," and plotted ley lines in search of harmonic convergence. Others interred cremated ashes, or performed obscure rites involving live gerbils and dead chickens. "We've had women standing on top of the mounds clutching daggers, and a guy praying over a crystal so big it looked like kryptonite," Ken said. "No animal sacrifices that we know of, but it wouldn't surprise me."

Oddest of all was the United Nuwaubian Nation of Moors, a group that claimed descent from Egyptians, aliens, and Native Americans.

The nation's leader styled himself, variously, as Dr. Malachi Z. York-El, Atume-Re, Chief Black Eagle, and an extraterrestrial from the Planet Rizq. At their Georgia compound, the Nuwaubians had built a sphinx and pyramids and adopted Egyptian dress. They often came to Etowah to commune with their kin, both earthbound and alien.

"They said a flying saucer was going to come down and pick them up off Mound A," Steve said, referring to the tallest mound. "It never came, unfortunately. We were going to help all these people pack up and wave good-bye to them."

The stream of strange visitors created management headaches at Etowah and other mound sites. Traditionally, rangers' main concern had been catching night thieves who dug for artifacts. Now, the problem was people *burying* crystals and other items, which technically had to be preserved and catalogued (most mounds are state-protected archaeological sites).

To complicate matters, Creek Indians—descendants of the Etowans, and the designated native overseers of the site—had declared the mounds ceremonially closed; they regarded any ritual there as a desecration. But rangers could only issue citations for trespassing or damage to state property; they couldn't interfere with visitors' First Amendment right to worship as they chose.

"It's sad, really," said Steve, who moonlighted as an ordained minister. "People want to make some kind of spiritual connection with these mounds, and honor the Indians who lived here. But, if anything, they're doing the opposite."

DE SOTO'S ARMY spent several months crossing Coosa's realm without engaging in a serious fight. But as they neared the Indian nation west of Coosa, signs abounded that their summer idyll was about to end. The first clue was the appearance of heavily fortified towns, enclosed in double walls of crisscrossed logs, cut through with slits for firing arrows. At one town, the Spanish were met by the son of Tascalusa, "a powerful lord and very feared in that land." Though the envoy promised aid to the Spanish, De Soto didn't trust him and dispatched two spies to accompany the chief's son back to his home.

Marching on, De Soto reached Tascalusa's capital, and found the ruler awaiting the Spanish on the balcony of his mound-top dwelling. Tascalusa was "so large," one Spaniard wrote, "that, to the opinion of all, he was a giant." Clad in a full-length feather cloak and turbanlike headdress, he perched on high cushions surrounded by retainers, one of whom sheltered him from the sun with a staff topped by a deerskin battle standard.

De Soto put on a show of his own, replaying his famed entrance before Atahualpa. He sent horsemen galloping into the plaza before Tascalusa's mound, "turning them from one side to the other" and toward the ruler's perch. Though "horses were held in great dread among those people," the Spanish display left the ruler unmoved. "With great gravity and unconcern," Tascalusa "from time to time raised his eyes and looked as if in disdain." Nor did he rise from his cushion when De Soto dismounted and approached.

Having established his preeminence, Tascalusa fed his guests and entertained them with dancers. De Soto reciprocated by staging jousting matches and horse races—another vain attempt to impress his host, who "appeared to think little of all this." The ruler thought even less of De Soto's inevitable demand for women and baggage-carriers. "He responded that he was not accustomed to serving anyone, rather that all served him."

For the first time in La Florida, De Soto had met a leader as haughty and headstrong as himself, and even craftier. The conquistador insisted that his host stay the night near the Spanish. Tascalusa complied, but not before sending messengers to a town called Mavila, five days' travel away. He told De Soto that his envoys would arrange for the army to be provided at Mavila with fresh porters, as well as a hundred women, "and those which [the Spanish] most desired."

As the army marched on, with Tascalusa in tow, "and always the Indian with the sunshade in front of his lord," one of De Soto's personal guards strayed in search of a runaway slave, and was slain by Indians. In a fit of anger, De Soto threatened to burn Tascalusa unless he turned over the killers. Once again, the ruler promised to comply—as soon as the army reached Mavila.

Whether he knew it or not, Tascalusa had found De Soto's weak spot. Cool and calculating in a crisis, the conquistador was quick to anger and rash when enraged. Ignoring his spies, who warned of "evilly disposed" Indians gathering at Mavila, De Soto raced ahead of his army with a vanguard of only forty men, impatient to collect all that Tascalusa had promised him.

Mavila, one of De Soto's men wrote, was "a small and very strongly palisaded town," situated on a plain. Houses outside the walls had been hastily torn down, in apparent preparation for battle. De Soto's captains advised him to camp outside the town. Replying "that he was tired out with sleeping in the open field," De Soto recklessly entered Mavila with Tascalusa and a dozen soldiers.

They were greeted by several hundred natives singing and proffering gifts of marten skins. The Mavilans also distracted their visitors with a dance "by marvelously beautiful women," allowing Tascalusa to slip into a council house to confer with his confederates. When De Soto demanded that he come out, Tascalusa refused. A captain sent in to fetch him discovered a crowd of armed men. Other houses were found to conceal more warriors, "a good five thousand."

Finally realizing he'd walked into a trap, De Soto "placed his helmet on his head and commanded that all should mount their horses." One Spaniard drew his sword and slashed an Indian. Then warriors rushed from their hideouts, "shouting loudly and discharging their arrows." Five Spaniards quickly fell; the others managed to escape through the town gate, wounded and having lost their mounts and weapons.

De Soto had to have twenty arrows plucked from his thick cotton tunic. Even so, he demanded a horse and lance, and slew several Indians who chased the retreating Spanish. But knightly bravado couldn't solve the dilemma De Soto now faced. While he'd been inside Mavila, the army's Indian porters had arrived and laid their burdens by the town walls. As soon as De Soto fled, the porters moved everything inside the walls, including weapons that soldiers had carelessly left in their packs. Mavilans struck off the porters' chains and armed them with bows. Then they closed the town gate, "began to beat their drums and to raise banners with a great yell, and to open our trunks and bundles and display from the top of the wall all that we had brought."

Storming Mavila looked suicidal: natives inside the well-fortified bastion hugely outnumbered the Spanish. But if the Spanish retreated, stripped of supplies and their ability to overawe natives, they would be left weak in a hostile territory ruled by the determined and canny Tascalusa.

De Soto's anxious lieutenants voiced "different opinions," but as usual the conquistador ignored their concerns and went on the offensive. The Indians had used guile to exploit his overconfidence; now he would turn the same tactic against them. With forty horsemen, De Soto rode up to Mavila's gate. A few Indians came out to skirmish, but didn't stray far from the safety of the town. Then the Spanish turned and galloped off, as if fleeing. When Indians poured out of Mavila in pursuit, the horsemen turned and charged, killing scores with their lances.

De Soto then encircled the town, his best-armed men on foot and his horsemen behind. The foot soldiers attacked in unison, using axes to smash the palisade and firebrands to torch the houses inside. As the fighting raged, so, too, did the flames, flushing Mavilans from their fortified shelter. Horsemen cut them down or drove them back into the inferno, "where, piled up one on top of the other, they were suffocated and burned to death."

The battle continued until dark, without a single Indian warrior surrendering. "We killed them all," one Spaniard tersely reported, "some with the fire, others with the swords, others with the lances." When a warrior realized he was the last still standing, he "climbed a tree that was in the wall itself, and removed the cord from the bow and attached it to his neck and to a branch of the tree and hanged himself."

One of De Soto's men estimated the Indian dead at twenty-five hundred; another put the toll at three thousand, not counting the many wounded whom soldiers "found afterward dead in the huts and by the road." If these figures are close to accurate, the massacre at Mavila, on October 18, 1540, rivals the Civil War battle of Antietam as the deadliest day of combat ever recorded on U.S. soil.

The victors had little to celebrate. More than twenty soldiers lay dead, including De Soto's brother-in-law and nephew. Many of the Spanish were "killed by arrow wounds in the eyes or mouth, for the Indians, knowing that their bodies were armed, shot at their faces." About two hundred others—almost half the surviving force—were badly wounded, many by multiple arrows; dozens died after the battle. Scores of horses had been killed or injured, too. And the army's baggage, including the pearls looted at Cofitachequi, had gone up in flames. De Soto's men, one wrote, "were left like Arabs, empty-handed and with great hardship."

They were also left to forage and find shelter in a hellscape out of Hieronymus Bosch. Mavila's smoldering pyre illuminated the battlefield. Exhausted and thirsty soldiers who sought to drink at a pond found its water "tinged with the blood of the dead." Others skinned slain horses to get at the meat. Ghastliest of all was the plight of the injured. Desperate for salve, soldiers "busied themselves in cutting open the dead Indians and taking the fat to use as ointment and oil in treating wounds."

De Soto was forced to linger a month at Mavila, waiting for his army to recover. While there, he learned that ships had landed on the Gulf coast, just six days' travel away. But De Soto was no longer ready to meet his supply fleet. He now had nothing to show for his journey, not even pearls, and his men might want to board the ships and flee to Cuba. If word of his ravaged and empty-handed state got out, De Soto's reputation, and his hope of finding new recruits to colonize La Florida, would be ruined. "Consequently," one of his men wrote, "he determined not to give news of himself so long as he did not find a rich land."

In late November, with winter approaching, De Soto once again turned away from the sea, marching his depleted army back into the American interior.

TRAILING DE SOTO from Coosa to Tascalusa, I eased out of the piedmont and piney woods, into the black-soil plain of central Alabama. Most De Soto scholars believe Mavila was located somewhere along the Alabama River between Selma and Mobile. But archaeologists haven't yet found a site with the mass of bones and Spanish artifacts one would expect. Fire and, later, frequent flooding may have destroyed all evidence of the battle.

Charles Hudson, the professor who mapped De Soto's route, thought the likeliest match for Mavila was a place now known as Old Cahawba, where remains had been found of a fortified Indian settlement that abruptly vanished about the time of De Soto's march. To reach it, I followed a roughly paved road until it dead-ended at a bluff by the Alabama. There was no trace of the Indian settlement, apart from a dimly visible moat, encircled by a glade of oak trees wreathed in Spanish moss.

The wealthy cotton town that arose on the same spot in the 1800s had likewise vanished, swept away by the Civil War and constant floods. All that remained were grassed-over mounds where a courthouse and brick stores once stood, and a few lonely columns of antebellum mansions.

Old Cahawba was one of the South's most haunting ruins, and a dolefully apt memorial to the bloodbath that may have occurred there in 1540. But I couldn't conjure Mavila. Hoping to catch some echo of battle, I'd instead found its opposite: a bucolic and silent refuge where nothing stirred, except a few deer startled by my boot steps.

RATHER THAN DRIVE on and leave Mavila unexamined, I decided to track down a man who had been recommended to me as an expert on sixteenth-century combat. Kent Goff was an army major who had served as a bayonet-drill instructor at West Point and an intelligence officer in the first Gulf War; now, when his military schedule allowed, he taught college history. I caught up with him in a classroom a day's drive from Old Cahawba, where we chatted quietly as his students took a World Civ exam.

A clean-cut midwesterner in pressed khakis, polo shirt, and spit-polished black shoes, Kent could recite long passages from *The De Soto Chronicles* almost verbatim. But he mined the Spanish accounts for very different clues than other students of the expedition.

"I read the *Chronicles* as after-action reports," he said, using a military term for detailed postmortems of battle. "You have two warrior societies meeting each other for the first time. It's a fascinating case study of combat."

One insight he'd gleaned was that tactics often trumped manpower and firepower. In most battles, Indians had the advantage of numbers, and their longbows had greater range and accuracy than the Spaniards' crossbows and clumsy muskets. Natives were also much more mobile than their heavily armored foes, at least in woods and swamps, where horses were of little use. What they lacked was experience of European-style warfare.

"Indians fought in the traditional style of the warrior individual," Kent said, "with great courage and in concert with family members." The Spanish, by contrast, fought as cogs in sixteenth-century Europe's most efficient military machine. "It was like the Romans versus the Celts. On an individual level, Celts were better fighters. But led in a group by centurions, the Romans could beat ten times their number."

At Mavila, he said, the Spanish formed a "combined arms team": foot soldiers, horsemen, and harquebusiers, launching a coordinated assault. On a signal—a musket shot—they attacked simultaneously from four directions. Soldiers with shields protected axmen from arrows as they chopped at the walls. Infantry poured through the breach.

"Indians had never encountered this kind of warfare," Kent said. The resulting surprise and disarray helped to explain the lopsided casualty figures. "When the Spanish pierced Indian lines and natives saw their fellow warriors and blood relations go down, they were stunned and broken," he said. "And they couldn't outrun a horse. So it became a massacre."

Also, while native archers had an edge in long-range duels, their foes were much deadlier in close combat. In addition to steel swords, De Soto's men wielded a versatile weapon called the halberd, a heavy lance topped with a hook, ax blade, and bayonet. Kent had studied a sixteenth-century manual on infantry tactics and demonstrated the use of the halberd, using me as a dummy.

"First, you thrust at the face," he said, jabbing the point of his imaginary weapon at my nose. I flinched and raised my arm, as a warrior would his shield.

"Now you can't see me well," he said, "so I can swing my halberd around and whack you on the head with the butt end." I stumbled back, as if stunned by the blow.

"Now I take another step forward, with extended arms, and bring down the ax blade." He made a motion like a man chopping wood. Kent's students looked up from their exams as their suddenly animated professor dispatched a visiting writer.

"Here's another move," Kent said, taking up his phantom weapon again. "You feint toward the head, then rotate the weapon, drop it down and use the hook to grab your enemy behind the knee, and then jerk. That upends him, and once he's down all you have to do is finish him off with the point." He pretended to skewer me, as if gigging a frog.

"The Spanish put a lot of thought into how to kill people efficiently," Kent said, resting his halberd. "And they would have left just horrible wounds on unarmored opponents. Arms, legs, heads, and guts strewn everywhere. The Spanish covered in blood and gore. But, judging from the *Chronicles,* these guys liked their work."

Kent acknowledged that this passion for close-range killing made the Spaniards "unpleasant people," at least by our standards. As a soldier, though, he admired their endurance and discipline. "Navy SEALs would be dropping with exhaustion after what these guys went through. This is a thousands-mile trek, right up there with the epic marches of military history."

Kent was also awed by De Soto's ability to hold his men together in the face of extraordinary obstacles. "The Spanish have no supply line, they're living off the land, they lose most of their gear at Mavila," he said. Yet the expedition continued for several thousand miles after that.

Kent checked the clock and began to gather his students' exams. "To most people, De Soto and his men seem like creatures from another world," he said. "To me, they're prototypical Americans—spirited and resourceful adventurers who never gave up and had absolute confidence in themselves."

DE SOTO LEFT Mavila having lost more than a hundred of the six hundred men he had landed in Florida the year before. The weather was turning cold and the army desperately needed food and shelter. The Spanish fortunes had fallen so far that one nobleman wore a torn Indian blanket and otherwise was "bare-headed, bare-footed, without hose or shoes, a shield at his back, a sword without a scabbard." He "had to look for his supper with his fingernails."

Marching northwest, into Mississippi, De Soto made winter camp at a settlement called Chicasa, where fleeing Indians had left a large supply of corn. But late one night, natives slipped past the Spanish sentries, "two by two and four by four, with some little jars in which they brought fire." They torched Chicasa, burning to death a dozen Spaniards, fifty-seven horses, and several hundred pigs. What remained of the army's gear, including saddles, weapons, and scarce clothing, also went up in flames. "If the Indians had known how to pursue their victory," one Spaniard wrote, "this would have been the last day in the lives of all the Christians."

Instead, the Indians withdrew, and it was at this juncture that the Spanish displayed the resilience and resourcefulness Kent Goff so admired. They hurriedly fashioned bellows from bear hides and built a makeshift forge; cut down ash trees to craft lances; made new saddles and shields; and wove grass into sleeping mats. A week after the fire, when the Indians resumed their attack, the Spanish were able to repel them.

Still, the fire at Chicasa, following so soon after the disaster at Mavila, tipped the balance of fear between invaders and natives. In spring, as De Soto marched west, "something occurred that they say has never happened in the Indies," one Spaniard wrote. Before Chicasa, natives had fought mostly when provoked and usually in defense of food and women. Now, it was they who initiated battle, brazenly erecting a stockade directly in the army's path. The three hundred warriors inside wore horned headdresses and painted themselves with stripes, "their faces black and the eyes ringed round in red in order to look more ferocious."

De Soto ordered a frontal assault, "saying that if he did not do so, they would become emboldened to attack him at a time when they could do him more hurt." The Spanish triumphed, at the cost of fifteen dead and many more wounded. Captured Indians told the Spanish they had sought a fight "only with the intent of proving themselves against us, and for no other purpose." De Soto's once resplendent army could no longer overawe natives simply by marching into their territory.

De Soto, however, had no choice but to plunge ahead, in search of large settlements; without their stores to pillage, his army would starve. He led his hungry and wounded men across northern Mississippi, through "many swamps and thick woods," until they reached a corn-rich province called Quizquiz. The Spanish immediately seized several hundred women as hostages. But in a shift that reflected the army's weakness, De Soto didn't keep his captives long. "For fear of war," he quickly released them, in hopes "he could have peace" and desperately needed supplies.

ALMOST IN PASSING, the army's chroniclers wrote that Quizquiz lay beside *el rio grande*—"the great river." In the Algonquian language, the river had a different name: Misi Sipi, meaning Great Water. Before embarking on my trip, I'd gone to see *Discovery of the Mississippi,* one of eight canvases in the U.S. Capitol rotunda that celebrate great moments in American history. The painting depicts De Soto dressed in satin and shining armor, surveying the Mississippi from astride a white stallion. A priest gazes heavenward as soldiers haul a cross and cannon to the river's bank, half-naked Indians cowering before them. Commissioned by Congress in 1847, the work is a minor classic of Manifest Destiny, glorifying the triumph of white civilization over Indian savagery.

The painting is also pure fiction, beginning with the natives' teepees and feathered bonnets—Plains Indian props, transplanted to sixteenth-century Mississippi. The Spanish trappings are just as inaccurate. By May 1541, De Soto's men looked more like natives than conquering Europeans, having lost or worn out their clothes and replaced them with buckskins and Indian blankets.

Nor did the Spanish raise a cross or perform any other rite upon reaching the river. They were sick and starved and cared only about "little walnuts" and a supply of maize they found in Quizquiz. The Mississippi, in any case, was already known to the Spanish. For two decades, mariners along the Gulf coast had observed the mouth of a

Discovery of the Mississippi, *a painting in the U.S. Capitol Rotunda by William Powell*

great waterway they called the River of the Holy Spirit, the same name given it by most of De Soto's men.

Most inaccurate of all was the painting's portrayal of cowering Indians. In reality, natives patrolled the Mississippi in an armada of two hundred canoes packed with warriors in battle regalia. The dugouts, bedecked with shields, awnings, and banners, "had the appearance of a beautiful fleet of galleys," wrote one of De Soto's men. Each afternoon, for the duration of the conquistador's monthlong stay by the Mississippi, Indians gave a great shout and rained arrows on the Spanish camp.

The river itself, as first described by the Spanish, was of little interest except as an obstacle. The lone recorded detail concerning De Soto's arrival at the river was his discovery of "an abundance of timber," suitable for rafts, which the army set about building. Then, before dawn on June 8, De Soto ordered the four barges loaded with "men who he was confident would succeed in gaining the land in spite of the Indians and assure the crossing or die in doing it."

Natives evidently hadn't expected a predawn crossing, and left the opposite shore undefended. But the river trip was nonetheless daunting. The Mississippi was larger than the Danube, wrote one awed Spaniard: so wide, another man added, that "if a man stood still on the other side, one could not tell whether he were a man or something else." He was also struck by the river's fish, including one ungainly species, "a third of which is head," with "large spines like a sharp shoemaker's awl." This is the first European description of a catfish.

Most fearsome of all was the river's current, which sent uprooted trees shooting through the roily water. Men in the rafts had to paddle almost a mile upriver before crossing, so they could land at a designated spot across from their camp. Finally, after five difficult hours, the Spanish succeeded in ferrying every man and beast across.

"They gave many thanks to God," one Spaniard wrote, "because in their opinion, nothing so difficult could ever be offered them again."

BY THE TIME I crossed into Mississippi, I'd compiled a small album of colorful claims on De Soto by the towns along his route. In Georgia, there had been the De Soto Nut House; in Alabama, the De Soto Caverns and their aboveground amusement park, with cartoon cutouts of Spaniards and Indians battling at "De Soto's Squirt Gun Maze." A nearby town displayed a block-length mural titled *Chief Coosa Welcomes De Soto to Childersburg*. This was strange, since I'd already visited Coosa's capital two hundred miles back, in north Georgia. But Childersburg, like many towns, refused to acknowledge the Hudson Route and stood by a decades-old claim that *it* was the true site of Coosa.

Mississippi was even stauncher in its defense of De Soto lore. Entering the town of Aberdeen, I pondered a sign stating, with startling specificity, that on December 16, 1540, De Soto "marched up what is now this street." Two hours on, I reached a town that outdid even Aberdeen: Hernando, seat of DeSoto County. Town fathers in the nineteenth century laid out Hernando in Spanish colonial style, with a twelve-street grid and a central plaza. The courthouse, decorated with murals of De

MISSOURI

OZARK MOUNTAINS

ARKANSAS

TENNESSEE

OKLAHOMA

DE SOTO
1541-2

Little
Rock

Friar's
Point

Memphis
Walls

Hernando

Oxford
Clarksdale
Aberdeen

Columbus

Arkansas
City

LUIS DE MOSCOSO
1542-3

Jackson

LOUISIANA

Mississippi River

MISSISSIPPI

TEXAS

New Orleans

0   50 Mi

0   80 Km

DE SOTO'S ROUTE
(3 of 3)

Soto, had a red star set in the marble floor, marking the exact spot where the conquistador slept on his way to "discovering" the Mississippi.

As to where, precisely, De Soto launched his army across the river, almost every county along the Mississippi awarded the honor to itself. Each competing claim was buttressed by the work of local antiquarians who had found irrefutable proof that the True Crossing began in their district. After spending several days studying these hermeneutic tracts, and trying to follow historic markers as elliptical as pirate maps, I began to appreciate why Charles Hudson had needed years to elucidate De Soto's path across the South.

Characteristically, the Hudson Route bypassed all the traditional claimants, instead meeting the river near an unsung community called Walls, just below Memphis. So I followed a small road west from Hernando until it dipped, suddenly, from a wooded bluff into the low open plain of the Mississippi Delta. A carpet of green and coffee-colored fields spread before me, wet and lush even in winter.

The Delta is one of the most fertile plains on earth, layered, like a rich chocolate cake, with alluvial soil scooped up by the river during its long course through the continent. The Delta is also the nation's poorest region, a legacy of its settlement by former slaves who were reenslaved after the Civil War, as cotton sharecroppers. When mechanical pickers displaced field laborers, many Deltans were left stranded in rural ghettos, of which Walls remained one.

Entering the town, I passed sagging weatherboard shacks, derelict public housing, and the sorriest trailer park I'd ever seen, with snarling dogs chained before battered single-wides. At the only open shop, a convenience store, I asked the woman at the counter if she could direct me to the site of De Soto's riverside camp.

"Say who?"

"De Soto. The Spanish explorer who discovered the Mississippi near here."

She chuckled, lighting a Kool. "There's a few Mexicans at the trailer park. Could be he's there. Ask me, I'd take a gun."

A lean, tattooed customer came over. "There's an old river landing down the road where we used to go and get drunk," she said. "Don't know the history, but that might be your spot."

Lacking other leads, I followed her directions, into a maze of back roads, none of which brought me to the river. Then I saw a dirt track leading to an earthen levee. At the top of the embankment stood a sign that read, "No Loaded Weapons or Shooting." As the road dipped down the levee's other bank, the Huck Finn in me stirred. The Mighty Mississippi, the Father of Waters, lay just ahead.

If only I could see it. My view was obscured by a black cloud pouring from a truck parked on the riverbank. Going over to see whether anyone needed help, I found two men in grimy camouflage standing by the truck's tailgate. They were stuffing something into a dented trash can from which billowed flames and foul-smelling smoke.

"What are you doing?" I asked.

"Cooking wire," one of them said. He poked in the can with a stick and held up a tangle of singed copper wire. "Scrap dealers won't buy it with the insulation on. So we come down here to burn off the plastic. Folks don't like you doing this near town, on account of the smell." Once stripped, he said, the wire brought 75 cents a pound, which struck me as a difficult and unpleasant way to make a living.

"What are *you* doing?" the man asked.

"Looking for where De Soto crossed the Mississippi."

He heaved another coil of wire into the can. "Coulda been here, coulda been anywhere. It's a big river."

I gazed out at the water. The river was turbid and swift and a mile or more wide, just as the Spanish described. But the bank was paved with ugly concrete slabs, held together by wire mesh: revetments, the men said, to guard against erosion. A barge loaded with coal churned past. The wind shifted, enveloping us in acrid smoke from the wire inferno. My inner Huck withered.

En route to Walls, I'd conceived a vague plan to cross the river in a small craft, so I could grasp a little of what the Spaniards experienced in their rafts. But the wire burners said they'd lived their whole lives by the Mississippi and rarely ventured on it. "Definitely not now, not in this water, no sirree," one of them said. "Not in anything smaller than a tugboat."

I tried my luck downriver, only to hear the same refrain at every

landing. The water was too high, too rough, too unpredictable, a vor-
tex of unseen dangers. Boats got caught in whirlpools or crushed by
hidden dikes; were capsized by huge waves from passing barges; were
speared by sunken trees, called blues, which filled with gas and exploded out of the deep, like torpedoes. "It looks like lazy ol' man river
out there," a grizzled fisherman warned, "but believe you me, that water will eat you right up."

I'D ALMOST RESIGNED myself to a ride on a faux steamboat, at one
of the Delta's casinos, when I met a man named Bubba, who told me
about a "river rat" named John Ruskey, who "might could take you
out." I didn't know what "river rat" meant—my first thought was
"drowned"—but I tracked him to the cellar of a former tire factory,
which he used as a workshop for hewing cypress canoes. A lean man
with a full beard, graying shoulder-length locks, and a feather stuck
rakishly in his wide-brimmed hat, John Ruskey looked like a Confederate sawyer. He was actually from Colorado, which explained why he
was willing to take me out on the Missisissippi when no one else
would.

"People around here think I'm crazy," he said, as we loaded a canoe on his truck. "They've heard so many horror stories since birth
that they don't get on the river unless it's in something motorized and
conditions are perfect." He handed me a life jacket. "Now, I have to
warn you, if you fall in, you probably won't be able to swim to the
bank. The current's too strong, it'd take an hour, and by that time hy-
pothermia and exhaustion will get you. So stay with the canoe and
don't let go of your paddle."

As we drove between cotton fields, John told me about his first
trip on the Mississippi, several decades before. Smitten by the romance of the river, he and a high school friend from Colorado had
built a raft from plywood and oil drums. They launched it in Wisconsin and had floated all the way to Memphis when, in the middle of a
chess game, the raft struck a submerged pylon. "It looked like someone had crushed soda crackers and scattered them on the river," John
said of the raft. He and his friend had to be fished out by a patrol boat.

John later settled in Mississippi to play guitar with the Delta's legendary bluesmen. But he couldn't stay away from the river. So he began making canoes and working as a guide on summer trips. "You're far safer in a canoe than a motorboat," he said, "because you're never going so fast that if you hit something you'll get into big trouble."

We reached Friar's Point, one of the many river towns that laid claim to De Soto. The setting, at least, matched my image of the Mississippi much more closely than other landings I'd visited. The bank was free of concrete revetments, casino paddle-wheelers, or men burning wire—just a sandbar strewn with driftwood.

It took us only a minute to launch the canoe and glide out into the water. Then we paddled upriver, along the shore, as De Soto's men had done. I had little experience in canoes, apart from summer-camp floats in Pocono ponds. But with John in back, performing the hard work, all I had to do was paddle and keep watch on the water ahead.

From shore, the river's surface had looked deceptively uniform. Up close, with John's guidance, I saw its variations. Glassy, seemingly calm patches denoted boils, reverse whirlpools spiraling up from the depths. Rough patches revealed eddies circling rocks, or the limbs of drowned trees. Shears formed at the point where the current hit an eddy. "It'll be a bit of work getting around this bend," John said each time the shore curved. Contrary to what I'd imagined, the current was strongest around bends rather than in the middle of the river.

There were no locks or dams on the lower Mississippi, leaving this stretch of river relatively untamed. The shore looked just as wild. Though the land had been logged many times, the Delta's topsoil was so rich that nature quickly reclaimed abandoned fields. John said the riverside teemed with white-tailed deer, turkey, beaver, boars, even the rare cougar. There were also a dozen different species of trees—a dense, lush forest much like the one the Spanish described.

"The lower Mississippi was once America's Amazon," John said, "twenty-two million acres of hardwood forest." As an expert canoe builder, he reckoned that some trees must have been six or more feet in diameter for Indians to make dugouts like those De Soto's men saw, each filled with dozens of warriors.

After paddling for several miles, we pulled the canoe onto a narrow beach of deep, sticky goop—what locals call gumbo, or Missis-sippi mud. John said most of the silt came from the Missouri River, which dredged the Plains before emptying into the Mississippi. "I fig-ure there's more of Montana in the Delta than there is of Mississippi," he said. This was a startling reminder of the river's immensity; it was al-most four thousand miles long and served as a drainage basin for close to half the continent.

The river was also a thoroughfare for three-quarters of the nation's grain. We watched 250-foot-long barges of barley crawl by, tied together to form massive flotillas. "If you get too close to them they can't even see you," John said. "On their radar, a canoe just looks like another log."

Once the barges passed, we shoved off and paddled straight across the river. Perched in the canoe's bow, eyes trained on the Arkansas shore, I realized we were slipping rapidly downriver, pressed by the wind and current. Logs and one entire tree chuted past, limbs flailing in the foamy water. It took us twenty minutes of hard paddling to reach an island only midway across the river.

The passage would have been far trickier for De Soto's men, who crossed at night. "Things get weird out here in the dark," John said. "You lose your sense of direction and get disoriented. You have to nav-igate by the shapes of trees and snags and their relation to each other." This from a river rat who had paddled the Mississippi for fifteen years. When the Spanish crossed, it was their virgin journey on the river.

After a short rest, we paddled close to the low Arkansas shore and then turned downstream. John lifted his paddle and the canoe drifted with the current, easing us back into the middle of the river. For the next few hours we had the Mississippi to ourselves, with no barges or other traffic, just woods and sky and water.

At sunset, we pulled the canoe onto a sandbar strewn with bits of petrified Mississippi mud, black and hard and molded in sculptural shapes. Stretching my pleasingly tired limbs on the sand, I watched the stringy clouds overhead turn scarlet and mauve. The water also changed colors, from its customary muddy hue to a glassy wash of pinks and oranges and pale blues. I needed only a corncob pipe to make my river fantasy complete.

Lolling on this lovely sandbar, I was struck, once again, by how rarely the Spanish described the beauty and grandeur of the continent they crossed. At best they'd note the land's agricultural potential, or call it "attractive." Many of De Soto's soldiers had trekked through the tropics and the Andes; by comparison, the less dramatic wilds of La Florida may have seemed unimpressive. Or perhaps, five centuries ago, travelers took stunning natural vistas for granted.

When I ran this by John, he offered a different theory. "They must have been too terrified most of the time to think of America as anything but threatening," he said. "They were fighting for survival."

This was certainly true of De Soto's men by the time they crossed the Mississippi, in the summer of 1541. Reaching the far shore, soldiers pulled the rafts apart to save scarce nails, and then slogged through "the worst road of swamps and water they had seen." At an Indian town, they fell greedily on "deer, lion, and bear skins," and cut them into jerkins, leggings, and moccasins. Six months before, the men had mocked a nobleman clad in an Indian blanket. Now, all were driven by necessity to go native.

In the twilight, we left the sandbar and glided along a back channel of the river. Late at night, John said, beavers gnawing trees created a chorus so loud that it sounded like an army chewing corn on the cob. As we returned to the main part of the river, a sliver of moon and a few faint stars appeared. The Arkansas shore sketched a low, dark line, barely visible at all.

"It'll be a little work getting around this point," John said, for the umpteenth time, as we fought the current around yet another bend. Beyond it lay the landing we'd launched from eight hours before. I fell gratefully ashore, like De Soto's men after crossing the Mississippi. "That was a breeze," John said, lugging the canoe past me. "You'll have to come back in summer so we can do some serious paddling."

WEST OF THE Mississippi, *The De Soto Chronicles* become hard to follow. Geographical coordinates blur and so do the names of Indian towns: Quixila, Quipana, Quitamaya, Quiquate, Chaguate, Coligua, Catalte. De Soto's army lurched this way and that, chasing rumors of riches or searching for a "populous district" to pillage. First northeast

Arkansas, then the boot heel of Missouri, then the Ozarks, where De Soto again hoped mountains might yield gold and silver. Then west to a plain where the population was "scattered" and warriors battled the Spanish with the ferocity of "wounded dogs."

After one fight, natives surrendered woolly blankets made from "cowhides," and told of a barren land a short way on, where the "cattle" roamed. De Soto had reached the boundary between the settled, corn-based people of the South and the nomadic hunters of the buffalo plain. He had also crossed a linguistic divide. None among the chain of a dozen interpreters De Soto had assembled since Florida could communicate with the tattooed nomads, except by signs.

With winter approaching, the army marched back from the Plains and made camp in east-central Arkansas, almost closing the crooked circle De Soto had traced since crossing the Mississippi six months before. The winter proved harsh, and scores of men died, including the interpreter Juan Ortiz. This was a loss De Soto "felt deeply," one of his men wrote, a rare mention of the conquistador's emotions.

Without Ortiz, De Soto was forced to rely for translation on an Indian youth seized two years before, who had learned a little Spanish. According to the *Chronicles,* it took the youth an entire day to relay what Ortiz "stated in four words," and "most of the time he understood just the opposite of what was asked." As a result, the Spanish frequently became lost, sometimes marching for days on trails that brought them back to where they'd started.

De Soto, in effect, was wandering blind, deaf, and mute in the middle of the continent. He'd lost more than a third of his men and all but forty of his 220 horses; those that remained were unshod for lack of iron. Unable to keep exploring with such a depleted force, De Soto concocted a desperate scheme. He would return to the Mississippi, build boats, and follow the river to the Gulf of Mexico. Then he would "send word to Cuba that we were alive," in hopes of resupply. Once equipped with fresh men and provisions, De Soto would resume his march west, into the arid territory where Cabeza de Vaca and his fellow wanderers had picked up vague rumors of riches.

In early spring of 1542, the Spanish retreated east through icy swamps, sometimes so deep in water they had to swim. Finally making camp by the Mississippi, De Soto felt sure the Gulf was just a short way downriver. But a local chief contradicted him, saying he knew nothing of "the sea," or of an Indian settlement large enough to sustain the army during the time needed to build boats.

Convinced the chief was lying to keep the Spanish from his settlements, De Soto sent his best captain and eight riders to scout south along the river. The men returned a week later, reporting that they had seen only "canebrakes and thick woods," and arms of the great river too broad to cross. There was no way out.

For the first time, even De Soto lost heart. His "grief was intense on seeing the small prospect he had for reaching the sea," wrote one of his men. "Worse, according to the way in which his men and horses were diminishing, they could not be maintained in the land without succor."

In his despair, the conquistador "fell sick." The *Chronicles* give no detail of his illness, only that it was serious. Even so, De Soto kept scheming. A powerful chief ruled the other side of the river; maybe he could be cowed into giving aid. De Soto sent an emissary, telling the chief that the conquistador "was the son of the sun and that wherever he went all obeyed him." The chief was unimpressed. If De Soto was the son of the sun, he replied, "let him dry up the great river and he would believe him." As for De Soto's demand that the chief cross the river to give obeisance, the Indian declared that "he was not accustomed to visit anyone." Rather, all paid homage to *him*.

By the time De Soto received this news, he was confined to his bed, "badly racked by fever." Enraged at having his authority challenged, he wanted to cross the river and punish the chief for his impudence. But he and his army were too weak, the river ran "deep, and very furious," and Indians who lived near the Spanish appeared to be preparing an attack.

From his deathbed, De Soto lashed out one last time. He sent a force to kill every male in a nearby settlement, "in order that by treating them cruelly, neither the one town nor the other should dare to attack him." His men dutifully butchered a hundred Indians, leaving a few to wander away wounded, "that they might strike terror into those who did not happen to be there."

Having committed his final atrocity, De Soto summoned his lieutenants to his bedside. "He asked them to pray to God for him and in His Mercy to pardon him his sins, and place his soul in glory." He also expressed "the sorrow he felt at leaving them in so great confusion as he was doing in a land in which they did not know where they were." De Soto anointed a successor, Luis de Moscoso, who had served with him in Peru. A day later the conquistador died, at the age of forty-two, not in battle but in bed, "in a land and at a time when his illness had very little solace."

His passing, however, gave comfort to his men. "There were some who rejoiced at the death," one wrote, since De Soto's successor, Moscoso, was "fond of leading a gay life," and "would prefer to be at ease in a land of Christians than to continue the hardships of the war of conquest and discovery, of which they had long ago become aweawried."

De Soto's death also posed a danger, since it might embolden the surrounding natives to attack. Moscoso hid the conquistador's corpse for three days and then buried it at night, telling the Indians that De Soto "had gone to the sky as he had often done before" and would shortly return. But the Indians knew De Soto had been sick, and they noticed a patch of disturbed ground in the Spanish camp. So Moscoso ordered De Soto's body to be disinterred in the dark.

"A considerable quantity of sand was placed with the blankets in which he was shrouded," one member of the army wrote, "and he was taken in a canoe and cast into the middle of the river."

According to another chronicler, the Spanish hollowed out an oak tree, placed De Soto's body inside, and nailed planks over the ends to create a crude coffin. Then they cast De Soto's casket into the water, "to give him the Rio Grande for a sepulcher," and watched the log box sink quickly to the bottom.

THE MORNING AFTER my canoe trip, I awoke with chapped hands, sore shoulders, and a strange itch produced either by splashes of the murky river or by the fleabag motel I'd stayed in. Creaking from the motel bed to my muddy, snack-strewn car, I checked the odometer:

three thousand miles since my start point in Naples, Florida, and more biscuits and gravy than I cared to recall.

I flipped open my coffee-stained road atlas to yet another state—Arkansas, my eighth—and plotted a route to yet another Indian mound. Since Etowah I'd visited dozens of ancient humps, bumps, and hillocks. I was mounded out: "awearied," like De Soto's men, of discovery. The conquistador didn't make it to the end of his army's trek. Nor, I decided, would I.

Arcing over the Mississippi on the Hernando De Soto Bridge, I made an abbreviated tour of the army's path in Arkansas before trying to find the site of De Soto's demise. Its location, like that of Mavila, was a tantalizing mystery. Of the many clues I'd read about, the most intriguing was a small item in a Masonic publication from the 1950s, telling of an ancient coffin that had washed up in a riverside field, containing a skeleton, sword, and bits of armor. The story said the coffin, allegedly De Soto's, had been taken to a Masonic hall in Arkansas City. This happened to be the seat of a riverside county that Charles Hudson had since identified as the likeliest site of the conquistador's last camp.

So I drove south through the Arkansas Delta, past endless wet fields of rice, and turned onto a small road across Bayou Boggy. The road ended at a decaying town with a sign by the levee: "Welcome to Historic Arkansas City." Beside this stood plaques displaying grainy photographs of the great Mississippi flood of 1927, which had drowned the river port. Before that catastrophe, Arkansas City had boasted twelve thousand inhabitants and dozens of fine shops and hotels, even a sports arena that had hosted a Jack Dempsey bout. Now its name was a rueful joke. There was no city anymore, just a struggling community of a few hundred people and no commerce apart from a liquor store, Laundromat, and grocery. "History's all we got left," said an old man sitting by the levee. "Not much present and no future, not that I'll live to see it."

I was surprised, then, to discover that the dying town still had two Masonic lodges—one for each race, the man explained. The black lodge had opened long after the alleged discovery of De Soto's coffin, so I tracked down a deacon of the white lodge. Roy McCallie had never heard about the coffin, but took me to see whether it was tucked away in some corner of the rundown former opera house that served as the lodge's headquarters.

The first floor had Masonic symbols on the walls, but when I asked their meaning, Roy said, "Not allowed to tell you—it's secret." He led me upstairs to the room that had served as the lodge's meeting hall in the 1950s, when the coffin was found. We searched the hall and an adjoining storeroom, but found only boarded-up windows, broken chairs, and a collapsing ceiling.

"When you join the lodge, they tell you all the things you got to do, and seems like part of that involved an old coffin." Roy said. He hadn't mentioned this before.

"So the coffin was part of a Masonic initiation?" I prompted.

"I'm thinking that's it." Roy went quiet, collecting his thoughts. "I had a stroke a while back. Things that happened yesterday I can't remember." He led me back downstairs. "If it *was* some initiation, that'd be secret business. Even if I remembered, I couldn't tell you."

I had no better luck at the town hall or at its cobwebbed museum. My last stop was the home of a very elderly woman named Dorothy Moore, who, Roy told me, was "a real conversive lady." She greeted me by hissing through her screen door, "I still have a pistol and know how to use it." Then she invited me in, served rum cake, and shared every memory of her ninety-five years, none of which had to do with the conquistador's casket.

"I'm the oldest person in Arkansas City, aboveground, that is," she said. "Seen plenty of coffins, but not the one you're after." She smiled, wrapping the last slice of rum cake for me to take on the road. "Young man, I do believe you've been led on. Just like those Spanish, always chasing their gold."

AT SUNSET, I bought a Budweiser at the liquor store and climbed the levee. I might not have found a coffin, but Arkansas City seemed a fitting place to toast the end of De Soto's journey, and my own. The conquistador's route across La Florida led him to the richest and most populous city-states of sixteenth-century North America. Retracing this path today, I'd crossed countless miles of rural blight and has-been towns that had never been much. Of these many backwaters, from the Black Belt to Appalachia to the Delta, the site of De Soto's death appeared the most forsaken.

As boys raced down the levee on dirt bikes, I took out my battered copy of *The De Soto Chronicles* and reread accounts of the conquista-dor's burial, in water that was "nineteen fathoms" deep. Beyond a fringe of trees, I could just make out a channel of the river and tried to imagine De Soto at the bottom, sleeping with the catfish. The Domini-can friar Bartolomé de Las Casas consigned De Soto to an even deeper grave. Calling him "butcher-in-chief," Las Casas wrote: "There can be no doubt that he is now in the depths of Hell enjoying the wages of his wickedness."

Like De Soto's exhausted soldiers, I couldn't mourn this mon-strous man. But I still felt awed by his doomed quest. At the Florida history fest, Tim Burke had likened De Soto to a drug lord, fatally ad-dicted to risk and riches. After trailing the conquistador for three thousand miles, I'd come to see him differently: as a Spanish Ahab, murderously chasing the unattainable until it devoured him. A victim of fever, both real and figurative, until swallowed in the end by the great river he'd "discovered."

De Soto, at least, sank before taking everyone down with him. After his death, the frayed Spanish army marched west, hoping to reach Mexico. In east-central Texas, they ran out of food and real-ized it was impossible "to traverse so miserable a land." Retreating to the Mississippi yet again, they made nails from chains, anchors from stirrups, rigging from mulberry bark, and sails from blankets. Then they boarded their makeshift vessels and floated downriver, under attack from Indians wielding bows and clubs studded with fish bone.

Reaching the Gulf, the Spanish sailed on for fifty-two days until they came to a coast and saw Indians "clad according to the Spanish custom, whom they asked in what land they were." The astonished na-tives replied in Spanish that the land was Mexico. At which point the survivors "leaped ashore and kissed the ground." De Soto's army, gone for over four years, had long since been given up for dead. Half of its men were.

DE SOTO'S FAILED march also extinguished the thirty-year dream of conquistadors in La Florida. Ponce de León, Narváez, De Soto, a slew of lesser figures—all had suffered the same fate. The land and its people defeated them. After a hiatus of several decades, others tried to penetrate the land De Soto had probed, only to be driven back again. While the Spanish succeeded in settling coastal Florida, the vast interior De Soto explored was written off as hostile and barren, a graveyard for Europeans.

It had become one for Indians, too. Even before fleeing La Florida, De Soto's men saw the scars their march left behind. During their retreat to the Mississippi in 1542, the Spanish couldn't find food because they had earlier burned towns and fields and "the land was left devastated." When they returned a year later, natives by the river had no corn to harvest; De Soto's final attacks the previous spring had left them unable to plant seeds. "Weak and enfeebled" Indians offered themselves as slaves in exchange for ears of corn the Spanish had taken. Many of these natives soon died, as did "almost all the Indians of service"—those the Spanish had seized earlier on their march— who perished from disease and exposure.

In the 1560s, Spaniards returning to the interior of La Florida, including veterans of De Soto's march, were stunned to find overgrown fields and vacant towns where before they'd traveled through populous provinces. Of mighty chiefdoms such as Tascalusa's, nothing but ruins remained.

After my meeting with Charles Hudson, I'd read everything I could to fill in what he'd called the Dark Age in Indian history that followed De Soto's march. Though much remained uncertain, the rapid collapse of Indian societies was probably due to multiple traumas, and not just epidemic disease. The thousands of Indians slaughtered and enslaved by De Soto were mostly young men, killed in battle or chained as porters. These losses drained chiefdoms of critical labor and vitality, making them vulnerable to famine and attack. Once rulers and priests could no longer sustain or defend their starving and diseased people, social and religious cohesion may also have unraveled.

As city-states disintegrated so, too, did the balance of power between native societies. One historian calls the post–De Soto South a "shatter zone," a Darwinian free-for-all in which Indians preyed on one another. Over time, remnant and incoming groups coalesced into tribes such as the Creek and Choctaw. But, compared with the agricultural empires they replaced, these were loose confederations.

It was into this radically altered world that English and French traders ventured, in the late 1600s and early 1700s, rediscovering the lands De Soto had marched through long before. A century after them came American pioneers, to whom the interior seemed a virgin wilderness, waiting to be conquered by their axes, plows, and flintlocks. Gone were the Apalachee archers, the massed warriors in stockaded Mavila, the two-hundred-canoe armadas patrolling the Mississippi. While many of the Indians who remained fought stoutly, most were ultimately subdued by guns, trade, alcohol, and forced removal to the West, where the process would repeat itself.

The famous painting of De Soto in the U.S. Capitol, riding imperiously past Indians, was truer than I'd realized. Not to the conquistador's arrival at the river in 1541, but to the transformation his march set in motion. De Soto didn't discover the Mississippi; he did much more. His mad, failed quest blazed a trail to the new world that America was to become.

PART III
SETTLEMENT

French colonists landing in Florida in 1564, from a drawing by an artist on the expedition, Jacques le Moyne de Morgues

CHAPTER 10

FLORIDA

FOUNTAIN OF YOUTH, RIVER OF BLOOD

> Who wants to go to Florida?
> Let him go where I have been,
> Returning gaunt and empty.
> —Nicolas Le Challeux,
> French colonist and poet (1565)

THE OLDEST KNOWN work by a European artist in North America is a watercolor of a near-naked giant, his arm slung around a tiny fop in tights. The giant is chiseled, like a body-builder, and covered in tattoos. He wears bracelets and anklets made of berries; a fringe of beetle wings skirts his muscled thighs. The little man beside him looks dressed for an Elizabethan farce: blue stockings, scarlet garters, slashed doublet, velvet tassels, and a plumed hat as showy as his twirled mustache.

I discovered this odd couple in an art history book, near the start of my crash course on early America. As startling as the image was, the accompanying text surprised me even more. It said the watercolor depicted the meeting of a Florida chief and a French captain, in 1564. The captain had just landed to found a colony of Huguenots, or French Protestants, who suffered religious persecution at home.

Hang on, I thought. This art historian has his facts mixed up. The first Protestant refuge in North America was established by English

Pilgrims at Plymouth, in 1620. Not by some French dandy in Florida, in 1564. Every schoolkid knows *that*.

I was, of course, wrong. And this time my reeducation took me across the Atlantic, to a terrain I'd last visited on college exams: the Reformation. Huguenots were followers of John Calvin, a French exile in Geneva who sought to cleanse Christian worship of ceremony, superstition, and papal "abomination." This purification extended to personal behavior. Huguenots formed morals boards to punish drinking, dancing, and fornication, and abolished all holidays, including Christmas. English Puritans later looked to French Protestants as a model.

But Huguenots were also, well, French. The captain in the watercolor was René de Laudonnière, who first appears in the historical record in 1561, when the Spanish seized a ship under his command. Cataloguing the contents of his wardrobe, they found a "tooled-leather collar from Morocco, a doublet of white taffeta decorated with crimson silk, a gray cloak with a velvet border two feet in width, and a pair of black woolen cloth shoes trimmed with velvet." Laudonnière's austere Calvinism evidently left room for Gallic vanity—as well as for a "poor chambermaid" he later brought with him across the Atlantic as his mistress.

Huguenots were also flexible in their relationship with France's monarchy. The Protestant leader in France, Admiral Gaspard de Coligny, sought radical reform of the established church and took up arms against Catholics. Yet he remained a fixture at the royal court and a close adviser to France's Catholic queen, Catherine de Médici. In 1562, Coligny won royal backing for the creation of a Huguenot colony on the Atlantic coast of North America (an earlier attempt in South America had failed).

The colony would give Huguenots an overseas haven and Catholics a way to get rid of them. But it also gave common cause to mercantile Protestants and a French Crown that had just emerged from a decade of war with Spain. By the middle of the sixteenth century, Spain had become bloated on American bullion, which came to Europe aboard galleons that followed the Gulf Stream, along the coast of Florida and the Carolinas. This shore was therefore highly strategic and potentially profitable: a base for maritime raiding, for salvaging the frequent wrecks, and for challenging Spain's suzerainty over the Americas.

As leader of the expedition, Admiral Coligny chose a Huguenot sea captain, Jean Ribault. Accompanying him was the dandy René de Laudonnière and another 150 or so Protestants. On May Day, 1562, the French arrived at a wide river that Ribault christened Rivière de Mai in honor of his landing date. He erected a stone column engraved with the fleur-de-lis, then coasted north, naming the rivers he passed for those of his homeland: the Seine, the Somme, the Loire, and so on. The finest he called Port Royal; its mouth, near Beaufort, South Carolina, is still known as Port Royal Sound.

In contrast to the Spanish voyages that preceded it, Ribault's was peaceful. The French, then as now, preferred conciliation to confrontation, and seemed to possess social graces that other Europeans lacked. Their accounts of meeting Indians are laced with phrases such as "wishing not to appear ungrateful," "knowing their feelings," and "we sought to appease them"—sentiments foreign to hard-handed conquistadors.

The French also conformed to national stereotype in their sensuous appreciation of natives. They admired "well-formed" women wearing skirts of moss; painted deerskins "so naturally charming and still so consistent with the rules of art"; and native cuisine such as alligator flesh, which one Frenchman likened to veal.

At Port Royal, Ribault chose a site for a fort and gave his men a stirring speech. Any who volunteered to stay would "always be revered as those who were the first to live in this strange land," he said. "Your fame shall hereafter shine inextinguishably in the heart of France." Thirty men heeded his call and Ribault sailed off, pledging to return in six months with supplies and reinforcements.

Instead, on reaching France, Ribault became caught up in the civil war between Catholics and Protestants that had erupted in his absence. Meanwhile, the colonists at Port Royal also fought among themselves, eventually murdering the officer whom Ribault had left in charge. After waiting in vain for relief from France, they built a small boat and set off for home.

Becalmed midway across the Atlantic, the French ran out of food and ate their shoes and jackets; "as for drink, some used sea water, others their urine." Ever since Columbus's landing in 1492, Europeans had expressed horror of cannibalism, which they believed to be rife among natives. Now they resorted to the practice themselves, selecting one man for slaughter so the others could live. "His flesh was equally divided among them. Then they drank his warm blood."

The survivors were eventually rescued by an English ship. Ribault, by then, was also in English hands, having fled the strife in France and offered his services to Queen Elizabeth. Distrustful of the French captain, she threw him in the Tower of London. So when the fighting ceased in France, and the Huguenot leader, Admiral Coligny, renewed his colonizing plans, he chose René de Laudonnière as commander.

This time about three hundred Huguenots sailed, including women, artisans, an apothecary, and a painter. Returning to the River of May in the summer of 1564, they found the column Ribault had erected two years before. Indians had garlanded it with magnolias, and adorned the base with baskets of fruit, vases of perfumed oil, and bundles of corn. They also greeted the French by kissing the column and raising their arms, as if in prayer. The watercolor I'd seen, of a tall chief with his arm around Laudonnière, depicted this worshipful welcome.

"Being delighted by this good treatment," Laudonnière chose the riverside as the site for a new settlement. "The place was so pleasant that melancholics would be forced to change their nature," he wrote. A forest of cedar, palm, and magnolia "gave a fragrance so delightful that perfume could not improve upon it." The riverside also abounded in vines laden with plump grapes. "On the request of my soldiers," the captain claimed, he named the loveliest part of this landscape after himself: "the Vale of Laudonnière."

The settlers built a fort called La Caroline, in honor of their king, and erected the birthright of every Frenchman: a bakery. They made wine and bartered with Indians for corn. Laudonnière kept a falcon as a pet. The French also shipped home sassafras, an alligator skin, and tobacco, which had just been introduced to France by an ambassador to Portugal, Jean Nicot, whose surname is the root of the word "nicotine."

But the French at La Caroline, like so many early colonists in America, proved incapable of sustaining themselves. Few knew how to farm or to catch the region's fish and game. In any event, they preferred to hunt for precious metal. Indians possessed small quantities of gold, which they claimed was abundant in the interior. In reality, the

The French building a fort in Florida, based on the original by an artist on the expedition, Jacques le Moyne de Morgues

Indians' gold plates and jewelry came from Spanish ships, many of which wrecked on Florida's coast en route from Mexico and South America.

Before long, the French ran out of trade goods to barter for food. They started stealing native crops and kidnapped an Indian chief to ransom for corn. Laudonnière, a clumsy diplomat, played one chief against another until he squandered the goodwill of all of them. He also lost the confidence of the colonists, some of whom stole off by sea to raid Spanish ships and outposts in the Caribbean. When one group of pirates returned, Laudonnière had their ringleaders shot and hung on a gibbet. As colonists, French Protestants were proving just as greedy and violent as the Spanish Catholics they so despised.

By the summer of 1565, a year after their arrival, the French were living on acorns, berries, and roots. Some "ate privately the bodies of newborn puppies," Laudonnière wrote. He decided to abandon the colony. But just as the French prepared to depart, three very different fleets appeared in the River of May, in rapid and unexpected succession.

The first was commanded by John Hawkins, an English privateer. Astonished that La Caroline's colonists were starving in so lush a land, one of Hawkins's men wrote scornfully of the lazy Gallic desire "to live by the sweat of other mens browes." This was a richly ironic comment, given that the English were on their way home from a slave-trading expedition in the West Indies.

Hawkins, however, pitied his fellow Protestants, giving them food and exchanging one of his ships for cannons from the fort. After he left, Laudonnière again prepared to sail home—at which point, the second fleet arrived. This one brought Jean Ribault, who had led the earlier French voyage to Florida. Released from the Tower of London, he'd been sent by the French to resupply the colony and to remove Laudonnière. Reports had reached France that La Caroline's commander was hoarding food and keeping his chambermaid as a mistress, while threatening to execute any of his men who cohabited with native women. Laudonnière denied the charges and then fell ill, "depressed by the false rumors that had been spread about me."

It was at this juncture that the third fleet appeared in the river. The fleet's flagship drew beside one of Ribault's vessels and a man aboard the arriving ship called out, "What people?"

"From France," replied an officer on Ribault's ship, who then asked the identity of his interrogator. The answer must have stunned him.

"Pedro Menéndez de Avilés, Captain-General of the King of Spain, who has come to hang all the Calvinists I find here."

AS A FRENCHMAN with a finely tuned sense of aesthetics, René de Laudonnière would be appalled by the present-day surrounds of the colony he founded. The "large and beautiful river" that the French called Rivière de Mai now blooms with algae, sewage, and factory waste. Its banks, so aromatic that Laudonnière thought perfume could not improve their fragrance, reeks of septic tanks and the industry of greater Jacksonville, a city mocked by its detractors as "an olfactory crime" and a "Dixie version of Newark."

My expectations were therefore modest as I crawled through Jacksonville's traffic in search of the fort at La Caroline, which lay near a spot marked on my map as Dredge Spoil Island. Navigating a sea of subdivisions, I reached a riverside park called the Fort Caroline National Memorial: no longer a Huguenot refuge, but a pleasing sanctuary from the sprawl and traffic of modern Florida.

The visitors center was empty, and I saw no one as I followed a trail to a triangular fort of log and sod, a few cannon poking over its ramparts. A park ranger sat nearby in a golf cart, smoking a cigarette. I asked him whether this was the historic La Caroline.

"You mean Fort Fake-ee?" he said, gesturing at the log stockade. "Park Service put it up in 1964." No trace of the original fort had ever been found, he said; nor was anyone sure whether this was its location. The reconstruction was "an educated guess at best," based on French descriptions of the fort and a drawing by the expedition's artist.

The ranger, Craig Morris, was a bespectacled man with thinning sandy hair and an irreverent take on Fort Caroline's history. "You gotta love the French," he said, lighting a fresh Camel. "They write about how they filleted fish and seasoned it with bay leaves. And they made two thousand gallons of wine here. That's a lot of hooch!" Even the names of French ships seemed characteristic: one was called the *Trout,* another *Shoulder of Mutton.*

Craig said few park visitors shared his appreciation of the French. Most arrived unaware of Fort Caroline's history, and many were dismayed to learn that Huguenots, not English Pilgrims, were the first to seek religious freedom on U.S. soil. "Americans love to bash the French," he said. This was particularly so during periods of French-American tension, such as had been sparked by war in Iraq.

"Jacksonville's a military town, patriotic and conservative," he said. "We've had people come here and realize it was a French site and turn around and go back to their cars in disgust. Some of them say things like 'How can you memorialize the French? They're always against us.' Or 'French are losers, they always surrender.' " Craig shook his head. "I tell them, 'Ever heard of Lafayette?' But they aren't listening."

Craig invited me into his golf cart for a tour of the rest of the park, mostly a maritime hummock of oak, hickory, pine, and palmetto. We ended atop a bluff crowned by a ten-foot concrete pillar: a replica of the column Ribault erected in 1562. The view stretched for miles toward the sea, a panorama of salt marshes and low islands. No ship could have approached La Caroline without being quickly spotted.

"I try to tell people that American history is incomplete unless you know what happened here," Craig said. "We associate freedom with the Pilgrims, but the French tried first and almost succeeded."

If they had, the continent's history might have unfolded very differently. "You'd have had the French in Florida and Canada, squeezing the English from both sides. And Jacksonville today would be like New Orleans. We'd be eating beignets instead of barbecue." He laughed. "And France would have been spared Euro Disney."

We lingered until five o'clock, when Craig had to close the park gate. He'd grown up nearby and often came to the bluff as a teenager, when the park stayed open after dark. "This was Jacksonville's lovers' lane," he explained. "Maybe it's this phallic column, got everyone hot and bothered. If you weren't here by six-thirty on a Saturday night you couldn't get a parking spot."

These days, Craig said, the park was a magnet of a very different kind. Jacksonville's large evangelical community held prayer sessions there, honoring the French as the country's first Protestants. Sometimes, they erected crosses by the river. "This is government property," Craig said. "Church and state have to stay separate." So rangers quietly took the crosses down. But this only strengthened the resolve of those who put them up. "They think Jacksonville is God's chosen city and it all began at Fort Caroline."

For the first time Craig became reticent. Through his church, he knew a woman who took a keen interest in the Huguenots, and he recommended I talk to her. "I was raised Southern Baptist, I thought I'd seen it all," he said. "But these folks are serious. *Real* serious."

PEDRO MENÉNDEZ, THE commander of the Spanish fleet that surprised the French at La Caroline, was an expert seaman, veteran soldier, and devout crusader of the Counter-Reformation. This made him the perfect agent for the mission he embarked on in the summer of

1565. Earlier that year, Menéndez had contracted with King Philip II to colonize and fortify Florida, and convert its inhabitants. Then, as news reached Spain of the growing French presence at La Caroline, the king strengthened Menéndez's military force and commanded him to expel all interlopers: "Free those lands, and give no quarter to the enemy to take root in them."

By the time Menéndez caught up with the French, Ribault's newly landed fleet had turned La Caroline into a formidable bastion of eight hundred soldiers and settlers, about equal in number to the Spanish force. Ribault's vessels were also nimbler than the heavy Spanish ships. After a brief engagement in the River of May, Menéndez retreated to an inlet he'd reconnoitered forty miles to the south. There, on a shore Menéndez christened St. Augustine, the Spanish set up camp.

Ribault, emboldened by his repulse of the Spanish, decided to give chase and defeat Menéndez before he could dig in or be reinforced. La Caroline's deposed leader, Laudonnière, opposed the plan. He warned of the fickle weather—it was September, the height of hurricane season—and the danger of leaving the fort undermanned.

"Having more regard for his own opinion than for the advice that I had given," Laudonnière wrote, Ribault sailed off with almost all the ships and soldiers at his disposal. He left the still ailing Laudonnière in command of only a few dozen men capable of bearing arms, as well as more than a hundred others, many of them women and children.

Ribault's bold stroke almost succeeded. He surprised several Spanish ships just outside St. Augustine and was about to attack when the tide shifted, forcing the French back from the shallow inlet. Then a hurricane hit the coast, driving the French ships far out to sea.

Like Ribault, Menéndez was a daring tactician and a "friend of his own opinion," his chaplain wrote. Gambling that the tempest would keep Ribault from resuming his attack or returning to La Caroline, Menéndez left St. Augustine undefended and took five hundred soldiers to seize the French fort, by land.

In coastal Florida, "land" is a relative term. The terrain Menéndez had to cross was swampy and swollen by rain. Toting muskets, pikes, swords, and ladders, the Spaniards slogged through stormy weather in water up to their waists. At dawn on the third day, they came within

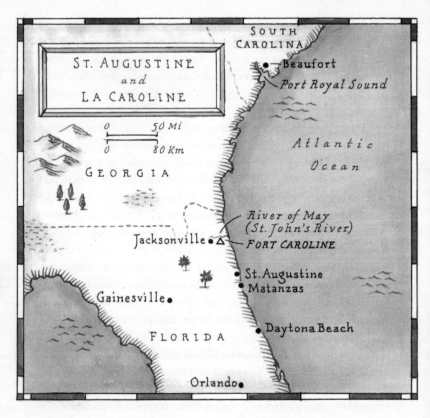

sight of the French fort and paused to pray for "victory over these Lutherans," as the Spanish generally referred to all Protestants.

Most of the French were asleep. Even the officer in charge of sentry duty had retired, "thinking that the Spanish would not come in such unusual weather," Laudonnière wrote. The Spanish quickly breached the fort and attacked men as they came from their beds.

Laudonnière rose from his sickbed and fought briefly before fleeing the fort, along with his chambermaid and several dozen others. They crept along the marshy shore and reached the few French ships left in the river. Seeing no other option, Laudonnière wrote, "we decided to return to France." Six weeks later the refugees reached Europe. "During the passage we had nothing to eat but biscuits and water."

Those left behind at La Caroline suffered a much worse fate. The few whom Laudonnière had judged capable of bearing arms included a cook, an aged carpenter, a beer maker, two shoemakers, a spinet player, and four youths "who served Captain Ribault in taking care of his dogs." They didn't put up much of a fight. "Some came out naked and others in shirts, saying 'I surrender,' " a Spanish priest wrote. "Notwithstanding this, there was a slaughter of 142."

Menéndez needed only an hour to take the fort and didn't lose a single man. A French survivor wrote that the Spanish "plucked out the eyes from the dead bodies, stuck them on their dagger points, and with exclamations and taunts" threw them at fleeing Huguenots.

Menéndez spared about fifty French, mostly women and children, though he did so reluctantly. "It causes me deep sorrow to see them among my people on account of their horrid religious sect," he wrote. He was also disgusted by the material evidence of heresy he found in the fort: "Lutheran books," playing cards "burlesquing things of the Church," and "a thousand other bad things" belonging to a Protestant preacher. "All this was ransacked by the soldiers," Menéndez wrote. "Nothing escaped them."

Leaving a garrison to hold the fort, he marched back to his base at St. Augustine, where he was met by a priest who donned his best cassock and raised a cross to bless the returning conqueror. In an account titled *Memoir of the Happy Result,* the priest wrote of Menéndez: "The fire and desire he has to serve Our Lord in throwing down and destroying this Lutheran sect, enemy of our Holy Catholic Faith, does not allow him to feel weary."

Menéndez's indefatigability was about to be tested again. Within a few days of his return, he learned from Indians that hundreds of French from Ribault's storm-wracked fleet had come ashore on the coast just south of St. Augustine.

THE DAY AFTER my visit to Fort Caroline I called Lyn Corley, the woman Craig Morris had told me was devoted to the Huguenots. "Have a Jesus-filled day," her answering machine said, asking me to leave "a joyous message." When Lyn called back, we arranged to meet at Fort Caroline. I found her at the park's gift shop, buying plastic helmets for a play at her church about the slaughter of the French.

A tall woman in her fifties, with molasses-colored eyes, Lyn was an unlikely champion of the Huguenot story. She spoke no French, had hated history in school, and was raised as a Southern Baptist, a creed that differed from Calvinism on such doctrinal matters as predestination. She'd also lived in Jacksonville for almost twenty years before learning of Fort Caroline's history. Her enlightenment occurred in 2001, when a visiting speaker at her church told of the Spanish massacre of the Protestants.

"I just sat there and wept," Lyn recalled, wet-eyed at the memory. "And I wondered, Why is this history hidden from us? These people died for their faith and we've forgotten them."

This wasn't strictly true; we were sitting on a bench in a national park named for the French fort. But to Lyn, the park was part of the problem: it was a secular government site and its plaques and museum dealt very delicately with religious issues. Also, no one knew for sure whether the park occupied the true location of the original La Caroline.

Lyn felt called to rectify this. "God asked me to claim a land so the city of Jacksonville could remember the Huguenots' sacrifice," she said. Then one day, escorting her grandchildren to a downtown playground, she'd gazed across the road and seen the spot she'd been guided to. "The land that God told me to claim was a power plant."

At first, Lyn thought she'd heard God wrong. A power plant? But then she learned that the plant occupied the site of Cow Ford, a nineteenth-century pioneer crossing that grew into Jacksonville. "In the Bible there are gateways to cities," she said, "and this was the gateway to ours."

Soon after her vision, the plant was torn down, leaving a large vacant lot. So Lyn, an interior decorator, took on a second career, lobbying officials to create a park on the plant site to honor the city's founders. She showed me a slick portfolio of photographs and sketches she'd assembled for this effort. "God told me how to do it."

The park was only part of Lyn's mission. A few months before my visit, she'd also helped organize a ceremony called "identification repentance." As she began telling me about the ceremony, using terms like "intercessors" and "blood covenants," I confessed that I couldn't picture the ritual she described.

"We'll watch it on video, then," she said. Driving to her church, King of Kings, we were met by her husband, Ted Corley, a part-time pastor with combed-back silver hair. He led us to an audiovisual room and put in a video marked "Reconciliation." On the TV screen appeared a woman in a long skirt, speaking from an altar about the horrors of Spanish conquest and "the darkness" it brought down on America.

"That's Ana Mendez," Lyn said. "She's a Spanish woman from a Jewish family who became a voodoo priestess in Mexico City and converted to Christianity while in a mental asylum. She's led identification repentances all over the world."

The camera panned across the church to twenty people walking down the aisle, clutching Bibles and Huguenot flags. These were French Protestants who had come to Jacksonville for the ceremony. They were joined at the altar by Hispanics from the congregation. Ana Mendez knelt beside them and said, "I have a great pain in my heart, I come here, I cannot lift my head because of what we have done. We have killed dreams, we have killed this holy land." Her voice rose, becoming a wail. "I cannot live with this anymore. Forgive us! Forgive us!"

One of the French then spoke. "For all of you of Spanish heritage, we forgive. Jesus paid the price. We forgive like He forgave us, today we declare here on this land, forgiveness from French Huguenots to all those descendants of the Spanish in America."

Up to this point, the ceremony seemed an emotional act of repentance and absolution. Then it became something else, more akin to an exorcism. "Now we order them to leave," Ana Mendez shouted. "All the powers of darkness the Spanish brought to this country, leave! All the religious spirits brought here to destroy the work of God, leave! Leave the shores of America!"

As the congregants wept and waved their arms, Mendez brought the story to modern times. "Forty years ago, prayer was taken from the United States. The work of the devil against prayer, we declare it finished! We renounce those spirits and cast them out and welcome worship, we welcome the Holy Spirit as king. To be ruler of America!"

Lyn turned off the tape. "That's identification repentance," she said. "To speak God's word over the future, to redeem the land from what the enemy has seized so that we can take up what was cut off."

I wasn't sure who "the enemy" referred to—Spain? Catholicism? The U.S. government?—or what, precisely, was to be "taken up."

Ted patiently explained. Jacksonville was part of a movement called "spiritual warfare" or "spiritual mapping," which held that Christians should attack "territorial spirits" sent by Satan. Christians needed to locate the source of their community's evil and cast it out, through prayer. I later read literature he recommended, which spoke of hitting "satanic command and control centers" with "smart bomb praying." In some cities, prayer targeted a gang, or a non-Christian cult, or the teachings of a liberal college. In Jacksonville, it was aimed at the long-ago slaughter of French Protestants by Spanish Catholics.

"The blood of martyrs for the Gospels was spilled here, long before the Pilgrims reached Plymouth Rock," Ted said. "The very fruit of our nation was sacrificed for what America is."

"Which is?" I asked.

"A nation built on faith. The French wanted this to be Zion. They thought they were going to establish in the New World what they couldn't in the Old." Ted paused, beaming at me. "Isaiah 62 says Jerusalem is Zion. We add Jacksonville."

I'd been to Jerusalem; it didn't much resemble Jacksonville. As a secular Jew, I also wasn't sure where I fit into this picture. But mostly I felt like a bystander. In the 1560s, the religious wars of Europe had spilled across the Atlantic. Now they'd spilled forward in time, animating holy warriors in present-day Florida.

"Philip II was the most evil man who ever lived," Lyn said. "He wanted the Catholic Church to control the world, and it's not over."

St. Augustine was about to hold an annual mass commemorating Menéndez's founding of the Spanish city. A day later, Lyn's church would hold its own remembrance, of Huguenots slaughtered by the Catholics.

"I used to love going to St. Augustine, but that was before I knew its history," Lyn said. "Now I stay away. That's the enemy's land."

WHEN PEDRO MENÉNDEZ learned that French sailors had come ashore near St. Augustine, he quickly marched off to meet them. Following the coast south, he found a French party huddled on the far side of a river too deep to ford. Menéndez hid his soldiers behind dunes and went to the water's edge with an interpreter. One of the French swam across and said Ribault's ships had been wrecked by the storm. He asked for safe passage so the 125 French castaways with him could return to La Caroline.

Menéndez replied that he had taken the French fort and executed its Protestants. "I had to make war with fire and blood," he said, "against all those who came to sow this hateful doctrine." Nor would he promise safe passage to the castaways.

The French offered their weapons—and, one account claims, a ransom—in exchange for their lives. Again, Menéndez demurred. The French should "give themselves up to my mercy," he declared, "that I might do with them that which our Lord ordered."

Exhausted, half starved, and unaware that Spanish soldiers lay in wait, the French surrendered to Menéndez's mercy. "Since they were all Lutherans," wrote a priest in the Spanish party, "his Lordship decided to condemn them all to death."

The priest, however, prevailed on Menéndez to spare any French who declared themselves "Christian"—that is, Catholic. A dozen claimed to be so. Menéndez, in a letter to King Philip, said only that he spared "great big men" and carpenters and caulkers "for whom we have much need." As for the rest, numbering about 110, "I had their hands tied behind them and had them stabbed to death."

Twelve days later, at the same river and on the same terms, another group of French castaways surrendered, including the fleet commander, Jean Ribault. Again, they were ferried across the water, tied up, and asked whether they were "Catholics or Lutherans." Jean Ribault replied "that all who were there were of the new religion," and began intoning a psalm. He was stabbed with a knife, stuck with a pike, and then beheaded. More than a hundred others were executed in similar fashion.

"He only spared the fifers, drummers and trumpeters," a Spaniard wrote of Menéndez, "and four more who said that they were

Catholics." One French survivor later reported that the musicians were "kept alive to play for dancing." The river where Menéndez slew the two parties of French became known as Matanzas, Spanish for "the Slaughters," a name it still bears today.

"He acted as an excellent inquisitor," a Spanish historian wrote of Menéndez in 1567, lauding his execution of unabashed heretics. "He was very merciful in granting them a noble and honorable death, by cutting off their heads, when he could legally have burnt them alive."

Menéndez, in his own account, emphasized the practical value of his actions. "I think it is a very great fortune that this man be dead," he wrote of Ribault. "He could do more in one year than another in ten, for he was the most experienced sailor and corsair known."

Lurid accounts of the Florida massacres soon circulated in France, inciting outrage and calls for revenge. In 1568, a French force attacked the Spanish garrison at the former La Caroline, surprising soldiers who "were still picking their teeth" after dinner. The French slaughtered hundreds of Spanish, hanging some of them from the same trees where Menéndez had hanged prisoners three years before.

This massacre salved French anger and pride but did nothing to halt Spain's reconquest of Florida. Menéndez, unlike De Soto, was as efficient a colonizer as he was a killer. He recruited Spanish farm families, paying their passage and furnishing them with land, livestock, and slaves—the first African slaves imported to a North American colony. He made peace with several of Florida's warlike tribes, in one case accepting a chief's sister as his wife, although he already had a wife in Spain. Within a few years, Menéndez had founded a string of fortified settlements along the Atlantic and Gulf coasts, and supported the establishment of missions as far north as the Chesapeake Bay, a few miles from the future Jamestown.

Most of these beachheads were short-lived, as was Menéndez, who died in 1574 while readying an armada to attack northern Europe. But the camp he'd hastily erected at St. Augustine in 1565 grew into a substantial garrison. By the late 1500s, several decades before Plymouth's founding, St. Augustine had a fortress, a church, a monastery, a hospital, shops, and more than a hundred dwellings, all laid out in strict accordance with Spanish town planning.

Even so, it was a precarious outpost, beset by mutinies, pirate raids, plague, fires, Indian hostility, and other woes. Much the same was true of every early colony on the continent. Between Ponce de León's "discovery" of Florida in 1513 and the founding of Jamestown in 1607, Europeans planted dozens of settlements across the future lower forty-eight states. Neither St. Augustine nor any of the others thrived. But alone among them all, the Florida city survived.

ST. AUGUSTINE TODAY is almost an exurb of Jacksonville, with a population one one-hundredth the size of the sprawling metropolis. But the two communities' very different histories have given St. Augustine a certain hauteur, and nouveau Jacksonville a degree of resentment. Since the early nineteenth century, St. Augustine has attracted artists, Gilded Age titans, and millions of tourists. Jacksonville got industry and a pro football team. Travel writers flocked to St. Augustine to extol the quaint charms of the country's oldest European settlement. Sports writers visited Jacksonville for the Super Bowl and derided the host city as so devoid of charm that it "makes Tampa look like Paris."

As if this abuse weren't cruel enough, it gave St. Augustine an undeserved historic primacy. As the park ranger Craig Morris pointed out, it was the French settlement at Fort Caroline that caused Menéndez to land at St. Augustine in the first place. And the colony that arose there was poorly sited, beside a harbor far inferior to Jacksonville's.

"If it wasn't for the French coming here," he said, "St. Augustine wouldn't exist. It'd just be a Bubba inlet, a podunk fishing village on a lousy little entrance to the sea." Craig also hated what the Spanish city had become. He called it "St. Tourist Trap."

On my first approach to St. Augustine, Craig's nickname seemed sadly accurate. The stone walls that once girded the old city had mostly crumbled, giving way to a moat of tourist schlock: mini-golf, alligator farm, chocolate factory, wax museum, and Ripley's Believe It or Not! The traffic circling the historic quarter was slowed by choo-choo trains out of *Thomas the Tank Engine* and buses marked "Trolley of the Doomed," one of twelve ghost tours on offer in St. Augustine. "We'll Drive You to an Early Grave!"

Breaching this gaudy perimeter, I entered a grid of narrow streets roughly a mile square. Architecturally, the Spanish quarter retained a pleasant Old World feel, its flat-fronted stone buildings painted in gay pastels and adorned with second-floor verandas—rather like the misnamed French Quarter of New Orleans, which was mostly built during a period of Spanish occupation in the late eighteenth century.

But the street scene in the country's oldest European city was indelibly modern American. The main colonial avenue, St. George, had become a pedestrian mall clotted with commerce that made a non-sense of the city's history: Old Tyme Photo, the Pirate Haus hostel, Fountain of Youth smoothies, Heritage Walk ("21 Unique Shops")—anything that evoked the past, no matter how anachronistically. Within minutes of stepping onto St. George, I found myself trapped in a scrum of shopping bags, boys in horned helmets waving plastic swords, and jostling tour guides dressed as Goths, Wild West sheriffs, and Cockney thugs.

Finally breaking free, I fled to the old town plaza, with its tolling bells and cathedral. In a handsome stone building I found the office of Bill Adams, director of heritage tourism for the city. He took me on a walk through old St. Augustine, pointing out the many buildings that had been saved from the bulldozer and restored in recent years.

"The preservation story here is a triumph," he said, ending our tour at a rebuilt Spanish tavern on St. George. "But history—real history—is a loser in this town." He gazed glumly at the horde crawling by on the street outside. "People don't come here to learn about the past. All St. Augustine gives them is a historical ambience for shopping."

The tavern was part of a two-acre museum Bill oversaw called the Colonial Spanish Quarter, a collection of reconstructed buildings where men and women in period dress demonstrated crafts and cooking. "We Make History Every Day!" its motto proclaimed. Bill had mixed feelings about living history, but saw it as a way to attract tourist dollars for the upkeep of historic properties.

"Unfortunately, it's a loser too," he said, as a woman in a long skirt and tight bodice served us beer from a cask. The colonial quarter attracted only a fraction of the 1.5 million people who crowded the shops along St. George each year, and a quarter the number who flocked to Ripley's Believe It or Not!

Bill blamed this on Disney World and Epcot Center, which many tourists visited before coming to St. Augustine. "People expect history to be fast-paced and entertaining, which is the opposite of Spanish colonial life." He drained his beer as reenactors came in for a break from weaving and blacksmithing. "Sometimes I think we should dress these people in leather masks and turn this into an Inquisition torture chamber. Then we'd have to beat tourists off with a stick."

Historic St. Augustine had another problem, which dated to 1821, when Spain ceded Florida to the United States. Americans started visiting the town, drawn by its warm climate and exoticism. Mostly Protestant New Englanders, they were shocked and titillated by St. Augustine's "popery," describing masked carnivals and a Good Friday custom known as "shooting the Jews," when locals hung effigies and peppered them with bullets. Ralph Waldo Emerson, who traveled to St. Augustine in 1827 to recover from tuberculosis, was one of many who relished the city's "dim vestiges of a romantic past" and ancient stones redolent of "a thousand heavy histories."

Hucksters quickly learned to trade on this nostalgia by wreathing the city in hoary fictions. At one time, four different buildings laid claim to being the oldest city's oldest house, including one allegedly built by Franciscan monks in 1565 (Florida had no Franciscans at that time, and no houses in St. Augustine survive from before 1700). Ponce de León's "fountain of youth" also cropped up at competing sites, even though the conquistador didn't land at St. Augustine, much less find a youth-restoring spring. The city started holding an annual commemoration of his "discovery," and the oil baron Henry Flagler built the famous Hotel Ponce de Leon, a faux-Moorish pile with a replica of the fountain and murals of the conquistador.

By 1930, St. Augustine's past had become so obscured by legend that the city named a "historical fact-finding commission" to distinguish truth from fiction. But locals resisted the commission's suggestions, leaving intact what a Florida Historical Society writer decried as rampant "flimflams" concocted "for the mercenary hoaxing of tourists." Seven decades later, it was still hard to tell bona fide from counterfeit history.

Old St. Augustine, in effect, was a buyer-beware attraction, a mile-square adjunct to Ripley's Believe It or Not!

Buying a ticket for the sightseeing train's "historic package," I chugged by the "Oldest House," the "Oldest Wooden School House," and the "Authentic Oldest Drugstore," then climbed off at "Ponce de Leon's Fountain of Youth." This was one of St. Augustine's biggest draws and a mecca for school groups studying Florida history. A sign at the ticket booth billed the park as the place where Ponce de León discovered North America and drank from an ancient Indian spring.

"Youth water?" a guide asked, offering me a plastic cup as I crowded into an enclosure called the spring house. The sulfurous water came from a well built over the spring. "When Ponce landed it was an overflowing pond," the guide said, pointing to a diorama with "life-sized" figures of the conquistador and Indians beside a pool of water. "The chief you see there was seven foot two and Ponce was four foot eleven. And that was in his boots and helmet."

Then he directed our attention to a stone cross on the ground, "left here by Ponce de León." It was fifteen stones long and thirteen across, signifying 1513, the year the conquistador landed. The guide also showed us a replica of an ancient silver saltcellar that had been found nearby, with a bit of parchment inside telling of Ponce de León's discovery of the fountain.

"I'm feeling younger already," quipped the woman beside me, holding up her cup. "I'm back in middle school history class!"

The source for most of this "history" was an eccentric Victorian, Louella Day McConnell, who opened the fountain park as a tourist attraction in the early 1900s, around the time she found the cross and saltcellar. At the St. Augustine Historical Society, I'd read a study that carefully debunked her many claims. It cited, among other things, an affidavit stating that the "fountain" dated only to 1875. The cross was made from a type of stone that didn't exist in sixteenth-century St. Augustine. The original saltcellar, since vanished, was decorated with an Indian wearing a nineteenth-century Plains head-dress.

All this was well known to local experts on St. Augustine history.

But none were willing to publicly contradict the fountain myth, since the family that owned the park and other historic attractions had sued detractors. So visitors kept sipping the fountain's water, hearing tales about stone crosses and seven-foot Indians, learning from a planetarium show at the park that Columbus sailed around "a world that had not yet been proved round," and stopping on the way out at Don Juan's Gift Shop to buy Fountain of Youth shot glasses and bottles of the elixir.

This might all have been harmless fun, were it not for the school groups and the site's genuine and much grimmer history. The guided tour ended at the planetarium, leaving visitors to wander the park grounds, a lovely expanse of moss-draped trees, ducks and ostriches, assorted statues and cannons, and at the back, an enclosure labeled "Timucuan Indian Burial Grounds."

Three decades after Louella Day McConnell "discovered" the cross and saltcellar, bones turned up on the property. Archaeologists later uncovered a large Indian village, adjoining Pedro Menéndez's first camp at St. Augustine and a mission built by the Spanish. Among the many graves were those of some of the first Indians in North America interred as Christians, arms crossed on their chests and graves empty of the tools and ornaments often found in precontact burials.

Early Europeans wrote that Florida's Timucan Indians were not only tall and powerfully built, but exceptionally long-lived; the French credulously recorded that some were 250 years old. But Spanish mission life brought disease, forced labor, and other ills. By the mid-1700s, only a few Timucuans remained.

An exhibit by the burial ground gave an unflinching account of this tragedy. But it was a decidedly secondary attraction for visitors, most of whom came for the waters and merrily ingested the fiction of a fountain of youth, beside a graveyard for Indians who perished prematurely as a result of European contact.

"It's sad and kind of sick, having one almost on top of the other," a park guide said, when I approached him during his break outside the spring house. "But no one seems to care."

Chris Meier was a twenty-year-old with a buzz cut who had come to work in St. Augustine because he loved history. Unfortunately for his job prospects, he possessed a hatred of phoniness to rival Holden Caulfield's.

"I work for a living telling lies," Chris said, "and what's worse, people believe me." Some visitors didn't just drink the youth water; they washed in it. And few questioned the canned history he delivered, except to ask, "Did Columbus land here, too, and drink from the fountain?" or "I thought the Pilgrims discovered America."

Chris was looking for another job in town. But he despaired of finding one that would let him tell a narrative truer to Florida's founding. "Ponce de León came for gold and slaves, not a fountain," he said. "Pedro Menéndez killed all the French except musicians for his private orchestra. How twisted is that?" Chris's face wrinkled in disgust. "These guys were psychopathic nutballs. Celebrating them is like idolizing Charles Manson."

A trolley tinkled up to the park gate, disgorging a new crowd of visitors. Chris went back in the spring house to fill plastic cups.

"Youth water, anyone?"

IF PONCE DE León was the mythical founder of St. Augustine, the true one was honored next door to the Fountain of Youth, at the Mission Nombre de Dios, or Name of God. This was believed to be the site of Menéndez's landing on September 8, 1565, and served as the venue for St. Augustine's annual commemoration of the Spanish arrival. Usually, the ceremony occurred in September, on the anniversary of the landing, but a hurricane had delayed it until mid-November.

The mission occupied a grassy shoreline, with an outdoor altar and a towering cross by the water. I was pleasantly surprised to find that the anniversary was a local event, sponsored by the city and the Catholic Church, rather than a tourist function. I was also surprised to find Lyn Corley, my evangelical guide in Jacksonville, who despite her view of St. Augustine as "enemy territory" had come to see the ceremony with a friend.

"Is there a Protestant section?" Lyn quipped, as a hundred or so people took seats by the outdoor altar.

"Yeah, back there," her friend replied, pointing at a nearby cemetery.

The ceremony opened with Spanish reenactors rowing ashore
a bald, heavyset man wearing a black cape and playing the part of
Menéndez. Reaching shore, they raised a flag and shouted, *"¡Viva
Menéndez! ¡Viva España!"* A priest held out a cross for the conquistador to kiss, and a narrator explained that the man playing Menéndez
was a thirteenth-generation native of St. Augustine and charter member of the Los Floridanos Society, a group of Spanish descendants.

"And he's proud of that?" Lyn hissed.

St. Augustine's mayor formally proclaimed the anniversary of the
city's founding and a local historian delivered a short address. "The
children who stepped ashore here would have their own grandchildren
by the time Jamestown was settled," she observed. "Here was the first
European town in North America, the place where Christianity began
in our nation."

None of the speakers mentioned the slaughter of the French. But
Lyn perked up when the historian noted that for six years the Spanish
relocated to nearby Anastasia Island, before returning to the city's
present site. "Hear that?" Lyn whispered to her friend. "This was *not*
a permanent settlement." Then, as the mass began, the two left their
seats and moved to a bench in the graveyard.

After communion, the priest invited the audience to share birthday cake with St. Augustine's "royal family." This referred to three
people in royal attire who, like the honorary Menéndez, belonged to the
Los Floridanos Society. "We're an elite group of Spanish who have always been here," one of the society's members explained.

Like so much in St. Augustine, this claim required a certain sleight
of history. In 1763, when Britain briefly won control of Florida, all but
three Spanish families in St. Augustine fled to Cuba. The city was later
repopulated by hundreds of refugees from a failed plantation that had
imported laborers from Greece, Italy, and the island of Minorca. This
mixed group—known collectively as Minorcans—grew into the non-
Anglo population of St. Augustine.

"In real life I'm a licensed massage therapist and think of myself as Minorcan," said Missy Hall, a royal family member wearing white gloves and a trailing gown. "But for today I'm Queen Mariana of Spain."

She was escorted by a teenaged girl wearing a dress made from drapery and a sullen adolescent boy clad in knee breeches and stockings. "My mom made me do this," he confided. "She takes this seriously." He straightened his crown, on order from the queen. "Today I have two moms, my real one and the queen. A great day. Just great."

Adding to his mortification was the role he'd been assigned to play. The woman who had started the tradition of dressing as Spanish royalty wanted to reenact a family like her own, with a mother and two teenaged children. The only historical family that matched was that of Queen Mariana, a late-seventeenth-century regent to her young son King Carlos II. Unfortunately, the family was inbred and Carlos, known as El Hechizado (the Bewitched), was mentally handicapped and had a jaw so deformed that he couldn't chew or speak properly.

"We're not supposed to tell people," the modern Carlos said, "but I'm a drooling retard." A band struck up "Happy Birthday" and he drew his sword to cut a giant cake decorated with the crest of St. Augustine. As he returned to his "throne," the queen told him to sit up straight. "A retard with two moms," he moaned. "Great day. Just great."

THE NEXT DAY I went to see the very different historical pageant held at Lyn Corley's church in Jacksonville. At King of Kings, the congregants were casually dressed and called out joyously as the pastor roamed the room, speaking through a Madonna-style headset.

"God is incorruptible, isn't that good news? Oh, that's so good!" he shouted, to loud amens. "This is the great joy, to know that someday we will be delivered from this world of sin. God, Mr. Big, the Creator, says it will all work out in the end."

Then the kids took over. Homeschooled under the direction of the church, they'd prepared a play based on the historical material Lyn had gathered. "It's a story of religious freedom," said a teacher acting as narrator. Adopting a French accent, she spoke about the Huguenots while a group of children in homemade costumes dragged cardboard boats past a bedsheet painted ocean blue.

"The world was Catholic, and if you were a Protestant trying to worship God in Europe, you were under persecution," the narrator intoned. As she told of the French voyages, the children brought out a cardboard fort and shook hands with Indians, played by black children from the congregation dressed in skirts stuck with moss. Then the children sang psalms together.

This happy scene was interrupted by the Spanish, sent by King Philip "because the Pope had decreed that Spain was entitled to everything." Children clad in black rushed in, waving plastic swords. The two sides fought lustily before the French fell down. Then the story moved to the slaughter at Matanzas.

"Menéndez gave Ribault and his men the chance to recant, but they chose to die rather than renounce the God they loved." As the children playing the French kneeled and recited a psalm, the Spanish ran them through with their plastic swords. "At Matanzas lies the blood of Jean Ribault and his men," the narrator concluded. "Blood has a voice, and the voice is one of freedom in Jesus Christ."

Lyn glowed as the congregation burst into applause. "Wouldn't it be great," she said, "if we could perform that in St. Augustine?"

AFTER WATCHING THE dueling ceremonies, I decided to leave the wars of religion behind and investigate a more secular controversy. The figure at its center was Michael Gannon, whom I went to see at his home in Gainesville. A tall, stooped man in his late seventies, Gannon had an unusual résumé. He'd worked as a radio sportscaster, Coast Guardsman, war correspondent in Vietnam, priest of the diocese of St. Augustine, and official historian for the Catholic Church of Florida, before leaving the priesthood and becoming a professor of history at the University of Florida.

In 1985, just before Thanksgiving, Gannon got a call from a Florida reporter who was seeking a fresh angle for a holiday story. "I told him, 'I know an *old* angle,'" Gannon recalled. While reading Spanish accounts of the landing at St. Augustine in 1565, he'd been struck by the mention of a thanksgiving mass, after which Menéndez "had the Indians fed and dined himself." In other words, fifty-six years before the Pilgrim feast at Plymouth, the Spanish performed a similar ritual in St. Augustine.

The Spanish left no details of their meal, but Gannon made an educated guess, based on what he knew of sixteenth-century diet and the foods listed on Spanish ship manifests. "It was probably a stew called *cocido*—salt pork and garbanzo beans, laced with garlic," he said, "accompanied by hard sea biscuits and red wine." Gannon had also made a close study of Timucuans and believed their contributions to the meal would have included corn, venison, and tortoise.

Gannon's comments to the reporter quickly hit the news wires and went national. "Was the First Turkey Really Salt Pork?" read a typical headline. Calls flooded in from across the country, particularly New England, where Gannon was dubbed "the Grinch who stole Thanksgiving." The historian didn't flinch from the controversy; he stoked it. When a TV interviewer in Boston told him that Plymouth officials had called an emergency meeting to discuss his remarks, the professor coolly replied: "By the time the Pilgrims came to Plymouth, St. Augustine was up for urban renewal."

In the years since, Gannon had often replayed his role as Thanksgiving provocateur. But he cheerfully acknowledged that the fuss was much ado about little. Other Europeans in pre-*Mayflower* America had also marked their arrival by offering prayers of thanksgiving. Some may have celebrated the occasion by feasting with Indians. At best, St. Augustine's thanksgiving was the first to occur at a permanent European settlement on the continent.

For Gannon, though, the controversy sparked by his remarks spoke to a more consequential lacuna in our memory of early America. "For too long Florida has been a finger of land remote from the national scene—not even a fly-over state, just a destination for beaches and Disney and all its satellite attractions," he said. "Our history has not been treated seriously. There's an inbred resistance in the powdered-wig states to accepting the primacy of Florida and St. Augustine in the story of America's settlement."

Gannon thought St. Augustine deserved some blame for this neglect, having misrepresented its own history and allowed Ponce de León to become "the creation myth of the city." Gannon could still sing out the tagline of the radio station he'd worked for as a young announcer: "WFOY, Wonderful Fountain of Youth, 1240 on your dial!" He'd since urged the city to embrace its genuine history and require that tour guides be tested on their knowledge. "It's taken a while," he said, "but the city has finally realized that its true hero was Menéndez."

Gannon was delightful company, a raconteur who debunked myths with erudition, wit, and the wonderfully resonant voice of a former priest and radio announcer. He even gave me a rendition of the Lord's Prayer in Timucuan, as written down by an early Spanish priest. But when I questioned his characterization of Menéndez as a hero, citing the massacres of the French at Matanzas, the tone of our conversation changed.

"Menéndez had reason to kill them," Gannon said. "He could hardly feed his own colony. And he had no means of guarding all those men. If he'd had AK-47s, he could do it, but not with swords and crossbows."

What about La Caroline? I asked. Hadn't Menéndez declared that he came to slaughter all the Protestants he found at the fort?

"That wasn't an act of religious violence," Gannon replied. "It was done in self-defense, to save his colony. Remember, it was the French who chased after Menéndez to St. Augustine with everything they had."

Gannon also bristled at the notion that the Huguenots were religious martyrs, as Jacksonville's evangelicals believed. "We don't know that the French died for their faith," he said. "They happened to be Calvinists, but Fort Caroline was a military bastion. It could have been a religious refuge, but I don't think it was intended as one."

In his view, the stirring religious story in Florida was what happened in St. Augustine. "It became the first mission base for spreading the faith and teaching European agriculture and craft and reading and writing," he said. "The Spanish did this not by forcing themselves on the Indians but by living among them as Peace Corps people do today. It was a great work of the human spirit."

The "true martyrs," he went on, weren't French Huguenots; they were Spanish missionaries, many of whom were killed by Indians. "They could have lived a life of some ease, but came out here in the snakes and mosquitoes and heat to improve the lot of the natives, spiritually and materially. Indians got great yields from their harvests thereafter."

This might have been so. But before long, there weren't many Indians left to take in the harvest. Lacking beasts of burden, the Spanish pressed natives into service as porters, carrying heavy loads between missions. The crowding of mission life, and close contact with Europeans, also bred disease.

Again, Gannon saw these events differently. "If there was a health disadvantage for mission Indians, it was from relative inactivity and new foods," he said. "Hunters and gatherers were fine physical specimens, but when they settled down they declined in bone size and strength."

Quizzing Gannon, I started to feel like a stubborn undergraduate, trying to poke holes in a lecture by a distinguished professor. His spirited, almost missionary defense of the Spanish also confirmed the view I'd formed during my long travels in their wake, from the Caribbean to the Southwest to Florida. When it came to the Spanish, there was no middle ground. Black legend or white legend. Barbarous inquisitors or knightly bearers of Catholicism and civilization. For the first time I felt eager to move on, to the "powdered wig" story of Anglo-America.

Gannon's phone rang, interrupting our debate. It was the week before Thanksgiving and the annual media circus had begun, with a call from a newspaper in Massachusetts.

"They wanted to know if I'd changed my views," Gannon said, hanging up the phone. "I told them I can't change what's in the documents."

Glad to be back on less contentious ground, I asked Gannon a final question: how did he and his family celebrate Thanksgiving?

"The traditional way, with turkey," he said. "Salt pork is not a favorite of mine. Garbanzo beans I can leave on my plate. Hardtack? No thanks." He smiled. "But I'll take the red wine and drink to Menéndez. And I hope I'll always be remembered as the Grinch who stole Thanksgiving."

CHAPTER II

ROANOKE

LOST IN THE LOST COLONY

> Licence my roaving hands, and let them go
> Before, behind, between, above, below.
> O, my America! my new-found-land . . .
> How blest am I in this discovering thee!
> —John Donne, Elegy,
> "To His Mistress Going to Bed"

WHEN AMERICANS RECALL their English forefathers, they conjure folk of modest means who fled the Old World to live and worship as they chose. These refugees brought Anglo virtues—stoicism, the work ethic, respect for the rights of man—and forged a society of freedom and opportunity that underpins our own.

This uplifting narrative isn't altogether true to the Jamestown and Plymouth settlers. But it's even further removed from their forgotten English predecessors: a motley crew of slave traders, tourists, castaways, and Tudor knights more akin to conquistadors than to hungry Virginians or pious Pilgrims.

In 1558, when Queen Elizabeth ascended the throne, the notion that England was to rule North America would have seem as farfetched as present-day New Zealand colonizing Mars. Elizabeth's island realm of only three million people didn't yet include Scotland, much less a global empire. England had just lost Calais, its last toehold on the European continent, and had no presence at all in North America, apart from cod-fishing boats off Canada.

England also had a long record of futility when it came to exploring the New World. In 1496, four years after Columbus's first sail, another Italian navigator, John Cabot, won a license from King Henry VII to "seeke out, discover and finde" new lands. Cabot reached Newfoundland the next year but barely ventured ashore, discovering only some animal dung and a fishing snare. He gave the snare to King Henry, who dispatched Cabot on a second voyage to America. The mariner never returned. "He is believed to have found the new lands nowhere but on the very bottom of the ocean," a contemporary observed.

In the decades that followed, most of the English who attempted voyages of discovery were dilettantes. Typical was Richard Hore, a leather seller and dabbler in cosmography who sailed in 1536 with thirty gentlemen "desirous to see the strange things of the world." Upon spotting a canoe paddled by "the natural people of the countrey," the gents gave spirited chase. Their prey got away, leaving only a boot and a "mitten" as souvenirs for the tourists.

Then food ran out, forcing the English to forage for herbs and roots. Some of those who went ashore mysteriously disappeared. One man, drawn by the "savour of broyled flesh," came upon a fellow scavenger and asked why he wasn't sharing his victuals. "If thou wouldest needes know," the cook replied, "the broyled meat that I had was a piece of a mans buttocke."

The English were spared further cannibalism by the arrival of a French fishing vessel, which they seized in place of their own and sailed home. The king, now Henry VIII, was forced to repay the angry French from "his own purse." After that, Henry lost what little appetite he had for American adventures and returned to the business of dissolving marriages and monasteries.

Elizabeth, like her father, was preoccupied by problems at home and wary of trespassing on Spain's claims to America. But she quietly abetted the looting of Spanish treasure by seamen on "journeys of pickery." The most accomplished of these thieves was John Hawkins, the privateer who visited the French at La Caroline in 1565. Hawkins's niche was seizing slaves from Portuguese ships and ports in Africa and then selling them in the West Indies, while plundering Spanish galleons along the way. The queen lent Hawkins a royal ship called *Jesus of Lubeck,* and later knighted him. His coat of arms bore an African bound in cords.

In 1567, Hawkins lost a sea fight with the Spanish and had to abandon a hundred of his men on the shore of the Gulf of Mexico. Some of them wandered north, becoming the first English party to travel the American interior. Three survivors eventually reached the Atlantic and hitched a ride home on a French vessel.

At first, their adventure attracted little notice. But in the 1570s, a small circle of influential Englishmen began advocating colonization of America. To buttress their case, they debriefed the last of the cast-aways still alive: David Ingram, a sailor from Barking, in Essex. A colorful storyteller, Ingram told of Indians wearing penis gourds, cannibals with "teeth like dogs teeth," and creatures such as elephants, red sheep, and "fire dragons." But what riveted his interrogators were his tales of America's wealth: pearls "as great as an acorn," rivers with gold nuggets "as big as a man's fist," and an Indian city with streets broader than London's and banquet halls perched on pillars of silver.

Ingram's vague coordinates seemed to place him in a legendary land of riches called Norumbega, which had appeared on European maps for fifty years, at roughly the site of today's New England. In this northern region, Ingram said, a river led west to the sea—evidence of the long-sought Northwest Passage. He also told of Welsh-speaking Indians. This dovetailed with yet another legend, about a Welsh prince named Madoc who had sailed to America in the twelfth century.

For proponents of colonization, the message of Ingram's account was plain. England had missed out on the easy wealth of the Indies, and its voyages to the far north of America had thus far yielded little except salt cod and fool's gold. But somewhere in between lay Norumbega, a rich land with a shortcut to the Orient, and a territory that, thanks to Prince Madoc's long-ago voyage and John Cabot's brief visit in 1497, was rightfully England's.

An early map of the North American coast, including "Terra Norumbega"

The first man to try and make good on this claim was Sir Humfrey Gilbert, a rash courtier who took as his motto *"Quid non,"* meaning "Why not?" Gilbert won his knighthood for ruthlessly suppressing the Irish; among his other atrocities, he made prisoners approach his tent on a path lined with the severed heads of their kinsmen. England's brutal campaign to quell and colonize Ireland in the sixteenth century became a training ground for many of the men who later went to America, where they likened Indians to "the wild Irish."

Gilbert, however, was a Renaissance killer. He dreamed of founding a college to teach sword-fighting, Hebrew, and other skills suited to a lettered knight. He also wrote florid treatises on sailing to Cathay (Columbus's old dream) and "How Her Majesty May Annoy the King of Spain." In the 1570s, he won a charter from the queen to discover "remote, heathen, and barbarous lands" not yet "possessed of any Christian prince," in other words uncolonized by France or Spain.

Early English ventures to America, like those of the Spanish, were privately funded. But the source of finance was different. De Soto paid for his expedition with the pot of gold he'd amassed in America; Gilbert turned to England's emerging entrepreneurial class, granting a monopoly on trade to the Merchant Adventurers of Southampton. He also peddled, to speculators and friends, vast grants of American land he hadn't yet seen, much less possessed.

Leaving the queen a portrait of himself, Gilbert sailed in 1583 with five ships, 260 men, and "for solace of our people, and allurement of the Savages," musicians, Morris dancers, hobbyhorses, and "petty haberdasherie." Four of the ships reached Newfoundland, where Gilbert took possession with an archaic English rite: the presentation to him of a twig and a piece of turf. He also proclaimed the first English laws in America, which included an ordinance that anyone who insulted the queen would "loose his eares."

But Gilbert hadn't come to settle dismal Newfoundland. His object was the golden land of Norumbega, somewhere to the south. En route, in rain and fog, the largest of his ships wrecked on shoals, drowning eighty men and taking down most of the fleet's provisions. Another ship had already sailed home with a cargo of sick men. Left with too few settlers and supplies to establish a colony, Gilbert reluctantly turned toward England, in an overloaded ship called the *Squirrel.*

Nearing the Azores, the *Squirrel* and its last remaining consort, a ship commanded by Edward Hayes, ran into "outragious Seas." One afternoon, "oppressed by waves," Hayes came within hailing distance of the *Squirrel* and saw Gilbert in the stern, calmly reading a book. "We are as neere to heaven by sea as by land," Gilbert cried out. That night, the *Squirrel* was "devoured and swallowed up of the Sea."

SIR HUMFREY'S GALLANT demise rarely merits more than a footnote in histories of early America. But his failure, like that of De Soto, had far-reaching consequences for the future United States. His royal charter passed to his half brother, Walter Raleigh, who cast his eye at a different territory "not actually possessed of any Christian prince"— the little-known coast lying north of Spanish-held Florida.

Raleigh, then aged about thirty, cut an even more extravagant figure than his older brother. In portraits, pearls stud his silk clothes, his fur cloak, his ears, even his long dark hair. Raleigh was one of Queen Elizabeth's closest minions; his courtly offices included "Esquire of the Body Extraordinary." He wrote poetry in praise of the queen's beauty and won enduring fame for escorting her across a puddle in Greenwich. "Meeting with a plashy place," reads the only account of their muddy stroll, "Raleigh cast and spread his new plush cloak on the ground, whereon the Queen trod gently." Elizabeth rewarded his attentions with properties and profitable sinecures.

Raleigh, like his brother, was a warrior-gentleman who fought duels and performed brutal service in Ireland. But he was prone to seasickness and preferred the comforts of court to the hardships of overseas travel. He was also a patient planner, unlike Gilbert. Rather than quickly launch a large expedition to America, he dispatched two ships on a reconnaissance voyage, of which one of his scouts, Arthur Barlowe, gave an eloquent account.

In the summer of 1584, the English arrived off the coast of today's North Carolina. Like other early voyagers, Barlowe smelled America before he saw it: a fragrance so sweet that it was "as if we had bene in the midst of some delicate garden." He found the sandy shore just as enchanting. A flock of cranes, stirred by a single musket shot, "arose under us, with such a crye redoubled by many Ecchoes, as if an armie of men had showted all together."

Natives along the coast accepted gifts of clothing and immediately set to fishing, offering the visitors their catch. Even more hospitable were native women who greeted the wet, weary English at an island "they call Roanoak." The natives "tooke off our clothes, and washed them, and dried them again; some of the women pulled off our stockings, and washed them, some washed our feete in warme water." Indians also marveled "at the whiteness of our skinnes, ever coveting to touch our breastes, and to view the same."

After a pleasant stay of several weeks, the English sailed home, carrying furs, plant samples, and "two of the Savages being lustie men, whose names were Wanchese and Manteo." There is no indication whether they came willingly or not.

Raleigh took the Indians into his home, dressed them in taffeta, and put them under the tutelage of a brilliant young scholar, Thomas Hariot, so that he could learn Algonquian and they English. Barlowe believed the Indian name for the region he'd scouted was Wingandacoa. Hariot soon learned this was actually a phrase meaning "You wear fine clothes."

In the event, Raleigh chose a new name for his American domain. He christened it Virginia, in honor of Elizabeth, the Virgin Queen. By the terms of Raleigh's charter, his grant extended six hundred miles from the site of his planned colony, though not to lands possessed by Spain. "Virginia" therefore denoted a territory stretching roughly from the Carolinas to Maine. The queen knighted Raleigh on the occasion of Twelfth Night, and Sir Walter fashioned a seal proclaiming himself "Lord and Governor of Virginia," a realm that existed only on paper and that Raleigh would never visit.

He also appealed to the queen to give more than her name to the American enterprise. As principal lobbyist, he enlisted "a very good Trumpet," Richard Hakluyt, a famous chronicler of European voyages of discovery, and a man who sought to stir England from its "sluggish security." In a pamphlet he presented to the queen, Hakluyt spelled out twenty-three reasons for "Western Planting," as the English termed colonization of America. This position paper was a capsule of the hardheaded thinking that would drive English expansionism and set it apart from that of other nations.

In contrast to the Spanish, Hakluyt didn't engage in legalistic or theological debate about the rights of America's "naturall people." Instead, he emphasized the economic benefits of colonization. America's timber, minerals, and other resources would free England from dependence on European sources. And trade between England and its colony would greatly expand commerce. Wool, for instance, would find a ready market among American settlers, "to whom warme clothes shal be righte welcome."

Colonization would also "unladen" England of its surplus people.

This population was a source of great anxiety in Elizabethan England, where rapid growth and economic change had vastly increased the ranks of "vagabonds." In America, Hakluyt wrote, these wandering poor and unemployed would find work and serve England, rather than being "devoured by the gallowes." Colonization had strategic value, too, creating a counterweight to Catholic Spain, and a base for harassing its ships.

But English colonization, as conceived by its pioneers, was principally a mercantile mission: about commerce rather than converts, and markets rather than military conquest. "Whosoever commands the trade of the world," Raleigh later wrote, "commands the riches of the world and consequently the world itself."

Though Hakluyt and Raleigh's vision was prescient, it was beyond the means of Elizabethan England. The queen, wary of Spain's growing naval power and ambitions in northern Europe, could ill afford a major effort in America. So Raleigh had to rely instead on his own purse and on the proceeds of piracy by seamen sent to Virginia. This lucrative high-seas looting would cause delays and complications that ultimately sealed the colony's demise.

RALEIGH'S FIRST COLONIAL fleet sailed in 1585, under the command of Sir Richard Grenville, a brutish noble who slew a man in a street brawl and chewed glass as a parlor trick. En route to Virginia, Grenville raided Spanish ships; after dropping off colonists, he soon left to loot some more. During his short stay ashore, he also burned the homes and corn of Indians who failed to return a silver cup stolen by "one of the Savages."

The 108 men he left at Roanoke Island included an apothecary keen to sample New World plants, a Jewish metallurgist from Prague, and the first scientific research team in America: Thomas Hariot, the Oxford-educated polymath and tutor to Manteo and Wanchese (both of whom returned to Roanoke with the English), and John White, a talented artist sent to sketch the specimens Hariot collected.

The colony's commander, Ralph Lane, was a military engineer and, at least initially, a competent leader. The English quickly built a fort and traded for enough food to weather the winter. Though hapless at hunting and fishing, they managed to plant some corn. In all, only four of the 108 men would die during their first year in America, a remarkable record in the annals of early settlement.

The colonists, however, soon became restive. Like the Spanish and French before them, many of the English were intent on easy riches, and disappointed to find only small traces of precious metals. The colony was also plagued by too many men "of a nice bringing up," Hariot wrote, accustomed to "daintie food" and "soft beds of downe." Finding no such comforts in Virginia, "the countrey was to them miserable."

Hariot, by contrast, found the New World delightful and catalogued its bounty under headings titled "Of Roots," "Of Fruites," "Of Beasts," "Of Foule." He saw value in everything, from pumpkins to pine tar. Above all he extolled tobacco, which he thought purged phlegm and "other gross humors, and openeth all the pores and passages of the body." Hariot believed smoking explained why "Indians are notably preserved in health, and know not many grievous diseases."

They would not remain so for long. The four colonists who died while at Roanoke, Hariot wrote, were "sickly persons before even they came thither." This may explain what happened when the English visited Indian settlements. "Within a fewe dayes after our departure from every such towne, the people began to die very fast, and many in a short space." Neither Hariot nor the Indians knew the cause.

"This marveilous accident," he added, put Indians in great fear and awe of the English. Not only did the strangers appear unafflicted, they also had no women among them. Some Indians "therefore were of opinion that wee were not borne of women," Hariot wrote, "but that wee were men of an olde generation many yeeres past, then risen againe to immortalitie." Since Indians often died of disease when colonists were many miles distant, natives also believed the English capable of "shooting invisible bullets into them"—which in a sense they were, with microbes rather than guns.

Colonists also inflicted damage by more visible means. Like the French in Florida, the English soured relations with their neighbors by stealing crops and fish. Then, fearing reprisal for these acts, Ralph Lane launched a preemptive strike and beheaded an Indian chief. By the summer of 1586, a year after their arrival, the English were short of food, anticipating a counterattack, and anxiously awaiting Sir Richard Grenville, who had promised to return with more men and supplies.

Instead, the fleet that finally appeared was commanded by the famous privateer Sir Francis Drake, who was on his way home from sacking Spanish ships and colonies, including St. Augustine. His loot included hundreds of African and Indian slaves; some were offloaded to make room for the Roanoke colonists, who decided to seize the chance to go home with Drake. Soon after they decamped, Grenville finally arrived, having been diverted by conflict with Spain and looting of foreign vessels. He left eighteen men at Roanoke to hold the fort Lane had just abandoned.

DESPITE THE HASTY exit of its settlers, the first colony at Roanoke wasn't an unqualified failure. Lane and his men brought back reports and samples of potentially valuable commodities, most notably tobacco. Raleigh quickly took to the weed and popularized its "drinking," as the English called smoking. So did Hariot, who conducted "many rare and wonderful experiments" demonstrating tobacco's medicinal virtues. He later died of nose cancer.

Raleigh's first colony was also an instructive test run for a second, more considered effort. The waters around Roanoke had proved too shallow and hazardous for shipping. But, eighty miles north, Lane's men had scouted a deepwater harbor and fine land along the "bay of the Chespians," a local tribe. Chesapeake Bay, as it became known, seemed an ideal base for harassing the Spanish and searching inland for minerals and the dreamed-of passage to the Orient.

Relocated, the colony would also be reconfigured. Lane had established, essentially, a military outpost: an all-male force of soldiers and gentlemen-adventurers, dependent on Indians and constant resupply from home. A lasting colony required settlers who could sustain themselves. The core of the next party would therefore be families, yeomen farmers, and craftsmen, led by John White, the artist on the 1585 voyage.

An illustrator might seem an unlikely leader for a colonial expedition. But White belonged to the Painter-Stainers' Guild and was able to recruit like-minded artisans, including Ananias Dare, a brickmaker and tiler who had married White's daughter, Elenor. The party ultimately included seventeen women, nine children, and two ex-convicts who had been jailed for theft. Raleigh provided ships and created a corporate entity, the grandly named "Cittie of Raleigh in Virginia." He also engineered the awarding of coats of arms to White and twelve governing "Assistants," effectively making them minor nobility in the miniature England they hoped to found.

The second colonial fleet departed late in the sailing season, in May 1587, and its pilot spent weeks trolling the Indies, ostensibly in search of provisions but also in hopes of Spanish loot. Finding neither, the ships sailed on to Roanoke, where the colonists had planned to stop before proceeding to the Chesapeake. But their pilot claimed the summer was too far gone for him to carry the settlers farther north. More likely, he was impatient to get back to pirating.

So the colonists disembarked at Roanoke, which presented a melancholy scene. Of the eighteen men Grenville had left the year before, no trace remained except bones. The fort's walls had been razed; deer fed on melons overgrowing the site. John White learned that natives had attacked the small garrison, led by Wanchese, one of the Indians who had earlier sailed to England. Just a few days after the new colonists' arrival, Indians ambushed a man while he was crabbing alone; they "gave him sixteene wounds with their arrows" and "beat his head in peeces."

The only allies remaining to the colonists were Manteo (the other Indian who had traveled to England) and his kinsmen on a barrier island called Croatoan. In accordance with Raleigh's command, the English baptized "our savage Manteo" and made him lord of Roanoke. The next week brought another christening. White's daughter, Elenor Dare, gave birth, "and because this childe was the first Christian borne in Virginia, she was named Virginia."

The English still planned to move on to the Chesapeake, "where we intended to make our seat and forte," White wrote. But the long voyage had drained their supplies, and it was too late in the summer to sow and gather crops. The colonists decided someone should return to

England with the ships that had brought them, to secure more aid. The obvious choice was John White. He was influential, knew where to direct a supply ship, and would be unlikely to abandon the colonists, since his family remained among them.

White at first refused, fearing for his reputation and also for his "stuffe and goods," which might be "spoiled" or "pilfered" in his absence. So the colonists signed a bond, the first civic document drawn up in English America. They pledged to safeguard White's goods and stated that they had entreated him to leave, "much against his will," to secure supplies "necessarie for the good and happie planting of us."

At the end of August 1587, White set sail, leaving behind his daughter, his infant granddaughter, Virginia Dare, and 113 fellow settlers. Neither White nor any other Englishmen would ever see the colonists again.

ROANOKE ISLAND IS nine miles long and two miles wide, most of it low and scrubby and verged by swamp. Bridges now link the island to mainland North Carolina and to the Outer Banks, a hundred-mile-long sandbar elbowing into the Atlantic. The island has two towns, Manteo and Wanchese, streets named for Sir Walter Raleigh and Queen Elizabeth, and a subdivision called Colony of Roanoke. It's a hard place to get lost in today.

The novelist William Styron, who was raised seventy-five miles north of Roanoke, once observed that the historical imagination works best when fed "short rations" of fact. This has certainly been true of the Roanoke story. John White's colony left a meager paper trail and almost no physical trace. Yet these scraps have nourished a centuries-long feast of myth, melodrama, and speculation, all of it purporting to reveal the fate of Roanoke's "lost colonists."

I began my own mystery tour at Fort Raleigh, the national historic site honoring the vanished settlement. In the centuries after the English fort's abandonment, it was picked over by artifact hunters, recycled as a Civil War bastion, and buried beneath a faux-Elizabethan tourist attraction that included log cabins, a building style unknown to early colonists. No sixteenth-century house sites have ever been found.

Because of coastal erosion, archaeologists believe much of the colony may lie beneath the waters of Roanoke Sound.

The small park at Fort Raleigh is nonetheless a mecca for amateur sleuths—and kooks. "We get three hundred and fifty thousand visitors a year, and almost as many theories," said a ranger at the park's visitors center. "Aliens picked up the colonists and deposited them on Atlantis—that's a popular theory. You get others who talk about transdimensional time warp and how the colonists went through a secret doorway." The ranger shrugged. "I tell them, 'Yeah, we lose a lot of people that way.'"

Fantasy also reigned at the grounds adjoining Fort Raleigh, called the Elizabethan Gardens. This park had originally been conceived in the 1950s, by the Garden Club of North Carolina, as a re-creation of the sort of garden a Roanoke colonist might have planted. But overeager donors and landscape architects introduced manicured hedges, sunken flowerbeds, gazebos, and Carrara marble fountains, creating a tamed pleasure garden that bore no resemblance to the humble plot of an Elizabethan homesteader.

Also fanciful was the statue of Virginia Dare that occupied one corner of the gardens. It depicted Virginia not as a baby, but as the sexy babe the artist imagined she became in America: firm breasts, fine rump, loins thinly veiled by a fishnet. Her luxuriant hair was beautifully coiffed, despite some twenty years in the wilderness. Indian-style necklaces and braids encircled her neck and arms. The statue, known as the "Dare Venus," had been judged too racy when it went on display in the 1920s, and was hidden for decades before finding a home in the gardens.

Fiction of a different sort prevailed on Fort Raleigh's other flank. In 1937, an outdoor drama called *The Lost Colony* opened at Roanoke to such acclaim that it has run every summer since, attracting four million visitors and many noted actors (Andy Griffith played Raleigh from 1949 to 1953). The play was so big that it has spawned a parallel "Lost Colony," much more extensive than the historic park, including a mock Tudor theater and stockade, drama workshops, and an official historian who went by the theatrically lowercase name of lebame houston.

"There's nothing to see at Fort Raleigh—it's the dullest national park in America," lebame said, when I met her at a café in Manteo. "The play's what keeps this island alive. It's a hymn to the common man and woman trying to make it in America."

lebame herself was anything but common, beginning with her bleached white hair and the enormous sunglasses that shielded half her face. As a child, she'd played Virginia Dare in *The Lost Colony;* she had gone on to write plays of her own. She also shared a house in Manteo with a red-haired actress known to all as Queenie or HRH, because she often played royal roles, including Elizabeth I in *The Lost Colony*.

Queenie—real name Barbara Hird—was a large woman with an imperial bearing and the accent of her native Yorkshire. She confessed to having known little of the lost colony before migrating to America as an adult. "Roanoke was overshadowed in English memory by the Spanish Armada, which invaded a year later," she explained. "Also, no one much likes Raleigh in England. He was a bounder, always putting himself forward—not traits the English admire."

Barbara found Roanoke refreshing by comparison. People were intrigued by monarchy and amused by her royal performances. "One must endure a good bit of kowing and towing," she said, as a passing waitress attempted a curtsey. Barbara and lebame also kept a throne in their living room, a tall, straight-backed, gold-leafed chair topped by a crown. "It's horribly uncomfortable," Barbara said, "but it is where I must sit when I am wearing my big scary dress and wig."

The two women were unconventional in another way. Though they'd researched and performed the Roanoke story, neither wanted its true ending to ever be revealed. "If anyone solved the mystery, we'd have to change the name of the play," lebame said. "It'd just be *The Colony*. Not nearly so catchy."

Like everyone else, however, the women had their own explanation for the colonists' disappearance. Barbara leaned over and whispered in my ear, "Mosquitoes carried them off. In summer, they're absolutely frightful here."

"Of course," Iebame added, "if you tell anyone, we'll have to lop off your head."

"By order of the queen," Barbara said.

AFTER LEAVING ROANOKE in August 1587, John White was waylaid by storms and piracy; he reached home to find England bracing for a Spanish invasion. Elizabeth, needing every available vessel to defend the coast, barred ships from leaving port. White, with Raleigh's help, nonetheless managed to load supplies and a dozen more colonists onto two ships commanded by privateers, who promised to carry their passengers to Roanoke. The sailors went plundering instead, lost a sea fight off Spain, and were forced to retreat home, with White among the injured.

England defeated Spain's Armada in the summer of 1588, but the seas remained tense and shipping restricted. White bided his time, completing illustrations of butterflies, fireflies, and cicadas he'd seen in America. Finally, after many false starts, he sailed for Roanoke again in 1590, as a passenger aboard yet another plundering expedition.

The ships spent months in the Caribbean and didn't crawl up the Atlantic coast until midsummer, amid "very fowle weather with much raine, thundering, and great spouts." Reaching the treacherous Outer Banks, White was buoyed by the sight of smoke rising from the dunes. But going ashore, he "found no man nor signe that any had bene there lately." The next day an English boat capsized in the rough surf, drowning seven men. White had to beg the captain to stay a little longer.

Reaching Roanoke Island, he and a group of sailors trolled the coast in small boats, singing out "many familiar English tunes" and blowing a trumpet. "But we had no answere," White wrote. Going ashore, he found log walls still standing, "very Fort-like." But the colony's houses had been dismantled, and bits of heavy guns and ammunition lay strewn about, "almost overgowen with grasse and weedes." The searchers also found chests that had been buried and then dug up, including three belonging to White, their contents "spoyled" and "my armour almost eaten through with rust."

Along the shore, White found something else: a tree on which "were curiously carved these faire Romane letters CRO." One post of the fort also bore an inscription: "In fayre Capitall letters was graven CROATOAN." Before leaving three years earlier, White had agreed on a "secret token" with the colonists: when they left Roanoke, they would carve "the name of the place where they should be seated." If they were "distressed in any of those places," they were to carve a cross as well. Neither of the inscriptions he found at Roanoke bore such an SOS.

"I greatly joyed that I had safely found a certaine token of their safe being at Croatoan," White wrote, "which is the place where Manteo was borne, and the Savages of the Iland our friends."

White prevailed on the captain to sail to Croatoan the next day. But an anchor cable broke and the ship almost ran aground. "The weather grew to be fouler and fouler," White wrote. With food and water running short, he consented to the captain's plan to sail to Trinidad for the winter and return in spring. But the storm "blewe so forcibly" that the battered ship was driven far out to sea, on "the due course for England," to which it returned after the requisite detours for piracy.

The journey of 1590 was not, White dryly observed, "my first crossed voyage" to Virginia. But it was to be his last. "I leave off," he wrote in 1593, "committing the relief of my discomfortable company, the planters in Virginia, to the merciful help of the Almighty, whom I most humbly beseech to helpe & comfort them."

IN THE CENTURIES since, White's handful of poignant dispatches has served as the starting point for seekers of Roanoke's lost colonists. But White's writing presents as many questions as clues. The tree carvings led him to conclude that the colonists had gone to Croatoan, a barrier island forty miles due south of Roanoke. Yet he wrote, in the same account, that when he'd left the colonists in 1587, "they were prepared to remove from Roanok 50 miles into the main." In other words, due *west*. Then again, his earlier report on the 1587 voyage stated that colonists planned to go to the Chesapeake Bay, eighty miles *north*. No matter how you parse White's writing, it leads in every direction except straight out to sea.

Two decades after White last saw the colonists, the English who settled Jamestown picked up other leads. Indians told of seven whites held captive in the interior, as copper workers, and also of a place where "People have houses built with stone walls, and one story above another, so taught them by those English" from Roanoke. A search party sent from Jamestown reported finding crosses cut in trees, but no English people. According to another account, the colonists had "peaceably lived and intermix'd" with the Chespians, or Chesapeake, a tribe at the mouth of the bay, only to be slaughtered by the Virginia chief Powhatan at about the time the Jamestown settlers arrived in 1607.

David Quinn, the leading scholar of Roanoke, spent decades sifting the available evidence and concluded that the last of these scenarios was the likeliest. The colonists had gone north to the bay, as originally planned, and been taken in by Chesapeake Indians, the rare tribe in eastern Virginia that resisted Powhatan's control. When the Jamestown settlers arrived, Powhatan may have feared that the Chesapeake Indians and Roanoke survivors would assist the newcomers. So he ordered them killed, just as the Jamestown settlers were later told.

As for the carvings John White found at Roanoke, Quinn theorized that on leaving the island, the colonists would have sent a small group to Croatoan, as a lookout for English ships. This party may have melded into the native population, rejoined the others by the Chesapeake, or been killed.

Quinn's tidy thesis has won over most scholars, but it's impossible to prove without archaeological evidence, which is thus far lacking. The homeland of the Chesapeake has vanished beneath the sprawl of southeast Virginia, now a busy shipping and naval center. As the park ranger I spoke to at Fort Raleigh told me: "If Quinn's theory is right, the lost colonists are buried under a mall in Norfolk."

It's also hard to square Quinn's account with White's enigmatic statement, upon returning in search of the colony, that the settlers "were prepared to remove from Roanok 50 miles into the main." Quinn dismissed this, believing White confused "the main" with the Chesapeake region. Also, most of the territory fifty miles inland from Roanoke is swampy wilderness, far from the sea or other advantages. It would have made no sense for the Roanoke settlers to go there.

But there was one man who strongly disagreed: Fred Willard, director of the Lost Colony Center for Science and Research, whom I went to see at his home office eighty miles west of Roanoke. A paunchy man with long gray hair and a thin wispy beard that looked like Spanish moss, Fred was a former marina owner who now worked full-time trying to crack the Roanoke case.

"Most of the people on Roanoke Island hate me," he said. "They say, 'You'll find the lost colony and ruin us.' They want to own the story." He had little time for professional archaeologists, either. "Territorial geeks," he called them. "Their scope is so narrow." Fred took a broader tack. "What we've done," he said of the Lost Colony Center, "is open a whole gamut, a holistic, multidisciplinary approach."

To demonstrate his technique, Fred took me out the next day for some field research. He emerged from his home carrying machetes, maps, a global positioning system, and other gear. "Our study area is a million and a half acres of swampland," he explained.

As our driver, Fred had recruited Susan Purcell, an effervescent redhead who'd met him at a local yacht club and been converted to his quest. "Fred's brilliant," she told me. "If he was looking for a comet, I'd follow him there, too." As she sped east into the countryside, Fred set out his essential thesis. The abandoned Roanoke settlers moved fifty miles inland to escape Indian enemies and the Spanish, who sent several ships looking for the English. "The colonists were running for their lives," he said. "Inland was the best place for them to hide."

They were joined in their flight by their Croatoan allies, whose domain extended to the mainland. Fred's evidence for this was a tangled paper trail, which showed that the last of the Croatoans—by then known as Hatteras Indians—had migrated in the eighteenth century from the Outer Banks to the interior. He believed they'd done so to join a preexisting settlement.

Fred also made use of satellite and infrared images, which he said revealed "anomalies" in the landscape fifty miles inland from Roanoke. His mission now was to probe this territory for artifacts or evidence of a fort, and also to DNA-test current inhabitants of the area, who he believed had Croatoan blood.

At least that's what I extracted from his rapid-fire monologue, which looped across centuries and counties and tribes, connecting dots that seemed obvious to him but not always to me. "You got to take Fred on faith," Susan said. "I don't always get where his thinking is headed, but you know he'll get there in the end."

After an hour of driving, we stopped to collect two more of Fred's acolytes, Eddie and Vickie Squires. Eddie, a muscular millwright and welder with deep-set brown eyes, had learned from Fred that his family could be traced back to a man identified in a 1739 document as a Hatteras "King." Vickie was an avid genealogist who had researched Eddie's family tree and found pictures of forebears with dark hair, olive skin, and wide, high cheekbones.

"I'm real proud of it," Eddie said of his lineage. "We always knew my grandmama was Indian, but it was all kind of hush-hush when I was a kid in the fifties and sixties. Back then, being Indian was about as bad as being black."

We drove on, through Hyde County, one of the poorest and least populated counties in North Carolina. Trailers and tar-paper shacks perched before fields of corn and cotton. Then, near the head of the Alligator River, we plunged into swampy barrens. One dirt road led to a locked gate, another to a lonely deer stand, a third to the place where we'd started. "Fred's great with old maps and hopeless with modern ones," Susan quipped, patiently driving us in circles. "The joke is that he found the lost colony and then lost it."

Finally, we picked up a dusty track that wound around fields and onto a low, heavily vegetated ridge. "A perfect place for the colonists to hide," Fred said. He walked us into the woods, talking about all the landscape's "anomalies." A line of walnut trees, for instance. "Someone had to plant them, but there's no known community that's ever been here." The soil was different, too, and the land rose sixteen feet

above the surrounding plain. "The English had to be high enough off
the water to grow corn," he explained.

Then he led us to what he called a berm, a barely discernible embankment that ran for over a hundred yards through the briars and
vines. "I'm thinking this is part of a bastion," Fred said. He did a
rough sketch of the Roanoke fort and held it up against the landscape. "This berm could be the longest line of the fort they built
here."

"Or it could be a logging skidder trail," Eddie pointed out.

"We'll have to do a flyover with ground-penetrating radar," Fred
replied. He studied a map and asked Eddie to take a reading off the
GPS. Nodding meaningfully, Fred said, "We're exactly fifty miles into
the main."

We were also, according to the car's odometer, 162 miles into a
road trip that had carried us only twenty-five miles from the Squireses'
house, which we'd left four hours before. It took us several more hours
to drive back, with long detours to remote grave sites, where Fred took
down names of families he believed had some connection to the Indians who moved here from Croatoan.

"We got that much closer today!" he exulted, as Susan drove us
through the twilight back to Fred's house. His wife, Carol, served us
cold cuts and talked about her passion for ferrets. Then Fred led me
upstairs to his computer station, which shared space with Carol's
caged pets. As Fred pulled up satellite images, I didn't know what to
make of them, or of him. For all the grand talk, the Lost Colony Center
for Science and Research seemed a one-man band, playing at a computer in a room full of ferrets.

BUT ONE ASPECT of Fred's quest intrigued me. Whichever direction
the colonists went, it was likely they'd settled among Indians. Most of
the English were young and single, including six of the women; eleven
others were children. Virginia Dare was a week old when John White
left in 1587, and, if she survived, a woman of twenty by the time the
Jamestown settlers arrived. Raised in America, in close company with

Indians, would she have remained, in any real sense, an English person? And what of her children?

"A whole Country of English is there, bred of those who were left," a character declares in the 1605 London play *Eastward Hoe,* one of whose authors was Ben Jonson. "They have married with the Indians and make them bring forth as beautiful faces as any have in England."

In 1701, a naturalist named John Lawson picked up the theme of intermarriage, though he viewed it less sanguinely. While visiting the Outer Banks and the remains of Roanoke's fort, Lawson met coastal Indians who said "several of their Ancestors were white People and could talk in a book, as we do; the Truth of which is confirm'd by gray eyes being found frequently amongst these *Indians,* and no others." Lawson concluded that Roanoke's colonists "were forced to cohabit" with natives, "for Relief and Conversation: and that in process of Time, they conform'd themselves to the Manners of *Indian* Relations. And thus we see, how apt Humane Nature is to degenerate."

In the nineteenth century, when Victorian sentimentalists revived the Roanoke story, race once again took center stage. A North Carolina writer, Sallie Southall Cotten, founded an association to honor "the first white child born on American soil" and penned an epic poem, "The White Doe," which imagined Virginia Dare as a babe of "tender whiteness" who blossomed into a maiden with golden tresses and eyes of "limpid blueness"—a stark contrast to the "squaws of darksome features" all around her. She was worshipped by Indians, not only for her pale beauty but also because she imparted to the "rude, untutored savage" the uplift and wisdom of a "higher type of being."

Virginia Dare, in other words, had become a symbol of racial purity and progress. Her name was even adopted as a brand of vanilla extract and, in more recent years, by an anti-immigration group that takes the white doe as its emblem.

In North Carolina, the celebration of Roanoke's lost white tribe also focused interest on Indians in the southeast part of the state, many of whom had pale eyes, light skin, and English surnames that matched those of Roanoke colonists. In 1885, North Carolina's general assembly designated them "Croatan Indians"—descendants of Manteo's people—and accorded the tribe marginally greater rights than the rest of the nonwhite population.

THE CROATAN HAD since changed their name to Lumbee, and few of them cared much about their alleged link to Roanoke. But Fred Willard gave me the name of a man who was tracing his own ties to Manteo's people. Charles Shepherd lived in the rural community of Free Union, an hour's drive west of Roanoke. He worked as a FedEx courier and invited me to visit on his day off, at the brick home he shared with his parents.

"Hi, I'm Charles Sweet Medicine," he said, greeting me at the door wearing shorts, T-shirt, moccasins, and a "Native Pride" cap. What made this a little startling was that Charles otherwise resembled a young version of the African-American activist Al Sharpton: dark-skinned, heavyset, with a long sloping forehead, a faint mustache, and swept-back hair. He also had a New York accent.

"I'm from Brooklyn, originally," Charles explained, leading me to a side porch. "But I never really belonged there." He laughed, wiping sweat from his brow. "I don't really belong anywhere."

At thirty-five, Charles was still trying to work out his complicated identity. Free Union, the longtime home of his mother's family, occupied land marked on old maps as an Indian settlement. Some of its early inhabitants were Croatoan refugees from the coast, who had been reduced by war and disease to a tiny band. Later, remnants of other tribes mixed in, as did free blacks. In the course of the nineteenth century, their designation on censuses ranged from "other free person" to "free person of color" to "mulatto or other" to "Negro." A few Indian customs and words lingered until about 1900, but Free Union's several hundred inhabitants gradually lost their connection to native history.

"We knew we were different, but we just accepted the way we were classified by others, which was black," said Charles's mother, Pearl, a copper-skinned woman who had moved to New York as a teenager and married a black shipyard worker.

Growing up in New York and Connecticut, Charles never quite fit in. Most of his classmates were of Polish or Italian extraction. His black peers were different, too, "into rap and inner-city culture, which wasn't my thing." Only on family visits to Free Union did he feel at home. He loved hearing stories about forebears who hunted with bows and arrows and treated illnesses with herbs and poultices. When he was sixteen, applying for his first job, Charles replied to the race question by checking "Other." Later, he went to work as a pharmacy technician at an Indian reservation in Connecticut and began attending powwows.

"The first time I heard someone beating a drum, I felt my heart was going to explode," he said. "That was me, where I was from." On forms, he began identifying himself as American Indian, though he felt this was unsatisfactory, too. "I'm probably two-fifths African, two-fifths Indian, and one-fifth European," he said. "The categories in this country are too rigid. I'm everything."

Five years ago, Charles had moved to Free Union, but he didn't really fit there, either. Few locals shared his passion for reclaiming their hidden Indian heritage. At powwows elsewhere in the state, Charles felt quietly shunned. "I can tell they don't really view me as native," he said. "I'm too black, and there's still that segregation, even among Indians."

Then he heard about Fred Willard's search for Indian communities that might have ties to Roanoke. Charles contacted Fred and compared notes: two autodidacts on related quests. "Free Union was an isolated place and didn't mix much with the outside world," Charles said, "so it might be the key to the puzzle."

He took me to a spare bedroom he'd converted into an office, cluttered with books, census reports, maps, old church records, and anthropological studies. He unearthed a volume of the sketches and watercolors John White made of Indians in North Carolina. First published in 1590, White's sensitive portrayals of Algonquians caused a sensation in Europe. He depicted Indians not as "savages" but as sympathetic individuals, performing domestic chores or at leisure, dancing and sitting around a fire. White's Indians often smile; in one portrait, a girl gaily clutches an Elizabethan doll given her by colonists.

"I like to think these people are my ancestors," Charles said. He used their fringed deerskin clothes as models for the regalia he wore to powwows, where he went by the name Sweet Medicine in homage to the

Indian dancers: an engraving of a drawing by John White, an English artist in Virginia, first published in 1590

traditional healers in his family. Charles also hoped to use White's art as a blueprint for his ultimate dream: the full-scale reconstruction of an Indian village, patterned on one called Secotan that White had drawn.

"In a way, we're halfway there," he said, taking me for a drive around Free Union's scattering of modest houses, separated by large gardens and plowed fields. "Tobacco and corn and beans, mostly," Charles said, "same as the Indians grew." White's drawing of Secotan showed tidy fields of these crops alongside loaf-shaped longhouses. "We could build a few of those, too."

Charles imagined the resurrected Secotan as a tourist draw and summer camp for kids who wanted to live as Indians had. The village might also inspire his neighbors to reclaim their native identity. As he went on excitedly, about the details of late-sixteenth-century life near the Carolina coast, only one thing was missing: Roanoke's lost colonists.

"For me, personally, they don't mean that much, I already know I have Scottish and Irish heritage," he said. "But it would be a huge

The Indian village of Secotan, near Roanoke, from a drawing by John White, published in 1590

bonus if it turned out we're connected." Charles laughed. "I'd love to see a TV newscaster announcing that the lost colony had finally been found. Then the camera would pan around Free Union. Can you imagine the reaction? People would be watching their TV sets and thinking, '*What*? Virginia Dare's descendants are *black*? No way!' "

I asked Charles what he'd say if the TV camera turned to him.

"I'd say, 'Yes, we're black, and also white, and Indian, too. A melting pot. Isn't that what it means to be American?' "

IN 1591, A year after John White's return from his final voyage to Roanoke, Sir Walter Raleigh impregnated and secretly married one of Queen Elizabeth's ladies-in-waiting. The queen was enraged by the couple's stealth and their failure to ask her permission to marry. She seems also to have been jealous of the match. In her pique, she threw Raleigh and his wife in the Tower of London.

Though they were released soon after, it took years for Raleigh to regain the queen's favor. His attention also turned away from the colony he'd named for her. Instead, he became caught up in the search for El Dorado, the legendary city of gold in South America. But he still held his charter to Virginia, and, as late as 1602, he dispatched an expedition to search for the Roanoke colonists and scout the coast for possible trade posts.

Elizabeth died the next year, bringing to the throne King James, who disliked and distrusted Raleigh—and despised the weed he'd made popular at court. James even penned a tract called *A Counterblaste to Tobacco,* which described smoking as "a custome lothsome to the eye, hatefull to the Nose, harmfull to the braine, daungerous to the Lungs, and, in the blacke stinking fume thereof," resembling the smoke of hell.

Soon after James's accession, Raleigh was arrested for plotting against the king and found guilty of treason, as well as of "holding heathenish, blasphemous, atheistical, and profane opinions." The judge's sentence gives some context to the brutality that the English and other Europeans visited on Indians. "Hanged and cut down alive," the judge told Raleigh, "your body shall be opened, your heart and bowels plucked out, and your privy members cut off, and thrown into the fire before your eyes; then your head to be stricken off from your body, and your body shall be divided into four quarters, to be disposed of at the King's pleasure."

On the day of his execution, Raleigh won a reprieve, but he returned to the Tower, where he remained for most of the next fifteen years. Then, in 1618, James found an excuse to reinstate the death sentence—a simple beheading this time, rather than drawing and quartering. Raleigh composed a final poem, smoked a last pipe of tobacco, donned his finest garments (black velvet cloak, taffeta pants, silk stockings), and climbed the scaffold, imploring his hesitant executioner, "Strike, man, strike!" His widow embalmed his severed head and stored it in a velvet bag, as a keepsake.

Sixteen years before his execution, when Elizabeth was still queen and Raleigh's colonial charter remained in force, he had written of Virginia, "I shall yet live to see it an English nation." Strictly speaking, he never achieved this dream: his grandly conceived "Cittie of Raleigh in Virginia" vanished with the Roanoke settlers, and he lost his charter to the colony upon his conviction for treason.

But Raleigh's failure, like that of his half-brother Humfrey Gilbert, nonetheless bore fruit. As he sat in the Tower, others took up his colonial mantle and headed, once again, for the Chesapeake. They enlisted Raleigh's "trumpet," Richard Hakluyt, and consulted the writing and art of Thomas Hariot and John White. Before long, colonists in the Chesapeake also discovered the crop that would ensure their survival: Sir Walter's beloved tobacco. As Raleigh climbed the gallows in October 1618, Virginia was maturing into a permanent settlement, the beginning of an English nation in America.

FROM FREE UNION I drove back east and over the bridge linking Roanoke Island to the Outer Banks, a very different world from the swampy woods and struggling towns of the interior. Here, there were few trees, just huge stands of condos and commerce: beach supply shops, malls, mini-golf courses, and a "Brew Thru" liquor mart, where

I bought a six-pack without leaving my car. All of this was built literally on sand, a thin line of shifting isles buffeted by ocean surf and
winds.

I followed the coastal highway south, toward Croatoan, where so
many threads of the Roanoke story seemed to lead. The road took me
through empty dunes and wind tunnels so fierce they shook my car
and peppered it with sand. Reaching Hatteras Island, I found a motel
for the night and then went searching for the remains of Croatoan's
main settlement. But the coordinates Fred Willard had given me were
characteristically vague. After wandering the shore for an hour without success, I drove down the road to ask for directions at a place
called the Frisco Native American Museum.

Inside, I was greeted by haunting Plains Indian music and a
Navajo blanket adorning one wall. A man appeared from a back office, leaning on a cane carved from a gnarled branch. He wore jeans,
cowboy boots, a silver belt buckle, and a string tie with a turquoise
clasp, and his long gray hair was gathered in a ponytail. From his appearance, and the museum's, I took him for a migrant from out West,
possibly a Native American. His response to my query about Croatoan
quickly disabused me.

"What did you say your last name was?" he asked.

"Horwitz."

"So you're searching for the lost tribe. Are you *meshugge*?"

I laughed and told him I might be crazy, but I wanted to see all the
places connected to the Roanoke colonists.

"I'm glad they're lost," he replied. "The natives should have
knocked them off before the English breathed on them. Instead, the
natives were dumb schmucks and said, 'Be my friend.' Whole lot of
good that did them."

Carl Bornfriend was about as Indian as Mel Brooks's Yiddish-
speaking chief in *Blazing Saddles*. But in his embrace of all things
Native American, he was kin to Charles "Sweet Medicine" Shepherd. "I don't dig white history," he said. "It's the native stuff I care
about." The son of a Jewish furrier in Philadelphia, he'd come to his
vocation young. "I grew up around dead animals, picking up
drowned rats and asking my father, 'What's this?' By the time I was

ten, I'd started collecting and preserving stuff, and over time it grew into this mess."

He led me through the museum, a converted shell shop that was now a warren of rooms crammed from floor to ceiling with exhibits, in little apparent sequence. Tomahawks, snake skins, buffalo skulls, stuffed alligators, turquoise jewelry, pipes, moccasins, Hopi drums— some of it valuable, a lot of it not. "Any museum curator will tell you to limit the number of things in each exhibit case, and the length of your captions, because people can't take it all in," Carl said. "I ignore that advice completely."

He also ignored the interest of visitors like me in the Roanoke mystery. "That's the first thing people always ask when they come here," he said. " 'What can you tell me about the lost colony?' "

He walked me to the only display that related to Roanoke: a wall hung with reproductions of John White's sketches of Indians. Unlike Charles Shepherd, Carl didn't regard White's art with reverence. "His natives look like Sumo wrestlers, or some suckers in London that White stopped and said, 'Put on a breechclout.' I don't think the natives looked anything like this. It was all White's imagination." He chuckled. "Or, should I say, a whitey's imagination."

Carl's scorn extended to the colonists White left behind. "We're supposed to feel sympathy for these people? *Oy vey*. The English came to pillage and they got what they deserved."

"Even Virginia Dare?" I asked.

Carl smiled. "Maybe the natives ate her. She was new and plump and tender. That dago, Columbus, the natives should have rubbed him out, too."

Carl's museum had one other display with some connection to the Roanoke story. He showed me a box full of shards, bones, and shells that Fred Willard had found after a 1993 hurricane, at the site of the Croatoan settlement I'd gone looking for. Archaeologists had since un-covered an early English ring and other European artifacts, though it wasn't clear whether these were trade goods acquired by Indians, or items left at Croatoan by refugees from Roanoke.

Carl didn't care either way. "I want to show what remains of the natives who were here before the whole horrific white story started," he said, closing up his museum for the day. "*They're* the lost people we should care about."

On his way home, he led me to the Croatoan site, tucked down a dirt road on the sheltered side of the island. Despite Manteo's friendship, Roanoke colonists wrote little of Croatoan, noting only that Indians went there to fish and hunt. By the mid-1700s, very few natives remained on the island. Now, there was only a thicket of live oak, greenbriar, and poison ivy. Much of the former Indian settlement lay under beach houses.

"White man's dreck," Carl said, before driving off. "As usual, that's all that's left."

AFTER WANDERING THE shore for a while, I walked across the road to the ocean side of the island. This was dominated by Cape Hatteras Lighthouse, at two hundred feet the tallest brick beacon in the nation. A board by the lighthouse offered a typical weather forecast: "Sunny. Cloudy, too. Rain possible." The cape's fickle and stormy weather, coupled with ocean currents that drove ships onto the twelve-mile shoal just offshore, had earned Hatteras its nickname: "Graveyard of the Atlantic." It was the resting place of some six hundred vessels, including Civil War ironclads and powerful steamships.

In my reading about Roanoke, I'd often wondered why sixteenth-century mariners seemed reluctant to supply or rescue the colony, or to stick around once they got there. Greed was the explanation usually given: time ashore was time away from piracy. But gazing from the lighthouse at the whitecaps off Hatteras, it seemed remarkable that Elizabethan seafarers had braved this coast at all, in wooden ships, without weather forecasts, or proper charts, or modern navigational gear, or a beacon. On top of the cape's many hazards, English ships visiting Roanoke often arrived here in hurricane season.

I ran through blowing rain, from the lighthouse to the wide beach facing the ocean. Here, at the exact elbow of the Outer Banks, I could scan 270 degrees of ocean, from south to east to north. If any of the lost colonists did come to Croatoan, this spot was where lookouts would have kept watch for ships.

John Lawson, the English naturalist who visited the island's gray-eyed natives in 1701, recorded "a pleasant Story that passes for an uncontested Truth amongst the Inhabitants." The vessel that brought the first English, he wrote, "does often appear amongst them, under Sail, in a gallant Posture, which they call *Sir Walter Raleigh's* Ship." If, as Lawson believed, the islanders were descended from lost colonists, the legend of the phantom ship may have spoken to the longing of their English ancestors, who watched and waited in vain for Sir Walter to come to their rescue.

The Roanoke story was filled with shadows like this: traces and rumors and clues, all feeding the mystery of the colonists' fate. But after working the case for ten days, I'd started to wonder whether trying to solve it wasn't just futile but misguided. For all the beguiling unknowns surrounding Roanoke, the story's eerie power derived from what was *known*.

Roanoke's colonists weren't so much lost as abandoned. By their patron, Raleigh; by the pilot who left them at Roanoke instead of the Chesapeake; by the many other mariners delayed or detoured by piracy en route to Virginia; by an English nation that gave low priority to their rescue; even by John White, who seems to have been easily daunted and resigned to their abandonment.

Nor was the colonists' stranding unusual in sixteenth-century America. The continent was filled with missing persons. The Spanish hunters who rode off from their ravine camp in the Texas plains and vanished in a sea of grass. Sailors cast ashore by frequent shipwrecks. A French boy the Huguenots left behind when they fled their first attempted colony. Three men whom Ralph Lane sent from Roanoke to the interior, and then abandoned when the colonists hastily caught a ride home with Sir Francis Drake. The hundreds of slaves Drake left ashore to make room for them.

Very few of these missing persons were ever seen or heard from again. Nor did anyone much bemoan their loss. Abandonment was an occupational hazard in early America: a cost of doing business, like salt pork or iron nails.

The Roanoke colonists, at least, were remembered and celebrated. Centuries after their disappearance, people still sought some connection to them, as literal or spiritual ancestors. As seminal Americans: the first English, the first white baby, the first to marry Indians, or, for Charles Shepherd, a source of triracial identity. I'd even come across an article in the *Journal of Croatian Studies* alleging that shipwrecked sailors from Dubrovnik had mingled with Indians of the Outer Banks, "who then acquired the name Croatoan."

As implausible as this sounded, it was kin, in one sense, to the many other fantasies about Roanoke: almost all of them imagined the colonists assimilating peacefully with natives and their Arcadian surrounds. But the known elements of Roanoke's story made it hard to conjure such a romantic or redemptive end. At Fort Raleigh, I'd read a recent tree-ring study, which showed that White's colonizing party arrived the same year as a severe drought, the worst in coastal North Carolina for eight hundred years. Starving colonists would have had to trade or steal from Indians whose own crops were lean. Also, if Virginia's Chesapeake tribe did take the English in, the natives would likely have been ravaged by disease even before any possible slaughter by Powhatan.

And what of the colonists who came here, to Manteo's homeland, to keep watch for English ships? Hunched against the sand at Hatteras, I swept my gaze from north to east to south and back again, like the modern lighthouse beam. It was spring, wet and windy, but mild compared to the winter storms and late-summer hurricanes that so often hit this coast. Even so, I found it hard to focus on the horizon for more than ten minutes, and doubted I could spot a distant vessel in the gray expanse of turbid sea and lowering clouds.

How long did the colonists keep watch, day after day, month after month? At what point did they finally surrender hope of rescue from across the sea, and give their fate over to the land and its people?

More questions I could never answer. As the weather turned worse, I abandoned the beach, retreated to the shelter of my car, and pointed it north, toward the Chesapeake.

CHAPTER 12

JAMESTOWN

THE CAPTAIN AND THE NATURALS

VIRGINIA—
Earth's only paradise!
—Michael Drayton,
"Ode to the Virginian Voyage" (1606)

JOHN SMITH WAS the pivotal figure in the founding of English America, and the most vivid: a short bushy braggart, a con man, an escape artist, an accomplished killer. Smith saved Jamestown and set the Pilgrims on course for Plymouth. He demonstrated, in both word and deed, that the New World demanded a new type of man— one like him. Self-made, scornful of rank, and ceaseless in his salesmanship, Smith was apostle and exemplar of the American Dream.

If this sounds hyperbolic, it should: everything about Smith was overstated, usually by himself. He penned one of England's first autobiographies, in the third person, starring Captain Smith as an early modern superhero, battling evildoers and impossible odds. England's advances in America were all due to him: the discoveries of others, he wrote, "are but Pigs of my owne Sow."

And there's the rub, as a contemporary of Smith's might have put it. The story of America's English birth depends on a blowhard who is easy to dislike, and even easier to doubt.

Smith's alleged rescue by Pocahontas is the most famous of his exploits, but it was far from his first or most incredible. The son of a yeoman farmer, he fled his apprenticeship to a merchant at the age of sixteen, "to get beyond the Sea." He became a soldier of fortune, expert at artillery, and joined Christian forces fighting the Ottoman Turks. In Hungary, Smith was promoted to captain and awarded a coat of arms, adorned with the heads of three Turks he had decapitated in consecutive duels.

Later, wounded and captured in Transylvania, he was sold into slavery and taken in chains to Constantinople, where he charmed his "faire Mistresse"—the first of several high-born women who "tooke much compassion on him." But when she sent Smith to serve her brother in Tartary, the captain became a degraded field hand. One day, after too much abuse, Smith beat out his master's brains with a threshing bat, stole his clothes and horse, and rode off "into the desert."

He wandered north to Muscovy, west to the Baltic, and south through the Holy Roman Empire, traversing an atlas of bygone principalities. "Being thus satisfied with Europe and Asia," Smith wrote, he sailed for Africa and ended up on a pirate ship off the Barbary Coast. He experienced all this and many more adventures by his mid-twenties, when he returned to England and soon after sailed for his fourth continent: North America.

In December 1606, as Smith departed for Virginia, England was still playing catch-up on the continent. Spain had consolidated its hold on Florida and the Southwest. The French were establishing trade posts along the St. Lawrence River and probing Maine, Massachusetts, and upstate New York. England held only its vague claim to Virginia, and to a stretch of Pacific shore that Sir Francis Drake had coasted in 1579, during his round-the-world voyage in the *Golden Hind*. Beset by "vile, thicke and stinking fogges," Drake landed in northern California, tacked a brass plate to a post, and named the coast Nova Albion. No English would return there for two centuries. In 1606, not a single English settler occupied the future United States, unless some of the Roanoke colonists remained alive after twenty years in the wild.

At home, however, much had changed since Raleigh's failed venture in the 1580s. The defeat of the Spanish Armada boosted England's confidence and sea power, and in 1604, King James concluded an uneasy peace with Spain. England's colonial philosophy had also matured. In place of the Raleigh model, reliant on piracy and the purse of a rich knight, merchants formed joint-stock companies to raise capital and to pool the risk and profit. The Virginia Company, chartered in 1606, had branches in London and Plymouth, the former focused on the Chesapeake and the latter on "North Virginia"—roughly, the coast from New York to Maine.

Despite this corporate footing, and support from the Crown, the company's Chesapeake venture went badly from the start. Three ships carrying 105 colonists left London in 1606 and instantly hit foul weather, delaying the fleet and fraying tempers. John Smith, accused of plotting against the ships' captains, was put in chains for the rest of the voyage and he came close to being hanged.

In the West Indies, where the fleet stopped to reprovision, the English suffered the first of many gruesome casualties to come. A "gentleman" died in "great extremity" when his "fat melted within him by the great heate and drought of the Countrey." Upon finally reaching the Chesapeake, in late April 1607, the English had no sooner landed than Indians crept up on them in the night, badly wounding two men.

Colonists confronted another surprise when they opened sealed orders from the Virginia Company, naming the seven men who would rule them ashore. Six were prominent, well-connected figures, mostly in their forties and fifties. The seventh was John Smith: a commoner, only twenty-seven, and still under arrest for mutiny.

For their "seating place," the English selected a point of land thirty-five miles upriver from the bay, where deep water ran so close to shore that ships could moor to trees. Uninhabited by Indians, and linked to the mainland by a tidal isthmus, the peninsula appeared easy to defend. And in spring, the surrounds seemed a "paradise," one colonist wrote, blanketed in "faire flowers," strawberries, and "the pleasantest Suckles."

Colonists erected a fort and sent a party upriver to scout for riches and the dreamed-of Northwest Passage. In late June, they loaded two ships with a sample of what they thought was gold, a supply of clapboard, and letters extolling the Virginia settlement, which they called James Fort, Villa James, and eventually, James Towne. "You yet maye lyve," William Brewster wrote a friend, "to see Ingland more renowned then any kingdome in all Ewroopa."

Six weeks later, Brewster was dead. Scores of his fellow colonists soon trailed him to shallow graves. "There were never Englishmen left in a forreigne Countrey," a survivor wrote, "in such miserie as wee were in this new discovered Virginia."

Jamestown's rapid descent from heaven to hell has traditionally been blamed on the colonists themselves. Their first mistake was a poor choice of real estate. The swampy Jamestown peninsula lacked springs or brooks, leaving the men to drink from the river, which was not only brackish but "at a low tide full of slime and filth." This caused ills such as dysentery, typhoid fever, and salt poisoning.

"Our men were destroyed with cruell diseases, as Swellings, Fluxes, Burning Fevers," wrote the colonist George Percy. "In the morning their bodies trailed out of their Cabines like Dogges to be buried." Other ills recorded at Jamestown included heatstroke and calenture, a tropical delirium that made men jump into the sea, thinking it a broad green pasture.

Virginia's assault on newcomers' health, not just that first summer but for years to come, was so remorseless that the English referred to a process of "seasoning." Colonists landed, fell ill, and either died or became "seasoned" to their environment. Most failed this grim initiation. Of the more than twenty thousand English sent to Virginia during the colony's first decades, roughly three-quarters perished. This death rate, notes the historian Edmund Morgan, was "comparable only to that found in Europe during the peak years of the plague."

Indian attacks contributed to the toll. Natives knew better than to build villages on Jamestown's swampy peninsula, but they hunted there and regarded it as their territory. During the colony's first summer, Indians used high marsh grass as cover to creep up and snipe at settlers. One man was shot by arrows while "going out to do natural necessity," another while "straggling without the fort." In one "furious assault" on the fort, Indians killed two and wounded ten.

The settlers also fought among themselves. Almost from the moment of its founding, Jamestown became an all-male divorce court, rife with deceit, betrayal, and petty accusations. The council's first president was overthrown amid charges that he denied another man "a spoonful of beer" and "a penny-whittle" (a cheap knife). He was also accused of hoarding scarce food, to which he replied: "I never had but one squirrel roasted." His replacement as president fared no better; he was exposed as hiding behind an alias. His unmasker was a man he had sentenced to death for treason, the first of many who would be hanged, shot, burned, or tortured at Jamestown.

One reason for this strife was the makeup of the colony. At the top stood gentlemen who expected deference and creature comforts even as others starved. George Percy, one of the colony's revolving-door leaders, wrote to his brother, the Earl of Northumberland, pleading for a loan so he could afford more than the common ration of oatmeal. "It standing upon my reputation," Percy explained, "to keepe a continual and dayle table for Gentlemen of fashion about me."

Percy and his ilk regarded their social inferiors at Jamestown as rabble, and some evidently were: debtors, drunken sailors and soldiers, convicts released from prison, and laborers press-ganged at ports or on London streets. This mob would have been hard for anyone to motivate and control, and the gentry appointed to do so were spectacularly ill suited to the task.

By September 1607, just four months after the colony's founding, most of the original settlers were dead. Only a few weeks' slim rations remained. Starved, sick, and set against one another, the besieged English were all but defenseless, "our men night and day groaning in every corner of the Fort," Percy wrote.

Then a miracle occurred—the first of several interventions that would rescue Jamestown from impending doom. "It pleased God," Percy wrote, "to send those people who were our mortall enemies to releeve us with victuals, as Bread, Corne, Fish, and Flesh in great plentie, which was the setting up of our feeble men; otherwise wee had all perished."

*A portrait of John Smith, the frontispiece of
his history of Virginia, 1624*

Why the previously hostile Indians chose to save the English isn't clear. They may have judged the survivors to be of more value alive than dead. English ships brought copper kettles, axes, and other goods, and the colonists' skill with cannons and muskets could be enlisted against enemy tribes. Also, Europeans had appeared in the Chesapeake before: Spanish Jesuits (slaughtered near Jamestown a generation earlier), mariners on reconnaissance voyages, and possibly refugees from Roanoke. As yet, these intruders had posed little threat, and could be easily starved out or expelled when necessary. Or so Indians may reasonably have supposed in the late summer of 1607, as they kept watch on fifty dying men who seemed utterly clueless, since they drank foul water and couldn't feed themselves.

What natives couldn't know is that their rescue of the English would unleash John Smith, the one man capable of mobilizing the beleaguered colony. In a leadership reshuffle, Smith took charge of supplying the fort and immediately set off to trade for food, the first of many trips that would carry him, over the next two years, across eastern Virginia, Maryland, and, possibly, Delaware. Given the obstacles Smith faced, his travels comprise one of the great sagas of survival and improvisation in early America.

In contrast to Roanoke, where the English had settled among relatively small tribes that greeted the strangers peacefully, the Jamestown colonists had planted their fort in the middle of the most powerful and populous society on the Eastern Seaboard. Powhatan, whose capital lay just twelve miles from Jamestown, ruled an empire that stretched from North Carolina to Maryland. He collected tribute from dozens of tribes and fifteen thousand or more Indians.

Most natives lived in small settlements along four broad rivers flowing into the Chesapeake: today's James, York, Rappahannock, and Potomac. These were the superhighways of seventeenth-century Virginia, and Smith traveled them all, in an open boat powered by sail and oar, usually with no more than a dozen men. His first stop, at a village near Jamestown, set the pattern for dozens of encounters to follow.

"The Indians, thinking us near famished," Smith wrote, offered only "small handfulls of beanes or wheat for a hatchet or a piece of copper." To avoid seeming desperate—which he was—Smith scorned the offer and anchored nearby. The next day he "let fly his muskets and ran his boat on shore," then marched on the village. Natives quickly offered venison and corn, at a favorable rate of exchange.

Smith's gunboat diplomacy violated orders from the Virginia Company in London, which commanded settlers to "have great care not to offend the Naturals." But Smith "loved actions more than wordes," he wrote, and valued firsthand experience over the opinions of "tender educats" 3,700 miles away. "I know no reason but to beleeve my own eies, before any mans imagination."

This scorn was somewhat disingenuous; a well-read man, Smith

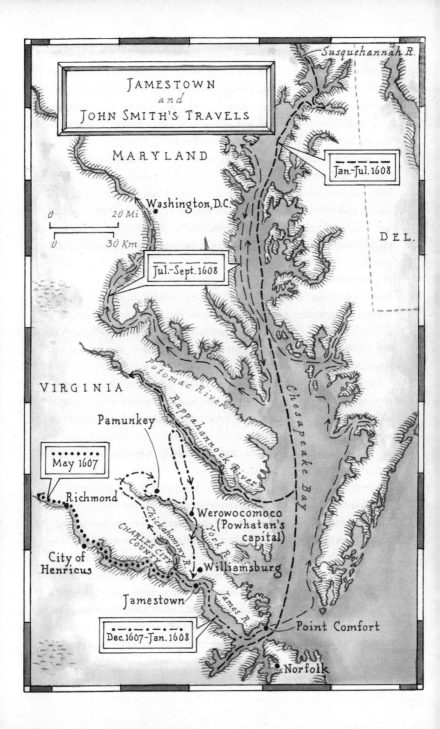

JAMESTOWN
and
JOHN SMITH'S TRAVELS

Susquehannah R.

MARYLAND

Jan.-Jul. 1608

●Washington, D.C.

0   *20 Mi*

0   *30 Km*

DEL.

Jul.-Sept. 1608

VIRGINIA

Potomac River

Rappahannock River

Pamunkey

May 1607

Chesapeake Bay

●Richmond

Chickahominy R.

CHARLES CITY COUNTY

York R.

●Werowocomoco
(Powhatan's
capital)

City of
Henricus

●Williamsburg

Jamestown

James R.

Dec. 1607-Jan. 1608

●Point Comfort

●Norfolk

admired the power politics of Machiavelli. He believed a soft approach toward the "Naturals" would invite their contempt and, ultimately, an attack. By intimidating natives, in pursuit of clear goals, he sought to win their respect and avoid an all-out conflict. "Onlie with fearing them," he wrote, "we got what they had."

To keep Indians in awe of the English, Smith adapted the skills at artillery and deception he'd honed as a soldier of fortune. He fired his boat's cannon into a tree full of icicles, to magnify the shot's impact; used rivers and encircling woods to create terrifying echoes; and stuck soldiers' helmets atop sticks, "to make us seeme many." He also reprised his gladiatorial skills, besting several chiefs in solo combat.

But Smith didn't succeed through bluff and bullying alone. He traded shrewdly, spreading goods among villages to stoke demand without dampening prices. His time abroad had also made him a skilled linguist. He compiled an extensive Algonquian lexicon, including enduring words such as *mockasin* and *tomahack,* and a term for friend, *chammay,* which may be the source of "chum."

Smith also had a gift for wiggling out of tight spots. During an exploratory trip late in 1607, he split his small force and went scouting alone with an Indian guide, only to be ambushed and shot in the thigh with an arrow. He grabbed his guide as a human shield while firing his pistols, but in the time it took him to reload he was surrounded and forced to surrender.

Smith's captor was Powhatan's brother Opechancanough, a proud warrior who would bedevil the English for decades to come. But the captain managed to engage the chief, at least by his own account. "I presented him with a compass dial," Smith wrote, "describing by my best means the use thereof, whereat he was so amazedly admired as he suffered me to proceed in a discourse of the roundnes of the earth, the course of the sunne, moone, starress, and plannets."

Smith was then taken on a long tour of Indian villages and brought before Powhatan. The "Grave and Majesticall" ruler, aged about sixty, wore "Chaynes of great Pearles about his necke" and perched on an elaborate dais, surrounded by wives and retainers. In Smith's first account of their meeting, published the next year, he wrote that

King Powhatan comands C: Smith to be slayne, his daughter Pokahontas beggs his life his thankfullnes and how he subiected 39 of their kings. reade ÿ history.
printed by James Reeve

Pocahontas saves John Smith, from Smith's 1624 account of the rescue

Powhatan welcomed him "with good wordes, and great Platters of sundrie Victuals."

Not until 1624, seventeen years after his capture, did Smith publish the story familiar to generations of American schoolchildren. "Two great stones were brought before Powhatan," he wrote. Then the chief's retainers grabbed Smith and laid his head on the rocks. "Being ready with their clubs, to beat out his braines, Pocahontas the kings dearest daughter, when no intreaty could prevaile, got his head in her armes, and laid her owne upon his to save him from death."

Smith's original account of his capture, in 1608, was heavily edited in London and published as propaganda for the Virginia Company.

His near execution isn't mentioned, though it's possible the scene was censored by editors. It's also possible that Smith lifted his story from the strikingly similar account of Juan Ortiz, the Spanish captive in Florida who became De Soto's translator. By 1624, when Smith published the dramatic version of his rescue, Ortiz's account was available in England, and Pocahontas had become a well-known and admired figure.

Even if Smith really did undergo the ordeal he described, he may have misunderstood its meaning. He was new to Virginia, the other members of his party had just been massacred, and Powhatan's warriors, by all accounts, were large and fearsome men. They shaved their heads on one side, growing their hair long on the other and decorating it with "the hand of their enemy, dried." They adorned their pierced ears with claws, dead rats, and live snakes. Powhatan's personal guards were also "the tallest men his Country doth afford," Smith wrote. When these "grim courtiers" seized him and laid his head on a stone, he had every reason to expect they were about to beat out his brains.

But Powhatan may never have intended to kill his captive. Mock executions are believed to have been part of a native ritual, to test prisoners' mettle prior to adopting them. By Smith's own account, no sooner had Pocahontas intervened than Powhatan—who moments before had seemed intent on slaying his captive—"was contented he should live to make him hatchets, and her bells, beads, and copper."

If Smith's "rescue" by Pocahontas is questionable, there's even less basis to the legend of a romance between the two. In Disney's animated movie version, Pocahontas is a busty and vaguely Asian Barbie, and Smith a blond Ken Doll. In a recent movie for adults, *The New World,* the darkly handsome Colin Farrell frolics with a voluptuous young actress in skimpy buckskins.

The real Smith, judging from portraits, was hirsute and homely. Of Pocahontas there are many descriptions, beginning with Smith's own: "A child of ten years old," he wrote, she was beautiful in "feature, countenance and proportion" and possessed "wit and spirit" that made her the "Nonpareil" of Virginia.

This is a flattering portrait—of a *child*. Another colonist later described her as a "young girle" cartwheeling naked through Jamestown, not yet old enough to wear the apron donned by female Indians at puberty. Her proper name was Matoaka, "Pocahontas" being a girlish nickname meaning "Little Lively One." The only hint that Smith saw her in a more mature light was his mention, years later, that his foes at Jamestown spread the unfounded rumor that he planned to make himself king of Virginia by marrying Pocahontas. In the event, she wed a different John. Smith went to his grave a bachelor.

Whether or not Pocahontas saved Smith from execution, she *did* rescue Jamestown. One night, she came to the fort to warn the English of a trap Powhatan was laying. At other times, she hid an English messenger and saved a captive boy whose fellow prisoners were killed. She also served as an intermediary and frequent visitor to the fort, bringing desperately needed food in exchange for trinkets. Smith's Algonquian lexicon includes a phrase that translates: "Bid Pokahontas bring hither two little Baskets, and I will give her white beads to make her a chaine."

With Pocahontas's aid, Smith's initiative, and the arrival of more settlers, the troubled colony began to find its feet. As other councilors died or were deposed, Smith rose to become president and acted quickly to mobilize the listless colonists. "He that will not worke shall not eate," the captain famously declared, "for the labours of thirtie or fortie honest and industrious men shall not be consumed to maintaine an hundred and fiftie idle loyterers."

Under Smith's stern rule, colonists performed military drills, built houses, and dug a well of "excellent sweet water." But what made Smith exceptional was his recognition that survival in America meant learning to live as *Americans*. Settlers sowed forty acres of corn, guided by two Indian prisoners who "taught us how to order and plant our fields." Natives also showed them how to clear land by cutting notches in tree trunks and stripping the bark so the trees would rot. At one point, Smith dispersed his men among villages, to live off the land and learn from Indians "how to gather and use their fruits as well as themselves." During his one-year tenure as leader, almost no English died, an unprecedented success.

Smith was also the first English colonist to see the folly of pursuing "gilded hopes" of mineral riches and the dream of a Pacific passage. America's true promise, he believed, lay in its soil, timber, fish, game, and other resources. And tapping this wealth required patient and humble labor, not the idle "Gallants," metal refiners, perfumers, and other supernumeraries the Virginia Company kept sending.

"I intreat you," Smith wrote his superiors in London, "send but thirty Carpenters, husbandmen, gardiners, fisher men, blacksmiths, masons and diggers up of trees, roots, well provided; then a thousand of such as we have."

Smith wasn't a democrat; he ruled despotically and treasured his feudal coat of arms. But he believed that power and privilege should flow from merit, not birth. It "is a happy thing," he wrote, to inherit wealth and honor. "But that which is got by prowesse and magnanimity is the truest lustre."

Smith's high opinion of himself, and his disdain for inherited rank, put him at odds with the well-born men sent by the Virginia Company to Jamestown. Typical was George Percy, the earl's son, who reviled the upstart captain as "an ambitious, unworthy and vayneglorious fellow, attempting to take all men's authorities from them." In 1609, Smith's foes engineered his removal as leader, and may have tried to kill him. During a river trip, Smith was asleep in his boat when someone "accidentallie" ignited his gunpowder bag, "which tore his flesh from his bodie and thighs, 9 or 10 inches square in a most pittifull manner." Ferried back to the fort, he was "unable to stand, and neare bereft of his senses." A ship was about to depart for England and Smith sailed home, never to return to Jamestown.

THOSE LEFT TO run the colony in the captain's stead quickly brought it to the brink of ruin again. Shortly before Smith's departure, they began a campaign of terror against Indians, burning villages, looting the tombs of "dead kings," and cutting off natives' heads and limbs to force tribes to hand over food. Smith, for all his harshness, knew that such tactics would invite retribution. Sure enough, natives responded by massacring trade parties, in one case stuffing the mouths of English corpses with food, as a warning to any others who "shold come to seeke for breade and reliefe amongste them."

George Percy, the new leader of the colony, also failed to store grain, let fishing nets rot, and so angered Indians that they killed the hundreds of hogs Smith had bred as a reserve food supply. As a result, the English found themselves, at the end of 1609, back where they'd been two years before, besieged and ill-provisioned inside their wretched fort. Except now there were five times as many settlers, competing for scarce food through a long winter known as "the Starving Time."

When rations ran out, colonists ate horses, dogs, cats, rats, and mice. They ate shoes, cooked starch from their collars into "a gluey porridge," and devoured excrement. When nothing else remained, they ate one another. "Some have Licked up the Bloode which hath fallen from their weake fellows," Percy wrote. Others disinterred corpses. The nadir was reached when a man killed his pregnant wife, "chopped the Mother in pieces and salted her for his food." Percy executed the man after extracting a confession by hanging him from his thumbs.

Of five hundred colonists at Jamestown when Smith left in the autumn of 1609, only sixty remained alive the following May, when a supply fleet arrived. The newcomers had endured a trauma of their own, having been shipwrecked on Bermuda for almost a year following a great storm (a stranding that inspired Shakespeare's play *The Tempest*). At Jamestown, they found the fort's gate hanging from its hinges, walls torn down for firewood, and crazed survivors, "so Leane that they looked Lyke Anatomies," running naked through the fort, crying, "We are starved. We are starved."

The incoming governor decided there was no hope of resurrecting Jamestown, and ordered its evacuation. This news was greeted with "a generall acclamation and shout of joy." On June 7, 1610, just over three years after Jamestown's founding, the English abandoned the fort, "with a peal of small shot." Like so many New World ventures before it, Virginia had failed.

Then came yet another deus ex machina. After sailing a short way toward the sea, Percy wrote, "Suddenly we espied a boat making towards us." Its captain was English, and he heralded the arrival of a fleet carrying 150 fresh settlers and a year's supply of provisions. "Whereupon," Percy wrote, "we all returned to James Town again."

MISBEGOTTEN, ABANDONED, AND miraculously rescued four centuries ago, Jamestown still feels like an orphan of early America. Plymouth, founded thirteen years afterward, is a rock star for tourists. So is Williamsburg, which lies just twelve miles from Jamestown, the settlement it supplanted as Virginia's capital in 1699. Even the meager remains at Roanoke Island, Jamestown's failed predecessor, attract as many tourists annually as the first permanent English colony in America.

One reason for this relative neglect is the bashing Jamestown has taken from generations of historians, particularly nineteenth-century New Englanders. Eager to anoint Plymouth as the birthplace of America, they cast the country's English beginnings as a regional morality play. Pilgrims, in frigid Massachusetts, scraped through by dint of pious, shared labor. Virginians, their degenerate Southern twins, were greedy, godless, class-ridden, and indolent, playing bowls in the streets as their settlement rotted around them.

In the Yankee view, not only was Jamestown a disgrace; its founding hero was a colossal liar, as evidenced by the many versions he gave of his rescue by Pocahontas. Henry Adams, who launched a famous broadside against Smith just after the Civil War, saw his salvo as "a rear attack on the Virginia aristocracy" he so despised. Though regional passions later cooled, many twentieth-century historians were just as harsh. In 1975, Edmund Morgan branded Jamestown a "fiasco" that endured despite the worst efforts of its colonists.

Jamestown's physical remains fared almost as poorly as its reputation. Semiabandoned by the late 1600s, most of the colony site was planted over with crops, and then buried beneath a Confederate fort. The isthmus linking the peninsula to the mainland washed away, leaving Jamestown an island. Not until 1893 did the quaintly named Association for the Preservation of Virginia Antiquities buy one corner of the island, which became a small historic park that still evokes its Victorian origins.

The park's statue of Pocahontas depicts the naked Indian girl as a woman of about twenty, demurely clad in a deerskin dress. Nearby stands a towering statue of John Smith, hand on sword hilt, gazing resolutely toward the river. The colony's restored church is hung with musty plaques put up by groups such as the National Society of Colonial Dames, honoring the "Ancient Planters of Virginia."

Until recently, there wasn't much else to see. When the archaeologist William Kelso first visited in the 1960s and asked about the English fort, a park ranger pointed at a cypress in the river and said, "You're too late—it's out there." The spit of land on which the fort stood was believed to have eroded into the James.

Forty years later, I found Kelso, a trim white-haired man in shorts and deck shoes, sifting dirt in a pit by the river. "I guess I'm someone who tends to question what he's told," he said. Raised in Ohio, Kelso had been taught the conventional line: "Jamestown was a failure," he recited, "a footnote to the triumph of Plymouth." Later, when he became an archaeologist in Virginia, Kelso kept hearing that the Jamestown site was a dry hole, just as he'd been told on his first visit. But in the 1990s, he and a team of colleagues went in for another look.

Over the course of a decade, they'd unearthed trench lines and post holes delineating the foundation of Jamestown's fort, only 15 percent of which had washed away. They also found house sites, scores of graves, and thousands of artifacts. As it turned out, there was more of historic Jamestown than had ever been found of Roanoke or the original Plymouth colony. To Kelso's contrarian eye, archaeology also contradicted much of the conventional wisdom about early Virginia.

"It's easy to find failure here," he said, "but that's not the whole story. There were capable, hardworking people and good decisions made."

Using his trowel as a pointer, Kelso traced the outline of the fort. It was triangular, occupied the island's highest ground, and was built with bulwarks, a moat, and an arc of defensive earthworks, all state-of-the-art military engineering in the early seventeenth century. The colonists had constructed the fort in three weeks—astonishingly fast, given that they had to dig a thousand-foot-long trench and cut and raise a fourteen-foot palisade. "Men who were loafing and disorganized," Kelso said, "couldn't have done this."

There were also signs that colonists quickly adapted to their environs. Shedding their hot, heavy armor, they refashioned it into buckets and other items. They sided their houses with Indian-style bark shingles, which were cooler than the thick clay walls common in England. And archaeologists had found considerable evidence of craft work and industry, including locally made brick, glass, nails, and barrels. "Their orders were to produce goods for export," Kelso said, "and they certainly gave it a college try."

If the supposed idleness of colonists had been exaggerated, their suffering was not. Kelso showed me dirt marks tracing grave sites, like chalk lines at a crime scene. So far, the remains of seventy-two people had been found, often piled together in shallow holes without clothing or shroud. Half were in their twenties or younger. Their bones bore signs of hard labor, poor nourishment, and violence. One woman had five teeth in her head. The knee of a young man was shattered by a bullet, the leg of another pierced by an arrowhead. A piece of skull, fractured by blunt trauma, was found in a trash pit, discarded after a failed effort to trepan the skull and save the man's life. Archaeologists had also found crude medical tools such as a *spatula mundani,* a narrow spoon used to treat extreme constipation by extracting hard stools.

By 1610, at the end of the Starving Time, survivors at Jamestown occupied a virtual necropolis: the dead outnumbered the living by roughly ten to one. "If you're looking for evidence of failure," Kelso said, waving his trowel across the crowded graves, "there it is."

But once again, on-site research gave nuance to the story. Tree-ring analysis showed that Jamestown, like Roanoke, was settled during the onset of a severe drought. Only two hoes had been found, evidence that the Virginia Company had failed to equip colonists for farming. Whatever crops the English sowed would have failed, heightening pressure to extract food from Indians, whose own harvests had also suffered; Smith noted in 1608 that natives had little to trade, "their corne being that year bad." The conflict between colonists and Indians was, at least in part, a desperate, Darwinian struggle.

"The bottom line is that Jamestown endured," Kelso said, returning to his work. "That's success, even if it wasn't pretty. And given what the people here had to overcome, it's a miracle any of them survived."

THE SUPPLY FLEET that forestalled Jamestown's abandonment in 1610 brought a new governor, Lord De La Warr, and a harsh shift in policy. To end the chaos, the colony's London council licensed the ruthless suppression of internal dissent and external threats. De La Warr and his successors introduced martial law, whipping colonists for infractions such as missing church. A second offense of blasphemy was punished by having a lancet thrust through the tongue. Colonists who deserted or robbed from the storehouse were hanged, burned, "broken upon wheles," and bound to trees until they starved. Even stealing flowers from another colonist's garden became a capital offense.

For Indians, the new regime was crueler still. Soon after De La Warr's arrival, the English attacked a neighboring tribe that had vexed the colony since its founding. A troop led by George Percy "put some fiftene or sixtene to the Sworde," burning houses and corn. After beheading one prisoner, Percy took the tribe's "Queen" and her children aboard an English boat. But his soldiers began "to murmur" over their being spared. "Itt was Agreed upon," Percy wrote, "to putt the Children to deathe the wich was effected by Throweinge them overboard and shoteinge owtt their Braynes in the water."

When Percy returned to Jamestown, Lord De La Warr was displeased; the "Queen," he said, should be burned. At first, Percy demurred. "Haveinge seen so much Bloodshed thatt day," he wrote, "I desyred to see no more and for to Burne her I did not holde itt fitteing." In what passed for mercy at Jamestown, Percy gave the queen "A quicker dispatche." Soldiers took her into the woods and "putt her to the Sworde."

Several years of savage warfare followed. Then, in 1613, Pocahontas came to the rescue again, though not of her own volition. An English mariner, Samuel Argall, learned she was visiting a tribe on the

Potomac and decided to "possess myself of her by any stratagem," to hold her in exchange for prisoners, arms, and tools Powhatan had seized from the English. With threats and bribes, Argall coaxed the Potomac chief to bring Pocahontas aboard his ship, where he feasted and then confined her. "She began to be exceeding pensive and discontented," a colonist wrote. Argall sent a messenger to Powhatan, telling of the kidnapping and demanding English captives and property, and a large quantity of corn. "Then he should have his daughter restored, otherwise not."

Powhatan returned seven prisoners, a few tools and weapons, and a little corn. But the English weren't satisfied. For almost a year, they awaited the full ransom. Then they took Pocahontas and 150 men to collect it in person. After a tense standoff and no answer from Powhatan, Pocahontas went ashore and met several of her kinsmen, curtly informing them: "If her father had loved her, he would not value her lesse than old swords, Peeces [guns] or Axes: wherefore shee would still dwell with the English men, who loved her."

One of the colonists certainly did. During Pocahontas's captivity, she'd lived with a minister who tutored her in English and Christianity. Then aged about seventeen, she also came to know John Rolfe, a recently widowed settler in his late twenties. Since arriving in Virginia a few years before, Rolfe had experimented with tobacco seeds from the Caribbean. He had also fallen desperately in love.

In an extraordinary letter to the colony's governor, Rolfe wrote that his feelings for Pocahontas "hav a long time bin so intangled, and inthralled in so intricate a laborinth, that I was even awearied to unwinde my selfe thereout." By confessing "these passions of my troubled soule," Rolfe put himself in some peril. The English regarded union with heathen natives as a grievous sin. Rolfe, a pious man, knew "the heavie displeasure which almightie God conceived against the sonnes of Levie and Israel for marrying strange wives." His love for the member of a "barbarous" and "accursed" people also exposed him to the scorn of settlers, who would "taxe or taunt me."

But Rolfe was besotted, unable to control "the many passions and

sufferings, which I have daily, hourely, yea and in my sleepe indured."
His torment, he assured the governor, wasn't "the unbridled desire of
carnall affection." Rather, he felt compelled to marry Pocahontas, to
save her soul and his own. She wanted to become Christian, he wrote,
possessed the "capablenesse of understanding" to do so, and gave a
"great appearance of love to me."

We have only Rolfe's words as evidence of her affection. According to another colonist, Pocahontas was already wife to an Indian warrior named Kocoum, of whom nothing more is known. Whatever her
feelings toward Rolfe, the prospect of their marriage was attractive to
everyone else. Both the Indians and the English were exhausted by
warfare, and seeking a way to save face. Having failed to collect the full
ransom for Pocahontas, the governor, "for the good of the plantation,"
approved her marriage, and so did Powhatan.

In April 1614, she was baptized "Rebecca" (after Isaac's biblical
bride, whom God told, "two nations are in thy womb," one "mightier
than the other") and wed Rolfe, with two of her brothers and an uncle
in attendance. "Ever since," a colonist wrote later that year, "we have
had friendly commerce and trade not only with Powhatan himself but
also with his subjects round about us; so as now I see no reason why
the colony should not thrive apace."

The colony did begin to prosper, thanks not only to the peace following the marriage but also to Rolfe's introduction of West Indian tobacco. The native Virginia strain, one colonist wrote, was "weak and
of a biting taste," and yielded only a small leaf per plant. The imported
species had a fuller, sweeter flavor and grew tall and bushy. Within a
few years, settlers were growing tobacco to the exclusion of other
crops and exporting it by the ton, at tremendous profit. Tobacco was
the gold that Europeans had so long sought in North America and
never found.

IN 1616, THE Rolfes sailed for London with their year-old son,
Thomas. The voyage was sponsored by the Virginia Company to
trumpet the colony's success and its "civilizing" of natives. The trip

also gave Powhatan a chance to spy on England. He sent along a trusted priest, Tomocomo, telling him to record the number of people he saw in England with "notches on a stick," so Powhatan could judge if the "multitudes" he'd heard about actually existed. The priest had to quickly abandon this census, and was likewise stunned by England's abundant crops and trees; he said Indians believed colonists "came into their country for supply of these defects."

Tomocomo was also charged with discovering the fate of John Smith, whom Powhatan and his people evidently admired. For months after the Rolfes' arrival, the captain kept his distance. When he finally appeared, his reunion with Pocohantas proved awkward. The naked Indian girl Smith had first met a decade before was now a wife, mother, and Christian, "and was become very formall and civill after our English manner." Upon meeting Smith, he wrote, she gave him a "modest salutation" and "without any word she turned about, obscured her face, as not seeming well contented."

Only later did she speak, reminding Smith of the many promises he'd made to Powhatan. "What was yours should be his," she said. "You called him father, being in his land a stranger." Yet Smith had left Virginia, and thereafter the English "did tell us alwaies you were dead." Indians doubted this, she added, "because your countriemen will lie much." On this sour note, Smith ended his brief account of their visit.

He noted with pleasure, however, that Pocahontas made a great impression on "divers courtiers" who met her in London. "They have seen many English ladies worse favored, proportioned, and behavioured." She went with lords and ladies to balls and plays, including the Twelfth Night masque held at Whitehall Palace.

Pocahontas also sat for a portrait, the only contemporary image of her that survives. The artist, or his patron, was intent on portraying Pocahontas as a thoroughly English gentlewoman. Unsmiling and stiffly posed, she sits swaddled in courtly attire—puffed sleeves, embroidered velvet mantle, starched lace collar, towering beaver hat—and clutches a fan of ostrich plumes. Except for her strong cheekbones and piercing almond eyes, she is barely recognizable as an Indian.

*A portrait of Pocahontas (a.k.a. Matoaka and
Rebecca Rolfe) in London, 1616*

By then, she may no longer have felt like one. Pocahontas had
known the English for half of her twenty years and lived among them,
as Rebecca Rolfe, for the past three. An exceptionally intrepid
woman—the mirror image of John Smith—she had inhabited three
distinct worlds in her short life: Tsenacomacoh (the Indian name for
Powhatan's realm), colonial Virginia, and Stuart England. Having
crossed the Atlantic, she gave signs of wanting to stay. In January 1617,
a Londoner wrote that John Rolfe was about to return with his wife to
Virginia, "sore against her will."

Then, as they waited for favorable winds, Pocahontas and Thomas
fell ill. No symptoms were recorded, but the Rolfes had earlier removed from London to a country village, "Being offended by the
Smoke of the Town." Pocahontas and her son may have suffered from
a respiratory ailment, possibly tuberculosis.

Upon finally setting sail, the Rolfes traveled only a short way down the Thames when Pocahontas became too ill to go on. She was taken ashore at Gravesend, to a dockside cottage or inn. According to a local church registry: "March 21.—Rebecca Wrothe wyffe of Thomas Wroth gent. A Virginia Lady borne, here was buried in ye Chauncell."

This brief entry, misspelling her name and confusing those of her husband and her son, is the only record in Gravesend of Pocahontas's death. Daughter to an Indian king, and a celebrity in London, she was just another traveler through the busy river port. The church where she was buried burned a century later, and its many graves became intermingled. To this day, no one knows precisely where Pocahontas's remains lie.

"My wife's death is much lamented," John Rolfe wrote in a letter two months after her burial. She had been comforted at the end, he said, by the apparent recovery of their two-year-old son. "All must die," she told her husband, "but 'tis enough that her childe liveth."

He almost didn't. Before the ship left the English coast, Thomas's health faltered. Rolfe reluctantly left him at Plymouth, in the care of an admiral, and arranged for a brother to collect him. Rolfe then returned to Virginia, where he became a prominent official, married for a third time, to an Englishwoman, and had a daughter before he died in 1622, never having seen Thomas again.

Thomas Rolfe recovered his health and moved back to Virginia at about the age of twenty, to a large plantation he'd inherited from his father. He seems to have identified wholly as an Englishman, and been accepted as one. He married the daughter of a leading colonist and made only one visit to his Indian relations, in 1641. Soon after, he became an officer in the colonial militia, which put down an Indian rebellion in 1644, effectively destroying the world in which his mother had been raised.

Thomas Rolfe died in about 1675, having become, an early Virginia historian wrote, "a Person of Fortune and Distinction in this Country."

JOHN ROLFE, HUSBAND of Pocahontas and pioneer husbandman of tobacco, was as critical to Virginia's survival as his wife, or the captain she allegedly saved. By experimenting with tobacco, Rolfe transformed Jamestown from a struggling startup venture to a thriving concern. His marriage ushered in a period of calm that gave the colony breathing space to grow and prosper. The union also offered hope to the English that their Indian neighbors could be peacefully "civilized" and Christianized.

But in the centuries following Rolfe's death, he was gradually airbrushed from American memory. By the time writers in the newborn United States began to celebrate Jamestown, many states had banned marriage between Indians and whites, which made the Rolfes' union discomfiting. John Smith, on the other hand, seemed a perfect fit for the role of American hero: a man of action and dash, self-made, individualistic, iconoclastic. His "rescue" by Pocahontas also softened the story of Indians' subjugation by Europeans. In art and writing, she blossomed into a nubile maiden, clasping the brave captain to her breast. The aftermath—her kidnapping, marriage to another man, and premature death—was all but forgotten.

"John Rolfe is not our ancestor," Vachel Lindsay wrote in a 1917 poem, "Our Mother Pocahontas." "We rise from out the soul of her."

At Jamestown's historic park, there is no statue of Rolfe, only of Smith and Pocahontas. Inside the nearby church, bronze and marble memorials to Smith and Pocahontas hang side by side, like connubial tombstones. A small plaque to Rolfe, erected by the Tobacco Association of the United States, looks on from the opposite wall.

When I returned to the park on Landing Day, the annual commemoration of Jamestown's founding in May 1607, one of the activities was a tour led by Richard Cheatham, in colonial garb, playing the part of John Rolfe. Only three other visitors followed him through the park. "At best, you'll find Rolfe in a few coloring books," Richard complained afterward, over a sandwich at Jamestown's Starving Time Café. "Rolfe was an innovator, open-minded in work and love. You'd think those are qualities that Americans would admire. But the only John at Jamestown anyone cares about is Smith."

There was one exception to this rule. Since Smith died childless, he was of only minor interest to Americans who cherished their blood ties to early Virginia. These descendants were a conspicuous presence on Landing Day: elegantly dressed, they formed a coven by a monument to Jamestown's founders, busily swapping genealogical credentials while studying the pins on one another's suits and dresses.

"I trace back to the Rolfes, Paines, Wares, and Woodsons."

"Really? I'm kin to the Winston line. I have Bolling, too."

"Are you in the DAR?"

"Hon, I don't have the bosom for all those pins."

Eavesdropping on their chatter, I was reminded of Maori in New Zealand, who introduce themselves at ceremonies by reciting thirty generations of ancestors. Virginia genealogy seemed, if possible, even more labyrinthine.

"There's your Colonial Dames, your Descendants of Ancient Planters, your Jamestowne Society, your First Families of Virginia," explained one of the Landing Day attendees, Betty Fitzgerald, ticking off a short list of ancestral societies. Each group had its own entry rules, usually to do with the arrival date and status of one's forebear. Some associations required a "double legacy," or blood tie to two distinguished Virginia families, many of which had intermarried in colonial times. "It's like voles in your yard," Betty said. "Lines go over and under each other and tunnel all around."

The most revered lineage was that tracing back to John Rolfe and Pocahontas. Their only child, Thomas, also had only one child, a daughter named Jane. She married a rich planter, Robert Bolling, and bore a son before dying the same year, probably from complications of childbirth. Bolling remarried and had seven more children. This meant that some Bollings descended from Pocahontas, and many did not.

"You have to ask people, 'Are you a "Red Bolling" or a "White Bolling"?'" Sam Tarry explained. His Bolling line was Red.

"Me too!" a woman chimed in. "Pocahontas is my eighth great-grandmother." This meant putting eight "great"s before "grandmother" to span the generations between her and Pocahontas.

Genetically speaking, a family tie this attenuated is almost meaningless: digging ten generations back yields an ancestral pool of thousands. But even a faint connection to Pocahontas has long been revered in Virginia. In 1924, the state passed "An Act to Preserve Racial Integrity," which segregated anyone with a trace of "non-Caucasian" heritage. Lawmakers inserted a clause known as the Pocahontas Exception, exempting white Virginians with "one sixteenth or less" of Indian heritage and "no other non-caucasic blood."

Even more baroque was the Degree of Pocahontas, a group that held an annual "Princess Pocahontas Memorial Day" at Jamestown. Soon after Landing Day, I went to see a local leader of the group at her house twenty miles east of the historic park. A tall, trim, dark-eyed woman in her sixties, Sandra Dye worked by day at a mobile-home park, but spent many nights attending to her duties as "Seated Pocahontas" of Onawa Council Number 38.

"My father and grandfather were Red Men," she said, as we settled on a couch in her den. "So I guess Pocahontas is in my blood."

Sandra didn't mean this literally. From the nine-hundred-page book on her coffee table, *History of the Improved Order of Red Men and Degree of Pocahontas,* I learned that the Red Men were a secret fraternity, founded in 1813 and descended from colonial groups that adopted Indian regalia as a symbol of freedom and defiance (the Sons of Liberty had done so most famously during the Boston Tea Party).

Only white males belonged to the Red Men. They formed "tribes" and "wigwams" led by a "Sachem" or "Great Senior Sagamore." In the late nineteenth century, the order spawned a women's auxiliary, the Degree of Pocahontas, which adopted its own titles.

"I'm a past 'Great Pocahontas' and 'Great Keeper of Wampum,'" Sandra said. This meant she'd served as head of the state council and as treasurer. Other ranks included Great Prophetess and Great Minnehaha. New members were initiated with "Indian" rituals and signs. Sandra couldn't tell me more. "It's secret."

Until recently, the Order of Red Men and the Degree of Pocahontas had a public face as well. Councils participated in parades and other civic events, the men wearing war bonnets and buckskins, the women clad in deerskin dresses and headbands. Then, in the 1990s, real Indians started to complain. "They don't like palefaces wearing their regalia, because it has special meaning," Sandra said.

Park officials at Jamestown asked degree members to stop wearing deerskins to the Princess Pocahontas Memorial Day. They now wore white dresses instead.

"It's sad, because when we wore our regalia we attracted a crowd," Sandra said. "Tourists would ask, 'What kind of Indian are you?' I'd say, 'I'm not, I'm of German and English descent.' But I thought we were drawing attention to Indians' plight. We weren't being disrespectful."

I asked Sandra if she still had her costume. "Oh, yes." Her face brightened. "I'll go get it." She went upstairs, returning a few minutes later wearing beads, moccasins, and a fringed leather dress slit up the thigh. "I have this beautiful costume and I never get to wear it anymore," she said, turning in a circle. "When I had longer hair I wore it in a ponytail."

Sandra sat on the couch and we resumed our conversation. A bit flustered by her transformation into an Indian maiden, I asked if she identified with Pocahontas.

"Absolutely. Freedom, friendship, and charity are the Degree's precepts, and we take those from Pocahontas."

"Why do you think she helped the English?"

"She was fascinated by John Smith, and justly so," Sandra said. "I'm enough of a romantic to think she didn't want this handsome stranger to have his head cut off."

The Degree had carried on Pocahontas's benevolent spirit. At one time, it provided food and clothing to Indian children; now most of its charity went to the Make a Wish Foundation. Members had also contributed to the upkeep of the church grounds in Gravesend, Pocahontas's burial site.

But the Red Men and women had fallen on hard times. Since their peak of half a million members in the 1920s, the Order and Degree had dwindled to fewer than twenty thousand. Sandra's council numbered only thirty-five, down from two hundred when she'd joined in the 1970s. The local Red Men "no longer have a functioning tribe," she said.

Sandra blamed this decline on modern domestic life. "We can't compete with *Survivor* and *American Idol*," she said. "And so many women work and have extra activities at home. No one has any time. The Lions and the other fraternal groups all have the same problem."

Sandra pressed her palms against her fringed dress. "At least, compared to the Moose and Shriners," she said, "we have the prettiest costumes."

THE NEXT DAY, I met another woman in a skin dress, one who could actually have passed for Pocahontas. In 1611, eager to establish a better base than fetid Jamestown, colonists founded the City of Henricus on high ground near the head of the James River, eighty miles to the west. They built a large settlement, including the first hospital in English America, and chartered its first college a year before the Pilgrims landed. It was at Henricus that John Rolfe experimented with tobacco and met Pocahontas.

In 1622, an Indian uprising ravaged the fledging city and it never recovered. All that stands now is a reconstructed fort and Indian village. When I arrived on a cool spring morning, the only person in sight was a beautiful young woman with olive skin, long black hair, and dark brown eyes. Clad in a fringed deerskin and wampum beads, she kneeled in a garden, tending pyramids of dirt.

"I'm a Creek Indian and we were mound builders," she joked of the piles. Actually, she was planting crops as Virginia Indians had, in small cones of soil to hold the moisture. She also scattered the mounds, since natives lacked draft animals or plows to form even rows. "I don't get to smoke this—only men did, mostly ceremonially," she said, plucking a thumb-shaped tobacco leaf. "But when you harvest it by hand, it gets into your pores and gives you a good buzz."

Melanie Wright had grown up near Jamestown, in a family of Creek descent from Georgia. But she felt more comfortable playing the role of a Virginia Indian, first at Jamestown and now at Henricus. "It's hard to interpret your own history: it's too personal, particularly the failures," she said. "Here, I'm someone else, and I have this village all to myself."

She led me past mounds of corn and squash and beans, which she tended along with tobacco. Few visitors were very excited by Indian agriculture. "But when I'm scraping the flesh off hides, and get covered in blood and guts," she said, pausing beside a stick hung with rawhide, "that really turns the guys on. They stand around and drool."

Their ardor tended to cool when she tanned the hides, using deer brains. Also, her knee-length skin dress and the fringed mantle covering her shoulders were much more modest than seventeenth-century native attire. "They don't pay me enough to wear just a little leather apron," she said. "Anyway, I'm a modern-day weenie Indian. It gets cold here, and I don't have any bear grease."

We ducked inside a *yehawken,* an oval structure made of boughs, with woven mats covering the dirt floor. Melanie fanned a fire with turkey feathers, the smoke rising through a hatch in the roof. "Welcome to my home away from home," she said, settling on a fur. "For all intents and purposes I spend my days in the seventeenth century."

Melanie enjoyed her work, but she didn't idealize the natives she portrayed, or regard them with solemn awe. "They were really into show and fanfare," she said. "Powhatan was always trying to impress the English with all his women and possessions. And you had to look great when going into battle—you couldn't wear the same thing you wore around your *yehawken*." She was also amused by natives' fondness for English mirrors, which had often been found in Indian graves. "I love the vanity of these people! Let's not turn them into boring, perfect specimens."

This unvarnished attitude extended to Pocahontas. Melanie suspected Powhatan's daughter was drawn to Jamestown by the chance to collect beads and other trinkets. Pocahontas also must have enjoyed the doting attention of the English, who had no girls among them.

"Powhatan had eighty children. They always say Pocahontas was his favorite. But gee, until when? Next week?" Melanie shrugged. "When the English kidnapped her, Dad didn't seem too upset. She must have thought, 'Whatever, I'll stay with the white folk. They think I'm special and give me lots of stuff.'"

This wasn't an ennobling image: more Paris Hilton than Mother Pocahontas. But it seemed as plausible as the romantic imaginings of groups like the Degree of Pocahontas, or the many theories that scholars had spun from slim historical evidence.

For all Melanie's irreverence, though, there was one thing she couldn't abide: visitors who asked, as they often did, "Are you a real Indian?"

"I tell them, 'No. I'm completely plastic.' If I say yes, then they always ask if I'm a 'full blood.' I feel like telling them, 'No, I donated a pint last week so I'm a little short right now.' "

Melanie's grandmother *was* a full-blood, but told neighbors her family was Cuban, which carried less of a stigma than being Indian. "Now people want you to be *real,* not a mix like everyone else in America. No one ever goes to the fort here and asks one of the colonial interpreters, 'Hey, are you a full-blooded Englishman?' "

She poked at the fire. "When I have to fill out a form and they ask for my race, I put 'human.' "

A school bus pulled up outside and Melanie composed herself. As we walked back past the garden, she stooped to pick up a soda tab. "I'm Indian, we love shiny things," she said, smiling again. Then, as I headed for the fort, she warned, "Don't let those filthy English cough on you!"

FROM HENRICUS I wound along backcountry roads, in search of Pocahontas's true people. That any of them remain is as miraculous as the survival of early Jamestown. Soon after Powhatan's death, in 1618, his brother Opechancanough became ruler, and in 1622 he led the uprising that destroyed Henricus and killed 350 English across Virginia, almost a third of all colonists. But the balance of power had tipped since 1607, when the first settlers lay starving and sick in Jamestown's fort.

New colonists quickly replaced those killed in the uprising, and they hit back hard at the Indians. The settlers' appetite for tobacco (a crop that quickly depletes soil) and the introduction of roving livestock also encroached on Indian fields and hunting grounds. When Opechancanough led another large-scale revolt in 1644, it ended with his death and the destruction of the empire he and his brothers had ruled.

"Upone pain of death," Virginia's assembly declared in 1646, Indians were barred from the territory between the York and the James Rivers. Dispossessed of much of their land, and depleted by warfare and disease, Powhatan's former confederacy dwindled to bands, outnumbered and encircled, as Jamestown's occupants had once been. In the early 1600s, John Smith recorded the names of some forty tribes he encountered during his travels. A century later, a colonist named

Robert Beverley found remnants of only eight. "The Indians of Virginia are almost wasted," he wrote. His rough census of Indian villages included notes such as "a small number yet living," or "much decreased of late by the small pox." He listed many of the tribes visited by Smith as "extinct."

Among those that survived was the Pamunkey, the core tribe of Powhatan's domain and the one he's believed to have been born into. In a 1677 treaty with the "Dread Soveraigne Lord Charles the II," the Pamunkey secured the right to remain unmolested on the land they still held, as well as the right to gather wild oats, rushes, and other plants "not usefull to the English." In exchange, Indians pledged amity and subjection to the king, and agreed to an annual rent of twenty beaver skins, to be delivered by tribal leaders to the colony's governor.

This tradition has continued ever since, though the Pamunkey now substitute deer for beaver, presented to Virginia's governor on the steps of the state capitol. The Pamunkey also still occupy their remnant of riverside land, in an oxbow twenty miles east of Richmond. To reach the reservation, I followed a country road until it ended at a settlement of modest houses. Apart from a small museum, there was little to distinguish the Pamunkey enclave from hundreds of other rural communities in Virginia. Nor did the first people I met—blue jean–clad, with lightly tanned skin and soft Virginia drawls—seem much different from their non-Indian neighbors.

One of them pointed me to the home of Warren Cook, the tribe's deputy chief, a handsome, strongly built man with graying black hair and long-lashed green eyes. "This reservation is different than most," he said. "It wasn't given to us—it's a place that was never *taken* from us." In this respect, the Pamunkey resembled the Zuni: the rare tribe that still inhabited land it had occupied when Europeans arrived.

Speaking with Warren, I sensed another parallel. Like the Zuni, the Pamunkey maintained a certain distance from both non-Indians and other tribes. Their relative isolation, geographic and social, was one reason the Pamunkey had survived. "We pretty much keep to ourselves," Warren said, "and these days, the rest of the world leaves us alone."

It seemed clear he wanted me to do the same. But when Warren said he had an errand to run, I asked whether I could tag along and see the reservation. He shrugged and said, "That won't take long."

We drove past well-spaced weatherboard houses and fields of knee-high wheat. Residents owned their houses but not the land, which reverted to the tribe on their death. Only eighty-five people lived on the reservation, about a tenth of the total number of Pamunkey. "That's not counting all the folks who *think* they're one," Warren said. "The world's largest tribe is the Wannabes."

People wrote to the Pamunkey from all over the world, claiming that they descended from Pocahontas and were therefore eligible for tribal membership—often because they thought it came with some economic benefit. The Pamunkey, however, had no casino and received only modest state aid. Also, to join the tribe one had to prove a recent forebear was Pamunkey.

Warren stopped beside an old monument to Pocahontas, inscribed with the words "Gentle and humane, she was the friend of the earliest struggling English colonists whom she nobly rescued, protected, and helped." A bas-relief depicted a long-haired woman with a headband. A local artist had modeled her face on a 1920s studio photograph of Warren's grandmother Pocahontas Cook.

"I like the artwork, but personally I would take the monument down," Warren said. "Pocahontas was an exceptional young woman, intelligent and adaptable, but she got carried away with the English." He said most Pamunkey shared his ambivalence. Some considered Pocahontas a traitor for helping the invaders and then marrying one. "Mostly, though, we're just tired of hearing about her all the time," he said, "instead of figures more representative of our people."

Warren drove me down by the river, to a grassy mound that was decorated with feathers and a leather pouch of tobacco. Here the Pamunkey believed Opechancanough had interred the bones of his brother Powhatan, and later been buried himself after being captured and then shot in the back at Jamestown. One colonist described Opechancanough as "a Man of large Stature, noble Presence, and extraordinary Parts." But in 1644, he was so old and weak when he led the uprising that he had to be carried into battle on a litter.

"It'd be nice if all the visitors to Jamestown paid more attention to

Powhatan and Opechancanough," Warren said. "They weren't on the boat to America—they met it, and did everything they could to drive the English back out to sea."

The legacy of their defeat was all too apparent from our secluded perch by the river. It had taken Warren twenty minutes to show me what remained of Powhatan's once mighty realm: a twelve-hundred-acre pocket, most of it uninhabitable wetland. "You have to get out on the water to really get a sense of the reservation," he said.

We sat quietly for a while, before I asked about the boat I'd seen parked in his yard. For the first time Warren smiled. "You're hard to get rid of," he said. "Just like those damned English."

A FEW DAYS later, at the wheel of his nineteen-foot skiff, Warren started to open up, and so did the scenery. It was late May, when Virginia's woods and scrub begin to close in, turning much of the state into a muggy, buggy inferno. But as we motored into the Pamunkey River, the woods gave way to a breezy expanse of placid brown water. Warren coasted swampy islets, pointing to long-stalked wild rice and a water lily called spatterdock. A plant that bloomed later in the year was marshmallow, from which Indians used to extract sugary goo, the forerunner of today's confection.

An osprey rose from its nest, arching massive wings and hovering over the water before diving in to catch a fish with its talons. There were also egrets and eagles and Canada geese swooping overhead. "Fish, fowl, plants, fields, game—everything Indians needed to live well," Warren said. "If land had been given to us by the government, like it was to most tribes, we'd never be in a place this nice."

Warren steered to the widest point in the river and cut off the engine. For 360 degrees there wasn't a sign of humanity, apart from our boat. "It would have looked about the same four hundred years ago," he said, "when the English started mucking around here."

For the first time in Virginia, I sensed how hard it must have been for John Smith to navigate this watery wilderness, which was almost devoid of landmarks. Heavy foliage obscured the shore, forming a low band of green that stretched for miles. High reeds camouflaged creeks emptying into the river. I wouldn't have known the channels were there if Warren hadn't told me.

This uniform, well-cloaked landscape made southeastern Virginia ideally suited to ambush. At one point, Smith described Indians raining "more than a thousand arrows" on his boat, which he'd learned to armor with a shield of tightly woven sticks, hemp, and grass. Near where Warren and I now drifted, his sixteen-man party had been surprised by seven hundred Pamunkey under Opechancanough. Smith challenged the chief to a duel on an island in the river, wagering copper against corn. "Our game shalbe the conqueror take all," he declared with characteristic bravado, before grabbing a long lock of the chief's hair and pressing a pistol to his breast. The "trembling king" ordered his warriors to lay down their bows and deliver up baskets of corn. Or so Smith later claimed.

He wasn't so adroit at escaping another hazard of travel in these parts: the tidal mudflats that he called "the Ooze," a mucky mantrap that ensnared the English and their boats. During one trip on the Pamunkey River, Smith was so "stuck fast in the Ooze" that he had to be rescued by natives who came "to bear me out on their heads."

He didn't say how they reached him, but an anthropologist in the 1920s described Pamunkey scampering across the mud, legs bent and weight on their shins, never letting one limb bear down for more than an instant. In the goopiest mire, called floating mud, they crawled on their bellies.

"If you stand up straight in it, like the English did, you sink right down to your ass," Warren said. "My father knew how to cross it, but I never could."

His father, who had served as chief for forty-two years, was also among the last of the Pamunkey to trap animals the traditional way. The reservation still abounded with the furry creatures Smith had described: "Powlecats, weesels and Minkes," and strange animals he knew only by their Indian names: *Aroughcun* (raccoon), *Opassom,* and *Mussascus,* a beast he likened to a "water Rat" that smelled "exceedingly strongly of muske." Warren's father stalked all these animals, but the muskrat most of all. At low tide, with Warren's help, he set out a wood contraption called a deadfall trap. When the muskrat went for the bait of wild parsnip, a log fell from a forked stick, clubbing the animal into the mud. Unlike a metal trap, the deadfall didn't rust or rip the pelt, which Warren's father sold for three dollars, with the meat bringing twenty-five cents.

"He gave the meat money to us kids," Warren said. "I bought my first car on muskrat money, about two hundred and fifty dollars I'd saved up."

No one used deadfall traps anymore, or made canoes from cypress, as Warren's grandfather did. But the Pamunkey caught shad in handmade nets and milked their eggs and sperm at the reservation's hatchery, to reseed the river's stock. They also hunted deer and duck on ancient tracts, and dug clay from the riverbank to make pots.

"There's no mystical tradition, or ritual, or language left—that was already gone by my grandparents' time," Warren said. "Being Indian for them was just a way of life, living off the land and the water. The little we do of that now is all that's left."

Warren started the motor and returned upriver. After pulling the boat out, he invited me back to his house for grilled croaker. While the fish cooked, he showed me family photos, beginning with black-and-white studio portraits of unsmiling, dark-haired forebears and ending with color pictures of his five smiling daughters, several of them blond. "The Indian blood is going out," he said.

For the past several generations, few Pamunkey had married other Indians. There weren't many in Virginia to choose from. Warren's wife was white, and all his daughters had married non-Indians. "It's getting harder and harder to define ourselves by blood," Warren said.

It was also becoming hard to maintain Indian identity as tribal members moved off the reservation or commuted to the city. Warren had worked in Richmond as an art therapist and employment counselor, among other jobs. "People want to freeze-frame Indians—they don't want me driving a nice car and living in a nice home," he said. "But my dad didn't want me to fish and trap. He wanted me to get an education and go into the world."

Warren went to a shelf and pulled down a volume of John White's drawings of sixteenth-century Algonquians. Flipping through portraits of tattooed, loinclothed natives, he said, "They're part of my history; I'm interested in them. But I can't relate to these people. We're talking about the Stone Age. How are you going to identify with that?"

Even so, Warren had reproduced one of White's drawings on his business card. A talented artist, he made jewelry of owls, spiders, and turtles, and painted natives in traditional regalia. When I pointed out that this seemed to suggest a strong identification with his distant fore-bears, Warren nodded. "Maybe I'm more Indian than I realize," he said. "It's part of me and it's not. We're all mixed up between two worlds."

TORRENTIAL SPRING RAIN set in, so I broke off my tour of Powhatan country and camped out at the state archives in Richmond. It didn't take me long to realize why Warren and other Indians I'd met seemed wary at first of inquisitive strangers. While Zuni resented prying anthropologists, Virginia's eight surviving tribes had been victimized by a much deadlier species: whites who sought to deny they were Indians at all. The most virulent assault had occurred within living memory, in the guise of science, and had almost succeeded.

"The savage aborigines," Walter Plecker wrote in a medical journal in 1925, were a "complete failure" at developing America's natural bounty. Only the "great Nordic race" was capable of that. But early settlers made a "fatal mistake" by introducing "other savages, many being recent cannibals." Over time, the mingling of African, Indian, and Caucasian blood had weakened America and threatened its purity and progress. "Race suicide" was imminent, "unless united, deter-mined and radical measures are adopted before it is not too late."

Plecker's article, "Racial Improvement," wasn't the work of a lonely crank. He was a leader of the movement known as eugenics, a warped offshoot of Darwinism that sought to strengthen the gene pool by weeding out "inferior" strains. Plecker was also Virginia's registrar of vital statistics, the keeper of its birth, death, marriage, and other rec-ords. This gave him the power and means to make the state a labora-tory for his race-cleansing fanaticism.

To Plecker, Indians posed the gravest threat. Virginia's Racial Integrity Act of 1924 denied white status to anyone with a trace of "non-Caucasian" blood, but permitted marriage between whites and Indians. Plecker believed the state's Indians were actually mixed-breeds with African ancestry, making them "Mongrel Virginians" and covert agents of racial infection.

His solution was to expose, persecute, and purge anyone he regarded as impure, even alerting cemetery administrators to racially suspect corpses that had been buried alongside Caucasians. Plecker also disinterred antebellum records, which often listed both natives and free blacks as "colored." Using this and other "evidence," he set about reclassifying Virginia Indians as "Negro." He changed birth certificates and forced local registrars, obstetricians, and midwives to do the same, so that children born to Indians were no longer Indian. In essence, Plecker waged statistical genocide against the few tribes in Virginia that had survived the earlier onslaught of war, disease, and dispossession.

"Hitler's genealogical study of the Jews is not more complete," Plecker boasted in 1943 of his "racial integrity" files, which tracked Virginians' "pedigrees" back more than a century.

Nazi atrocities discredited eugenics, and in 1946, Plecker finally retired, at the age of eighty-six. But his thirty-four-year reign of terror had a long afterlife. By altering or destroying records, he had damaged the paper trail Indians needed to gain federal recognition. Many natives fled the state to escape harassment, and most of those never returned. Others hid their Indian ancestry and melted into the white population. By the end of the twentieth century, only a few thousand Indians remained in Virginia: three-tenths of one percent of the population.

Even more insidious was the wedge Plecker drove between Indians and blacks, who often lived side by side in Virginia. To guard against the slightest suspicion of "impurity," which would subject them to the third-class citizenship of blacks, Indians during the first half of the twentieth century had quarantined themselves. They formed their own churches and schools (or sent children to Indian schools in other states), avoided social contact with blacks, and enacted tribal statutes forbidding members to marry them.

"You had to be careful of the company you kept," Gertrude Custalow told me. An elderly Mattaponi Indian, she lived at a reservation down the road from the Pamunkey. "If you were too close to a black person, you were ostracized by the tribe because it would give the state an excuse to take away our land."

The scars of Plecker's campaign lingered to the present day, and so did habit and tradition. Many Indians still kept their distance from blacks, and some tribes continued to forbid intermarriage. No such strictures applied to contact with whites. The result was a strange realignment. Indians whose ancestors had battled Europeans for survival were now thrown together with their historic persecutors. And while laws and taboos restricting contact between whites and blacks had eased, those sundering natives and blacks remained.

This divide was starkest in Charles City County, just west of Jamestown, where I headed once the rain subsided. The Chickahominy Indians who inhabited the county in the 1600s were entirely driven from their land, unlike the Pamunkey. But some returned in the 1800s, to what had become a plantation county where blacks outnumbered whites by two to one. Natives formally reconstituted the Chickahominy tribe in the late 1800s, aided by whites who wanted to divide the county's nonwhite majority. But it wasn't entirely clear who qualified as Chickahominy. Families split, with some members joining the tribe, and others not.

"This is my grandmother's cousin; he was chief of the Chickahominy," Richard Bowman said, showing me pictures on his living room mantel. "And this is my father-in-law, the one in the war bonnet. His grandmother and my father's grandmother were sisters."

What made this odd was that Richard also displayed a plaque of appreciation from the NAACP. He'd headed the local branch of the civil rights group in the 1960s, and led the fight to integrate schools in the county, an effort Indians joined whites in opposing.

Now a trim, bald man in his eighties, Richard had light brown skin, brown eyes, and high cheekbones—not unlike the people pictured in bonnets and buckskins in his living room photos. But he identified with a different tribe. "My grandmother was born a slave in 1860 on a plantation near here," he said. "Others of my family were free blacks. I'm proud to be their descendant, too."

Richard took me for a drive in his truck, past the Chickahominy tribal center and powwow grounds. Most of the people who lived in his rural community were tribal members, including the current chief, another relative of Richard's. "I wouldn't want better neighbors," he said. "But we don't socialize. They're still frightened someone will call them 'colored.'"

Richard acknowledged he might have Indian blood, too. "I've probably got all the major groups in me," he said. "Race is a frame of mind. You are who you think you are. America's a free country." But it hadn't always been so, and he wanted to ensure that remembrance of early Virginia included this legacy. "Jamestown wasn't just about English and Indians," he said. "A lot of other people's roots go deep here, too."

THIS WAS AN aspect of Jamestown's story that had, until recently, attracted little notice. Just a year after the colony's founding, a supply fleet brought eight Poles and Germans to the fort. Recruited for their skill at producing finished goods for export, they founded a glassworks at Jamestown, the continent's first industrial enterprise. These forgotten Germans and Poles were, in a sense, forerunners of the immigrant tide that would fill America's factories in the nineteenth century.

In 1619, another new labor force arrived. A ship under joint Dutch and English command landed at Point Comfort, east of Jamestown. The vessel, John Rolfe wrote, "brought not any thing but 20. and odd Negroes," which the governor of the colony acquired in exchange for food. In another dispatch, Rolfe referred to the cargo as "Negars," the first recorded use of the N-word in America.

The Africans had been pirated from a Portuguese slave ship en route from Angola to Mexico. Little is known of their fate in Virginia, which didn't start codifying slavery until 1661. Some of the Africans may have been enslaved for life, others held as indentured servants, like poor whites, laboring for seven or more years before winning their freedom. A few early Africans became substantial landowners; one family moved to Maryland and named its seventeenth-century holding Angola.

But as Virginia's plantation economy boomed, the status of blacks deteriorated. In 1705, the colony declared that slaves "shall be held, taken, and adjudged, to be real estate." By 1790, when the newly created United States took its first census, there were almost 300,000 slaves in Virginia—40 percent of the state's population.

If Point Comfort, where Africans were first sold in Virginia, was slavery's Plymouth Rock, Charles City County represented its first great hub. Richard drove me along the James, where early colonists founded vast plantations, using Africans to grow tobacco and build some of the oldest and grandest estates in the South. One of these plantations passed down to a signer of the Declaration of Independence, who made a careful inventory of his 110 slaves, including several listed as "mad," "crippled," or "worthless." The riverside estates later spawned forgettable presidents, William Henry Harrison and John Tyler. Several of the manors are now tourist attractions, with guided tours led by women in hooped skirts.

"Folks pay these days to see what slaves built," Richard said. "Not that you'll hear a lot about that on the tours. Mostly, they tell you about the furniture."

Driving back inland, he turned down an avenue that led to a colonnaded brick mansion, more modest than those by the river. In the side yard we found a ruddy, white-haired man struggling with a swimming pool cover. Richard strode over and thrust out his hand. "I'm Richard Bowman," he said. "My grandmother was born on this plantation."

"Isn't that something?" the man replied, smiling broadly as he grasped Richard's hand. "I'm James Bailey, pleased to meet you."

James was a retired Richmond stockbroker who had bought a thousand acres of what was once a twelve-thousand-acre plantation. He showed us a beautiful boxwood garden, then led us to a wooden outbuilding with a single large room and a sleeping loft above. "This here was one of the slave quarters," he said. "We've found records dating it to at least 1720."

Richard stepped inside, standing before the stone hearth. "My grandmother might have been here," he said, "her feet could have patted over this floor."

James nodded. "You can almost reach back and touch the past."

If there was discomfort in their encounter, I couldn't detect it. They chatted amiably about hunting and fishing and mutual acquaintances. Then Richard said he was on the committee planning the county's upcoming commemoration of Jamestown's four hundredth birthday. He asked if he could bring people here to see the plantation where their ancestors had lived and labored.

"That's a great idea!" James said. The two men exchanged phone numbers and Richard drove back down the long avenue and through the woods, back to his modest frame house. "A generation ago I don't know if I'd have had the spunk to do that, and he wouldn't have responded that way," Richard said. "Times has certainly changed."

RICHARD'S PARTING COMMENT stuck with me as I completed my tour of Powhatan's vanished domain. Times had indeed changed in the way Richard meant, with the civil rights movement and the transformation it brought to the state. But viewing the same landscape through the lens of Virginia's beginnings, and of my long, strange journey across America, I kept seeing shadows cast by much more distant events.

Four centuries after the wedding of John Rolfe and Pocahontas, marrying "out" was still a raw issue in southeast Virginia. The tobacco Rolfe planted was mostly gone, but the plantation slavery its cultivation spawned had left three races still jostling with one another, over the past as well as the present. Each person and group I'd encountered— Richard Bowman, the Pamunkey, the Descendants of Ancient Planters—was staking a claim to the same historic ground. As if to give Woody Guthrie's famous song about America a new refrain: "This land is *my* land."

I'd heard a similar chorus throughout my rambles: from Spanish and Pueblo in New Mexico, Catholic and Protestant in Florida, black and white and red and shades in between in North Carolina. When it came to memory of the country's founding, Guthrie's ribbon of highway wound back to a land that was made by *me*.

As a mere third-generation American, I didn't have a horse in this race to the start line. Ellis Island was my family's Plymouth Rock. This gave me the freedom, I thought, to rummage through other people's attics without prejudice. Perhaps, in a roundabout way, I was honoring my own heritage, too. Some of my ancestors in czarist Russia were dissident "bomb throwers," or so my family claimed. In homage to this, I liked exploding American icons and myths.

But in Virginia, the role of serum administrator started to sour on me. A few days after visiting Richard Bowman, I went to Richmond for a museum lecture on Pocahontas. In the crowd of elderly whites wearing bow ties and big hats, I spotted three women who looked different. Going to sit with them, I learned that they were members of the Chickahominy. We chatted amiably about the tribe, until I realized one of the women was someone Richard Bowman had told me was a distant relative. When I mentioned this, her smile stiffened.

"There's a lot who are Indian and don't want to admit it," she said.

"*Is* he related to you?" I asked.

"Some went to the other side, went black. That's their choice."

I was about to ask a blunt follow-up, a reporter scenting blood, when the interrogator in me withered. She wasn't a public official or a corporate criminal. She was an eighty-seven-year-old woman who had lived through a vicious racial witch hunt. If there was a malefactor in the room, it was me: a latter-day Plecker, demanding to know whose blood was one-sixteenth this or one-thirty-second that.

"It was all paper," she whispered, as the lecture began, gently completing the interview for me. "And paper could kill you."

AFTER THE LECTURE, I decided to leave Virginia and its ghosts behind. From here, the story of early America pointed north, to the conventional starting point of the national narrative, and the last stop of mine.

But Jamestown shadowed this story, too. Of the many lapses in America's memory of its beginnings, one of the most glaring is this. The founding father of New England wasn't William Bradford or

Myles Standish or others aboard the *Mayflower*. It was a man long reviled by Yankee historians: the peripatetic John Smith.

In 1614, five years after his departure from Jamestown, Smith voyaged to the northeast Atlantic coast and scouted the shore in a small boat, as he'd so often done around the Chesapeake. "Few have adventured much to trouble it," he wrote of this northern region. His description of the coast explained why. Rocky and barren, it was "a Countrey rather to affright than delight." He also passed stretches of beach dune, which appeared just as desolate. "High hills," he wrote, "overgrowne with shrubby Pines, hurts and such trash."

Nonetheless, Smith saw promise in this forbidding landscape. Its rocks could provide building material; food such as cod, clams, and lobster abounded; there was ample timber and land. "Tender educats" might "complaine of the piercing cold," Smith wrote, but for "health and fertilitie" the region was well suited to the English. He became an ardent promoter of its colonization and penned several tracts on how to accomplish this. All that was needed for a settlement to prosper was "honest industry" and the leadership of a man such as himself.

The territory required one other thing: a new name. Though generally known in England as "the North Part of Virginia," the cool, rugged coast bore little resemblance to the Chesapeake. Also, in 1614, "Virginia" was still synonymous in English minds with disease, famine, and hostile Indians.

While charting the northern coast, Smith observed that its latitude was the same as the Pacific shore Sir Francis Drake had sailed in 1579 and called Nova Albion. And so, in a stroke of geographic marketing that rivaled Eirik the Red's christening of Greenland, Smith Anglicized Drake's name and gave it to the cold, stony region he hoped to sell to his countrymen. He called it "New England."

Smith never realized his dream of pioneering the place. Others followed his advice, and his fine charts, but sailed without the headstrong captain. Left to watch from afar, he kibitzed to the end, titling his last work *Advertisements for the unexperienced Planters of New-England, or any-where.*

In 1631, at the age of fifty-one, Smith died in poverty, willing most of his meager estate to cover the cost of his funeral. "Here lyes one conquered, that hath conquered Kings," his epitaph reads. "Subdu'd large Territories, and done things/Which to the World impossible would seem."

CHAPTER 13

PLYMOUTH

A TALE OF TWO ROCKS

The rock underlies all America: it only crops
out here.
—Wendell Phillips,
speech to the Pilgrim Society of Plymouth (1855)

WHEN I RETURNED to Plymouth, three years after my first brief visit, the place felt altogether different. Plymouth Rock, the replica *Mayflower,* the monuments studding the shoreline—they were familiar to me and yet not, like childhood haunts I'd revisited as an adult, only to discover that memory had played tricks on me.

It took me a while to figure out why. Plymouth hadn't changed; *I* had. Before, I'd rolled into town as a passing traveler, a twenty-first-century motorist pausing to glimpse the shore where long-ago Pilgrims stepped off a wooden ship to found a new country. Now, arriving at the end of a long journey forward in time, I saw Plymouth through jaundiced eyes, not as the cornerstone of early America, but as its cap-stone, piled on a cairn erected by all those who came before.

For a day or two, this made me a grumpy tourist. I had to resist quibbling with shopkeepers whose T-shirts bore Plymouth's motto: "America's Home Town." *Not to Virginians it isn't. Or to Hispanics, or Indians.* At Pilgrim Hall, I barely glanced at the museum's trove of colonial relics, instead searching until I found a small wall panel acknowledging pre-*Mayflower* visitors to America. *That's all?*

Returning to the Rock, I wanted to lecture the tourists trying to land coins on its uneven surface, which Plymouth legend held was a token of good luck. *Blarney, like everything else about that rock.* Then I retreated to a pub on Plymouth's main street, and needled the man on the next stool, a local tour-bus driver wearing a red, white, and blue jacket. What about Jamestown, I asked. Or St. Augustine?

"Forget all the others!" he finally shouted, slapping his hand on the bar. "*This* is the friggin' beginning of America."

I slunk from the bar to my room at the Governor Bradford Motor Inn. Lecturing locals about the flaws in their version of history was futile, not to mention obnoxious. Better to just take in the spectacle of Plymouth, like everyone else, and try to grasp what made the Pilgrim story so enduring.

I also had some research to finish, about the first English voyages to Massachusetts, which paved the way for the Pilgrims' arrival and survival in Plymouth. This, at least, was a source of spiteful solace, affording me another story that was more colorful than the pious Pilgrim myth. English Massachusetts, that most Puritan of colonies, had first been settled because of syphilis.

In the sixteenth century, Europeans believed the remedy for a disease could be traced to the malady's geographic source. Since syphilis was thought to have come from America, so must its antidote. In 1577, Europe's leading expert on New World plants extolled the virtues of sassafras, an aromatic plant that Indians used for a range of medicinal purposes. "The roote of this Tree," wrote the Spanish physician Nicolás Monardes, cured many ills, foremost among them "the evill of the Poxe."

Monarde's ebulliently titled herbal, *Joyfull news out of the newe found worlde,* helped drive the price of sassafras to 20 shillings a pound. When Roanoke colonists found the tree in abundance, hopes soared that it thrived in "the North Part of Virginia" as well. Since this little-known territory was linked in English minds to Norumbega, the legendary land of riches, the region might also yield mineral wealth.

And so, in 1602, Bartholomew Gosnold set sail from England with thirty-one men, including an apothecary and twenty settlers to found a year-round trading post. His sailors were "none of the best," wrote a gentleman aboard Gosnold's ship, the *Concord.* After crossing the Atlantic, they sounded for days before making landfall "upon an unknowen coast." Or so the rocky, fog-bound shore of southern Maine seemed to its first recorded English visitors.

Within hours of their arrival, another vessel appeared. Rigged with mast and sails, it looked to the English like a European fishing boat. Even more startling was its crew: Indians with painted faces, one of them clad in black serge breeches, waistcoat, hose, and shoes. The natives climbed "boldly aboord" the *Concord,* displaying no sign of fear or wonder. "They spake diverse Christian words," wrote one of the astonished English, "and seemed to understand much more than we."

With words and signs, the Indians explained that they'd traded with Basque fishermen, whose boats had trolled the northeast Atlantic coast for decades. As so often before, a land "unknowen" to the late-arriving English wasn't so to other Europeans.

Gosnold, sensibly "doubting the weather" in Maine, decided to try his fortunes elsewhere. Sailing south, he reached a sandy headland where the sailors caught so much fish that Gosnold called it Cape Cod. His next stop was a lovely vine-draped island, which he named "Marthaes vineyard," in honor of his daughter. Even more enticing was a nearby isle that Gosnold christened Elizabeth. "Sassafras trees plentie all the Island over," one passenger exulted, "a tree of high price and profit." It was here that the English chose to build their trading post and fort.

Natives of the isle—today's Cuttyhunk, outermost of an island chain still called Elizabeth—traded furs for trinkets and helped cut and carry sassafras until more than a ton had been loaded on the *Concord.* At this point, some of the settlers who had agreed to stay behind with Gosnold changed their minds; they were poorly provisioned and feared that others might cheat them of the cargo's profit. So, after a stay of only a few weeks, Gosnold reluctantly abandoned the island and its welcoming natives, who escorted the departing ship in their canoes.

"They made huge cries and shouts of joy unto us," one of the English wrote. "We with our trumpet and cornet, casting up our cappes in the aire, made them the best farewell we could."

Like so many early encounters, the *Concord*'s gentle island cruise quickly gave way to much harsher contact. Gosnold's ambitions turned to Jamestown, where he died during the colony's first summer. Those who sailed after him to New England seized on a new commodity, which sailors hauled aboard like so much lobster or cod.

"They were strong and so naked as our best hold was by their long haire," a mariner wrote of five natives the English kidnapped in 1605.

One captain paraded his exotic catch through the streets of London, to recoup part of the cost of his voyage. Another took Indians to Spain to sell as slaves; among these was a young native of Massachusetts named Tisquantum.

Seized in 1614, Tisquantum somehow escaped slavery in Spain and made his way to London and then Newfoundland, where he boarded an English ship headed toward his homeland. During his five-year absence, the New England coast had been hit by a devastating plague, probably introduced by European fishermen or sailors. Thomas Dermer, captain of the ship that carried Tisquantum south in 1619, described villages "not long since populous now utterly void," or inhabited only by dying natives covered in "sores" and "spots." Reaching Tisquantum's home, formerly a large and thriving settlement called Patuxet, Dermer found its inhabitants "all dead."

It was to this ravaged shoreline that the *Mayflower* passengers came late the following year. Initially headed for the mouth of the Hudson River, they'd been blown off course to Cape Cod and started probing the Massachusetts shore for a place to settle. At Patuxet, they found fresh water and woods cleared by the now absent Indians. Unloading their ship, they built shelters on the site of the extinct settlement.

In March, after a harsh winter that killed half the English, a lone Indian appeared, naked except for a leather apron. To the colonists' astonishment, "he saluted us in English, and bade us welcome." Samoset, as he called himself, was a refugee from Maine, where he'd met Englishmen before, acquiring a few of their words and a taste for their beer.

Five days later, he returned with an even more surprising figure: "the only native of Patuxet." This was Tisquantum, whose kidnapping by the English in 1614 had spared him the epidemic that killed off his kinsmen. Like so much about America, the arrival of this miraculous survivor struck the pious settlers as providential. A plague had given them Patuxet as a home, and now the last of its people had appeared to guide them in the wilderness. Tisquantum spoke English, was willing to act as interpreter and intermediary with other Indians, and taught settlers how to plant corn and fertilize it with fish.

"Squanto," wrote the colonists' leader, William Bradford, using an

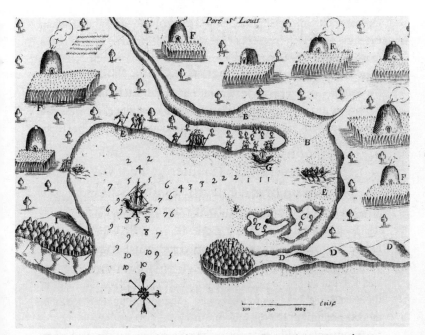

Samuel de Champlain's chart of Port St. Louis (Patuxet) in 1605, showing native fields and homes before disease wiped out the settlement

abbreviation of Tisquantum's name, "was a special instrument sent of God for their good beyond their expectation."

Eighteen months later, Squanto "fell sick of an Indian fever, bleeding much at the nose," Bradford wrote. He was dead within a few days. Though Squanto endures in American memory as savior of the Pilgrims, the name of his homeland vanished with its people. The French explorer Samuel de Champlain, who visited Patuxet in 1605, called it Port St. Louis. Then came John Smith, whose place names tended to stick. On his 1614 map of New England, the shore became "Plimouth." The Pilgrims retained Smith's name, though they also referred to their home as "New Plimoth" or "Plimoth Plantation."

Like St. Augustine and Jamestown before it, Plimouth was a poor choice for permanent settlement. Its harbor was shallow and hard to navigate, and arable land was limited to coastal fields. When Puritan colonists arrived in force a decade after the *Mayflower,* they settled a much better harbor forty miles to the north, at the mouth of a river John Smith had named the Charles. This colony quickly overshadowed the Pilgrim settlement and grew into greater Boston, of which Plymouth (as it was eventually spelled) became a satellite. It remains one today, a formerly industrial town that has found new life as a bedroom community for the metropolis an hour's drive away.

ON MY RETURN, once I got over my initial annoyance at Plymouth's claims to historic primacy, the town started to grow on me. Unlike St. Augustine's, its old commercial district hadn't been given a franchise facelift. Nor was Plymouth overgroomed and quainted-up, the fate of so many New England towns. Centuries-old houses looked their age, well lived-in still, with peeling paint and warped clapboards. Most of the town's historic sites were likewise antique and unimproved, memorials not only to the Pilgrims but to a bygone tourist sensibility.

Atop Cole's Hill, overlooking the Rock and harbor, I plunked quarters into an old telescope to "bring distant points of interest within range." The nearby wax museum had closed, denying me the chance to see paraffin Pilgrims planting corn. But the rest of Cole's Hill remained a museum piece, its every boulder and bench and bronze inscribed with high-flown sentiment.

"Reader!" exhorted the inscription on a sarcophagus holding the bones of settlers who died during the colony's first months. "History records no nobler venture for faith and freedom than that of this pilgrim band." Invoking the "weariness and painfulness," the "hunger and cold," that settlers endured, the epitaph concluded: "May their example inspire thee to do thy part in perpetuating and spreading the lofty ideals of our republic throughout the world!" This message seemed likely to be lost on the well-fed tourists driving past in their climate-controlled cars.

At the crown of Cole's Hill stood the largest monument of all, a towering bronze of Massasoit, "Great Sachem of the Wampanoags" and "Protector and Preserver of the Pilgrims." The statue had been

erected in 1921 by the Improved Order of Red Men, the fraternity of
white men I'd encountered in Virginia. Ten feet tall, and perched on a
boulder bigger than the Rock, the sculpted sachem had six-pack abs
and taut, rippling glutes. A companion statue of William Bradford, below the hill, was as tiny as Massasoit's was tall: a four-foot-six Pilgrim
shrunken by a shortfall in the memorial budget.

Most townspeople, I discovered, had a sense of humor about Plymouth's motley collection of marble and granite. They poked fun at
the grandiose, neoclassical canopy covering the Rock and its sand pit,
dubbing it the Greek Outhouse. Nor did all locals staunchly defend
Plymouth's first-in-America status, as the tour-bus driver at the pub
had done. Instead, they pointed out the apt initials of their town's
leading shrine.

"P.R.," Roger Silva said. "That's why people remember us. We had
good public relations people on the *Mayflower*. They got our story out."

I met Silva at a café where locals gathered each morning for coffee.
Like most Plymoutheans, he didn't trace his ancestry to the Pilgrims.
The son of a Portuguese immigrant, he'd followed his father into Plymouth's rope factory, and since served as a town selectman. The town's
industry had also drawn Irish, Italians, Germans, and Finns. Plymouth,
for all its *Mayflower* fame, was more blue-collar than blue-nosed.

The one man in the coffee shop with Pilgrim forebears was the target of gentle derision. "Everett's so old he *came* on the *Mayflower*,"
one of his friends jeered. "Everett," another man yelled, "be sure to
tell him how hard that first winter was!"

As a town, Plymouth also took pains to puncture the romantic
myths that had grown up around its early settlers. Paintings and legend depict the Pilgrims stepping from the *Mayflower* straight onto the
Rock, and many visitors still believe this actually happened. But a historic marker near the Rock, and a booklet sold at museum shops,
spelled out in detail the amusing truth behind the boulder's enshrine-
ment.

The first of the *Mayflower* passengers to step ashore at Plymouth
were scouts, who arrived in a small boat. When the *Mayflower* followed,
the ship anchored a mile out in the shallow bay, and the English were
shuttled ashore. In any event, the Pilgrims never mentioned the Rock—

or any coastal rock—in their copious writing about Plymouth. Rather, the story of the hallowed stepping-stone derived from oral testimony, recorded many generations later, in the manner of an Icelandic saga.

"About the year 1741," the story went, a church elder named Faunce asked to be carried to the shore, where a wharf was soon to be built. Pointing to a large rock, he said it was the very stone that "had received the footsteps of our fathers on their first arrival." Faunce then "bedewed it with his tears and bid to it an everlasting adieu."

Elder Faunce was ninety-five at the time. Even if his memory was intact, he'd been born a quarter century after the Pilgrims landed. His father, from whom he'd heard the story, wasn't a witness, either; he came to Plymouth three years after the *Mayflower*. And the story of Faunce's identification of the stone was itself based on a boyhood memory, that of a deacon who recalled, many decades later, having been "present on the interesting occasion" of the old man's teary farewell.

At the time of Faunce's adieu, no one else much cared about the Rock, which was promptly buried beneath the new wharf. But on the eve of the American Revolution, "animated by the glorious spirit of liberty," Plymoutheans tried to free the stone with thirty yoke of oxen. In so doing, they split it. Unable to pry loose the bottom half, they toted the top part to the town square, where it became a venerated and much vandalized symbol of liberty, with souvenir-seekers chipping off pieces to carry home.

When locals later moved the mutilated stone to safer ground, behind a fence at Pilgrim Hall, they dropped it from a cart, adding a fresh crack. Eventually, the wandering slab was reunited with its other half at the waterfront and cemented to it. The wharf was torn down and the Greek Outhouse erected, creating the venue where tourists have looked down at the much-abused Rock ever since.

"I always tell visitors it used to be bigger," Dan Cuetera said. "Anyway, sailors don't land ships on a rock. They're always trying to *avoid* rocks."

Dan worked as a historical interpreter aboard the replica *Mayflower*, which was moored near the Rock. As part of his job, he inhabited the role of one of the many "Strangers," or non-Pilgrim passengers, who sailed on the *Mayflower*, seeking economic opportunity rather than religious liberty. "I am not one of these separatists from Holland," Dan said, assuming his period voice, "though God's grace and profit do jump together."

Like other interpreters, Dan had taken dialect training at Plimoth Plantation, a living history park outside town. There were many accents to learn, since the original settlers came from different regions of England. Dan's favorite was East Anglia, source of the generic pirate accent. "I swallow me r's and har'ly p'onounce 'em a'tall." He laughed. "That's the fun part of the job. No one would be doing this if it wasn't for *Monty Python.*"

Dan wasn't quite so keen on the dress-up part of his job, which had also been meticulously researched. The male Pilgrim stereotype—black clothes, tall stiff-brimmed hat adorned with a buckle—was rich person's attire, the stuff of portraits, not daily life. Plymouth's settlers were mostly modest country folk, and when Dan played one, he wore a floppy hat, loose pants, and shapeless jacket, all the color of dead leaves. "Not a flattering look," he said. "The breeches are baggy around the butt and the jacket would make Adonis look stoop-shouldered."

Pilgrims' plain ways extended to music, which Dan performed as part of a period troupe. In church, Pilgrims sang only psalms and never in perfect harmony. "A psalm is the word of God, not to be ornamented with the work of man," Dan explained. "That is what Papists do." So his group mostly sang English country songs, without musical accompaniment. The singers called themselves the Puritones.

While Dan enjoyed mocking the Pilgrims, he thought their dour Calvinism explained why Plymouth, rather than Jamestown, had been anointed the country's birthplace. "The Virginia story is a lot more exciting, but as a founding myth it's a lousy fit," he said. "No one wants to build a national story around a man killing and eating his pregnant wife, or colonists too lazy to grow their own food. Shiftlessness isn't part of the American self-image."

Plymouth, by contrast, carried a message that suited a nation of striving immigrants. "Here, the story line is 'Live in excruciating poverty for years and work hard and eventually your family will prosper.'"

This uplifting narrative required careful editing. After first landing at Cape Cod, the hungry English looted Indians' buried stores of corn. Also, the epidemic that preceded the English to Plymouth not only provided them a harbor, fresh water, and cleared fields to sow; it gave them a chance to settle in without immediately inciting natives, as had happened so often at earlier beachheads. The Pilgrims' nearest neighbors, Massasoit's people, lived miles inland and had been ravaged by disease. They were in no position to resist the newcomers, even if they'd been so inclined, and they greeted the Pilgrims peacefully.

"If it wasn't for the plague," Dan said, "the story here might have been a lot uglier from the start, like Jamestown's."

Before long, it became so. Within a few years of the *Mayflower*'s arrival, colonists clashed with Indians and stuck the bloody head of a defeated foe on a pike atop Plymouth's fort. But the Pilgrim story familiar to most Americans had been radically abridged, encompassing only the colony's first year: the Pilgrims sailed, signed the Mayflower Compact, landed at Plymouth Rock, suffered through winter, and celebrated the first harvest with kindly Indians.

"Thanksgiving, I can't thank thee enough," Dan said, donning his drab hat and dead-leaf jacket to perform with the Puritones at a sold-out autumn banquet. " 'Tis what keeps us weary Pilgrims employed."

THANKSGIVING WAS THE third and most exalted of Plymouth's trinity, holier even than the *Mayflower* and the Rock. It carried the story of America's founding out of Plymouth and into millions of homes, renewing memory of the Pilgrims each autumn over turkey, sweet potato, and pumpkin pie.

The only people who might be surprised by this would be the Pilgrims themselves. They wrote thousands of words about the colony's first years, and all of two paragraphs about their famous repast. They didn't record its date or call it a thanksgiving, which to Calvinists signified a solemn religious observance. They didn't even specify turkey as one of the dishes served.

"Our harvest being gotten in," one settler wrote, "our governor sent four men on fowling, so that we might after a special manner rejoice together." The hunters had great success. But there's no mention of whether they bagged turkey rather than geese or duck.

Nor did Pilgrims initially intend for Indians to share in the bounty. Massasoit and ninety men turned up unannounced, almost tripling the number of mouths to feed. The Indians went out and hunted deer, adding venison to the menu for the three days of feasting that followed. Fish was also abundant, and corn, in some form, was doubtless consumed. But of the many familiar trimmings—pumpkin pie, sweet potatoes, cranberry sauce—there is no written evidence.

Like Plymouth Rock, the Pilgrim feast was also forgotten for many generations. New Englanders continued to hold harvest feasts and days of religious thanksgiving—to mark, among other events, their bloody victories over Indians. But it wasn't until the early nineteenth century that writers rediscovered the 1621 meal, recasting it as the "first Thanksgiving," an antecedent to what had become a Yankee tradition of homecoming feasts, with turkey often served as the centerpiece.

The key figure in this revival was Sarah Josepha Hale, a New Hampshire native who wrote "Mary Had a Little Lamb." As editor of an influential women's periodical, she waged a long campaign to turn the New England rite into a national holiday. Finally, in the midst of the Civil War, Abraham Lincoln proclaimed the last Thursday of November 1863 as Thanksgiving: a day to solemnly acknowledge the sacrifices made for the Union and to give "humble penitence for our national perverseness." He made no mention of turkey or Pilgrims.

The holiday took hold—despite resistance from Southerners—and evolved into a secular celebration of American abundance. The Plymouth story also became a touchstone for immigrants. According to a 1934 citizenship manual, "every new American needed to know" about Pilgrims, who exemplified the ethos of hard work and liberty.

Shopping was part of the American Dream, too. So in 1939, at the urging of merchants, FDR moved Thanksgiving ahead a week, to lengthen the Christmas shopping season. And there it has remained, a day of national gluttony, retail pageantry, TV football, and remembrance of the Pilgrims, a folk so austere that they regarded Christmas as a corrupt Papist holiday.

WHILE THE PILGRIMS and their abstemious ways have faded from the American scene, the Indian tribe they dined with in 1621 remains on the premises. In 1970, the 350th anniversary of the Pilgrim landing, a Wampanoag leader convened a Thanksgiving protest beside the Massasoit statue atop Cole's Hill. After declaring the fourth Thursday in November a "Day of Mourning" and giving speeches denouncing the Pilgrims, the protestors pulled down the English flag from the replica *Mayflower,* threw sand on the Rock, and turned over tables at a Thanksgiving dinner they'd been invited to at Plimoth Plantation. A holiday intended to celebrate harmony between newcomers and natives had turned into its opposite.

The Day of Mourning became an annual rite. In 1996, protestors marked it by disrupting a sedate Plymouth tradition, a local procession to church called the Pilgrim Progress. When activists tried to repeat this the next year, police moved in with pepper spray and handcuffs, provoking a much-publicized and embarrassing mêlée. In its wake, the town officially recognized the Day of Mourning and erected yet another plaque on Cole's Hill, acknowledging that for Indians, "Thanksgiving Day is a reminder of the genocide of millions of their people, the theft of their lands, and the relentless assault on their culture."

Tensions had since eased, and Plymoutheans now marked the weekend before the autumn holiday with an elaborate "America's Hometown Thanksgiving Parade." I arrived to find thousands of people lining the streets as floats and marchers streamed past, representing every era and every organization for miles around. Pilgrims, waving gaily from a mock *Mayflower,* jostled with unicyclists, vintage cars, marching bands, Revolutionary War soldiers, and Boston cops wearing kilts and blowing bagpipes, cheered on by onlookers in windbreakers and Red Sox caps.

In this cheerful, gaudy scene, one group of marchers stood out. All male, the marchers wore black suits and top hats and strode two by two, trailing a cannon and a banner marked "Old Colony Club." They looked like Victorian mourners who had taken a wrong turn and fallen in with a mob of Plymouth townies.

"This isn't our big day," one of the black-suited men said, as I struggled along the crowded curb, trying to keep up.

"What is?" I asked.

"Forefathers' Day. Much older than Thanksgiving and more significant."

This was news. But I couldn't gather more in the crush and noise of the parade. The man gave me the club's address and invited me to join the group for Forefathers' Day, a month hence. The gathering, oddly, began at 5:30 A.M. "Dress warmly and bring earplugs," he advised, tipping his top hat and marching on.

The intervening weeks gave me time to research the enigmatic club and its holiday. Both dated to 1769, when seven men in Plymouth formed a private club to avoid "the many disadvantages and inconveniences that arise from intermixing with the company at the taverns in this town." The date they chose for their annual meeting was December 22, anniversary of the first English settlers' arrival at Plymouth.

To mark the occasion in 1769, club members fired a cannon, raised a silk flag emblazoned with "Old Colony 1620," and retired to enjoy a "decent repast" of clams, oysters, cod, eels, venison, succotash, Indian pudding, cranberry tarts, and apple pie. Though substantial, the food was chosen to reflect the fare eaten by early settlers, and "dressed in the plainest manner . . . in imitation of our ancestors." Repeated in following years, the tradition became known as Forefathers' Day (the term "Pilgrims" wasn't applied to the *Mayflower* passengers until the nineteenth century).

"Top of the morning to you!" said the man who greeted me in the foyer of the Old Colony Club building on Plymouth's main street. It was 5:15 A.M. and the club was already crowded with men in tuxedoes. Given the formal attire, and the club's snobby origins, I'd expected to find WASPish *Mayflower* descendants sipping tea from bone china, in finely appointed rooms from the pages of *Yankee Clipper*. Instead, the interior of the white clapboard building had sloping floors, water-stained wallpaper, and simple furnishings. Portraits of club presidents hung askew. Walls, shelves, and glass cases were stuffed with dusty items donated or abandoned by former members: pipes, tobacco tins, elephant tusks.

"We're a men's club; our wives aren't here to make us behave or clean up," one of the members said, showing me an antique card room with standing ashtrays and yellowed rules on the wall for the club's only game, called bestia. "It's extinct everywhere but here," my guide said. "Appropriate, I guess."

If the club was a throwback, it was no longer the blue-blooded establishment of earlier centuries. Members had to be upstanding citizens of Plymouth or nearby Duxbury, and could be denied entry if a single member slipped a black cube into the club's old wooden ballot box. But many of the men I met had Irish, Italian, or Portuguese surnames, including the club's most distinguished member, the Reverend Peter Gomes, a brown-skinned, gray-haired man wearing round horn-rims and carrying a cane. A renowned clergyman who preached at the Harvard Memorial Church in Cambridge, he spoke in orotund phrases, even at 5:30 in the morning.

"Convening at this hour gives off the odor of ancient activity," he said. "And it's a pleasant form of lark that permits us to boast for the rest of the year about rising in the cold and dark."

Gomes's lineage was a mix of African-American and Portuguese from the Atlantic island of Cape Verde. This made him a rather unusual celebrant of the *Mayflower*'s arrival. As Malcolm X observed: "We didn't land on Plymouth Rock; that rock landed on us." But having grown up by the famous stone, Gomes saw the Pilgrims differently.

"I've always liked them, if not necessarily their descendants," he said. "They were full of adventure, a little naïve, not altogether successful—unlike the Puritans of Boston. They did the best they could, but weren't really hustlers. Yet Americans have chosen to remember them."

This was an intriguing take, and I wanted to hear more. But it was almost six A.M., time for the Forefathers' Day rites to begin. A man called out, "Let's go, Pilgrims," and everyone donned top hats, scarves, and overcoats. It was still dark out, the tail end of the longest night of the year. "Balmy," one of the men declared, his breath clouding in the frigid air.

By the standards of late December in New England, the weather was indeed temperate; only a little below freezing, without wind or snow. The men, about a hundred in all, lined up behind flag bearers, a small band, and, at the head, the club's oldest member, a stooped ninety-nine-year-old with a cane and cape. At the command "Forward march!" they proceeded along the main street and down a lane to the crest of Cole's Hill. Four men wheeled forward the small cannon I'd seen at the Thanksgiving parade.

The club president intoned an abridged version of the proclamation issued in 1769, invoking the memory of Plymouth's forefathers but omitting the original expressions of loyalty to the Mother Country. Then the gun crew captain shouted, "Ram the charge! Prick the charge! Fuse the cannon! Fire!"

A deafening blast roared out across the harbor where the first settlers sailed in, followed by a cloud of smoke. The cannon fired a second and third time, the club members waving their top hats and crying, "Hip, hip, hooray!"

This was, in part, an expression of relief. I'd been told the cannon sometimes failed; at one July 4 parade, it had fired prematurely, wounding the hand of a member of the gun crew and propelling a ramrod above the heads of holiday marchers. This time the blasts were harmless, although they no doubt woke anyone sleeping within a mile of the hill.

"They'll not forget the Pilgrims, that's for sure," Reverend Gomes quipped, pulling at his watch fob. It was 6:16 A.M. and light was just starting to pink the rim of the harbor. The men resumed marching, past the sarcophagus of Pilgrim bones, up Leyden Street, the oldest in Plymouth and named for the Dutch town from which the Pilgrims departed, then back along the main street, past Sean O'Toole's pub and Di Marzio Insurance and Bangkok Thai Cuisine.

"Our labors are done," Gomes said, as we returned to the club, having walked no more than a half mile. "What I love about the Old Colony is that it has no redeeming merit. You can join the Kiwanis if you want to perform good works. We do that in our other walks of life. Here, nothing is required, only this annual observance."

Like the club's founders, the men retired for a "decent repast," though not quite the daylong gorging of 1769. After a breakfast of sausage, eggs, baked beans, and ham, they dispersed to home or work, and returned at day's end for a traditional dinner of succotash.

In the seventeenth century, succotash—its name derived from an

Algonquian word, possibly meaning "mixed"—denoted a pottage of beans, corn, and meat. A staple of the Indian diet, succotash wasn't beloved of early settlers. "Broth," William Wood called it in 1634, "made thick with fishes, fowls, and beasts boiled all together, some remaining raw, the rest converted by over-much seething to a loathed mash."

In the centuries since, "succotash" had become a catch-all label for a range of American dishes, but in Plymouth it still hewed to native and colonial tradition. "The old recipe says to cook corned beef in one pot and fowl in another," Cynthia Sykes said, stirring a tan-colored soup in the Old Colony's basement kitchen. "I do that, but not the other part, which says to put the pots outside, hanging on broomsticks to cool."

She'd cooked the beef and chicken, as well as venison, for four hours, then mixed their juices with navy beans, turnip, and hominy, or hulled corn. "I serve this brown goop in bowls, with the meat on the side," she said. "That's the traditional way. And no salt or spices."

Succotash was originally just the soup course on Forefathers' Day, but now it was the main meal, followed by apple pie. "In the old days, people did physical work from dawn to dark, they could eat ten courses without killing themselves," Cynthia said. "Not these guys."

At seven P.M., she rang a cowbell, and the men, who had been drinking upstairs, clumped down the narrow stairs like hungry prep-school boys. They seated themselves around small wooden tables, diving into baskets of bread even before someone rose to say grace. "This is a godless place," murmured the Reverend Gomes, whose table I shared. "Beyond the reach of prayer."

Then the men passed plates of meat and forked it into the bowls of gruel Cynthia had dispensed. The result wasn't particularly appetizing: basically chunks of well-cooked flesh floating on a pool of brown soup. But it tasted much better than it looked. The corned beef provided salt, and the beans and turnip and hominy formed a soothing sort of porridge. "In my youth, everyone in town ate this on Forefathers' Day," Gomes said. "It was a way to clean out the refrigerator before Christmas."

The Rock was another fixture of his childhood in Plymouth, and one he regarded as instructive. "Growing up here, we were given a useful distinction between symbol and reality," he said. "The Rock, like many icons, is important not because it's big and impressive, but because of what it represents."

As Gomes paused to add more meat to his bowl, I asked him the question I'd put to others in Plymouth. Setting aside local pride, why elevate the Pilgrims to iconic status and ignore all the others who came to America before them?

Gomes responded by telling me about his appearance, some years ago, in a television debate with the owner of Berkeley Plantation in Virginia. Not only had Jamestown preceded Plymouth, the Virginian observed; documents showed that in 1619, colonists landing at nearby Berkeley had designated their arrival date a day of annual thanksgiving.

"This man was energetically anti-Yankee," Gomes recalled. "So I decided magnanimity was the best response. I said, 'Of course, the gentleman from Virginia is quite correct. But it doesn't matter. Americans love *us*.'"

I wasn't sure I followed his argument. "So you're saying we should honor myth rather than fact?" I asked.

"Precisely." The reverend smiled benignly, as I imagined he might at a bewildered parishioner. "Myth is more important than history. History is arbitrary, a collection of facts. Myth we choose, we create, we perpetuate."

He spooned up the last of his succotash. "The story here may not be correct, but it transcends truth. It's like religion—beyond facts. Myth trumps fact, always does, always has, always will."

THE DESSERT COURSE arrived, and more wine. Men rose to deliver inebriated toasts or simply to shout, "We are table number one!" Tired from the long day, I left before the speeches and cards and cigars, and walked down to the harbor, digesting my dialogue with Gomes, along with the succotash. In December, the waterfront was empty and dark, except for floodlights illuminating the Rock and the coins scattered in the sand around it.

Gomes had articulated a thesis I'd been groping toward during the course of my travels, but had kept resisting. Now, shivering beside

Plymouth Rock, it seemed inescapable. I could chase after facts across early America, uncover hidden or forgotten "truths," explode fantasies about the country's founding. But in the end it made little difference. Myth remained intact, as stubbornly embedded as the lump of granite in the pit before me.

Maybe I'd gone about my research all wrong. Instead of combing history's fine print, like an investigative journalist, I should have studied the Greek classics, or anthropology, or elementary psychology. Myth didn't grip only modern Americans; it had possessed the long-ago Europeans I'd been traipsing after.

A shortcut to Cathay, cities of gold, Norumbega, Columbus's terrestrial paradise—these were visions I'd dismissed as medieval superstition. But they'd driven Europeans all over the Americas, with unintended and shattering consequences. Even Bartholomew Gosnold, searching for a tree that would cure syphilis, helped set in train the events that led to Squanto's kidnapping, his assistance to the Pilgrims, and their successful settlement of the shore I was standing on almost four centuries later. Myths didn't just trump fact; they helped create it.

The modern map of America ratified ancient mirages. Rhode Island, which is not an island, got its name from a geographic mixup with Block Island, which Giovanni da Verrazzano thought resembled the Greek isle of Rhodes. "California" is believed to derive from Calafia, queen of the tall, black Amazons whom sixteenth-century Spaniards conjured as occupants of today's Golden State. And two continents bore the name of Amerigo Vespucci, who penned fantasies about lands he never saw. All these names were now fixed, and likely to remain so.

As a fact-bound journalist, I'd dutifully recorded the legends littering my path across America. But I'd failed to appreciate why these myths persisted. People needed them. In St. Augustine, I'd doubted that many of my fellow visitors to the "Fountain of Youth" really believed Ponce de León found an elixir, or that the sulphur water they quaffed from plastic cups would roll back the years. But it was harmless fiction, so why spoil the fun with facts?

Like everyone else, I'd tossed the water down with a smile, even with the faint hope that the foul-tasting minerals might do some good, like cod liver oil or vitamin C. Anyway, the fountain was the rare chapter of the conquistador story that offered hope and renewal and a little comedy, rather than conquest and cruelty. Was it so surprising that visitors preferred the fountain myth to the grim reality on display nearby, of Indians exterminated by European contact?

At St. Augustine, and at the Florida history fest where tourists steered clear of my conquistador armor, I'd sensed something else. Americans didn't so much study history as shop for it. They did this at Plymouth, too, ticking off sites like items on a grocery list: the Rock, the *Mayflower,* Pilgrim Hall, Plimoth Plantation.

The past was a consumable, subject to the national preference for familiar products. And history, in America, is a dish best served plain. The first course could include a dollop of Italian in 1492, but not Spanish spice or French sauce or too much Indian corn. Nothing too filling or fancy ahead of the turkey and pumpkin pie, just the way Grandma used to cook it.

I HAD MY own comfort food, which I consumed when the season allowed. After long days tracking the sixteenth century, I'd switch on a motel TV to watch baseball, or doze off over newspaper box scores. Despite steroids and other scandals, baseball was for me unchanging and unchallenging, a well of pleasant boyhood memories. A soothing lullaby, like the lines I'd learned in grade school about American history. *O beautiful for pilgrim feet ... When, in the course of human events ... our fathers brought forth on this continent ...*

One night, while reading about baseball, I sensed a link between my nostalgia for the game and the historical quest I'd been on. In his essay "The Creation Myths of Cooperstown," Stephen Jay Gould pondered why Abner Doubleday was celebrated for "inventing" baseball one day in 1839. Doubleday never claimed to have done so, and the man who gave him posthumous credit for creating the sport was later judged criminally insane. In any event, there was clear evidence that our "national pastime" evolved over decades, from English games with funny names like rounders and stool ball. Yet the romantic legend of young Abner, a future Civil War general, creating an entirely new and American game, in an upstate New York cow pasture, was so potent that humble Cooperstown became home to baseball's Hall of Fame.

Gould attributed this to "the psychic need for an indigenous creation myth." Humans, whether contemplating the genesis of their customs or of their species, yearn to locate "an explicit point of origin," rather than accept that most beginnings are gradual and complex. "Creation myths," he concluded, "identify heroes and sacred places, while evolutionary stories provide no palpable, particular thing as a symbol for reverence, worship, or patriotism."

As with baseball, so, too, with America's birth. The country's European founding was slow and messy: a primordial slime of false starts and mutations that evolved, over generations, into English colonies and the United States. Once on its feet, the newborn American nation looked back in search of origins, and located its heroes and sacred places on the stony shore of Massachusetts. The Pilgrim Fathers of 1620 begat the Founding Fathers of 1776. Cooperstown had Doubleday's cow pasture, Plymouth its hallowed Rock.

And that's where I'd ended up. While walking off my Forefathers' Day dinner, I found myself drawn by the lights inside the Greek Outhouse. On a late December night, bathed by the icy tide in seaweed and styrofoam, the Rock looked even more pitiful than it had on my earlier visits. But for the first time I regarded the battered stone with grudging respect. You could yank at it with thirty yoke of oxen, crack it, chip pieces from it, or bury it in sand, as Indian protestors had done. But you couldn't dislodge it from American memory.

I reached into my pocket for a penny. Fingers chilled, I fumbled the toss, watching the coin skid off the Rock and into the rimy surf. I stood for a moment, thinking of luck, and Pilgrim feet, and my own feet, numb with cold, then turned and set them on the way toward home.

NOTE ON SOURCES

When navigating the source material on early America, it's easy to feel as the Vikings often did in the North Atlantic: *hafvalla,* lost at sea. The literature on Europe's discovery of America spans ten centuries, twenty-odd countries, and roughly as many genres, from saga to science fiction. No two translations or editions of explorers' writings read alike. There are also countless charts, runes, graves, and other remains to decipher. It helps to have a working knowledge of Icelandic, Algonquian, and radio-carbon dating.

Possessing none of these skills, I've been unusually reliant on the spadework of historians and the generosity of archaeologists, archivists, linguists, and other specialists I consulted in the course of my research. This book also reflects my training as a journalist. "When in doubt," a hard-nosed city editor once advised me, "leave it out." I've tried to bring that same caution and skepticism to a historical subject that is riddled with controversies, fantasies, and outright forgeries. For this reason, I've given little or no space to the so-called Vinland Map, the Chinese discovery of America, Columbus's crypto-Judaism, and other popular but poorly sourced notions about the hemisphere and its early explorers.

A reporter's love of paper trails has also influenced my selection of which among scores of expeditions to retrace. The journeys of Coronado, De Soto, John Smith, and others in this book generated hundreds of documents that survive to this day. Unfortunately, the voyages of men such as Henry Hudson and the Portuguese Corte-Reales did not.

That being said, my decision to focus on ten or so historical episodes, rather than to attempt a comprehensive survey, has inevitably resulted in a number of significant figures being left out—most notably, Samuel de Champlain, the Frenchman who explored the coast and rivers of New England and wrote vividly about his adventures (including the founding of the Order of Good Cheer, the first gastronomic society in North America). For readers interested in Champlain's voyages, and other topics that merit much more attention than I've given them, I've offered some suggestions below.

Finally, before I dive into specific sources, a word on proper nouns. The names of explorers, and of the people and places they encountered, vary tremendously depending on language, translation, idiosyncratic spelling, and alphabet (or the lack of it). Hernando De Soto, on second reference, should properly be Soto, not De Soto. The ruler called Powhatan by the English was known to his own people as Wahunsenacawh. However, for the sake of clarity, I've almost always hewed to common usage. Also, when not specifying tribal names, I've frequently used the term "Indians," as Native Americans generally do themselves.

The chapter notes below are intended as a highlights reel of my research. Full citations for the books mentioned, and for other works I consulted, are in the bibliography that follows.

PROLOGUE

The story of America's discovery and settlement by Europeans stretches across such a vastness of time and territory that most scholars have probed pieces of it rather than the whole, rather like the explorers themselves. A notable exception is Samuel Eliot Morison, the great Harvard historian, mariner, and misogynist (he refused to teach Radcliffe women). Morison is to America's early exploration what Shelby Foote is to the Civil War: an old-fashioned storyteller who writes with exceptional verve, sweep, and wit. Morison's writing, like Foote's, can feel dated, particularly in its dismissive treatment of natives. But for an overview of New World exploration, there's no better place to start than with Morison's magisterial *The European Discovery of America,* a two-volume work divided into northern and southern voyages.

Other general works I found particularly useful during the initial, omnivorous phase of my research were Alan Taylor's *American Colonies: The Settling of North America,* John Bakeless's *The Eyes of Discovery,* and *The Discovery of North America,* edited by W. P. Cumming, R. A. Skelton, and D. B. Quinn. One of the best compilations of writings by and about explorers is online: *American Journeys,* a digital library sponsored by the Wisconsin Historical Society. This user-friendly site includes maps and historical background to each selection. Go to www.americanjourneys.org.

An indispensable geographical resource is *The Atlas of North American Exploration,* by William H. Goetzmann and Glyndwr Williams, which combines summaries of almost every exploring expedition in North American history with colorful, easy-to-read maps.

On Native American history and culture, I turned most often to the *Handbook of North American Indians,* a twenty-volume work published by the Smithsonian Institution. Though often dense, and occasionally dated (the first volume appeared in 1978), the *Handbook* examines every region, era, and tribe in North America, from every perspective: archaeological, demographic, linguistic, political, religious, musical, and so on.

There are a number of excellent books about environmental history and the interchange of plants, animals, and microorganisms known as the Columbian Exchange. Pioneering works in this field include Alfred Crosby's *Ecological Imperialism: The Biological Expansion of Europe, 900–1900* and William Cronon's *Changes in the Land: Indians, Colonists, and the Ecology of New England.* More recent is Charles Mann's *1491: New Revelations of the Americas Before Columbus,* an excellent and balanced overview of current scholarship on the Columbian Exchange, disease, and New World demography.

My material on Verrazzano is mostly drawn from Lawrence Wroth's *The Voyages of Giovanni da Verrazzano,* which includes not only the navigator's writings but a comprehensive look at what's known about his life and voyages, as well as the geographical thinking of his day.

CHAPTER I

The most comprehensive translation of the Norse sagas is *The Complete Sagas of Icelanders,* a five-volume work published in Iceland that includes forty sagas and forty-nine related tales. The last volume ends with an invaluable reference section, including maps, a timeline of historical events relevant to the sagas, illustrations of ships and homesteads, and a glossary defining terms such as "Althing," "berserk," "scorn-pole," and "sworn brotherhood."

Most readers, however, will find more than enough in Penguin's abridgement of the *Complete Sagas,* titled *The Sagas of the Icelanders.* This one-volume edition opens with excellent essays by novelist Jane Smiley and historian Robert Kellogg. As Smiley observes, the sagas' blend of plainspoken prose and fantastical imaginings introduce us to "a world a thousand years separated from ours, both intensely familiar and intensely strange." For readers interested only in the Norse discovery of America, Penguin has also published a very short edition, *The Vinland Sagas,* with a lively and informative introduction by Magnus Magnusson and Hermann Pálsson.

For a broader understanding of the Norse and their world, I relied in particular on *Vikings: The North Atlantic Saga,* a wide-ranging and well-illustrated collection of essays by leading experts on the Norse, edited by William Fitzhugh and Elisabeth Ward. One of the volume's authors, Birgitta Linderoth Wallace, was especially helpful to me, sharing her archive and wisdom about all things Norse during my visit to Halifax, Nova Scotia. Thanks also to Gísli Sigurðsson of the Árni Magnússon Institute in Reykjavik.

On native history and culture, I am indebted to Ruth Holmes Whitehead, who met with me in St. John's and whose work includes *Stories from the Six Worlds, The Old Man Told Us,* and *Elitekey: Micmac Material Culture from 1600 AD to the Present.* My understanding of the archaeological record was also informed by other experts I interviewed in Newfoundland: Priscilla Renouf, Kevin McAleese, Gerald Penny, and Martha Drake.

On the Beothuk, I mainly drew on James P. Howley's *The Beothucks or Red Indians,* Ingeborg Marshall's *The Beothuk,* and Ralph T. Pastore's *Shanawdithit's People: The Archaeology of the Beothuks.* An excellent overview of Newfoundland history, both native and European, is Kevin Major's *As Near to Heaven by Sea: A History of Newfoundland and Labrador.*

The story of Helge Ingstad's search for and discovery of the Norse site in L'Anse aux Meadows is told in his own words, in *Westward to Vinland.* While Ingstad received (and claimed) most of the credit for having found the Viking site, others had speculated before that northern Newfoundland was home to the Norse, including W. A. Munn, a cod liver oil refiner in Newfoundland, and Jørgen Meldgaard, a Danish archaeologist.

The Thomas McGovern essay I cite at the end of this chapter is "The Vinland Adventure: A North Atlantic Perspective," published in the *North American Archaeologist,* vol. 2 (4), 1980–81.

CHAPTER 2

The best collection of primary sources relating to Columbus is *Journals and Other Documents on the Life and Voyages of Christopher Columbus,* translated and edited by Samuel Eliot Morison. Another excellent source is *New Iberian World: A Documentary History of the Discovery and Settlement of Latin America to the Early 17th Century.* For a short edition, with background on navigation and geography, see *The Log of Christopher Columbus,* translated by Robert Fuson.

Morison's *Admiral of the Ocean Sea: A Life of Christopher Columbus* is the standard modern biography of the navigator, and is particularly useful for its nautical insights (Morison retraced Columbus's voyages in a yacht). But the book was published in 1942, a half century before the wave of new and more critical scholarship that attended the five-hundredth anniversary of Columbus's sail. One of the best of these recent works is *The Mysterious History of Columbus* by the *New York Times* science writer John Noble Wilford, who writes with rare balance and clarity about the navigator and his legacy. Also noteworthy is the historian Felipe Fernández-Armesto's biography *Columbus,* an elegant, erudite, and concise portrait of the explorer and his beliefs.

Other works relating to Columbus that I found useful were Stephen Greenblatt's *Marvelous Possessions: The Wonder of the New World,* Tzvetlan Todorov's *The Conquest of America,* and Ilan Stavans's *Imagining Columbus: The Literary Voyage,* a scholarly survey of writing about the navigator. For scathing critiques of Columbus and his impact, see Kirkpatrick Sale's *The Conquest of Paradise: Christopher Columbus and the Columbian Legacy* and David Stannard's *American Holocaust: Columbus and the Conquest of the New World.*

A fascinating subgenre of Columbus literature is scholarly debate over the intellectual impact of his voyages on the Old World. Did his discoveries transform Europe's image of itself and the universe, or were Columbus's voyages filtered through a medieval and classical worldview so entrenched that his exploration served mostly to buttress preexisting beliefs? Anthony Grafton surveys this and other aspects of the European cosmos in *New Worlds, Ancient Texts: The Power of Tradition and the Shock of Discovery.* Balanced, accessible, and beautifully illustrated, this is one of the most illuminating books I read in the course of my research.

The quote that is the basis for the title of my book, about Columbus thanking God for the end to "a voyage so long and strange," comes from "To the Indies," an essay in *The Aztec Treasure House,* by Evan Connell.

CHAPTERS 3 and 4

In addition to the sources cited above, I relied on *The Dominican Republic: A National History,* by Frank Moya Pons; *Why the Cocks*

Fight: Dominicans, Haitians, and the Struggle for Hispaniola, by Michele Wucker; and *Colonial Santo Domingo,* a guide published in the Dominican Republic. Also helpful to my understanding of the modern D.R. were my conversations with Hamlet Hermann, a writer, political analyst, and former government minister in Santo Domingo.

For the native history of Hispaniola, see *The Tainos: Rise and Fall of the People Who Greeted Columbus,* by Irving Rouse, and *Columbus's Outpost Among the Tainos: Spain and America at La Isabela, 1493–1498,* by Kathleen Deagan and José Maria Cruxent.

My principal source on Vespucci was *Letters from a New World: Amerigo Vespucci's Discovery of America,* edited by Luciano Formisano. For an outrageous and incisive commentary on Vespucci, listen to Jack Hitt's radio essay, which aired on PBS's *This American Life* on July 12, 2002. Hitt likens Vespucci's letters to those published in *Penthouse Forum,* and regards the Italian as the first great salesman in American history. "The naming of America wasn't a mistake," Hitt concludes. "It was prophecy." A link for the program, "Give the People What They Want," is at www.thislife.org.

The little-known work of Father Ramón Pane can be found in "Columbus, Ramón Pane and the Beginnings of American Anthropology," by Edward Gaylor Bourne, in *Proceedings of the American Antiquarian Society,* 1906. Pane's writing is also tucked within *The Life of the Admiral Christopher Columbus by His Son Ferdinand,* translated by Benjamin Keen.

For Bartolomé de Las Casas, I turned to the Penguin Classic edition of *A Short Account of the Destruction of the Indies,* translated by Nigel Griffin, with an excellent introduction by Anthony Pagden.

CHAPTER 5

The books I found most useful for a general understanding of Spain and Spanish conquest are J. H. Elliott's *Imperial Spain, 1469–1716* and *Empires of the Atlantic World: Britain and Spain in America, 1492–1830,* Henry Kamen's *Imperial Spain, 1469–1716,* and Hugh Thomas's *Rivers of Gold: The Rise of the Spanish Empire.* A provocative, revisionist study is Matthew Restall's *Seven Myths of the Spanish Conquest*. My understanding of the Spanish has also been informed by Professor Douglas Cope, whose lectures on colonial Latin America I attended at Brown University in the fall of 2007.

For the history of Spanish exploration and settlement of what is today the United States, the outstanding work is David J. Weber's *The Spanish Frontier in North America,* which touches on everything from the sixteenth-century origins of the black legend to Spanish revival architecture in the twentieth. Weber is exceptionally balanced, avoiding the romanticizing or reviling of the Spanish that characterizes so much writing on this subject. For one-stop shopping on the Spanish in North America, there is no better book than this.

In a very different vein, Carlos Fuentes's *The Buried Mirror: Reflections on Spain and the New World* is a freewheeling, literary meditation by one of Latin America's leading novelists. "The Hispanic world did not come to the United States," Fuentes observes. "The United States came to the Hispanic world. It is perhaps an act of poetic justice that now the Hispanic world should return."

Cabeza de Vaca's narrative of his journey across America was published in several editions, under different titles. Among the many translations, one of the most recent and fluid is by Martin A. Favata and José B. Fernández, *The Account: Alvar Núñez Cabeza de Vaca's Relacion.* Cyclone Covey's earlier translation, *Adventures in the Unknown Interior of America,* is useful for its introduction, annotations, and thoughtful epilogue by William Pilkington.

For devoted students of Cabeza de Vaca, the indispensable work is *Alvar Núñez Cabeza de Vaca: His Account, His Life, and the Expedition of Pánfilo de Narváez,* translated and edited by Rolena Adorno and Patrick Pautz. This three-volume study presents *The Account* in Spanish and English and includes an examination of everything to do with Cabeza de Vaca and the Narváez expedition.

A new and less academic work is Paul Schneider's *Brutal Journey: The Epic Story of the First Crossing of North America*. Well-paced and thoroughly researched, *Brutal Journey* is also notable for its nuanced treatment of Narváez, who tends to come off as a cartoon conquistador in many works about Cabeza de Vaca.

CHAPTERS 6 and 7

As I mention in the text, the New Mexico scholars Richard Flint and Shirley Cushing Flint are unparalleled in their knowledge of Coronado and his expedition. I have drawn heavily on their work, in particular *Documents of the Coronado Expedition, 1539–1542,* a meticulous and exhaustively annotated translation of letters, accounts, muster rolls, and other papers relating not only to Coronado's travels but also to those of Fray Marcos, Estevanico, and Hernando de Alarcón. The *Documents* includes the original Spanish, maps, a glossary, and biographical and geographic data on the people and places named in the documents. This is the bible of Coronado studies.

Richard Flint is also the author of *Great Cruelties Have Been Reported: The 1544 Investigation of the Coronado Expedition,* and he and Shirley have edited two collections of essays, *The Coronado Expedition to Tierra Nueva: The 1540–1542 Route Across the Southwest* and *The Coronado Expedition from the Distance of 460 Years.* For a less detailed treatment of the expedition, see *The Journey of Coronado,* translated and edited by George Parker Winship. It has a concise historical introduction and fluid, lightly annotated translations of the conquistador's letters and accounts by his men.

The Flints and their fellow members of the Center for Desert Archaeology are also at the forefront of the search for sites along Coronado's trail. During my own trek, I attended lectures on this quest by John Madsen, Gayle Hartmann, and William Hartmann, a planetary scientist at the University of Arizona. "Coronado's journey was the Apollo expedition of his day," he says, "and Mexico City was a sixteenth-century mission control, shipping out men to explore the unknown." Hartmann has written a novel about the Spanish in the Southwest, *Cities of Gold,* and designed an excellent Web site about Coronado, http://www.psi.edu/coronado/coronado.html.

For a different approach, see *To the Inland Empire: Coronado and our Spanish Legacy,* by Stewart Udall, a former secretary of the interior and renowned environmentalist. Udall makes a passionate case for recognition of the early Spanish and calls 1542—when Coronado,

De Soto, and other Spaniards were roaming across America and the Pacific—"a Himalayan moment" in geographical discovery. "Never again would any country have a year—or even a century!—when its explorers would range so far or add so much to the store of knowledge about earth's unknown places."

Another distinctive take on Coronado is Douglas Preston's *Cities of Gold: A Journey Across the American Southwest.* This book combines history and travel adventure, rather like my own, except that Preston is much more intrepid: he retraces Coronado's route through Arizona and New Mexico on horseback. By turns comic and poignant, *Cities of Gold* is particularly strong in its evocation of the Southwest's pioneer and ranching cultures.

An excellent overview of native societies encountered by the early Spanish is Edward H. Spicer's *Cycles of Conquest: The Impact of Spain, Mexico, and the United States on the Indians of the Southwest.* For a provocative look at the Spanish impact on the Pueblo peoples, see Ramón A. Gutiérrez's *When Jesus Came, the Corn Mothers Went Away.* On the Zuni, I often consulted *A Zuni Atlas,* by T. J. Ferguson and E. Richard Hart. For the story of the controversial Smithsonian anthropologist I refer to in the text, see *Zuni: Selected Writings of Frank Hamilton Cushing,* edited by Jesse Green.

CHAPTERS 8 and 9

The principal sources for De Soto's expedition are the writings of three men who accompanied the conquistador: Luis Hernández de Biedma (a royal factor), Rodrigo Rangel (De Soto's secretary), and a Portuguese known only as a "gentleman of Elvas." There has been a great deal of scholarly debate about the accuracy of these accounts, and how much they borrow from one another. But taken together they provide a rich and plausible narrative of the expedition.

The same can't be said of a fourth, widely used source, which is too often lumped together with the others. Long after De Soto died, the half-Spanish, half-Incan historian Garcilaso de la Vega drew on memories of survivors to write a book-length narrative of the expedition. He also drew on his own very literary imagination, stretching scenes that merit only a few lines in the others' accounts into entire chapters that read like chivalric romances. I've used Garcilaso very sparingly, in a few instances where he's directly citing the information of others or is writing about events corroborated in the three principal accounts.

Translations of Biedma, Rangel, Elvas, and Garcilaso, as well as other documents relating to De Soto's life and expedition, are collected in *The De Soto Chronicles: The Expedition of Hernando de Soto to North America in 1539–1543*. This indispensable two-volume work includes essays by many of the leading experts on De Soto and Spanish conquest. For a cautionary deconstruction of the sources on De Soto, see *The Hernando de Soto Expedition: History, Historiography, and "Discovery" in the Southeast*, edited by Patricia Galloway.

The best biography of the conquistador is David Ewing Duncan's *Hernando De Soto: A Savage Quest in the Americas*. Duncan bridges popular and academic history, writing a biography that is carefully researched, balanced, and also a lively and accessible read. Almost half of the book deals with De Soto's life before his arrival in La Florida. Charles Hudson's *Knights of Spain, Warriors of the Sun: Hernando de Soto and the South's Ancient Kingdoms* focuses almost exclusively on the La Florida expedition, and is particularly strong on the native societies De Soto encountered. Hudson's earlier research on this subject can be found in *The Southeastern Indians*.

As I've noted in the text, Hudson has also devoted more study than anyone else to reconstructing De Soto's route. While the Hudson Route remains contentious, it's the current best fit of the documentary and geographical evidence. The story of Hudson's quest is told by his wife, Joyce Rockwood Hudson, in her engaging travelogue, *Looking for De Soto: A Search Through the South for the Spaniard's Trail*.

While tracking De Soto, more than at any other point in my book, I had to leave out a wealth of material gathered from historians, archaeologists, and park officials along the conquistador's route; if I hadn't, telling the story of the expedition would have consumed two volumes rather than two chapters. However, my discussion of De Soto and his impact on the South has been informed by many of these sources, in particular Charles Fenwick, former superintendent of the De Soto National Memorial in Bradenton; Bonnie McEwan, director of Mission San Luis in Tallahassee; Jeff Mitchem, station archaeologist at the Parkin Archaeological State Park in Arkansas; Dave Moore, archaeologist at Warren Wilson College in North Carolina; and John Connaway, survey archaeologist with the Mississippi Department of Archives and History, in Clarksdale. I'm also indebted to two professors I consulted at the University of Mississippi, Jay Johnson and Robbie Ethridge (whose "shatter zone" thesis I refer to in the text), as well as Vernon Knight at the University of Alabama.

There is no better way to grasp the sophistication and grandeur of mound culture than to visit its remains, not only at large complexes such as Moundville in Alabama and Ocmulgee in Georgia, but also at small parks like the one in Parkin, Arkansas. For more reading on mound culture, see Robert Silverberg's *The Mound Builders* and Mann's *1491,* which is particularly good on Cahokia.

CHAPTER 10

The most accessible sources for the writings of René de Laudonnière and other Frenchmen in sixteenth-century Florida are two books by Charles Bennett, *Laudonnière and Fort Caroline: History and Documents* and *Three Voyages.* The former includes a history of the French colony and documents relating to its founding and destruction, including Spanish accounts.

On the artwork of the French painter in Florida Jacques le Moyne de Morgues, see *Discovering the New World,* edited by Michael Alexander, and *The New World: The First Pictures of America,* edited by Stefan Lorant. The watercolor I refer to, of Laudonnière and a Timucuan chief, is held by the New York Public Library. Some scholars believe this is not Le Moyne's original work, but a copy made from a tinted engraving of his drawing, which was printed by Theodore de Bry in 1591. The best book on the natives the French and others encountered in northeast Florida is *The Timucua,* by Jerald Milanich.

For the Spanish in Florida, the best modern treatment is Eugene Lyon's *The Enterprise of Florida: Pedro Menéndez de Avilés and Spanish Conquest of 1565–1568.* Lyon takes a revisionist tack, emphasizing the commercial aspects of Menéndez's mission. Also useful to me were

Paul E. Hoffman's *A New Andalucia and a Way to the Orient: The American Southeast During the Sixteenth Century* and Woodbury Lowery's *The Spanish Settlements within the Present Limits of the United States.*

Very little is known about Juan Ponce de León and no eyewitness accounts of his voyages survive. An early Spanish history of Ponce de León's exploration is available on the *American Journeys* Web site. Also see Morison, *Southern Voyages,* and Leonard Olschiki, "Ponce de León's Fountain of Youth: History of a Geographical Myth," published in *The Hispanic Historical Review* in 1941.

On St. Augustine, I turned to *The Oldest City: St. Augustine, Saga of Survival,* a collection of scholarly essays edited by Jean Parker Waterbury. I also found a wealth of information at the St. Augustine Historical Society, one of the best archives I visited in the course of my travels. The historical society member I cite with regard to the "flimflams" in St. Augustine is Charles Reynolds; his "Fact Versus Fiction for the New Historical St. Augustine" was published in 1937. A contrary view, offering evidence of the Fountain of Youth's veracity, is "The First Landing Place of Juan Ponce de León on the North American Continent in the Year 1513," a booklet available at the present-day Fountain of Youth park.

CHAPTER II

Any study of early English voyages to the New World begins with the encyclopedic work of Richard Hakluyt, the great Elizabethan chronicler of exploration. *The Principall Navigations, Voyages Traffiques & Discoveries of the English Nation,* first published in 1589, is a multivolume compilation of Hakluyt's and others' writing about every explorer and adventurer known or believed to have set off before 1600. Sprawling and eccentrically organized, it is best read in excerpts, like those reproduced on the *American Journeys* Web site or in collections such as *The Discovery of North America.*

One of the editors of *The Discovery,* David Beers Quinn, is a twentieth-century Hakluyt who edited and updated his predecessor's research and wrote roughly as many words on English exploration. Of his many books, the most useful to me included *England and the Discovery of America, 1481–1620,* and *The Voyages and Colonising Enterprises of Sir Humphrey Gilbert.*

Quinn, who died in 2002, was also the dean of Roanoke studies, collecting primary accounts in *Virginia Voyages* and providing a comprehensive history in *Set Fair for Roanoke: Voyages and Colonies, 1584–1606.* Quinn's writing can be elliptical, but the depth of his scholarship makes his work indispensable.

More accessible to the general reader is Ivor Noël Hume's *The Virginia Adventure: Roanoke to James Town,* a lucid and lively retelling of early colonization, interspersed with archaeological insights. Karen Ordahl Kupperman's *Roanoke: The Abandoned Colony* is an excellent short treatment, putting Roanoke in the context of English and native society. Raleigh Trevelyan's *Sir Walter Raleigh* is a recent and very fine biography of Roanoke's sponsor.

On memory of Roanoke, Robert Arner's booklet, *The Lost Colony in Literature,* offers a wry survey of the many books, poems, and other works inspired by the colony's disappearance. For an overview of current scholarship and archaeology related to the colony, see *Searching for the Roanoke Colonies,* a collection of essays edited by E. Thomson Shields and Charles R. Ewen. More on the work of Fred Willard's Lost Colony Center for Science and Research can be found at its Web site, http://www.lost-colony.com.

For a groundbreaking study of the trauma experienced by early English colonists at Roanoke, as well as at Jamestown and Plymouth, see "Seasons of Misery: Catastrophe and the Writing of Settlement in Colonial America," a 2006 Ph.D. dissertation at Yale University by Kathleen M. Donegan.

CHAPTER 12

John Smith, as I've indicated in the text, is the best and most vexing source on early Jamestown. His hundreds of pages of writing about the colony are disorganized, his sentences impossible to parse, and his spelling and syntax so idiosyncratic that English can seem a foreign language. It therefore helps to have a strong editorial hand, which Philip Barbour provides in his well-annotated three-volume study, *The*

Complete Works of Captain John Smith, the gold standard for scholarship on the captain.

A recent compilation from the Library of America is *Captain John Smith: Writings, with Other Narratives of Roanoke, Jamestown, and the First English Settlement of America.* Edited by James Horn, it has the merit of collecting Smith and many other writers in one volume. For a short sample of Smith's work, see Karen Ordhal Kupperman's *Captain John Smith: A Selected Edition of His Writings,* which is very well chosen, edited, and introduced. On Jamestown's first decade, the handiest collection of primary sources is *Jamestown Narratives: Eyewitness Accounts of the Virginia Colony,* edited by Edward Wright Haile.

Of the many secondary works on Jamestown, one of the best is David A. Price's *Love and Hate in Jamestown: John Smith, Pocahontas, and the Start of a New Nation,* a concise, readable, and excellently researched look at the very tangled and hard-to-tell story of Virginia's early years. For the general reader, there is no better introduction to the subject. Among the best analyses of John Smith and his legacy is J. A. Leo Lemay's *The American Dream of Captain John Smith.* For an incisive look at the historiography of Jamestown, see Jill Lepore's essay in *The New Yorker,* "Our Town," April 12, 2007.

On Powhatan and the tribes he ruled, no one has written more than Helen Rountree, whose works include *Pocahontas's People: The Powhatan Indians of Virginia Through Four Centuries* and *The Powhatan Indians of Virginia: Their Traditional Culture.* For Powhatan's famous daughter, see *Pocahontas: The Evolution of an American Narrative,* by Robert S. Tilton, and *Pocahontas: The Life and the Legend,* by Frances Mossiker.

The recent Jamestown quadricentennial brought a flood of new books on the colony. The one that adds freshest insight is William Kelso's *Jamestown: The Buried Truth,* in which the archaeologist expands on many of the points he made in my interview with him, which took place a year before the book's publication. Also new is Tim Hashaw's *The Birth of Black America,* which tells of the "Black Mayflower" that brought Africans to Jamestown in 1619. For more on Virginia's first Africans, see two articles published in the *William and*

Mary Quarterly: "The African Experience of the '20. and Odd Negroes' Arriving in Virginia in 1619" by John Thornton (1998) and "New Light on the '20. and Odd Negroes'" by Engel Sluiter (1997).

Walter Plecker's article "Racial Improvement" was published in the *Virginia Medical Monthly* in November 1925. An equally shocking tract is *Mongrel Virginians,* published the next year by two of his colleagues, Arthur H. Estabrook and Ivan E. McDougle. For an excellent study of Plecker and eugenics, see J. David Smith, *The Eugenic Assault on America: Scenes in Red, White, and Black.* Historical background on the divide between blacks and Chickahominy Indians can be found in *Charles City County, Virginia: An Official History,* edited by James P. Whittenburg and John Coski.

CHAPTER 13

An account of Bartholomew Gosnold's 1602 voyage, by one of its participants, John Brereton, can be found on the *American Journeys* Web site, along with accounts by other early English travelers to New England. I also drew on my interviews with archaeologist Jeffrey P. Brain, of the Peabody Essex Museum in Salem, Massachusetts, who has searched for the site of Gosnold's outpost on Cuttyhunk.

The starting point for any research on Pilgrim Plymouth is William Bradford's *Of Plymouth Plantation, 1620–1647,* and a journal of the colony's first year he co-authored with Edward Winslow, published as *Mourt's Relation.* Scholarly classics on the Pilgrims and later Puritan settlers include John Demos's *A Little Commonwealth: Family Life in Plymouth Colony* and Edmund Morgan's *The Puritan Dilemma: The Story of John Winthrop.* For the general reader, two recent books of note are Nathaniel Philbrick's bestselling *Mayflower: A Story of Courage, Community, and War* and Godfrey Hodgson's *A Great and Godly Adventure: The Pilgrims and the Myth of the First Thanksgiving.*

On Plymouth Rock, see *Memory's Nation,* by John Seelye, and a Pilgrim Society booklet, "Plymouth Rock: History and Significance," by Rose Briggs. My material on the Old Colony Club is mostly drawn from the work of the Plymouth historian Jim Baker, who was very generous with his time and research on the town and its history. Some of his work can be found at http://www.oldcolonyclub.org.

Finally, a few suggestions for further reading about some of the people and places I mentioned only in passing, or not at all. For Samuel de Champlain, see Morison's biography *Samuel de Champlain: Father of New France,* and the work of the Champlain Society in Canada; its Web site is at www.champlainsociety.ca. Samples of Champlain's wonderful writing can also be found at the *American Journeys* Web site, as can that of Jacques Cartier, the sixteenth-century French explorer I refer to in the Newfoundland chapter.

For other early explorers of Canada, and the search for the elusive Northwest Passage, see Morison, *Northern Voyages,* and the accounts excerpted in *The Discovery of North America.* One of the most extraordinary of these northern voyagers was Martin Frobisher, whose story is wonderfully told in Robert Ruby's *Unknown Shore: The Lost History of England's Arctic Colony.*

Little is known about Henry Hudson, the English navigator in service to the Dutch who searched for the Northwest Passage and, in 1609, sailed up the New York river named for him. The only surviving account of this voyage, by crewman Robert Juet, is available on the *American Journeys* Web site. For more on the Dutch, see Jonathan Israel's *Dutch Primacy in World Trade, 1585–1740.* The *American Journeys* site also includes an account of Sir Francis Drake's visit to the California coast in 1579. An excellent recent biography is *Sir Francis Drake: The Queen's Pirate,* by Harry Kelsey.

Two places I visited in New England, but was unable to include, deserve special mention. Jeffrey Brain, the archaeologist referred to above in relation to Cuttyhunk, has also led the excavation of Fort St. George, in Popham, Maine, the forgotten English colony that predated Plymouth by thirteen years. For historical background on the Popham colony, and information on the continuing archaeological work, see www.maine.gov/museum/anthropology/pophamcolony.

Dighton Rock is a site of a very different sort, a boulder by the Taunton River in Massachusetts that is covered in ancient etchings. These inscriptions have been attributed, variously, to Phoenicians, to the Norse, to sixteenth-century Portuguese, and to Wampanoag Indians. Dighton Rock and the small museum enclosing it are an entertaining introduction to the many mysteries and myths surrounding America's early exploration. I visited the site with its modern champion, Dr. Manuel Luciano da Silva, who has written a lively study, *Portuguese Pilgrims and Dighton Rock*.

BIBLIOGRAPHY

Adorno, Rolena. "The Negotiation of Fear in Cabeza de Vaca's *Naufragios*." *Representations*, No. 33 (winter 1991): 163–99.

Adorno, Rolena, and Patrick Pautz. *Álvar Núñez Cabeza de Vaca: His Account, His Life, and the Expedition of Pánfilo de Narváez*, 3 vols. Lincoln: University of Nebraska Press, 1999.

Alexander, Michael, editor. *Discovering the New World, Based on the Works of Theodore de Bry.* New York: Harper & Row, 1976.

Anderson, Ruth Matilda. *Hispanic Costume 1480–1530.* New York: The Hispanic Society of America, 1979.

Arner, Robert D. *The Lost Colony in Literature.* Raleigh: North Carolina Department of Cultural Resources, 1985.

Axtell, James. *Beyond 1492: Encounters in Colonial North America.* New York: Oxford University Press, 1992.

Bailyn, Bernard. *Atlantic History: Concept and Contours.* Cambridge: Harvard University Press, 2005.

———. *The Peopling of British America: An Introduction.* New York: Vintage Books, 1988.

Bakeless, John. *The Eyes of Discovery*. New York: Dover Publications, Inc., 1961.

Barrett, James H., editor. *Contact, Continuity, and Collapse: The Norse Colonization of the North Atlantic*. Turnhout, Belgium: Brepols Publishers, 2003.

Benedict, Philip. *Christ's Churches Purely Reformed: A Social History of Calvinism*. New Haven: Yale University Press, 2002.

Bennett, Charles E. *Laudonnière and Fort Caroline: History and Documents*. Tuscaloosa: The University of Alabama Press, 2001.

Bennike, Pia. *Palaeopathology of Danish Skeletons: A Comparative Study of Demography, Disease and Injury*. Copenhagen: Akademisk Forlag, 1985.

Bolton, Herbert. *Coronado, Knight of Pueblos and Plains*. Albuquerque: University of New Mexico Press, 1990.

———. *The Spanish Borderlands*. New Haven: Yale, 1921.

Boorstin, Daniel J. *The Discoverers*. New York: Vintage Books, 1985.

Bourne, Edward Gaylord. "Columbus, Ramón Pane and the Beginnings of American Anthropology." Worcester: Proceedings of the American Antiquarian Society, 1906.

Bradford, William. *Of Plymouth Plantation 1620–1647*. New York: The Modern Library, 1981.

Briggs, Rose T. *Plymouth Rock: History and Significance*. Boston: The Nimrod Press, 1968.

Bushman, Claudia L. *America Discovers Columbus: How an Italian Explorer Became an American Hero*. Hanover: University Press of New England, 1992.

Cabeza de Vaca, Álvar Núñez. *The Account: Álvar Núñez Cabeza de Vaca's Relación*. Translated by Martin A. Favata and José B. Fernández. Houston: Arte Público Press, 1993.

———. *Adventures in the Unknown Interior of America*. Translated by Cyclone Covey. Albuquerque: University of New Mexico Press, 1983.

Carter, W. Hodding. *A Viking Voyage*. New York: The Ballantine Publishing Group, 2000.

Cervantes, Miguel de. *Don Quixote*. Translated by Edith Grossman. New York: HarperCollins Publishers Inc., 2003.

Clayton, Lawrence A., Vernon James Knight Jr., and Edward C. Moore, editors. *The De Soto Chronicles: The Expedition of Hernando de Soto to North America in 1539–1543*, two vols. Tuscaloosa: The University of Alabama Press, 1993.

Columbus, Christopher. *The Log of Christopher Columbus*. Translated by Robert Fuson. Camden, Me.: International Marine Publishing, 1992.

Columbus, Ferdinand. *The Life of Admiral Christopher Columbus by his Son Ferdinand.* Translated by Benjamin Keen. New Brunswick, N.J.: Rutgers University Press, 1959.

Connell, Evan S. *The Aztec Treasure House.* Washington, D.C.: Counterpoint, 2001.

Connor, Jeannette Thurber, editor. *Pedro Menéndez de Avilés, Adelantado, Governor, and Captain-General of Florida, Memorial by Gonzalo Solís de Merás.* Deland, Fla.: The Florida State Historical Society, 1923.

Cotten, Sallie Southall. *The White Doe or the Legend of Virginia Dare.* Philadelphia: J. B. Lippincott Co., 1901.

Cronon, William. *Changes in the Land: Indians, Colonists, and the Ecology of New England.* New York: Hill and Wang, 1983.

Crosby, Alfred. *The Columbian Exchange: Biological and Cultural Consequences of 1492.* Westport, Ct.: Greenwood Press, 1973.

——. *Ecological Imperialism: The Biological Expansion of Europe, 900–1900.* London: Cambridge University Press, 1986.

Cushing, Frank Hamilton. *Zuñi: Selected Writings of Frank Hamilton Cushing.* Edited by Jesse Green. Lincoln: University of Nebraska Press, 1979.

Da Silva, Manuel Luciano. *Portuguese Pilgrims and Dighton Rock.* Bristol, R.I.: Manuel da Silva, 1971.

Davies, Hunter. *In Search of Columbus.* London: Sinclair-Stevenson Ltd., 1991.

Davis, Robert E. *History of the Improved Order of Red Men and Degree of Pocahontas 1765–1988.* Waco: Davis Brothers Publishing Co., Inc., 1990.

Deagan, Kathleen, and José María Cruxent. *Columbus's Outpost Among the Taínos: Spain and America at La Isabela, 1493–1498.* New Haven: Yale University Press, 2002.

Deloria, Philip J. *Playing Indian.* New Haven: Yale University Press, 1998.

Demos, John. *A Little Commonwealth: Family Life in Plymouth Colony.* Oxford: Oxford University Press, 1970.

Diamond, Jared. *Collapse: How Societies Choose to Fail or Succeed.* New York: Viking, 2005.

——. *Guns, Germs, and Steel: The Fates of Human Societies.* New York: W. W. Norton & Co., 1997.

Díaz del Castillo, Bernal. *The Conquest of New Spain.* Translated by John M. Cohen. New York: Penguin, 1963.

Donegan, Kathleen M. "Seasons of Misery: Catastrophe and the Writing of Settlement in Colonial America." Ph.D. dissertation, Yale University, 2006.

Duncan, David Ewing. *Hernando de Soto: A Savage Quest in the Americas*. Norman: University of Oklahoma Press, 1996.

Elliot, J. H. *Empires of the Atlantic World: Britain and Spain in America 1492–1830*. New Haven: Yale University Press, 2006.

———. *Imperial Spain 1469–1716*. London: Penguin Books, 1963.

Estabrook, Arthur H., and Ivan E. McDougle. *Mongrel Virginians: The Win Tribe*. Baltimore: The Williams & Wilkins Co., 1926.

Ewen, Charles R., and John H. Hann. *Hernando de Soto among the Apalachee*. Gainesville: University Press of Florida, 1998.

Fernández-Armésto, Felipe. *Columbus*. Oxford: Oxford University Press, 1991.

———. *Pathfinders: A Global History of Exploration*. New York: W. W. Norton & Co., Inc., 2006.

Ferguson, T. J., and E. Richard Hart. *A Zuni Atlas*. Norman: University of Oklahoma Press, 1985.

Fitzhugh, William W., and Elisabeth I. Ward, editors. *Vikings: The North Atlantic Saga*. Washington, D.C.: Smithsonian Institution Press, 2000.

Flannery, Tim. *The Eternal Frontier: An Ecological History of North America and Its People*. Melbourne: The Text Publishing Co., 2001.

Flint, Richard. *Great Cruelties Have Been Reported: The 1544 Investigation of the Coronado Expedition*. Dallas: Southern Methodist University Press, 2002.

Flint, Richard, and Shirley Cushing Flint, editors. *Documents of the Coronado Expedition, 1539–1542*. Dallas: Southern Methodist University Press, 2005.

———. *The Coronado Expedition From the Distance of 460 Years*. Albuquerque: University of New Mexico Press, 2003.

———. *The Coronado Expedition to Tierra Nueva: The 1540–1542 Route Across the Southwest*. Boulder: University Press of Colorado, 2004.

Formisano, Luciano, editor. *Letters from a New World: Amerigo Vespucci's Discovery of America*, translated by David Jacobson. New York: Marsilio Publishers, Corp., 1992.

Fraser, Walter B. *The First Landing Place of Juan Ponce de Leon on the North American Continent in the Year 1513*. St. Augustine: Walter B. Fraser, 1956.

Fuentes, Carlos. *The Buried Mirror: Reflections on Spain and the New World*. New York: Houghton Mifflin Co., 1992.

Galloway, Patricia, editor. *The Hernando de Soto Expedition: History, Historiography, and "Discovery" in the Southeast*. Lincoln: University of Nebraska Press, 1997.

Goetzmann, William H., and Glyndwr Williams, editors. *The Atlas of North American Exploration: From the Norse Voyages to the Race to the Pole.* Norman: University of Oklahoma Press, 1992.

Gould, Stephen Jay. "The Creation Myths of Cooperstown." *Natural History,* November 1989.

Grafton, Anthony. *New Worlds, Ancient Texts: The Power of Tradition and the Shock of Discovery.* Cambridge: The Belknap Press of Harvard University Press, 1992.

Grant, John. *An Introduction to Viking Mythology.* New York: Shooting Star Press, Inc., 1990.

Greenblatt, Stephen. *Marvelous Possessions: The Wonder of the New World,* Chicago: The University of Chicago Press, 1991.

Gutiérrez, Ramón A. *When Jesus Came, the Corn Mothers Went Away: Marriage, Sexuality, and Power in New Mexico, 1500–1846.* Palo Alto: Stanford University Press, 1991.

Haile, Edward Wright, editor. *Jamestown Narratives: Eyewitness Accounts of the Virginia Colony.* Champlain, Va.: RoundHouse, 1998.

Hale, Sarah Josepha. *Northwood: A Tale of New England.* Boston: Bowles & Dearborn, 1827.

Hakluyt, Richard. *The Principal Navigations Voyages Traffiques and Discoveries of the English Nation,* eight vols. London: J. M. Dent and Sons Ltd., 1927.

Hann, John H., and Bonnie G. McEwan. *The Apalachee Indians and Mission San Luis.* Gainesville: University Press of Florida, 1998.

Hashaw, Tim. *The Birth of Black America: The First African Americans and the Pursuit of Freedom at Jamestown.* New York: Carroll & Graf, 2007.

Haywood, John. *The Penguin Historical Atlas of the Vikings.* London: Penguin Books, 1995.

Heath, Dwight B., editor. *Mourt's Relation: A Journal of the Pilgrims at Plymouth.* Bedford, Ma.: Applewood Books, 1963.

Henige, David. *In Search of Columbus: The Sources for the First Voyage.* Tucson: The University of Arizona Press, 1991.

Hodgson, Godfrey. *A Great and Godly Adventure: The Pilgrims and the Myth of the First Thanksgiving.* New York: PublicAffairs, 2006.

Hoffman, Paul E. *A New Andalucia and a Way to the Orient: The American Southeast During the Sixteenth Century.* Baton Rouge: Louisiana State University Press, 1992.

Howley, James P. *The Beothucks or Red Indians.* Toronto: Prospero, 2000.

Hreinsson, Viðar, editor. *The Complete Sagas of Icelanders.* Reykjavik: Leifur Eiriksson Publishing, 1997.

Hudson, Charles. *Knights of Spain, Warriors of the Sun: Hernando de Soto and the South's Ancient Chiefdoms*. Athens: University of Georgia Press, 1997.

———. *The Juan Pardo Expeditions*. Tuscaloosa: The University of Alabama Press, 1990.

———. *The Southeastern Indians*. Knoxville: The University of Tennessee Press, 1976.

Hudson, Joyce Rockwood. *Looking for De Soto: A Search Through the South for the Spaniard's Trail*. Athens: University of Georgia Press, 1993.

Hudson, Marjorie. *Searching for Virginia Dare: A Fool's Errand*. Wilmington, N.C.: Coastal Carolina Press, 2002.

Hume, Ivor Noël. *The Virginia Adventure: Roanoke to James Towne: An Archaeological and Historical Odyssey*. Charlottesville: University Press of Virginia, 1994.

Ingstad, Helge. *Westward to Vinland*. London: Jonathan Cape Ltd., 1969.

Israel, Jonathan I. *Dutch Primacy in World Trade, 1585–1740*. New York: Oxford University Press, 1990.

Jones, Gwyn. *A History of the Vikings*. London: Oxford University Press, 1968.

Kamen, Henry. *Spain 1469–1714: A Society of Conflict*. London: Longman Group UK Ltd., 1991.

Karr, Ronald Dale, editor. *Indian New England 1524–1674*. Pepperell, Ma.: Branch Line Press, 1999.

Kelsey, Harry. *Sir Francis Drake: The Queen's Pirate*. New Haven: Yale University Press, 1998.

Kelso, William M. *Jamestown: The Buried Truth*. Charlottesville: University of Virginia Press, 2007.

Kennedy, Roger G. *Hidden Cities: The Discovery and Loss of Ancient North American Civilization*. New York: The Free Press, 1994.

Kupperman, Karen Ordahl. *Indians and English: Facing Off in Early America*. Ithaca: Cornell University Press, 2000.

———. *Roanoke: The Abandoned Colony*. Savage, Md.: Rowman & Littlefield Publishers, Inc., 1984.

Kupperman, Karen Ordahl, editor. *America in European Consciousness 1493–1750*. Chapel Hill: The University of North Carolina Press, 1995.

Las Casas, Bartolomé de. *A Short Account of the Destruction of the Indies*. Edited and translated by Nigel Griffin. London: Penguin Books, 1992.

Laudonnière, René. *Three Voyages*. Translated by Charles E. Bennett. Tuscaloosa: The University of Alabama Press, 2001.

Lemay, J. A. Leo. *The American Dream of Captain John Smith*. Charlottesville: University Press of Virginia, 1991.

Lepore, Jill. *Encounters in the New World: A History in Documents*. New York: Oxford University Press, 2000.

———. "Our Town." *The New Yorker*, April 12, 2007.

Lopez, Barry. *The Rediscovery of North America*. New York: Vintage Books, 1992.

Lorant, Stefan. *The New World: The First Pictures of America*. New York: Duell, Sloan and Pearce, 1965.

Lowery, Woodbury. *The Spanish Settlements Within the Present Limits of the United States*, 2 vols. New York: G. P. Putnam's sons, 1903–05.

Lyon, Eugene. *The Enterprise of Florida: Pedro Menéndez de Avilés and Spanish Conquest of 1565–1568*. Gainesville: University Press of Florida, 1974.

Madariaga, Salvador de. *Christopher Columbus: Being the Life of the Very Magnificent Lord Don Cristóbal Colón*. New York: The Macmillan Co., 1940.

Major, Kevin. *As Near to Heaven by Sea: A History of Newfoundland and Labrador*. Toronto: Penguin Books, 2001.

Mandeville, John. *The Travels of Sir John Mandeville*, translated by C.W.R.D. Moseley. London: Penguin Books, 1983.

Mann, Charles C. *1491: New Revelations of the Americas Before Columbus*. New York: Alfred A. Knopf, 2005.

Marshall, Ingeborg. *The Beothuk*. St. John's: Newfoundland Historical Society, 2001.

Maxwell, Kenneth. "¡Adios Columbus!" *The New York Review of Books*, January 28, 1993.

McAleese, Kevin E., editor. *Full Circle: First Contact*. St. John's: Newfoundland Museum, 2000.

McGovern, Thomas H. "The Vinland Adventure: A North Atlantic Perspective." *North American Archaeologist*, Vol. 2 (4), 1980–1.

Milanich, Jerald T. *The Timucua*. Oxford: Blackwell Publishers, 1996.

Milanich, Jerald T., and Susan Milbrath, editors. *First Encounters: Spanish Explorations in the Caribbean and the United States, 1492–1570*. Gainesville: University Press of Florida, 1989.

Miller, Lee. *Roanoke: Solving the Mystery of the Lost Colony*. New York: Arcade Publishing, 2000.

Mitchem, Jeffrey M. "The Ruth Smith, Weeki Wachee, and Tatham Mounds: Archaeological Evidence of Early Spanish Contact." *The Florida Archaeologist*, Vol. 42, No. 4, December 1989.

Mitchem, Jeffrey M., and Brent R. Weisman, Donna L. Ruhl, Jenette Savell,

Laura Sellers, and Lisa Sharik. "Preliminary Report on Excavations at the Tatham Mound." Gainesville: Florida State Museum, Department of Anthropology, 1985.

Morgan, Edmund S. *The Puritan Dilemma: The Story of John Winthrop*. Boston: Little, Brown and Co., 1958.

———. "Slavery and Freedom: The American Paradox." *The Journal of American History*, Vol. 59, No. 1 (June 1972), pp. 5–29.

Morison, Samuel Eliot. *Admiral of the Ocean Sea: A Life of Christopher Columbus*, two vols. Boston: Little, Brown and Co., 1942.

———. *Samuel de Champlain: Father of New France*. Boston: Little, Brown and Co., 1972.

———. *The European Discovery of America. The Northern Voyages A.D. 500–1600*. New York: Oxford University Press, 1971.

———. *The European Discovery of America. The Southern Voyages A.D. 1492–1616*. New York: Oxford University Press, 1974.

Morison, Samuel Eliot, translator and editor. *Journals and Other Documents on the Life and Voyages of Christopher Columbus*. New York: The Heritage Press, 1963.

Mossiker, Frances. *Pocahontas: The Life and the Legend*. New York: Da Capo Press, 1996.

Moya Pons, Frank. *The Dominican Republic: A National History*. Princeton: Markus Wiener Publishers, 1998.

Munn, W. A. *Wineland Voyages: Location of Helluland, Markland and Vinland*. St. John's: The Evening Telegram Ltd., 1914.

National Park Service. "De Soto Trail: De Soto National Historic Trail Study." National Park Service, Southeast Regional Office, 1990.

Ober, Frederick A. *In the Wake of Columbus*. Boston: D. Lothrop Co., 1893.

Olschki, Leonardo. "Ponce de Leon's Fountain of Youth: History of a Geographical Myth." *The Hispanic American Historical Review*, Vol. 21, No. 3 (August 1941), pp. 361–85.

Pagden, Anthony. *European Encounters with the New World*. New Haven: Yale University Press, 1993.

———. *Peoples and Empires: Europeans and the Rest of the World, from Antiquity to the Present*. London: Phoenix Press, 2001.

Parry, John H., and Robert G. Keith, editors. *New Iberian World: A Documentary History of the Discovery and Settlement of Latin America to the Early Seventeenth Century*. Vol. II. New York: Times Books, 1984.

Pastore, Ralph T. *Shanawdithit's People: The Archaeology of the Beothuks*. St. John's: Atlantic Archaeology Ltd., 1992.

Philbrick, Nathaniel. *Mayflower: A Story of Courage, Community, and War*. New York: Viking, 2006.

Plecker, Walter A. "Racial Improvement." *Virginia Medical Monthly*, November 1925.

Pollard, John Garland. "The Pamunkey Indians of Virginia." Bureau of Ethnology Bulletin 17. Washington, D.C.: Smithsonian Institution, 1894.

Preston, Douglas. *Cities of Gold: A Journey Across the American Southwest*. Albuquerque: University of New Mexico Press, 1992.

Price, David A. *Love and Hate in Jamestown: John Smith, Pocahontas, and the Start of a New Nation*. New York: Vintage Books, 2005.

Quinn, David Beers. *England and the Discovery of America, 1481–1620*. London: George Allen & Unwin Ltd., 1974.

———. *Set Fair for Roanoke: Voyages and Colonies, 1584–1606*. Chapel Hill: University of North Carolina Press, 1985.

———. *The Lost Colonists: Their Fortune and Probable Fate*. Raleigh: The North Carolina Division of Archives and History, 1984.

———. *The Voyages and Colonising Enterprises of Sir Humphrey Gilbert*, Volume I. London: The Hakluyt Society, 1940.

Quinn, David B., W. P. Cumming, and R. A. Skelton, editors. *The Discovery of North America*. New York: American Heritage Press, 1971.

Quinn, David B., and Alison M. Quinn. *Virginia Voyages from Hakluyt*. London: Oxford University Press, 1973.

Reid, Alastair. "Reflections: Waiting for Columbus." *The New Yorker*, Feb. 24, 1992.

Renouf, M.A.P., *Ancient Cultures, Bountiful Seas: The Story of Port Au Choix*. St. John's: Historic Sites Association of Newfoundland and Labrador, 1999.

Restall, Matthew. *Seven Myths of the Spanish Conquest*. Oxford: Oxford University Press, 2003.

Reynolds, Charles. "Fact Versus Fiction for the New Historical St. Augustine." Mountain Lakes, N.J.: Charles Reynolds, 1937.

Rountree, Helen C. *Pocahontas's People: The Powhatan Indians of Virginia Through Four Centuries*. Norman: University of Oklahoma Press, 1990.

———. *Pocahontas, Powhatan, Opechancanough: Three Indian Lives Changed by Jamestown*. Charlottesville: University of Virginia Press, 2005.

———. *The Powhatan Indians of Virginia: Their Traditional Culture*. Norman: University of Oklahoma Press, 1992.

Rouse, Irving. *The Tainos: Rise and Decline of the People Who Greeted Columbus*. New Haven: Yale University Press, 1992.

Ruby, Robert. *Unknown Shore: The Lost History of England's Arctic Colony.* New York: Henry Holt and Co., 2001.

Russell, Peter. *Prince Henry "the Navigator."* New Haven: Yale University Press, 2001.

The Sagas of Icelanders: A Selection. New York: Penguin Putnam Inc., 2000.

Sale, Kirkpatrick. *The Conquest of Paradise: Christopher Columbus and the Columbian Legacy.* New York: Plume, 1991.

Sauer, Carl O. *Sixteenth-Century North America: The Land and People as Seen by the Europeans.* Berkeley: University of California Press, 1971.

Sawyer, Peter. *The Oxford Illustrated History of the Vikings.* Oxford: Oxford University Press, 1997.

Schneider, Paul. *Brutal Journey: The Epic Story of the First Crossing of North America.* New York: Henry Holt and Co., 2006.

Seelye, John. *Memory's Nation: The Place of Plymouth Rock.* Chapel Hill: University of North Carolina Press, 1998.

Shields, E. Thomson, and Charles R. Ewen, editors. *Searching for the Roanoke Colonies: An Interdisciplinary Collection.* Raleigh: North Carolina Department of Cultural Resources, 2003.

Sider, Gerald M. *Lumbee Indian Histories: Race, Ethnicity, and Indian Identity in the Southern United States.* Cambridge: Cambridge University Press, 1993.

Silverberg, Robert. *The Mound Builders.* Athens: Ohio University Press, 1970.

Sluiter, Engel. "New Light on the '20. and Odd Negroes' Arriving in Virginia, August 1619." *The William and Mary Quarterly,* Vol. LIV, No. 2, April 1997.

Smith, J. David. *The Eugenic Assault on America: Scenes in Red, White, and Black.* Fairfax: George Mason University Press, 1993.

Smith, John. *Captain John Smith: A Select Edition of His Writings.* Edited by Karen Ordahl Kupperman. Chapel Hill: University of North Carolina Press, 1988.

———. *Capt. John Smith: Writings with Other Narratives of Roanoke, Jamestown, and the First English Settlement of America.* Selected by James Horn. New York: The Library of America, 2007.

———. *The Complete Works of Captain John Smith (1580–1631),* three vols. Edited by Philip L. Barbour. Chapel Hill: The University of North Carolina Press, 1986.

Speck, Frank G. *Chapters on the Ethnology of the Powhatan Tribes of Virginia.* Indian Notes and Monographs, vol. 1, no 5. New York: Heye Foundation, 1928.

Spicer, Edward H. *Cycles of Conquest: The Impact of Spain, Mexico, and the United States on the Indians of the Southwest, 1533–1960*. Tucson: University of Arizona Press, 1962.

Stannard, David E. *American Holocaust: Columbus and the Conquest of the New World*. New York: Oxford University Press, 1992.

Stern, Theodore. "Chickahominy: The Changing Culture of a Virginia Indian Community." *Proceedings of the American Philosophical Society*, Vol. 96, No. 2, April 21, 1952.

Strachey, William. *The Historie of Travell into Virginia Britania*. London: The Hakluyt Society, 1953.

Sturtevant, William C., general editor. *Handbook of North American Indians*, twenty vols. Washington, D.C.: Smithsonian Institution, 1978–2006.

Swanton, John R. *Final Report of the De Soto Expedition Commission*. Washington, D.C.: Smithsonian Institution, 1985.

Taylor, Alan. *American Colonies: The Settling of North America*. New York: Penguin Putnam Inc., 2002.

Thomas, David Hurst, editor. *Columbian Consequences*, three vols. Washington, D.C.: Smithsonian Institution Press, 1989–91.

Thomas, Hugh. *Rivers of Gold: The Rise of the Spanish Empire*. London: Weidenfeld & Nicolson, 2003.

Thornton, John. "The African Experience of the '20. and Odd Negroes' Arriving in Virginia in 1619." *William and Mary Quarterly*, Vol. LV, Number 3, July 1998.

Tilton, Robert S. *Pocahontas: The Evolution of an American Narrative*. Cambridge: Cambridge University Press, 1994.

Todorov, Tzvetlan. *The Conquest of America*. Translated by Richard Howard. New York: Harper and Row, 1984.

Trevelyan, Raleigh. *Sir Walter Raleigh*. New York: Henry Holt and Co., 2004.

Turner, Frederick Jackson. *The Frontier in American History*. New York: Robert E. Krieger Publishing Co., Inc., 1976.

Udall, Stewart L. *To the Inland Empire: Coronado and Our Spanish Legacy*. New York: Doubleday & Co., Inc., 1987.

The Vinland Sagas: The Norse Discovery of America. Translated by Magnus Magnusson and Hermann Pálsson. London: Penguin Books Ltd., 1965.

Waterbury, Jean Parker, editor. *The Oldest City: St. Augustine, Saga of Survival*. St. Augustine: The St. Augustine Historical Society, 1983.

Weber, David J. *The Spanish Frontier in North America*. New Haven: Yale University Press, 1992.

Whitehead, Ruth Holmes. *Elitekey: Micmac Material Culture from 1600 AD to the Present.* Halifax: The Nova Scotia Museum, 1980.

———. *Stories from the Six Worlds: Micmac Legends.* Halifax: Nimbus Publishing Ltd., 1988.

———. *The Old Man Told Us: Excerpts from Micmac History 1500–1950.* Halifax: Nimbus Publishing Ltd., 1991.

Whitfield, Peter. *New Found Lands: Maps in the History of Exploration.* New York: Routledge, 1998.

Whittenburg, James P., and John M. Coski, editors. *Charles City County, Virginia: An Official History.* Salem, W.Va.: Don Mills, Inc., 1989.

Wilford, John Noble. *The Mysterious History of Columbus: An Exploration of the Man, the Myth, the Legacy.* New York: Alfred A. Knopf, 1991.

Wilson, Ian. *John Cabot and the Matthew.* St. John's: Breakwater, 1996.

Winship, George Parker, translator and editor. *The Journey of Coronado 1540–1542.* Golden, Co.: Fulcrum Publishing, 1990.

Wood, Michael. *Conquistadors.* Berkeley: University of California Press, 2002.

Worster, Donald. *Dust Bowl: The Southern Plains in the 1930s.* New York: Oxford University Press, 1979.

Wroth, Lawrence. *The Voyages of Giovanni da Verrazzano 1524–1528.* New Haven: Yale University Press, 1970.

Wucker, Michele. *Why the Cocks Fight: Dominicans, Haitians, and the Struggle for Hispaniola.* New York: Hill and Wang, 1999.

Young, Gloria A., and Michael P. Hoffman, editors. *The Expedition of Hernando de Soto West of the Mississippi, 1541–1543.* Fayetteville: The University of Arkansas Press, 1993.

ACKNOWLEDGMENTS

Like the explorers in this book, I would have been lost without the local guides, translators, and intermediaries I met in the course of my travels. In addition to those mentioned in the text and source notes, I'd like to thank Alba Moquete Brown for her help in Santo Domingo and two generous and engaging Southerners: Billy Atkinson in Childersburg, Alabama, and DruAnna Overbay, who guided me through the Melungeon country of East Tennessee. I regret that I wasn't able to include our adventures in this book. Also, while I've paid homage to Timothy Burke of Calderon's Company in the text, he was a tremendous help with every aspect of my De Soto research. His group's Web site is a rare and colorful repository of information about conquistadors, from dress to diet to dogs. It can be found at http://mywebpages.comcast.net/calderon.

I wrote much of this book during a fellowship at the Radcliffe Institute for Advanced Study, the most stimulating place I've ever had the pleasure to hang out at. Deep gratitude to the Institute's then dean, Drew Gilpin Faust; to Judith Vichniac and the rest of the Radcliffe staff; and to my fellow fellows, who entertained and inspired me with their research and companionship. While at Harvard, I also had the great fortune to become the oldest student of Jill Lepore, who let me into her incomparable history writing seminar. She has enriched me ever since with her friendship, scholarship, and editorial pen.

I finished this book during a semester-long sinecure at the John Carter Brown Library, the unparalleled archive of early Americana at Brown University. Thanks to the library's staff, fellows, and director, Ted Widmer, a bohemian star in the constellation of American historians. Most of the images in this book are from the library's exceptional collection. I'm also grateful for my long-ago professor at Brown, Philip Benedict, who taught me early European history a quarter-century ago and tutored me all over again for this project, from his new perch at the Institut d'histoire de la Reformation, in Geneva.

The saints who read this book while it was still a work-in-chaos include my mother, Elinor Horwitz, and brother, Josh Horwitz; Maria Wherley, teacher and coon-skinner of Spruce Creek, PA.; and Victoria Sprow, who also helped with translation and Widener-diving. Thanks as well to my writer pals—Joel Achenbach, Jack Hitt, Michael Lewis, Bill Powers, Martha Sherrill—for their friendship, editorial advice, and title caucusing.

I am, once again, indebted beyond measure to my super-agent Kris Dahl and über-publisher John Sterling, the duo that launched this long and strange voyage and brought it ashore with their characteristic patience, optimism, and constructive prodding. Thanks also to the Henry Holt cult of editors, designers, and assistants, and to Jolanta Benal for another painstaking copyedit and fact-check.

Finally, and forever, love and worshipful gratitude to my wife, Geraldine, the Plymouth Rock of this endeavor and every other in my life.

ILLUSTRATION CREDITS

86   Courtesy of John Carter Brown Library at Brown University. From Gonzalo Fernández de Oviedo y Valdés, *Historia general y natural de las Indias,* Seville, 1535.

115 Courtesy of John Carter Brown Library at Brown University. From Bernardo de Vargas Machuca, *Milicia y descripcion de las Indias,* Madrid, 1599.

119 Courtesy of John Carter Brown Library at Brown University. From Juan de Tovar, *Historia de la benida de los yndios,* Mexico, ca. 1585.

148 Courtesy of John Carter Brown Library at Brown University. From Theodor de Bry, *Brevissima relacion,* Frankfurt, 1598.

156 Courtesy of Glasgow University Library, Department of Special Collections. From Diego Muñoz Carmargo, *Descripción de la Ciudad y provincial de Tlaxcala,* Mexico, ca. 1580.

162 Photograph by Ben Wittick. Courtesy Palace of the Governors, Santa Fe, negative number 016054.

181 Courtesy of John Carter Brown Library at Brown University. From Francisco López de Gómara, *Primera y segunda parte de la historia general de las Indias,* Zaragoza, 1553.

207 Courtesy of John Carter Brown Library at Brown University. From Antonia de Herrera y Tordesillas, *Historia general de los hechos de los castellanos,* Madrid, 1601–15.

235 Courtesy of Georgia Department of Natural Resources.

246 Courtesy of the Architect of the Capitol. By William H. Powell, commissioned 1847, purchased 1855.

263 Courtesy of John Carter Brown Library at Brown University. From Theodor de Bry, *America,* Pt. 2, Frankfurt, 1591.

269 Courtesy of John Carter Brown Library at Brown University. From Theodor de Bry, *America,* Pt. 2, Frankfurt 1591.

296 Courtesy of John Carter Brown Library at Brown University. From *Delle navigationi et viaggi,* Venice, 1606.

317 Courtesy of John Carter Brown Library at Brown University. From Theodor de Bry, *Grands Voyages,* pt. 1, Frankfurt, 1590.

318 Courtesy of John Carter Brown Library at Brown University. From Theodor de Bry, *Grands Voyages,* pt. 1, Frankfurt, 1590.

331 Courtesy of John Carter Brown Library at Brown University. From John Smith, *The generall historie of Virginia,* London, 1624.

335 Courtesy of John Carter Brown Library at Brown University. From John Smith, *The generall historie of Virginia,* London, 1624.

347 Courtesy of John Carter Brown Library at Brown University. From John Smith *The generall historie of Virginia,* London, 1624.

375 Courtesy of John Carter Brown Library at Brown University. *Les voyages du sieur de Champlain,* Paris, 1613.

INDEX

Entries in *italics* refer to illustrations.

Read more ...

Patrick Leigh Fermor

A TIME OF GIFTS: ON FOOT TO CONSTANTINOPLE –
FROM THE HOOK OF HOLLAND TO THE MIDDLE DANUBE

The classic memoir of an enchanted journey across pre-war Europe

In 1933, at the age of eighteen, Patrick Leigh Fermor set off from the heart of London on an epic journey – to walk to Constantinople. It was to be a momentous experience, and one that would change the course of his life.

A Time of Gifts is the rich and sparkling account of his adventures as far as Hungary, after which *Between the Woods and the Water* continues the story to the Iron Gates that divide the Carpathian mountains and the Balkans. At once a coming-of-age memoir, an account of a journey, and a dazzling exposition of the English language, Patrick Leigh Fermor is acclaimed for his sweep, intelligence and observation, and the remarkable way in which he captures the moment in time.

'Nothing short of a masterpiece' Jan Morris

'A treasure chest of descriptive writing . . . The resplendent domes, the monasteries, the great rivers, the hospitable burgomasters, the sun on the Bavarian snow, the storks and frogs, the grandeurs, the courtesies, all are revealed with a sweep and verve that are almost majestic' *The Specator*

Order your copy now by calling Bookpoint on 01235 827716 or visit your local bookshop quoting ISBN 978-0-7195-6695-0 www.johnmurray.co.uk

Read more ...

Patrick Leigh Fermor

BETWEEN THE WOODS AND THE WATER: ON FOOT TO CONSTANTINOPLE – THE MIDDLE DANUBE TO THE IRON GATES

Continuing the classic memoir of an eighteen-year-old's enchanted epic journey across Europe in 1933

The journey that Patrick Leigh Fermor began – to cross Europe on foot with an 'emergency' allowance of a pound a day – proved so rich in experiences that they have overflowed into more than one volume.

The opening of *Between the Woods and the Water* finds him crossing the Danube where the first volume – the acclaimed *A Time of Gifts* – left off. Remote castles, mountain villages, monasteries and towering ranges that are the haunt of bears, wolves, eagles, gypsies and a variety of sects are all savoured in the approach to the Iron Gates dividing the Carpathian mountains from the Balkans. This journey has captivated generations.

'The finest travelling companion we could ever have . . . His head is stocked with enough cultural lore and poetic fancy to make every league an adventure' Christopher Hudson, *Evening Standard*

'A book so good you resent finishing it' Norman Stone

Order your copy now by calling Bookpoint on 01235 827716 or visit your local bookshop quoting ISBN 978-0-7195-6696-7 www.johnmurray.co.uk

Read more ...

Philip Mansel

CONSTANTINOPLE: City of the World's Desire

**This acclaimed history charts the interaction between the
vibrantly cosmopolitan capital of Constantinople and its
ruling family**

In 1453 Mehmed the Conqueror entered Constantinople on a white
horse, beginning an Ottoman love affair with the city that lasted until
1924, when the last Caliph hurriedly left on the Orient Express. For
almost five centuries Constantinople, with its enormous racial and
cultural diversity, was the centre of the dramatic and often depraved
story of an extraordinary dynasty.

'The victory, the defeat, the magnificence, the squalor, the cruelty
and the tolerance of the Ottoman years are all recorded there,
Constantinople is one of those cities to which I always long to return,
and the longing grows on every page' Noel Malcolm, *Sunday Telegraph*

'Marvellous . . . The experience of the whole city grows with the
book . . . you always feel close to the beat of Constantinople's raffish
and mysterious heart' Michael Ratcliffe, *Observer*

*Order your copy now by calling Bookpoint on 01235 827716 or
visit your local bookshop quoting ISBN 978-0-7195-6880-0
www.johnmurray.co.uk*

Read more ...

Margaret MacMillan

PEACEMAKERS: Six Months that Changed the World

The Samuel Johnson prizewinner

Between January and July 1919, after the war to end all wars, men
and women from all over the world converged on Paris for the Peace
Conference. For six extraordinary months the city was effectively the
centre of world government, as the peacemakers wound up bankrupt
empires and created new countries.

They pushed Russia to the sidelines, alienated China and dismissed
the Arabs, struggled with the problems of Kosovo, of the Kurds, and
of a homeland for the Jews. The peacemakers, so it has been said,
failed dismally; failed above all to prevent another war. Margaret
MacMillan argues that they have been made scapegoats for the
mistakes of those who came later. They tried to be even-handed, but
their goals – to make defeated countries pay without destroying
them, to satisfy impossible nationalist dreams, to prevent the spread
of Bolshevism and to establish a world order based on democracy and
reason – could not be achieved by diplomacy.

This book offers a prismatic view of the moment when much of the
modern world was first sketched out.

'A fascinating piece of history' Tony Blair, *Guardian*

'Enthralling . . . detailed, fair, unfailingly lively . . . full of brilliant
pen-portraits' *Daily Telegraph*

*Order your copy now by calling Bookpoint on 01235 827716 or
visit your local bookshop quoting ISBN 978-0-7195-6237-2
www.johnmurray.co.uk*

Read more . . .

Tim Mackintosh-Smith

YEMEN: TRAVELS IN DICTIONARY LAND

Winner of the Thomas Cook/ *Daily Telegraph* Travel Book Award: an Arabian grand tour in which every page is dashed – like the land it describes – with the marvellous

Arguably the most fascinating but least known country in the Arab world, Yemen has a way of attracting comment that ranges from the superficial to the wildly fictitious. Crossing mountain, desert, ocean and three millennia of history, Tim Mackintosh-Smith portrays hyrax hunters and dhow skippers, a noseless regicide and a sword-wielding tyrant with a passion for Heinz Russian salad.

'This book is a classic' *Independent*

'Masterful' *Sunday Times*

'*Yemen* . . . is assured and agile: witty, quirky, gossipy, learned, poetic . . . [Tim Mackintosh-Smith] has created a work that will endure' *The Times*

'Mackintosh-Smith seems incapable of writing a dull sentence, and in him the scholar, the linguist and the storyteller swap hats with marvellous speed' *New York Times*

Order your copy now by calling Bookpoint on 01235 827716 or visit your local bookshop quoting ISBN 978-0-7195-9740-4 www.johnmurray.co.uk